Learning BASIC

Learning BASIC

Don Inman

SAMS

A Division of Macmillan Computer Publishing

11711 North College, Carmel, Indiana 46032 USA

Trademarks

All terms mentioned in this book that are known to be trademarks or service marks are listed below. In addition, terms suspected of being trademarks or service marks have been appropriately capitalized. SAMS cannot attest to the accuracy of this information. Use of a term in this book should not be regarded as affecting the validity of any trademark or service mark.

PowerBASIC Lite is a trademark of Spectra Publishing.
PowerBASIC is a registered trademark of Spectra Publishing.
GW–BASIC, MS-DOS, and Microsoft are registered trademarks of Microsoft Corporation.
IBM is a registered trademark of International Business Corporation.

Publisher
Richard Swadley

Publishing Manager
Joseph Wikert

Managing Editor
Neweleen A. Trebnik

Acquisitions Editor
Linda Sanning

Development Editor
Ella M. Davis

Senior Editor
Rebecca Whitney

Production Editors
Gail Burlakoff
Katherine Stuart Ewing

Copy Editor
Becky Freeman

Technical Reviewer
David Leithauser

Formatter
San Dee Phillips

Editorial Assistant
Rosemarie Graham

Book Design
Scott Cook

Cover Art
Dan Armstrong

Production
Jeff Baker
Claudia Bell
Brad Chinn
Brook Farling
Sandy Grieshop
Denny Hager
Audra Hershman
Betty Kish
Phil Kitchel
Juli Pavey
Howard Peirce
Cindy Phipps
Anne Owen
Joe Ramon
Tad Ringo
Dennis Sheehan
Louise Shinault
Kevin Spear

Production Coordinator
Mary Beth Wakefield

Indexer
Johnna VanHoose

*Composed in MCP Digital and ITC Garamond by
Macmillan Computer Publishing*

Printed in the United States of America

*Screen reproductions in this book were created by means of the
program Collage Plus from Inner Media, Inc., Hollis, NH.*

v

Overview

Contents

7   Program Control Structures, 173

8   Subroutines, Functions, and Procedures, 197

16   PowerBASIC Lite Reference, 413

Acknowledgments

I would like to thank Robert S. Zale, copyright holder, and Kurt Inman, systems programmer, for the development of PowerBASIC and PowerBASIC Lite.

I would also like to thank all the Macmillan editors for their constructive criticism and help in developing the manuscript for this book.

Introduction

About This Book

This book is a tutorial guide to the most commonly used features of PowerBASIC. The book's slow-paced style enables beginners to learn the fundamental concepts of the language. Also, the book provides information that more advanced users can utilize in making a transition from the language they have been using to the advanced, modular structures of PowerBASIC.

Your PowerBASIC Lite package includes a PowerBASIC Lite software disk, which you can use to create useful programs, and this book, which shows you how to use the software. You can use PowerBASIC on IBM and IBM-compatible personal computers. The language provides significant enhancements to previous versions of the BASIC language. The included PowerBASIC Lite software is a special, tutorial version of PowerBASIC and contains most of the programming features of the full PowerBASIC version. Use PowerBASIC Lite to test its features. Then if you like this version, you can order the fully implemented PowerBASIC that adds the use of external files and other advanced features.

Two files on your software disk contain the PowerBASIC Lite language and a Help system for the language.

- PBLITE.EXE contains the integrated development environment you use to write, edit, compile, and run programs from your computer's memory. This is the file you load from DOS to use PowerBASIC Lite.

- PBLHELP.PBH contains help information. This file is accessed automatically from the PBLITE.EXE file when you press the Help key (F1) while using PowerBASIC Lite.

The book contains discussions and demonstrations of the most commonly used features of PowerBASIC Lite. The first two chapters introduce you to the PowerBASIC Lite menu system and show the basic way you enter, save, and run programs and provide a guide for using the help system while writing and editing programs.

Chapter 3 provides an introduction to programming. Chapters 4 through 9 are devoted to the use of numbers, strings, operators, and programming structures. Chapters 10 and 11 explain the use of data files, and Chapters 12 and 13 introduce you to graphic screen modes and their use. PowerBASIC Lite contains powerful debugging tools to help you find program errors and locate them in your program. Common program errors and debugging techniques are discussed in Chapter 14. The final chapters (15 and 16) point you toward more advanced use of PowerBASIC and provide a reference of keywords.

You do not have to know a lot about computers to use this book. You should, however, know a little bit about your Disk Operating System—how to copy disk files at least. A little knowledge of some version of BASIC is helpful. However, the pace of the tutorials is slow, and the detailed instructions are easy to follow. When you combine the use of the book's tutorials with frequent use of PowerBASIC Lite's help information, you quickly learn the fundamental concepts of PowerBASIC.

About BASIC

BASIC (Beginner's All-purpose Symbolic Instruction Code) was developed in 1963 and 1964 at Dartmouth College by professors John G. Kemeny and Thomas E. Kurtz. It is an instructional tool for training novice programmers.

With the introduction of the personal computer, the use of BASIC became widespread. A wide variety of personal computers appeared, and many versions of BASIC were developed, each version customized to fit the hardware of a particular personal computer.

Eventually, the variety of computers stabilized and GW–BASIC (BASICA on IBM computers) became the "standard" version of BASIC. GW–BASIC retains the simplicity, ease of use, and general-purpose power of previous BASIC versions while adding features.

PowerBASIC takes advantage of the development of interpreted BASIC, keeping those things necessary to remain compatible with earlier BASIC versions. Also, it provides new structures, more efficient performance, and quicker execution.

When you decide to purchase the complete PowerBASIC language package from Spectra Publishing, you receive a PowerBASIC User Manual and a PowerBASIC Reference Guide. Much of the technical material in this book is from those manuals.

Chapter 1

Getting Started

You can learn to read, understand, and write BASIC programs by following the step-by-step tutorials in this book. Use this chapter to get started. You are introduced immediately to PowerBASIC Lite, an easy-to-use, modern version of BASIC. You will enter, save, and run two short PowerBASIC Lite programs. A summary of the topics and a short set of exercises is at the end of the chapter.

These topics are discussed in this chapter:

- The advantages of PowerBASIC Lite

- A description of files in this package

- Loading PowerBASIC Lite

- The integrated development environment and its components

- Entering your first program

- Saving and running the program

- Program errors

- Returning to DOS from PowerBASIC Lite

Why Use PowerBASIC?

There are two basic methods of translating high-level computer languages (such as BASIC) into the machine-language code that computers understand.

Interpreters scan one program statement at a time, translate it to machine-language code, and then execute the machine-language code of that statement. The interpreter repeats this sequence for each statement in the program.

Compilers scan all statements of a program, translate the complete program to machine-language code, and then execute the machine-language code of the complete program.

Many versions of BASIC, including GW-BASIC, are *interpreted languages*. When a computer runs an interpreted BASIC program, it must read each instruction and convert it to machine-language code that the computer understands. Even when the computer encounters the same instruction many times (such as within a loop), it must read the instruction and convert it, each time, before it can be executed. This repetition consumes time. Consequently, interpreted programs are executed more slowly than compiled programs.

PowerBASIC Lite is a *compiled* BASIC. When you run a PowerBASIC Lite program, all the instructions in the program are compiled immediately to machine-language code and executed in the language the computer understands. A compiled PowerBASIC Lite program runs much faster than a corresponding interpreted BASIC program.

In the past, compiling involved many steps, switching from one file to another to perform each separate step. It was a complicated and time-consuming process. PowerBASIC Lite makes compilation a simple process. Your PowerBASIC Lite package supplies you with an *integrated development environment* (IDE) with its compiler, text editor, debugger, pull-down menus, windows, input boxes, and context-sensitive help. Using the integrated development environment lets you write, run, and debug your programs from within the same environment.

PowerBASIC Lite makes more efficient use of storage space than BASIC interpreters. When you write PowerBASIC Lite programs, you can use many comments and appropriate spaces to produce clear programs that are easy to read and understand. You also can separate functional program blocks with blank lines.

Your program with all its comments, indentations, and blank lines is your *source code*. The PowerBASIC Lite compiler ignores all comments, indentations, and blank lines. The formatting remains in the source code of your programs, however, even after compiling. Therefore, you can easily read and modify your source code whenever you want. The compiled source code is *object code*, intended solely for the computer, to make your program run swiftly.

When you have some favorite GW-BASIC programs saved in ASCII format, PowerBASIC Lite can read them. Often, you can load your favorite GW-BASIC programs into the PowerBASIC Lite editor with no changes and run them in a compiled form. Some GW-BASIC statements and keywords are not supported by PowerBASIC Lite because it handles their functions in a different way. Some GW-BASIC programs, therefore, may require modification to run under PowerBASIC Lite.

Once you use PowerBASIC Lite, with its added features, you will want to rewrite your GW-BASIC programs to use these features.

Files in the PowerBASIC Lite Package

Before trying to use PowerBASIC Lite, first make a backup copy of the PowerBASIC Lite disk. Once you have successfully copied the disk, store the original disks in a safe place. When you run PowerBASIC Lite on a floppy disk system, use the backup disk.

To use PowerBASIC Lite on a hard disk system, make a new subdirectory on your hard disk. Use the DOS Make Directory command and type the name of the subdirectory (PBLITE in this example), as follows:

```
C:>MD \PBLITE
```

Next, copy the files from the backup disk to the PBLITE subdirectory.

```
C:>CD PBLITE
C:\PBLITE>COPY A:*.* C:\PBLITE
```

Two of these files are used to create programs and provide explanatory material:

- PBLITE.EXE—contains all that is necessary to write, run, and modify your PowerBASIC Lite programs.

- PBLHELP.PBH—contains help material to assist you with writing or modifying programs.

The example programs in the book are also included on the disk. These files are compressed and combined into one file: BAS.COM. When BAS.COM is uncompressed, many files with the .BAS extension will appear in your PBLITE directory. These files are the correct PBLITE programs found in the listings throughout the book.

In the course of this book, you will be asked to type programs yourself. As you learn more, you will make changes to these programs. The .BAS files on the disk are the "final" versions of the programs. Therefore, you should place the .BAS files in the subdirectory, \PBLITE\ANSWERS. While you are in your \PBLITE directory, use the DOS Make Directory command again. Type the following:

```
C:\PBLITE>MD ANSWERS
```

Now change to this subdirectory and copy the file BAS.COM into it by typing

```
C:\PBLITE>CD ANSWERS
C:\PBLITE\ANSWERS>COPY A:BAS.COM C:\PBLITE\ANSWERS
```

Finally, to uncompress the file, type

```
C:\PBLITE\ANSWERS>BAS
```

The .BAS files have now been moved to a subdirectory of the PBLITE directory to avoid accidentally overwriting them.

Loading PowerBASIC Lite

The installation procedure for PowerBASIC Lite is not complicated. After you prepare the backup disk or copy the backup disk files to your hard drive, you are ready to begin.

Use the following steps to load PowerBASIC Lite from a floppy disk system.

1. Insert your backup disk in the appropriate disk drive.

2. Access the drive selected in step 1.

3. At the DOS prompt, type the file name **PBLITE**.

4. Press Enter.

Use the following steps to load PowerBASIC Lite from a hard disk drive.

1. Access the subdirectory of the backup disk.

2. At the subdirectory's DOS prompt, type the file name **PBLITE**.

3. Press Enter.

When PowerBASIC Lite is loaded, the opening screen appears with the copyright information displayed in a rectangle at the center of the screen (see figure 1.1).

Press the Esc key (almost any other key also will work) to remove that information, and then you see the opening screen.

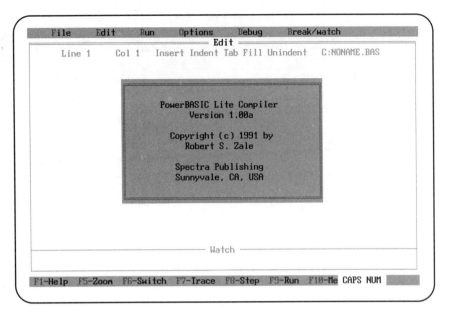

Figure 1.1. The opening PowerBASIC Lite screen.

The Integrated Development Environment

Study the opening screen after removing the copyright information (see figure 1.2). It contains five essential parts:

1. The Main menu on the bar at the top of the screen

2. The Edit window, which is the large upper rectangular area

3. The Status line at the top of the Edit window

4. The Watch window, which is the smaller rectangle below the Edit window

5. The Help line at the bottom of the screen

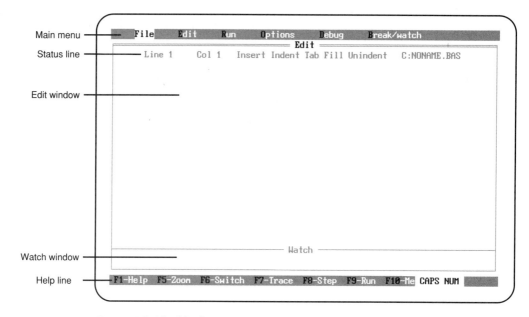

Figure 1.2. The blank PowerBASIC Lite screen.

The Main Menu

Look at figure 1.2. When you first load PowerBASIC Lite, the File item on the Main Menu bar is highlighted. You select a menu item by pressing either the right- or left-arrow key to move the highlight to the desired item on the Main Menu. Try these steps now:

1. Press the right-arrow key once. The highlight moves from the File item on the Main menu to the next item on the right, Edit.

2. Press the right-arrow key several times. Each time, the highlight moves one item to the right until it is on the last item, Break/watch (see figure 1.3).

When you press the right-arrow key again, the highlight cycles back to the File item, at the beginning of the menu. The highlight moves in the opposite direction when you press the left-arrow key.

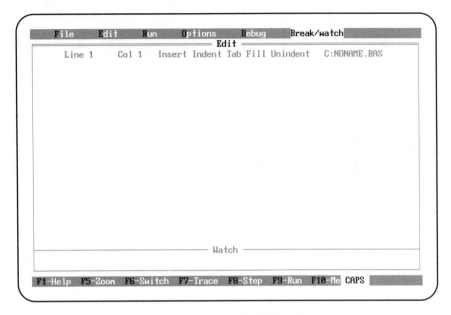

Figure 1.3. The Break/watch menu item is highlighted.

The Edit Window and Status Line

After moving the highlight around the menu bar, move it to the Edit menu item and press Enter. The highlight disappears from the Main menu bar, and a cursor appears in the Edit window in the leftmost column just below the status line (see figure 1.4).

Notice the first two items on the status line; Line 1, Col 1 is the cursor's position in the Edit window. You usually begin writing a PowerBASIC program at this position. However, we save writing a program for later so that you can spend some time exploring the Edit window and status line. At Line 1, column 1, type **abc**.

As each letter is typed and displayed, the cursor moves one space to the right. The column number in the status line increases by one as the cursor moves. After you type the letter *c*, the cursor should be at column 4, shown by the column number on the status line (see figure 1.5).

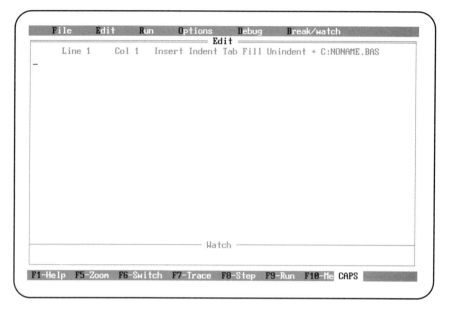

Figure 1.4. The Edit window ready for text.

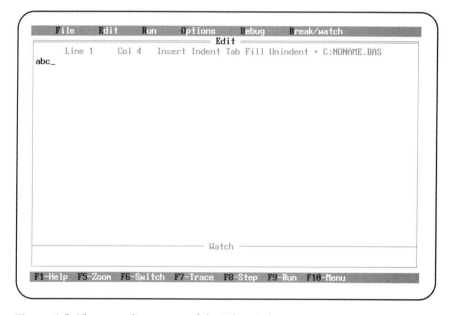

Figure 1.5. The status line at top of the Edit window.

After typing the letters *abc*, keep your eye on the column number on the status line and hold down the **d** key until the column number on the status line reaches 77. Then release the d key. If you hold the key down too long, press the Backspace key until the cursor is at column 77. The extra characters are erased as you press the Backspace key. The cursor should be at column 77 (see figure 1.6).

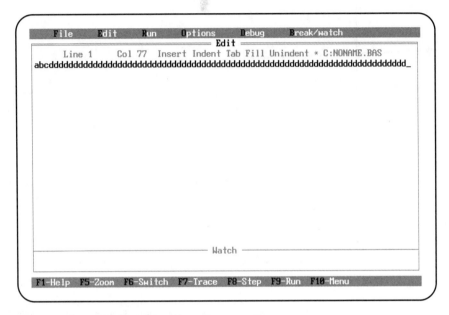

Figure 1.6. Column number 77 on the status line.

With the cursor at column 77, type **e**.

The cursor moves to column 78, but the line of text shifts left one position to make room for more characters. The letter a disappears off the left side of the screen, as shown in figure 1.7.

With the cursor at column 78, type **f**.

The text again scrolls to the left so that more characters can be inserted. The column number changes to 79, and the letter b disappears off the left edge of the screen.

Press the Enter key.

The text scrolls back to the right, displaying columns one through 77, and the cursor moves to the second line (see figure 1.8). The letter *f* in column 78 is not displayed, but it is still there. The Edit window displays only 77 columns of a line at one time.

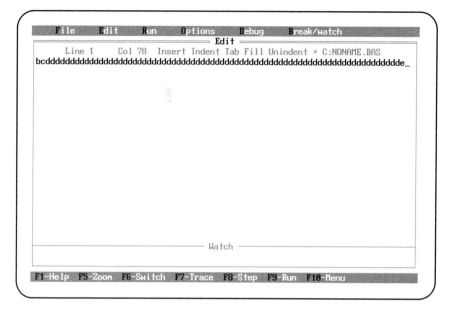

Figure 1.7. Text scrolls when the line is full.

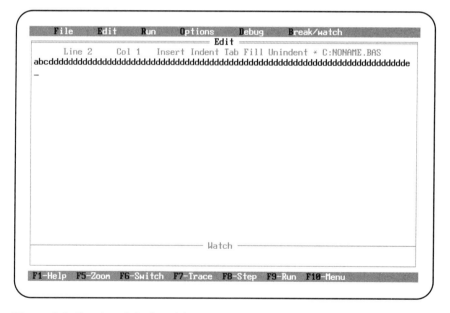

Figure 1.8. Text in original position.

Notice that the status line changes to Line 2, Col 1. The status line gives you instant information about current editing conditions.

Also, notice that the name of the current program is displayed at the extreme right of the status line. Because you haven't named a program yet, the current edit session is given the default name NONAME.BAS.

You can quickly erase the garbage on the screen by following these steps:

1. Move the cursor to Line 1, Column 1.

2. Hold down the Ctrl key and press **Q**. Then release each key. The Ctrl symbol and Q (^Q) appear on the left of the status line in the edit window (see figure 1.9).

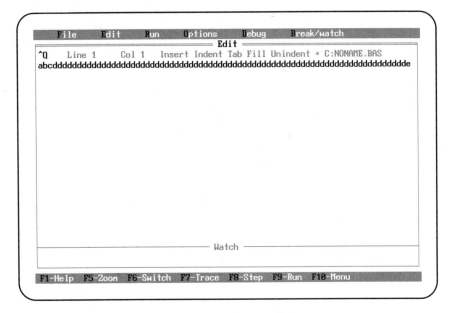

Figure 1.9. The Control-Q indicator on the status line.

3. Type the letter **Y**.

Ctrl-QY is the symbol for the key strokes in steps 2 and 3. This keystroke combination quickly erases the line on which the cursor resides.

Our experiment is concluded. You have seen how text is displayed in the Edit window. To leave the Edit window, press the F10 key. The cursor disappears from the Edit window, and the highlight returns to the Edit item on the Main menu.

The Watch Window and Help Line

The Watch window displays the values of variables during program execution. The Watch window is described in Chapter 14, "Dynamic Debugging."

The Help line at the bottom of the screen displays function keys that help you in the current environment setting. The Help line shown in figure 1.2 exists when you position the cursor on the Main menu bar or the Edit window. The Help line changes when the cursor is positioned in other parts of the environment. You made use of the last item on the Help line (F10-Menu) to return from the Edit window to the Main menu. Other items on the Help line are discussed as you use them.

The Menu System

You use menus and dialog boxes to provide information and commands when operating within PowerBASIC Lite's integrated development environment. You have accessed the Edit window from the Main menu and entered data in the Edit window. This section describes other menus you will use frequently and demonstrates how to use them.

You select menu items in one of three ways:

1. When any item on the Main menu is highlighted, you can make a selection by using the left- or right-arrow key to move the highlight to the desired item and pressing Enter.

2. To make a selection from the Main menu after any of its items is highlighted, press the key corresponding to the first letter of the desired item. To escape from a pull-down menu, press the Esc key.

    For example, to select the File menu when any item on the Main menu is highlighted, press **F** (for File). This step pulls down the File menu. You do not have to press Enter.

3. When the highlight is not on an item on the Main menu, you can make a selection by using thc Alt key in combination with the red, uppercase letter on the desired menu item.

Using the File Menu

You access the File menu by one of the previous methods. The File menu appears under its menu name (see figure 1.10).

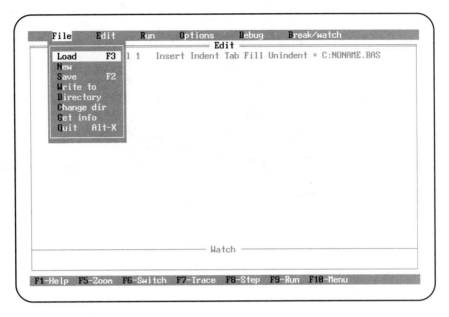

Figure 1.10. The File menu.

When you access the File menu, the first item (Load) is highlighted. Scan the list of items on the File menu. You use some of them often. You use others less often, and you may not use some of them at all. Notice that three of them are followed by a *hot key*. A hot key provides a shortcut to executing a menu command. You can use these rather than select menu items by cursor movement.

Command	Hot Key
Load	F3
Save	F2
Quit	Alt-X

You can access these items from outside the File menu by pressing the appropriate hot key.

Pay particular attention to the last item on the list, Quit. This selection enables you to exit PowerBASIC when a session is finished.

The File menu offers choices for loading existing files, creating new files, and saving a file currently in the editor. You move between File menu items by using the up- and down-arrow keys. The first item on the File menu is Load. When you load a file, it is read into the editor. When you finish creating a file, you save it by selecting Save.

13

Use the up- or down-arrow key to move the highlight to Load if it is not already there. Then press Enter. An input box appears, requesting the name of the file you want to load (see figure 1.11).

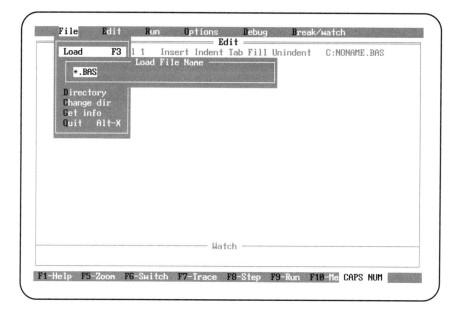

Figure 1.11. Load file name dialog box.

Type the name of the disk drive you are using to save your program files and the file name. For example, type **B:PBL0101** when you use drive B. Then press Enter.

A Verify dialog box appears, as shown in figure 1.12.

PowerBASIC Lite is very protective. Even though you erased the experimental lines you typed in the Edit window, PowerBASIC Lite wants to know whether you want to save what is on-screen—even when nothing is there.

Type **N**. This step removes the dialog box and clears the screen. The cursor is at line 1, column 1, ready for you to enter a program. Notice that the file name you enter for the program is displayed on the right end of the status line.

The PB0101 program does not exist yet, even though its name is displayed. By using the Load command, you can assign a name to a program that doesn't exist. You could have used the New command from the file menu. However, the new program would have automatically been provided with the default name, NONAME.BAS.

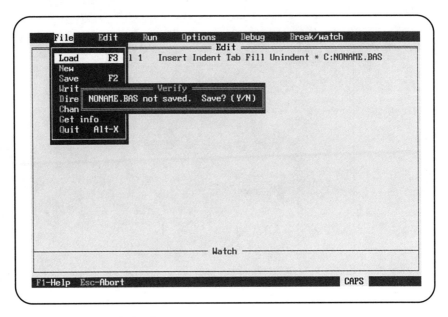

Figure 1.12. Verify dialog box.

A New Program

The editor has two text-entry modes: *Insert* and *Overwrite*. When you first select Edit from the Main menu, the Insert entry mode is active. When you use the Insert mode, text is entered at the cursor. Any text under the cursor or to its right is pushed to the right to make room for the new text. You can detect the active mode by looking at the status line. When the Insert mode is active, the third item displayed on the status line is the word Insert (see figure 1.13).

To change from Insert entry mode to Overwrite mode, press the Insert key (Ins on some keyboards). In Overwrite mode, any text lying under the cursor is overwritten as you type. When Overwrite mode is active, a blank space is displayed as the position of the third item on the status line, as shown in figure 1.14.

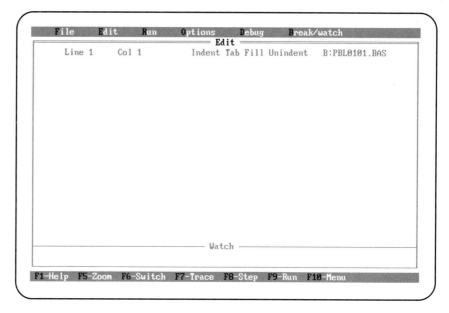

Figure 1.13. The status line for Insert mode.

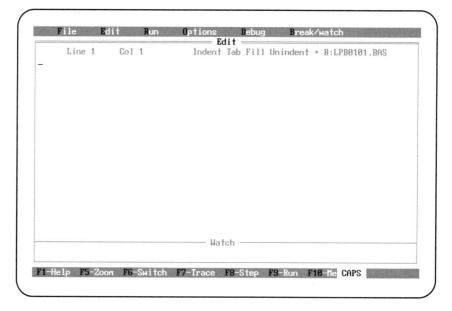

Figure 1.14. The status line for Overwrite mode.

Use the Insert key as a toggle switch to change entry modes.

1. When you are in Insert entry mode, pressing Insert toggles Overwrite entry mode On.

2. When you are in Overwrite entry mode, pressing Insert toggles Insert entry mode ON.

Use whichever mode you feel comfortable with.

If you are not already in the Edit window with the cursor positioned at line 1, column 1, select Edit from the Main menu. You are then ready to enter a program.

Type each line of listing 1.1 and press the Enter key at the end of each line. Type each line slowly and carefully. If you make a mistake while using Insert mode, use the backspace key to erase. Then type the correction. You can correct mistakes by typing over the mistake in Overwrite mode. Do not run the program yet.

Listing 1.1. The Print Date and Time program.

```
REM ** Print Date and Time **
' Learning BASIC, Chapter 1.
' File: PBL0101.BAS
CLS                             ' Clear the screen
PRINT "Date"                    ' Print the word in quotes
PRINT DATE$                     ' Print today's date
PRINT                           ' Print a blank line
PRINT "Time"                    ' Print another word in
quotes
PRINT TIME$                     ' Print the current time
END                             ' End the program
```

A Little About the Program

If you have programmed in BASIC before, you might notice that this program lacks line numbers. Line numbers are an integral part of the editing and execution of interpreted BASIC programs. You can use line numbers in a PowerBASIC Lite program. The built-in screen editor of PowerBASIC Lite, however, makes line numbers unnecessary.

The first three lines of the program are *remarks* to identify the program. These lines are not executed. The computer ignores the remarks when it compiles and runs the program. Remarks begin with the REM keyword or with an apostrophe (').

Of the remaining lines of the program, only the statements to the left of the apostrophes are executed. The apostrophes and all text to the right of the apostrophes are for your benefit. They tell you what the statement tells the computer to do.

PowerBASIC Lite ignores all text on a line that follows an apostrophe. Remarks enable you to add comments to a program so that you can recall how the program works when you return to it later.

There are three general kinds of program-control structures: *sequencing*, *looping*, and *conditional branching*. This program is at the simplest level, as a sequence of single-line statements. It uses only the sequence structure. That is, each statement is executed in sequence. After the compiler skips the three remarks, it compiles the statements from top to bottom, ignoring the comments following the executable statements. This is what the compiler sees:

```
CLS
PRINT "Date"
PRINT DATE$
PRINT
PRINT "Time"
PRINT TIME$
END
```

The loop and conditional branch structures will be described when they are introduced.

Even if you type the program correctly, you cannot be sure that it will compile and run correctly. Before you run a program, you should save it to disk. Sometimes an incorrectly written program can "hang up" the computer so that you have to restart the computer from DOS. If you haven't saved your program, you have to type it again from the keyboard. If you have long programs, you should save them frequently during their creation to prevent loss from unexpected interruptions.

Saving the Program

You save PowerBASIC programs from the File menu. Use the following steps to save the program in listing 1.1:

1. Return to the Main menu bar (by pressing F10).

2. Access the File menu (by pressing the arrow keys or typing **F**).

3. Move the highlight to Save, and then press Enter (or type **S**).

The menu is cleared and the disk drive whirs as your program is saved to the disk in the drive you named. Even though you save your program to disk, the program is still visible in the Edit window. Now it's time to test the program with a run.

Running the Program

Access Run on the Main menu by pressing Alt-R. The Run menu appears as shown
in figure 1.15.

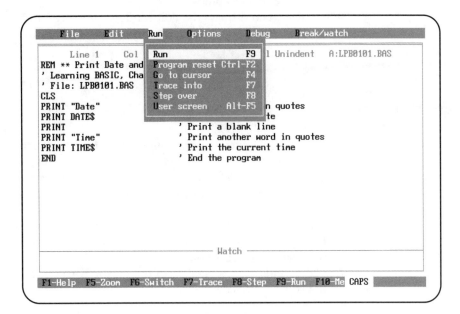

Figure 1.15. The Run menu.

The first item on the Run menu, the Run command, invokes the compiler for
the program or file you currently are editing. When the program compiles correctly,
it runs immediately. You use this command to run your program. While the Run
command is highlighted, press Enter.

The Edit window disappears, and you should see the following output of your
program in the User screen window:

```
Date
05-10-1991

Time
17:25:33
```

The User screen window is blank except for the information you ask to print.
The words you enclose in quotes are printed. A blank line separates the date and
time. Two built-in system variables, DATE$ and TIME$, were used to print the current
date and time stored inside the computer.

To return from the User screen to the Edit window, press any key.

When you return to the Edit window, your program is still there. Although it is not immediately apparent, the output of your program remains in the User screen window. You can toggle between the Edit window and the User screen window by pressing Alt-F5. Try it a few times.

When the screen displays the Edit window, pressing Alt-F5 displays the User screen. When the User screen is displayed, press any key to return to the Edit window.

Program Errors

If you typed listing 1.1 correctly and followed all the other instructions perfectly, everything went smoothly and you had no problems. Usually, some small errors creep into even the simplest programs. Sooner or later, everyone makes mistakes. Therefore, your next program contains an error that PowerBASIC Lite will find for you.

Press F10 to leave the Edit window and return to the Main menu, unless you are already there. Then type **F** to access the File menu. Move the highlight down to the New command and press Enter.

The Edit window goes blank with the cursor at row 1, column 1. Type the program in listing 1.2 exactly as shown.

Listing 1.2. The Sum and Average Temperatures program.

```
REM ** Sum and Average Temperatures **
' Learning BASIC, Chapter 1.  File: PBL0102.BAS

REM ** Use a Loop Structure **
CLS
Sum = 0
FOR day = 1 TO 7
  READ temperature
  Sum = Sum + temperature
NEXT day
Ave = Sum / 7
PRINT Sum, Ave
END

DATA 72.5, 83.3, 82.1, 75.7, 74.8, 83.2
```

This program contains a *loop* structure. The body of the FOR...NEXT loop is indented so that it can be clearly read and understood. The loop is executed seven times as specified in the FOR statement that marks the top of the loop. The value of the variable, day, increases by one each time through the loop because of the NEXT statement that marks the end of the loop. When the value of day reaches 8, the execution of the program proceeds to the statement following the loop. The sum and average of the temperatures are printed, and the program ends.

After you enter the program (including the error), press F10 to move to the Main menu, and then access the File menu by typing **F**.

Notice the present file name, found at the right end of the Main menu. The file name contains the active disk drive, along with the file name NONAME. When you use the Save command on the File menu, the program is saved under that name. Rather than Save, move the highlight down to the Write to... command and press Enter.

A New Name dialog box appears with a blinking cursor (see figure 1.16).

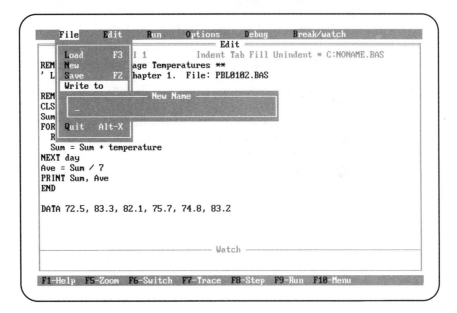

Figure 1.16. The New name dialog box.

Enter the disk drive you want to use to save the program, a colon, and the file name to use for saving. For example, to save the program with the name SUMAVE01 to a disk in drive B, type

```
B:SUMAVE01
```

The program is saved, and the new name appears at the right end of the status line, replacing NONAME.

Now it's time to try a run. Press F10 to access the Main menu. Then type **R** to access the Run submenu. After highlighting the Run item on the Run submenu, press Enter to run the program.

Instead of compiling and running, the following error message appears at the top of the Edit window, replacing the status line:

```
Error 4: Out of data
```

The cursor is blinking on the program line:

```
Read temperature
```

This message indicates the statement being executed when the error occurred.

Press the Esc key to remove the error message. The Run item on the Main menu item is highlighted, indicating that you return to where you were before the error occurred. Type **E** to return to the Edit window.

If you haven't spotted the error yet, study the program carefully. Remember, the FOR...NEXT loop is executed seven times. Now, look at the DATA statement. Count the number of temperatures in the list; there are only six. Therefore, when the computer tries to read data on the seventh pass through the loop, there is no more data, and you receive the error message. You must add one more temperature to the list.

Move the cursor to the right of the last temperature (83.2). Type **, 80.9** and press Enter.

Be sure to add a comma after 83.2 but not after 80.9. The DATA line should now read:

```
DATA 72.5, 83.3, 82.1, 75.7, 74.8, 83.2, 80.9
```

After making this correction, run the program again. The Edit window is erased, and then the program compiles and runs. The User screen window appears with the sum and average of the temperatures displayed on the top line, as shown in the following line.

```
552.5          78.92857
```

A comma separates the variables Sum and Ave in the program's PRINT statement. The comma causes each value to print in its own *print field*. The leftmost print field begins at column 1. Each print field is 14 characters long. The second print field therefore begins at column 15.

Positive numbers are printed with a leading blank space. That space is filled with a minus sign (–) for negative numbers. Because both values printed by the program are positive numbers, a blank space precedes each of them. The value of Sum that you see begins at column 2, and the value of Ave you see begins at column 16.

Because you saved the program when it contained the error, you should save it again with the correction. You gave it a name earlier, so save the program this time by using the Save command on the File menu. Remember that you

- Save a program with the Save command if it has been named.

- Save a program with the Write to... command if it has not been named.

This section completes the tutorial for this chapter. Use either of the following methods to return to DOS from PowerBASIC Lite.

1. From the Edit window, press Ctrl-X.

2. From anywhere, access the Quit command on the File menu and press Enter.

Summary

The BASIC language was designed in 1963 and 1964 as an easy-to-use instructional tool. PowerBASIC Lite is a modern, compiled version of BASIC with more powerful structures and faster execution times than the earlier, interpreted versions of BASIC.

The files in your PowerBASIC Lite package contain an editor, a compiler, and a help system that are linked together to make an integrated development environment. This environment enables you to create, edit, and run programs in an efficient manner through a system of menus. Individual menus are accessed through a Main menu that you can reach easily from anywhere in the environment.

You write and edit programs in the View window, and program results are displayed in the User screen window. You save programs that have been named to disk by using the Save command on the File menu. You save programs that have not been named by using the Write to... command on the File menu.

In this chapter, you

- Experimented with text in the Edit window.

- Entered and edited programs from the Edit window.

- Used the Load, New, Save, and Write to... commands of the File menu.

- Used the Run command of the Run menu.

- Discovered dialog boxes that pop up at appropriate times to provide or request information.

- Saw an error message displayed to help you find program errors.

This initial exposure to PowerBASIC Lite is a first step that leads to expanded exploration of the creation and editing of programs in the following chapter.

Exercises

1. Name the two basic methods of translating high-level languages, such as BASIC, into machine-language code.

2. Why do programs written in PowerBASIC Lite run faster than those written in an interpreted version of BASIC?

3. Where is the PowerBASIC Lite status line located?

4. What is the purpose of the F10 key in editing a program?

5. What command on the File menu should you use to save a program that has not been named?

6. What is the maximum number of characters that can be displayed on one line in the Edit window?

7. What action does the Ctrl-Q Y keypress combination perform?

8. On which menu is the New command located?

9. What key combination do you use to move from the Edit window to the User screen window?

10. Which menu contains the command that enables you to exit from PowerBASIC and return to DOS?

Chapter 2

Using PowerBASIC Lite

You had a taste of programming in the first chapter. Now it's time to learn more about using the PowerBASIC Lite development system. The editor has some powerful features you will read about in this chapter. You will learn to move the cursor within your program and to insert, move, and delete pieces of your program. Most programmers continually modify their programs as they think of new ways to do things. No doubt you are—or will be—the same way.

The following topics are discussed in this chapter:

- Selecting menus and browsing the File and Run menus

- Loading a previously saved program and running it one step at a time

- Editing a program—insert, delete, and block operations

- Using the Help index to find information about a wide range of PowerBASIC Lite programming components

- Copying statement syntax from help screens and pasting the information into the Edit window

- Breaking a program into functional parts

- Spacing printed output in different ways

Moving Through the Menus

As you learned in Chapter 1, "Getting Started," you can move from one item on the Main menu to another by pressing the arrow keys. You will use the File and

Run menus more often than any of the others. You should acquaint yourself, however, with items on the other menus so that you know which one to use when the need arises. You learned in Chapter 1 that there is no Edit menu. The Edit item on the Main menu puts the cursor in the Edit window for editing purposes. Let's explore the File and Run menus.

If you haven't already run PowerBASIC Lite from DOS as instructed in Chapter 1, do so now. Remember that the name of the file you load is PBLITE. After loading the file, press any key to remove the copyright information. The File item on the Main menu is highlighted. Press Enter to pull down the File menu (see figure 2.1).

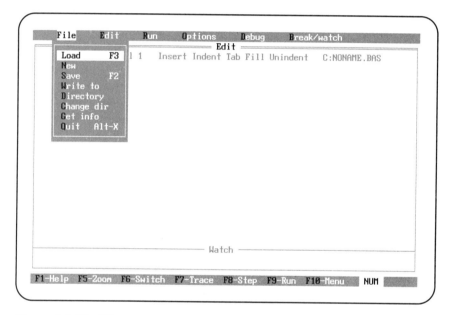

Figure 2.1. The File menu.

Exploring the File Menu

After highlighting the Load command on the File menu, press the Help key (F1). Pressing this key loads information about the Load command from the PBHELP file. A window labeled PowerBASIC Help appears, with a description of the Load command (see figure 2.2). You used the Load command in Chapter 1 to enter the file name (PBL0101) of your first program, Print Date and Time.

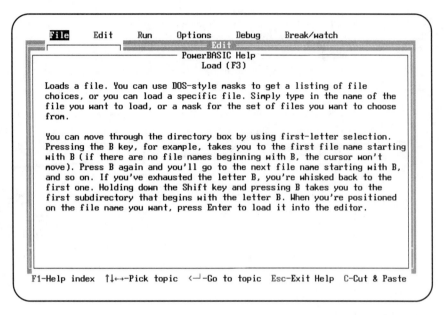

Figure 2.2. The Load help window.

Note: The term *mask* in the Help window refers to the use of *wildcards*. See "wildcard" in your DOS technical manual.

When you finish reading the information in the Load help window, press Esc to remove the window.

Use the down-arrow key to move the highlight in the File menu down to the New command. Press F1 to see the information in the New help window. A brief, two-line description tells you that New places in the editor a new, empty file named NONAME by default. (You used the New command in Chapter 1 to clear the screen in preparation for entering the Sum and Average Temperatures program.) When you finish reading the information in the New help window, press Esc to remove the Help window and return to the File menu.

Move the highlight on the File menu down to the Save command. Then press F1 to see the information in the Save help window. You see another short, two-line description about the use of the Save command. (You used the Save command to save a program in Chapter 1.) When you finish reading the information in the Save help window, press Esc to remove the window. Move the highlight on the File menu to the Write to... command. Then press F1 to see the information in the Write to... help window. The description tells you that this command writes the file in the editor to a new file name. (You used this command to save a program in Chapter 1.) When you finish reading the information in the Write to... help window, press Esc to remove the window.

Move the highlight on the File menu to the Directory command. You have not used this command yet. Press F1 to see the Directory help window (see figure 2.3).

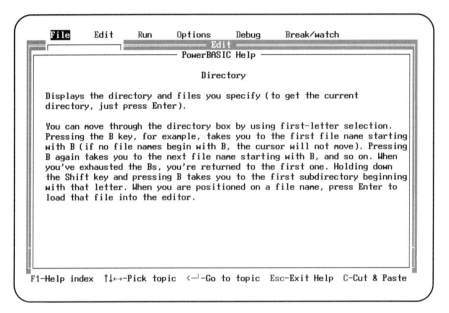

Figure 2.3. The Directory help window.

You use this command later in this chapter, in the section named "Loading a Program," to see a directory of your saved program files. When you finish reading the information in the window, press Esc to return to the File menu.

Move the highlight down to the Change dir command, and press F1 to see the information in the Change dir window (see figure 2.4).

Your use of this command depends on how many disk drives you use and how you organize your files. The Change dir command is described in the "Loading a Program" section of this chapter. When you have read the information in the window, press the Esc key to return to the File menu.

Move the highlight down the File menu to the Get info command. Press F1 to see the information in the first of four Get info help screens. The first screen is shown in figure 2.5.

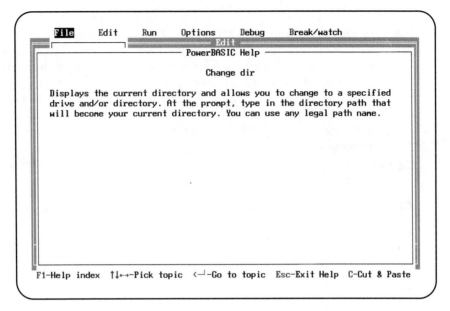

Figure 2.4. The Change dir help window.

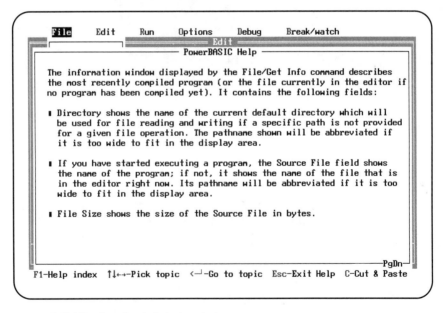

Figure 2.5. The first Get info help window.

Notice the help clue in the lower-right corner of the Get info help window (PgDn). When you finish reading the information in this window, press the PgDn key to see the second screen of Get info help. Do the same for the third and fourth screens of help. When you finish reading all four screens, press Esc to return to the File menu.

Move the highlight down to the Quit command and press F1 to see information in the Quit help window. You used the Quit command near the end of Chapter 1 to return to DOS from PowerBASIC Lite. When you finish reading the information in the Quit help window, press Esc to return to the File menu in preparation for the next section.

Exploring the Run Menu

After you access the Main menu and it is pulled down, press the right-arrow key to move the highlight to the Run item. Then press Enter to display the Run menu shown in figure 2.6.

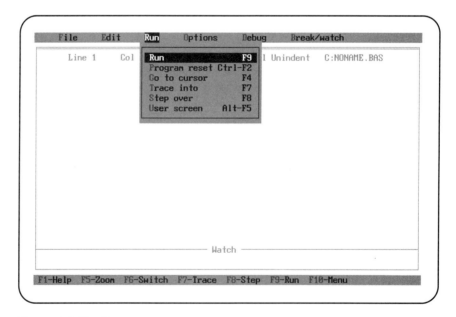

Figure 2.6. The Run menu.

The first item, Run, is highlighted. Press F1 to access the Run help window (see figure 2.7).

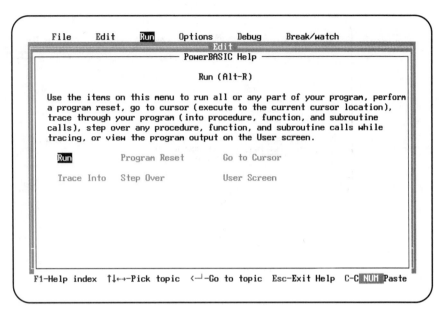

Figure 2.7. The Run help window.

You used the Run command on the Run menu in Chapter 1, but you should read the description in the Help window. When you finish, press Esc to return to the Run menu.

Move the highlight down to the Program reset command and press F1 to see information in the Program Reset help window. This command tells PowerBASIC when you finish with a particular debugging run and cancels the current debugging session. You use this command in Chapter 14, "Dynamic Debugging." When you finish reading the information in this help window, press Esc to return to the Run menu.

Move the highlight down to the Go to cursor command and press F1 to see information in the Go to Cursor help window. Notice that this command begins (or continues) execution of your program from the current line where the cursor resides. You also will use this command in Chapter 14, "Dynamic Debugging." When you finish reading the information in this help window, press Esc to return to the Run menu.

Move the highlight down to the Trace into command and press F1 to see information in the Trace Into help window, shown in figure 2.8. You will use this command in the "Tracing into the Program" section of this chapter.

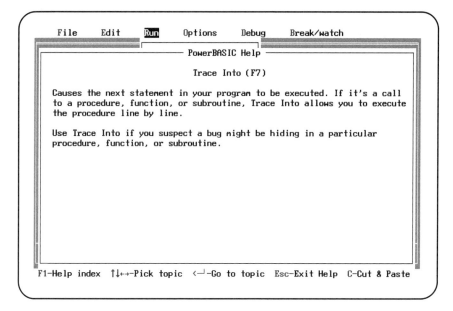

Figure 2.8. The Trace Into help window.

When you finish reading the information in this help window, press Esc to return to the Run menu.

Move the highlight down to the Step over command and press F1 to see information in the Step Over help window. The window shows that this command works like the Trace Into command with one exception: When the statement is a procedure, function, or subroutine call, the entire routine is executed in one step. The debugger pauses at the statement following the routine call. You will use this command, too, in Chapter 14, "Dynamic Debugging." When you finish reading the information in this help window, press Esc to return to the Run menu.

Move the highlight down to the last command, User screen, and press F1 to see information in the User Screen window shown in figure 2.9. You used the shortcut key combination, F5, in Chapter 1 to toggle between the Edit window and the User Screen window, where a program's output is displayed.

When you finish reading the information in this help window, press Esc to return to the Run menu.

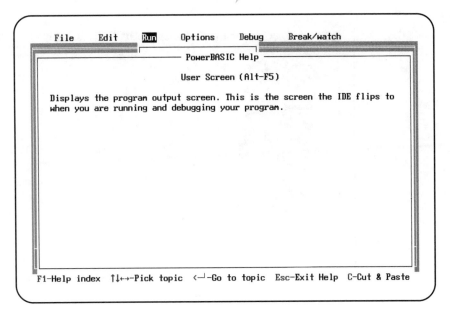

Figure 2.9. The User Screen help window.

Using a Previously Saved Program

When you want to load a program you previously saved and you know the name of the program, you usually use the Load command on the File menu to load it. However, suppose you cannot remember the filename. You use the Change dir and the Directory commands on the File menu to find the name of the program.

Loading a Program

Use the arrow keys to move to the File item on the Main menu. Press Enter and use the down-arrow key to move the highlight down to the Change dir command, as shown in figure 2.10.

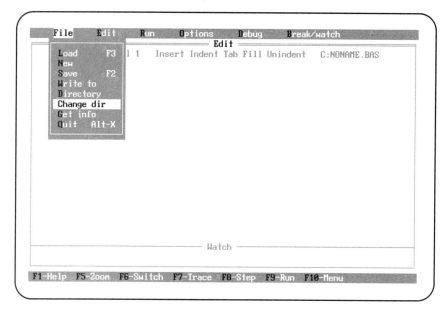

Figure 2.10. The Change dir command highlighted.

Press the Enter key. A New Directory dialog box appears with the current directory displayed, as previously described in the Change dir help window. When you are using a hard disk drive, the dialog box might look like the one in figure 2.11. The information varies for different system configurations.

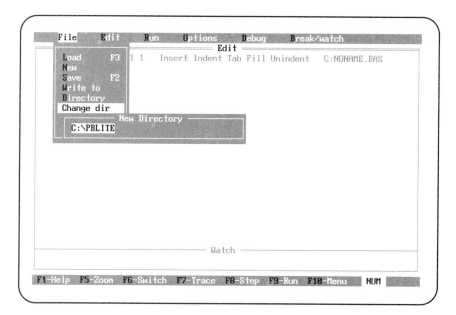

Figure 2.11. The New Directory dialog box displays the current directory.

The Change dir help window also explains you can change directories by typing in a new directory path. Suppose you are storing your programs on a disk in drive B and want to make drive B the current, active drive. With the disk in drive B, you type

```
B:\
```

and press the Enter key.

When you are using a different drive, use the letter appropriate for that drive.

The file directory disappears and the cursor blinks in the Edit window. The current drive in this example changes from the subdirectory named PBLITE on drive C to the root directory of drive B. Every disk has one, and only one root directory. You may subdivide the root directory into subdirectories. You usually use subdirectories to organize files on a hard disk drive. When you don't create subdirectories, all your files store to the root directory. The root directory of a drive is the backslash (\), as in the information just entered.

Disk drive B is now the active drive. You can now load any program directly from drive B without designating the drive in the file name of the program.

Press Alt-F to pull down the File menu again. Then move the highlight down to the Directory command and press Enter. An Enter File Name dialog box appears as shown in figure 2.12.

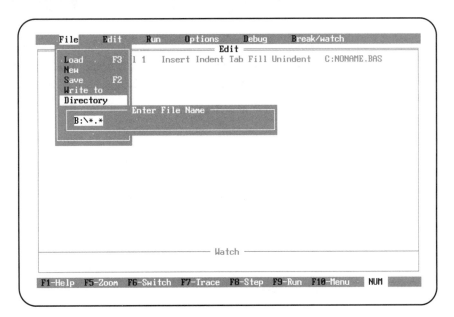

Figure 2.12. The File Name dialog box.

The asterisks are called wildcards. The left asterisk indicates you want to see files with any name. The asterisk following the period indicates you want to see files with any extension. Using asterisks in both places means you want to see all files in the B root directory. Press Enter to see all the files on drive B. Figure 2.13 shows a list of the files saved in Chapter 1. Your list may be longer. When you see the file name of the first program you entered in Chapter 1, PBL0101.BAS, use arrow keys to move the highlight to that program name and press Enter.

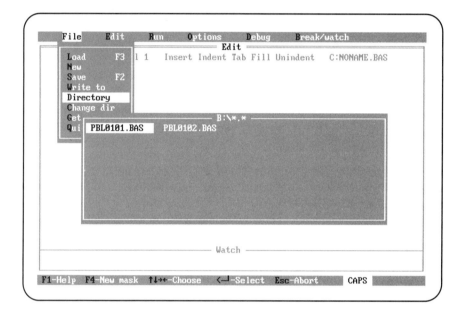

Figure 2.13. A list of files on drive B.

When you don't see the file name of that program, go through your disks to locate that file. Put that disk in your active drive, press Esc to remove the dialog box, access the Directory command on the File menu again, and press Enter. This time, move the highlight to the program name and press Enter.

The dialog disappears and the program file, PBL0101.BAS, is displayed in the Edit window.

Tracing into the Program

The Trace Into command on the Run menu enables you to watch the computer execute your program step-by-step. Use it now to step through the Print Date and Time program.

Press Alt-R to access the Run menu, move the highlight down to the Trace into command. Notice the hot key (shortcut method for accessing Trace Into) is F7. Use it in this demonstration to step through your program.

Press the Enter key after highlighting the Trace Into command. The screen blinks and the cursor and highlight move down to the CLS statement in your program, as shown in figure 2.14.

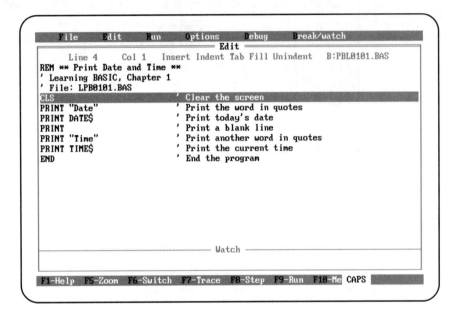

Figure 2.14. The CLS statement highlighted.

The computer skips the three remarks at the beginning of the program and pauses at the CLS statement, the first executable statement in the program. Press the F7 key. The screen blinks again, the CLS statement is executed, and the cursor and highlight move down to the PRINT "Date" statement.

To see that the output screen is cleared by CLS, you view it by pressing Alt-F5. Do it now to see the blank output screen. Then press any key to display the Edit screen again.

Press the F7 key again. The screen blinks again. This time, the PRINT "Date" statement is executed, and the cursor and highlight move down to the PRINT DATE$ statement, as shown in figure 2.15.

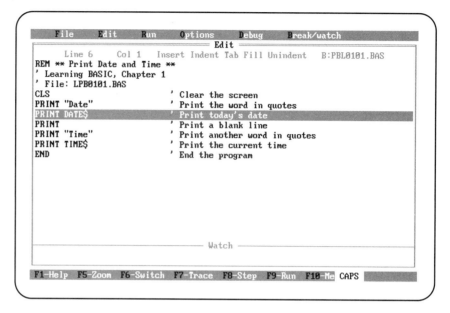

Figure 2.15. The PRINT DATE$ statement highlighted.

When the `PRINT "Date"` statement is executed, the word in quotation marks (Date) is printed. Press Alt-F5 to see the Output screen. You see the single word

```
Date
```

Press any key to move back to the Edit window. Then press F7 again. The screen blinks, the `PRINT DATE$` statement is executed, and the cursor and highlight move down to the `PRINT` statement that has nothing following it.

Press Alt-F5 to view the output screen. You should see two lines at the top of the screen:

```
Date
12-22-1991
```

The date you see on the screen will be different depending on the day you look at this program. Press any key to return to the program in the Edit window.

Press F7. The `PRINT` statement is executed. The cursor and highlight move to the `PRINT "Time"` statement. A `PRINT` statement used by itself prints nothing, but does send a carriage return to the computer. When you look at the Output screen, you see no change from the previous one. After highlighting the `PRINT "Time"` statement in the Edit window, press F7; the `PRINT "Time"` statement is executed. The cursor and highlight move to the `PRINT TIME$` statement. Press Alt-F5 to see the Output screen.

```
Date
12-22-1991

Time
```

The word Time is added to the Output screen. Notice that the PRINT statement by itself causes a blank line to be displayed between the date and the word, Time. Press any key to move back to the Edit window.

Press F7. The PRINT TIME$ statement is executed. The cursor and highlight move to the END statement. The current time is added to the Output screen.

Press F7 one more time to execute the END statement. The Output screen appears:

```
Date
12-22-1991

Time
16:22:27
```

The computer's time is expressed in hours, minutes, and seconds. The time format is for a 24-hour day. The time displayed in this example is 4 p.m. plus 22 minutes and 16 seconds.

Press any key to return to the Edit window. You can see that the highlight is missing. You have traced through each step of the program as it is executed by the computer. Leave the Print Date and Time program in the Edit window for use in the next section.

Moving Within a Program

Begin your explorations of the editor by using the short cursor moves described in the following section, "Short Moves."

While you explore, observe the changes that take place in the status line of the Edit window, especially the Line and Col values:

- Line indicates the number of the line on which the cursor lies relative to the top of the file, not the top of the screen. For short programs, the entire file may show on the screen. Longer programs may extend beyond the screen.

- Col indicates the column number of the current cursor position relative to the leftmost column of the file, not the screen. In this book, statements for programs are restricted to the screen except where a demonstration of long statements appears.

41

Short Moves

You can make most cursor movements in more than one way. Table 2.1 lists ways the cursor can move with either the arrow-key or Control-key combinations. Ctrl-E means, "Hold down the Ctrl key while pressing the letter E, and then release both keys."

Table 2.1. Making short cursor moves.

Method 1	Method 2	Resulting Action
Right arrow	Ctrl-D	Move right one character
Left arrow	Ctrl-S	Move left one character
Down arrow	Ctrl-X	Move down one line
Up arrow	Ctrl-E	Move up one line

Move the cursor to line 1, column 1 of the Print Date and Time program. Then try the following sequence of cursor movements. Remember to keep an eye on the line and column values of the status line as the cursor moves.

1. Press the right-arrow key once. The cursor moves one position to the right. The Col value on the status line changes to 2 (see figure 2.16).

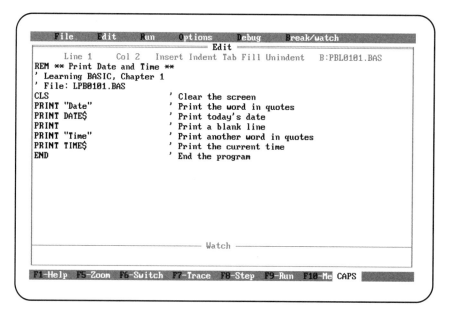

Figure 2.16. The cursor at column 2.

2. Press the right-arrow key several times. Each keypress moves the cursor one position to the right. As the cursor moves, the Col value on the status line changes to reflect its new position.

3. Hold down the right-arrow key until the cursor moves past column 77 of line 1. See how far it moves to the right. The cursor can move to the right until column 248. It remains at that position even when you press the right-arrow key. It is not good programming practice to enter text beyond the right edge of the Edit window (column 77 for the normal window).

4. Hold down the left-arrow key (under the R of the first remark) until the cursor moves back to column 1 of line 1:

```
REM ** Print Date and Time **
```

5. Press the left-arrow key again to see whether anything happens. When the cursor reaches column 1, it remains there for further presses of the left-arrow key.

6. Try moving the cursor with Ctrl-D and Ctrl-S. Ctrl-D works the same as the right-arrow key. Ctrl-S works the same as left-arrow.

Use the following steps to move the cursor vertically within your program. Begin with the cursor at line 1, column 1.

1. Press the down-arrow key. The cursor moves down one line. The value of Line on the status line increases by one, as shown in figure 2.17.

2. Try the Ctrl-X combination. Pressing the down-arrow key or Ctrl-X moves the cursor down one line. The value of Line on the status line increases by one each time the cursor moves down a line.

3. Press the up-arrow key. The cursor moves up one line. The value of Line on the status line decreases by one.

4. Try the Ctrl-E combination. Pressing the up-arrow key or Ctrl-E moves the cursor up one line. The value of Line on the status line decreases by one each time the cursor moves up a line. The cursor cannot move beyond the beginning of the file by up arrow or Ctrl-E.

5. Press the down-arrow key until the cursor no longer moves downward (see figure 2.18). When you press down-arrow or Ctrl-X, the cursor can move to the end of the file (one line at a time). The cursor cannot move beyond the end of the file when you use down arrow or Ctrl-X.

Learning BASIC

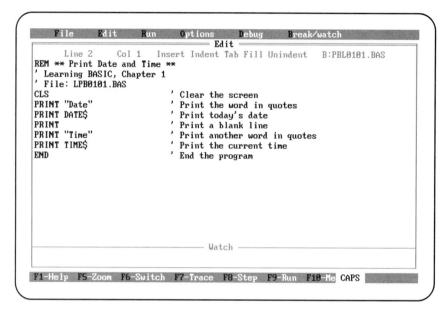

Figure 2.17. The cursor at line 2, column 1.

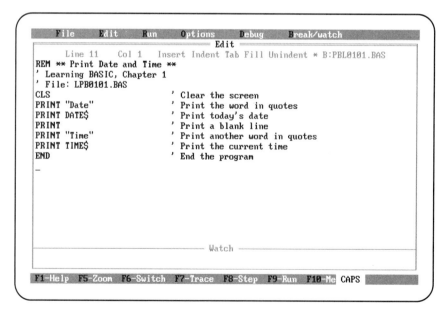

Figure 2.18. The cursor at the end of the file.

44

6. Press the up-arrow key or the Ctrl-E combination until the cursor has moved to Line 1, Col 1.

Larger Moves

This section describes some key combinations you can use to move the cursor in larger steps (see table 2.2).

Table 2.2. Making larger cursor movements.

Key Combination	Resulting Action
Ctrl-F	Move right one word
Ctrl-A	Move left one word
Ctrl-Q D or End	Move to end of line
Ctrl-Q S or Home	Move to beginning of line
Ctrl-Q X	Move to bottom of window
Ctrl-Q E	Move to top of window

The last four items in table 2.2 use a different symbolism. The Ctrl-Q portion means the same as the previous key combinations: Hold down the Ctrl key, press Q, and then release both keys. After this step, press the key of the last letter of the symbolism.

For example: Ctrl-Q D means hold down Ctrl while pressing Q. Release both keys, then press the letter D.

When the cursor is not at the beginning of the first line of the Print Date and Time program, move it there with the keypress combinations from table 2.1.

With the cursor at line 1, column 1, use the following sequence of cursor movements (using the key combinations from table 2.2).

1. Press the combination: Ctrl-F once. Ctrl-F moves the cursor right one word.

```
REM ** Print Date and Time **
```

A word is a sequence of characters separated by one or more of the following:

```
space <> . ; , () {} ^ ' * + -/ $
```

Therefore, the cursor skips the two asterisks and spaces to the word Print. The value of Col (8) on the status line changes to reflect the new column.

2. Press Ctrl-F four more times. Each time you press Ctrl-F, the cursor moves to the right one word until it reaches the end of the line. When the cursor reaches the end of a line and you press Ctrl-F, it moves to the first word of the next line. Try it. The value of Line and Col on the status line change to reflect the new cursor position.

```
REM ** Print Date and Time **
' Learning BASIC, Chapter 1
```

3. With the cursor at line 2, column 3, press the Ctrl-A combination once. Ctrl-A moves the cursor one word to the left. When the cursor is on the first word of a line, it moves to the end of the previous line (line 1, in this example).

4. Press Ctrl-A until the cursor is at the beginning of line 1. The cursor moves left one word until it reaches the first word of line 1. Press the combination once more. When the cursor is at the beginning of the first line of a file and you press Ctrl-A, the cursor does not move.

5. Now try the combination: Ctrl-Q D. When you press the Ctrl-Q key combination, the symbols for this combination (^Q) appear at the extreme left of the status line, as shown in figure 2.19.

   This symbol tells you that the editor is ready for you to use another keypress associated with a special key-combination command. While the symbol is on the status line, type **D**.

   The symbols disappear from the status line, and the action that the key combination causes takes place. Pressing Ctrl-Q D moves the cursor to the end of the current line (the end of line 1 in this example). The new column position (30) is shown on the status line.

6. While the cursor is at the end of the line, press Ctrl-Q and then S. Pressing Ctrl-Q S moves the cursor to the beginning of the current line. The new column position (1) is shown on the status line.

7. Press Ctrl-F to move the cursor right one word in the program's first line:

```
REM ** Print Date and Time **
```

Now press Ctrl-Q and then X. Pressing the Ctrl-Q X combination moves the cursor to the bottom of the window at the current column (see figure 2.20).

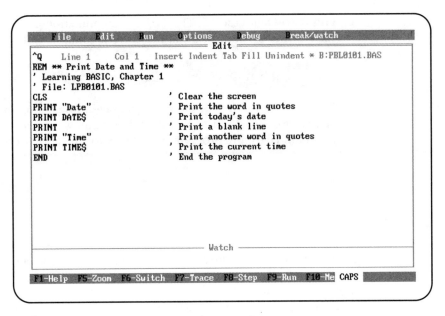

Figure 2.19. The Ctrl-Q symbol on the status line.

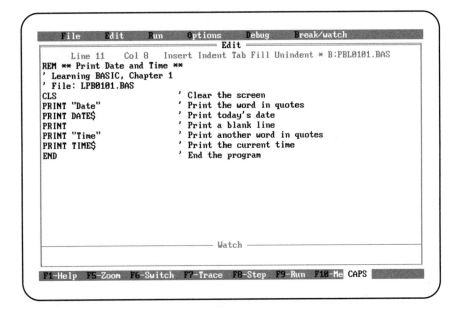

Figure 2.20. The cursor at the bottom of the Edit window.

8. Press Ctrl-Q and then E. The Ctrl-Q E combination moves the cursor to the top line of the window at the current column:

```
REM ** Print Date and Time **
```

Press Ctrl-A to move the cursor to the beginning of the line. Some very large moves are discussed in the next section when they are added to the program. Leave the program in memory for the additions.

Editing a Program

You know how to move the cursor to any point within a program. Now you can use what you've learned to edit an existing program. Use program 1.2 for this editing session. First, observe the status line at the top of the Edit window. Use Insert editing mode when you follow the directions for the first part of this tutorial. If the item to the right of the column number on the status line is not Insert, press the Insert key to change to Insert editing mode. The status line should look like the one in figure 2.21.

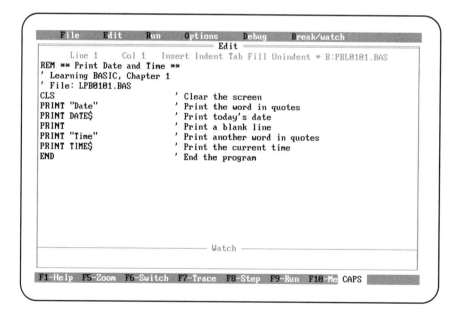

Figure 2.21. Insert showing on the status line.

Do not press Enter unless instructed to do so. You want to change the title of the program. Move the cursor to the blank space following the word Date in line 1 using one of the cursor moves you learned:

```
REM ** Print Date_and Time **
```

Type a comma. Because you are in Insert mode, a comma is printed and all characters to the right of the cursor are pushed one space to the right.

```
REM ** Print Date,_and Time **
```

Press the Delete key four times to delete the word and and the blank space to its left. Use the right-arrow key to move the cursor to the blank space to the right of the word Time:

```
REM ** Print Date, Time_**
```

Type **, and Temperature Data**

After inserting the comma and words, the title line now looks like this:

```
REM ** Print Date, Time, and Temperature Data_**
```

Now use the arrow keys to move the cursor to the number 1 following the word Chapter in line 2. Because you are using Insert mode, press Delete to remove the number. Then, type **2**.

The second line now looks like this:

```
' Learning BASIC, Chapter 2_
```

Next, practice using the cursor moves to move the cursor to the third line of the program so that you can change its file name. The file-name system for this program and other programs in this book includes the letters *PBL* (for *PowerBASIC Lite*), the chapter number, and the program number within the chapter.

Move the cursor to the number 1 of 01 representing the chapter number.

```
' File: PBL0101.BAS
```

Press Delete to erase the number 1. The characters to the right of the cursor move left one place to fill the empty space.

Type **2**.

The characters to the right of the cursor move one place to the right to make room for the **2**. The remarks at the beginning of the revised program now read

```
REM ** Print Date, Time, and Temperature Data **
```

49

```
' Learning BASIC, Chapter 2
File: PBL0201.BAS
```

Insert and Delete Shortcuts

You have used the Insert key to toggle between Insert and Overwrite editing modes. You have inserted and deleted characters in a program. You know how to use hot keys as shortcuts for editing larger chunks of text.

Table 2.3 shows key combinations you use to insert and delete characters, words, and lines of text.

Table 2.3. Key combinations used to insert and delete.

Method One	Method Two	Resulting Action
Insert	Ctrl-V	Toggle between entry modes
-	Ctrl-N	Open a blank line for text
Back Space	Ctrl-H	Delete character left of cursor
Delete	Ctrl-G	Delete character under cursor
-	Ctrl-T	Delete word right of cursor
-	Ctrl-Q Y	Delete to end of line
-	Ctrl-Y	Delete complete line
-	Ctrl-Q L	Restore line

Change from Insert to Overwrite editing mode now by pressing the Insert key. Move the cursor to the letter C of the CLS statement. Then press Ctrl-N. You can see in table 2.3 that pressing Ctrl-N opens a blank line above the CLS statement. The cursor is at the beginning of the blank line. Press the down-arrow key once so that the cursor is again at the C of CLS. Press Ctrl-N again. Another blank line is opened with the cursor at its first position.

Type **REM ** **Initialize **.

This remark sets off a block of statements that perform initialization functions. In this program, CLS clears the screen. In future programs, you use more statements of this type. The opening lines of the program now look like this:

```
REM ** Print Date, Time, and Temperature Data **
' Learning BASIC, Chapter 2
' File: PBL0201.BAS

REM ** Initialize **_
CLS                           ' Clear the screen
```

Press Ctrl-F, and then press the down-arrow key to move the cursor to the P of the PRINT "Date" statement.

Press Ctrl-N twice to open two blank lines.

Press the down-arrow key to move the cursor to the beginning of the second blank line.

Type **REM ** Main program **.

The blank line and this remark clearly set off the main program from those statements that initialize the program. This step makes the program easier to read and understand. Press Ctrl-F to move the cursor to the P of the PRINT "Date" statement. Then press Ctrl-N to open a blank line.

Type ' **Print date and time**.

This remark further subdivides the functions the computer will perform, but it is not necessary in a short program such as this one. Longer programs, however, should be documented clearly with remarks so that you can easily find where a specific action takes place.

Press Ctrl-F to move the cursor to the beginning of the next line, PRINT "Date". Then press the right-arrow key to move the cursor to the blank space to the right of the word Date.

```
PRINT "Date"_               ' Print the word in quotes
```

Press the Backspace key until the cursor is positioned at column 1. You erase one character each time you press the Backspace key. When the cursor reaches column 1, press the Delete key. The apostrophe and all characters on the line to its right move toward the cursor. Keep pressing the Delete key until the characters on the line reach the cursor and are erased one by one. Press the Delete key once more to remove the blank line.

As you know, you use the Backspace or Delete key to erase individual characters. The first four lines of the Main program block should look like this:

```
REM ** Main Program **
' Print date and time
PRINT DATE$                 ' Print today's date
PRINT                       ' Print a blank line

Print today's date PRINT              ' Print a blank line
```

Press the down-arrow key to move the cursor to the P in the word PRINT on the fourth line of the Main program block. Press Ctrl-Q and then Y to delete this line. The key combination Ctrl-Q Y deletes all characters from the cursor position to the end of a line. Because the cursor is on the first character, the complete line is deleted—even the remark at the right end of the line. The cursor is at the first column of the remaining blank line.

```
REM ** Main program **
' Print date and time
PRINT DATE$                  ' Print today's date

Print "Time"                 ' Print another word in quotes
```

Press the Delete key to remove the blank line. The PRINT "Time" line should move up with the cursor under the letter P.

Press Ctrl-Y to delete this entire line. The PRINT TIME$ line moves up when you make the keypress. The cursor should be at the P.

Press the down-arrow key to move the cursor down to the E in the END statement. Then press Ctrl-T. This keypress deletes the word to the right of the cursor. The word END is deleted. The apostrophe and the remark move to the beginning of the line.

Press Ctrl-T several times until all words in the remark are deleted. The cursor now rests at column 1 of the resulting blank line. You have used many of the insert and delete hot keys to modify the original program. These lines should be displayed:

```
REM ** Print Date, Time, and Temperature Data **
' Learning BASIC, Chapter 2
' File: PBL0201.BAS

REM ** Initialize **
CLS

REM ** Main program **
' Print date and time
PRINT DATE$
PRINT TIME$
```

You can exercise some of your typing skills by completing the program in the next section.

Adding to a Program

You squeezed the original program down to its bare essentials. With the cursor at the beginning of the blank line following the PRINT TIME$ statement, type each of the following lines. Press Enter at the end of each line.

```
' Sum and average temperatures
Sum = 0
FOR day = 1 TO 7
  READ temperature
  Sum = Sum + temperature
NEXT day
Ave = Sum / 7
PRINT
PRINT "Sum is"; Sum
PRINT "Average is"; Ave
END

DATA 72.5, 83.3, 82.1, 75.7, 74.8, 83.2, 80.9
```

You may recognize these lines as the bulk of the Sum and Average Temperatures program from Chapter 1.

PowerBASIC has several kinds of numbers. The default number type is called *single precision*. Single-precision numbers are precise to six or seven places. The simplest type of numbers are integers. Integers are the counting numbers, zero, and the negatives of the counting numbers. Integers occupy less storage space than single-precision numbers. A program can execute arithmetic operations with integers faster than it can with single-precision numbers. Therefore, you should use integers in your programs wherever possible.

You can declare variables in your programs to be integers by appending a percent sign (%) to the end of the variable name. In the block of statements you just added, the values of the temperature variable contain decimal portions. Therefore, they are single-precision numbers and should not be declared integers. The values of the day variable used in the FOR...NEXT loop are always integers (1, 2, 3, 4, 5, 6, or 7). Use your newfound editing techniques to place a percent sign after each occurrence of the variable day (it appears in two places). Make changes so that the two lines read

```
FOR day% = 1 TO 7
```

and

```
NEXT day%
```

Then you should have the program shown in listing 2.1.

Listing 2.1. Print Date, Time, and Temperature Data

```
REM ** Print Date, Time, and Temperature Data **
' Learning BASIC, Chapter 2
' File: PBL0201.BAS

REM ** Initialize **
CLS                              ' Clear the screen

REM ** Main program **
' Print date and time
PRINT DATE$                      ' Print today's date
PRINT TIME$                      ' Print the current time
' Sum and average temperatures
Sum = 0
FOR day% = 1 TO 7
  READ temperature
  Sum = Sum + temperature
NEXT day%
Ave = Sum / 7
PRINT
PRINT "Sum is"; Sum
PRINT "Average is"; Ave
END

DATA 72.5, 83.3, 82.1, 75.7, 74.8, 83.2, 80.9
```

Save the program under the file name PBL0201 using the Write To command from the File menu. Then run the program. The date is printed on the first line and the time on the second line. A blank line is printed, followed by the sum of the numbers on the fourth line and the average of the numbers on the fifth line of the Output screen. For example,

```
12-23-1991
13:17:57

Sum is 552.5
Average is 78.92857
```

Press any key to return to the Edit window.

Very Large Cursor Moves

Your program extends beyond the limits of the Edit window, and you need some new cursor-movement keys to move from one window to the next. You move the cursor from its current position to the beginning of the file by pressing Ctrl-Q R (or PgUp). When the cursor is not at line 1, column 1, press Ctrl-Q R or PgUp to move it there.

```
REM ** Print Date, Time, and Temperature Data **
```

To move to the end of the file, press Ctrl-Q C. Even though the end of the file does not show on-screen, pressing Ctrl-Q C moves the cursor to the end of your file. Try switching back and forth between the beginning and end of the program in listing 2.1 with Ctrl-Q R and Ctrl-Q C.

Scrolling

You also can scroll the window up or down one line at a time. Think of scrolling as either scrolling text in one direction or moving the window in the opposite direction. Ctrl-W scrolls the window up one line, and Ctrl-Z scrolls the window down one line. When the top line of the file is visible in the Edit window, Ctrl-W does not scroll the window. When the bottom line is visible in the Edit window, Ctrl-Z has no effect. Try both keypress combinations to see how scrolling commands work.

You also can scroll down a complete screen by pressing Ctrl-C or PgDn. To scroll up a complete screen, use Ctrl-R or PgUp.

Using PowerBASIC Lite Help

As you begin to program using the tutorials in this book, you may need additional help. You already used the PowerBASIC Lite help system to learn the functions of the commands on the File and Run menus. You also know that there is no Edit menu. Accessing Edit from the Main menu merely moves the cursor into the Edit window.

Option Menu Help

You have looked closely at the Run and File menu items. Three other items are on the Main menu: Options, Debug, and Break/watch. The last two items are described in Chapter 14, "Dynamic Debugging." Some features on the Options menu, however, might interest you.

Just after loading PowerBASIC Lite, the File item on the Main menu is highlighted. If you are anywhere else in the PowerBASIC Lite environment, return to the Edit window and press F10 to move the highlight to the Main menu. Then move the highlight to the Options item using the right-arrow key. Press Enter to pull down the Options menu. The highlight is on the first command, Array Auto-dim. Press F1 to see the help information on this item. The Array Auto-dim help screen is shown in figure 2.22.

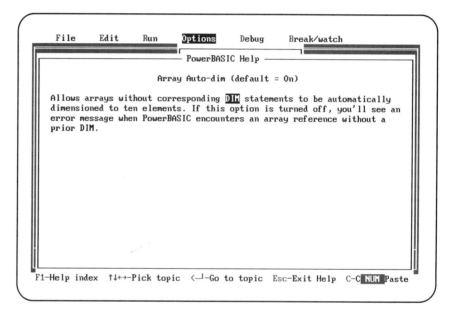

Figure 2.22. Array Auto-dim help information.

Read the information. As you can see, you can toggle the auto-dim feature off and on. When this feature is on, all arrays are dimensioned automatically to ten elements. When the feature is off and you fail to dimension an array in your program, you see an error message when you try to run the program. Even when the auto-dim feature is on, you may encounter a dimensioning error message when you try to use an array element with a subscript larger than the dimensioned value. It is good programming practice to dimension all arrays in your programs whether this feature is off or on. Then you can easily find the arrays you are using in your program.

Notice the highlighted keyword DIM. When you want to review the function of the DIM statement, press Enter. When you finish reading the necessary information, press Esc to return to the Options menu. Move the highlight down to the Stack Size command and press F1 to see the help information on this command. The stack is a special area of memory that holds return addresses, parameter passing, and local variables within structured statements. You probably do not need to change the stack size. Advanced programmers may allocate more stack space when a program is heavily nested (has loops within loops), uses many local variables, or performs recursion (loops back on itself). When you finish reading the Stack size information, press Esc to return to the Options menu.

Move the highlight down to the Music Buffer command and press F1 to see the help information on this command. This information pertains only to SOUND and PLAY statements. When you use either of these statments, the notes in the statement for making sound are stored in this special area of memory so that the computer can keep playing a string of notes while executing other program statements. This procedure is called "playing sound in the background." By enlarging the buffer, you can play a longer string of notes. By decreasing the size of the buffer, you free more memory for other purposes.

When you finish reading the Music buffer information, press Esc to return to the Options menu. Move the highlight down to the Com buffer command and press F1 to see the help information on this command. This information pertains to transferring data to and from your computer when it communicates with an outside source. When you use your computer for communications, you may want to change the Com buffer size. When you finish reading the Com Buffer information, press Esc to return to the Options menu.

Move the highlight down to the last command, Tab size, and press F1 to see the help information on this command. As you can see, you can change the number of spaces produced when you press Tab. When you finish reading the Tab Size information, press Esc to return to the Options menu.

Now it's time to learn more about using the PowerBASIC Lite help system. You obtain information from the help system from almost anywhere within the PowerBASIC Lite development environment.

Loading a Program for Help

You used the help system in the section called "Moving Through the Menus" earlier in this chapter, to learn which menu commands perform which functions. You used the help system in the preceding section, "Option Menu Help," to find help information about commands on the Options menu.

Now let's explore the use of the help system from within the Edit window. First, you must have some program statements in the window in order to search for help related to those statements.

Turn on your computer and load PowerBASIC Lite. Then use either of the following methods to load the program you saved as PBL0201.BAS:

- Directly from the DOS directory or subdirectory that contains your PBLITE.EXE file, type **PBLITE** followed by a space, the appropriate disk drive, a colon, and the program's name. For example, from a hard disk drive directory named PBLITE, load PBLITE and your program from drive B by entering this command:

```
C:\PBLITE>PBLITE B:PBL0201
```

When you have no hard drive and PBLITE.EXE is on a disk in drive A, load PBLITE from drive A and your program from drive B by entering this command:

```
A:>PBLITE B:PBL0201
```

- Access PBLITE.EXE first. Then use the Load command from the File menu to enter the saved program's file name.

Context-Sensitive Help

Regardless of which method you use, the program is loaded. The cursor blinks away at line 1, column 1 under the R of the first REM statement.

When you access help information about the menu commands, you press the F1 key. When you access information about statements within the Edit window, you press Ctrl-F1. Because the cursor is on the REM keyword, press Ctrl-F1 now.

A help window containing information about the REM statement is displayed over the Edit window (see figure 2.23).

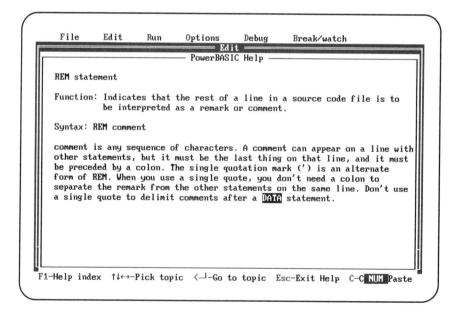

Figure 2.23. REM help information displayed.

REM is used in this book to mark the beginning of main sections of the program, and the apostrophe is used to mark the beginning of subsections within a main section, as in the Print Date, Time, and Temperature Data program:

```
REM ** Main program **
' Print date and time
```

You use the apostrophe also for comments following an executable statement, as in the same program:

```
CLS                                    ' Clears the screen
```

When you finish reading the help information on REM, press Esc to return to the program in the Edit window.

Move the cursor down to the CLS statement in the Initialize program block. Then press Ctrl-F1 to see help information for this statement. This simple statement displays only three lines (see figure 2.24).

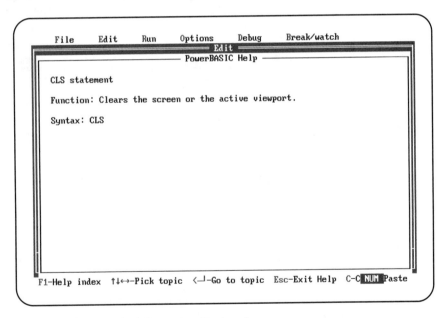

Figure 2.24. CLS help information displayed.

You should always initialize your output screen with the CLS statement to remove any information left by the last program run. This statement appears in the Initialize block of the programs in this book. When you finish reading the help information on CLS, press Esc to return to the program in the Edit window.

Move the cursor down to the PRINT statement in the Main program block. The cursor can be on any of the letters in the keyword PRINT. Then press Ctrl-F1 to see help information for this statement. Because you can use the PRINT statement in many ways, there are two pages of information about its use. The first three lines of the first page are displayed (see figure 2.25).

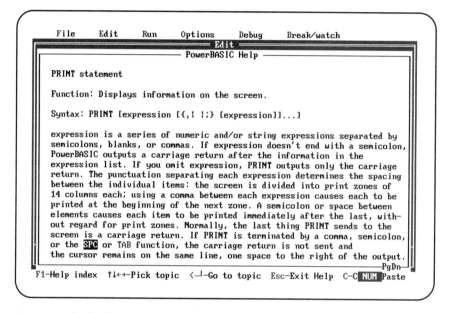

Figure 2.25. The first three lines of PRINT help.

The first three lines of all the statement help windows contain the name of the statement, its function, and its syntax. Programming languages understand statements you write only when you use the proper syntax. A "syntax error" message appears when you try to run a program that has improper syntax in one of its statements. PowerBASIC is helpful: the cursor blinks on a program line containing a syntax error. Notice the symbols in the Syntax line of the PRINT statement in figure 2.25.

- Square brackets ([and]) enclose the parts of the statement that are optional.

- An expression contains one or more constants, variables, or functions. For example, the DATE$ system variable in PRINT DATE$ is an expression.

- Braces ({ and }) indicate that one of the enclosed quantities must be used.

- A broken vertical line (¦) separates the quantities within braces.

- Commas (,) separate constants or variables when they occur in a list.

- A semicolon (;) separates constants or variables in a list.

- An ellipses (...) indicates that more items of the same kind are optional.

As statements are introduced in this book, descriptions of their specific syntax use are included also.

When you finish reading both pages of PRINT help information, press Esc to return to the Edit window. Then move the cursor to the DATE$ system variable and press Ctrl-F1.

The help information shows the syntax for setting the date and the syntax for retrieving the date. Because DATE$ is a system variable, you can use it also as an expression in a PRINT statement:

```
PRINT DATE$
```

Notice that you can use any of four forms to set the date. When you finish reading this information, press Esc to return to the Edit window. Similarly, access help information about TIME$, FOR, READ, NEXT, END, and DATA. You might see some unfamiliar computer terms. Don't worry about them: this book discusses the terms as it uses them.

What do you suppose happens when you press Ctrl-F1 when the cursor is not on a PowerBASIC Lite keyword? Try it. For example, move the cursor to one of the numbers in the DATA list and press Ctrl-F1.

The computer accesses the Index for PowerBASIC Help with the highlight on the first item, Help on Help (see figure 2.26).

Searching Help Screens

The main index shows a list of topics you should use when you encounter programming problems (see figure 2.26). Press the Enter key to see the Help on Help information in figure 2.27.

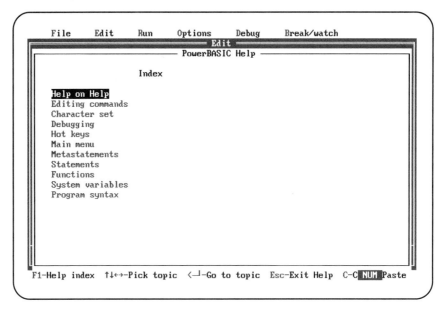

Figure 2.26. The Help Index.

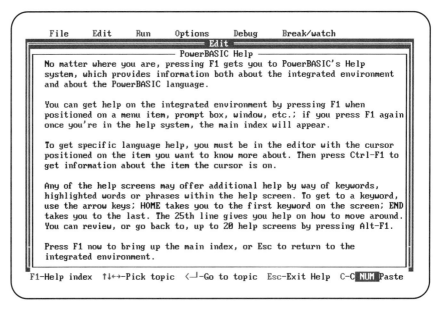

Figure 2.27. Help on Help information.

The information tells how to access PowerBASIC help from anywhere in the integrated environment and from within the Edit window. As you can see, some information requires more than one screen for display. You use the PgDn or PgUp keys to move from page to page. After reading the information on help, press F1 to go back to the Index list (main index). Press the down-arrow key to move the highlight to Editing commands. Then press Enter.

The first of six screens of information about editing commands describes how to access the editor (Edit window) and how to move from the editor back to the Main menu. You have done this several times. Press the PgDn key to see succeeding pages.

You have used many editing commands in this chapter, and you will use several others in later chapters. When you finish scanning all six pages of editing-command information, press F1 to return to the index. Move the highlight down the Index list to the Character set command. Then press Enter to access the first of four pages of character-set information (see figure 2.28).

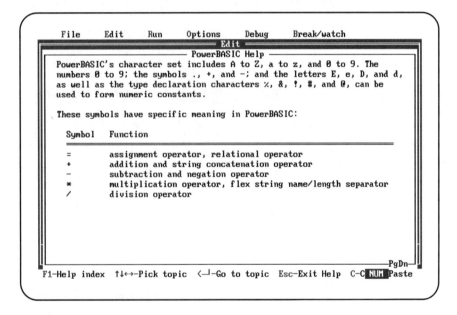

Figure 2.28. The first page of Character Set information help.

You have used some of the characters described on this page in your first three programs. These characters are described in later chapters. When you finish reading the information on all four screens of Character set help, press F1 to return to the Index.

Move the cursor down to Debugging and press Enter. You used the Trace Into feature to single-step through a program earlier in this chapter. You use other debugging features in Chapter 14, "Dynamic Debugging." When you finish reading this screen of debugging information, press F1 to return to the Index.

Move the cursor down to Hot keys and press Enter. You have already used many of the hot keys. These keys, described in three help screens, provide shortcut methods to perform actions that otherwise would require several keystrokes. When you have scanned the three screens of Hot key information, press F1 to return to the index.

Use these steps to scan the Main menu and Metastatements commands on the main index. You have learned about using the Main menu, and you may or may not need the information about metastatements while using PowerBASIC Lite. When you finish reading the help information about these items, press F1 to return to the index.

Move the cursor down to Statements and press Enter to see the first page of PowerBASIC's statements. You should recognize some of the statements on this screen. You can view information about any of the listed statements by pressing the arrow keys to move the highlight to the desired statement. Press the down-arrow key six times to move the highlight from the ARRAY statement to the DEFINT statement. Then press Enter to display the information in figure 2.29.

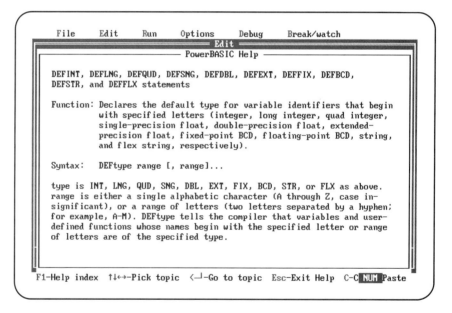

Figure 2.29. Help information about DEFtype.

This screen describes several statements you can use as type declarations for variables that begin with a specified range of letters. As you learned earlier, the default type for variables is single precision. You declared the variable day in the program saved as PBL0201.BAS by placing a percent sign after the variable name (day%). The statements described on this page enable you to declare variables whose names begin with specified letters.

Many programmers like to specify all variables as integers with a DEFINT statement:

```
DEFINT A-Z
```

As mentioned earlier, integers occupy less memory, and statements containing integer variables execute quicker than those containing other variables types. When you want a variable to be another type, you use one of the variable-declaration characters to override the DEFINT statement for that particular variable. You will observe this practice in most programs from now on.

When you finish reading the information about DEFtype statements, press F1 to return to the main index. When you want to see the second and third pages of statements, move the highlight to Statements. Then press the PgDn key to view the other screens. When you finish reading all the information on statements, press F1 to return to the index.

Move the highlight down to Functions and press Enter. There are two pages of help on this item. You learn how to use many of these functions in later chapters. When you finish reading all the information on statements, press F1 to return to the index.

Move the highlight down to System variables and press Enter. There is one screen of information for this item. You used the two system variables DATE$ and TIME$. You also looked at their help information by pressing F1 when the cursor was at the statement in the Edit window. When you finish reading all the information, press F1 to return to the index.

Move the highlight down to the last item on the index, Program syntax, and press Enter. There are three pages of help on this item. Read them all and then press Esc to return to the Edit window.

Copying Text from Help Screens

You may find it helpful to copy the syntax from a help screen when you want to use a PowerBASIC statement. Clear the editor to prepare for writing a new program by selecting New from the File menu. Then enter each of the following lines, and press Enter at the end of each line:

```
REM ** Experiment with FOR...NEXT Statement **
' Learning BASIC, Chapter 2.  File:PBL0202.BAS
REM ** Initialize **
CLS: DEFINT A-Z

_
```

Notice that two statements can be on the same line, as the Program Syntax help screen described earlier. The two statements CLS and DEFINT A-Z are separated by a colon. The cursor should be at the beginning of the next line. Be sure that it is there before continuing.

Press F1 to access the help system. Press F1 again to display the help index. Then move the highlight down to Statements and press Enter.

The first screen of Statements help is displayed. Move the highlight down to the FOR/NEXT statement in the first column. Press Enter to access help on this statement. This step displays the screen shown in figure 2.30.

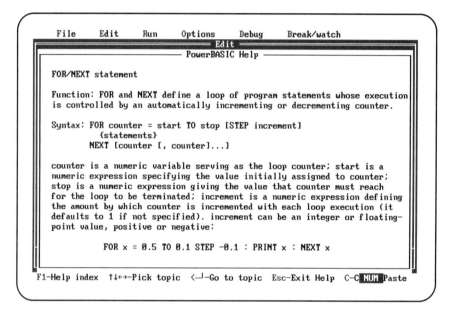

Figure 2.30. Help information on FOR/NEXT.

Positioning Your Cursor to Copy

Notice that you cannot see a cursor in the help information screen in figure 2.30. You can make a cursor appear when you type the letter *C*. When you do, the cursor appears in the upper-left corner of the help window.

Move the cursor down to the line labeled Syntax. Press the right-arrow key to move the cursor over to the letter F of the keyword FOR. You are ready to mark a block of text to prepare it for copying to your program.

Marking a Block of Text

When the cursor is positioned at the beginning of the block you want to copy, type **B**. This step marks the beginning of the block and highlights the first letter of the block (**F**).

Press the down-arrow key two times. Each time, the letter the cursor moves to is highlighted. Then hold down the right-arrow key until all three lines of syntax are highlighted (see figure 2.31).

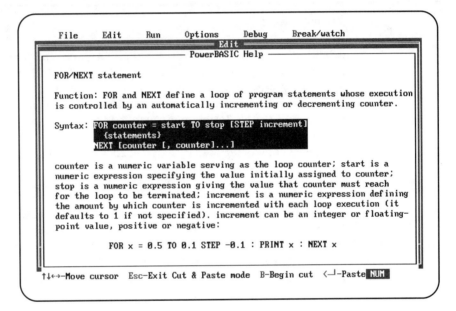

Figure 2.31. FOR/NEXT syntax highlighted.

The marked block is ready to be copied.

Pasting a Block of Text

After you mark the block, press Enter to copy it to the Edit window. This procedure pastes a copy of the marked block in the cursor's position in the Edit window. If you didn't place your cursor at the desired position before copying the block, the block is copied to the wrong place. Don't panic! You can move the cursor in the Edit window to the position at which you want the block and press Ctrl-K V to move the block to that position. Here are the lines in your program:

```
REM ** Experiment with FOR...NEXT Statement **
' Learning BASIC, Chapter 2.  File:PBL0202.BAS
REM ** Initialize **
CLS: DEFINT A-Z
FOR counter = start TO stop [STEP increment]
  {statements}
NEXT [counter [, counter]...]
```

Customizing a Block

You can still edit the statements in the highlighted block. The general terms of the syntax statements must be changed to specific variables and numbers you want to use in your program. You can use the name counter as a variable in your program, but the values you use for that variable are single-precision values. To override the DEFINT A-Z statement, you add a single-precision declaration character to counter.

Move the cursor to blank space following counter in the FOR statement. Type

```
!
```

Now counter is defined in this line as a single-precision variable.

You want to replace the syntax words start and stop with numeric values. In this loop, start counting at zero (0) and stop at 2. To make the change, move the cursor to the letter s of the word start. Type

```
0
```

Delete the word start by one of the methods you learned in this chapter. The zero you just typed replaces start. Move the cursor to the letter s of the word stop. Type

```
2
```

Then delete the word stop. Because the value of start is less than the value of stop, the value used as increment in the STEP clause must be positive. You are going to increase the value of counter each time through the loop by 0.1. Move the cursor to the left bracket ([) before the keyword STEP. Delete the left bracket. Move the cursor to the letter i of the word increment, and type

```
0.1
```

The value is inserted, and the cursor is still at the letter i of increment. Press Ctrl-Q Y to delete everything on the line from the cursor position to the right.

Move the cursor to the beginning of the second line of the FOR/NEXT loop. It should be positioned at the left brace mark, before the word statements. Type

```
PRINT counter!
```

Then press Ctrl-Q Y to delete everything to the right of the cursor on this line. You can place more than one statement between the FOR statement and the NEXT statement, but use only this one statement in this program.

Move the cursor to the next line, to the leftmost left bracket:

```
NEXT [counter [, counter]...]
```

Delete just that one bracket. Then move the cursor beyond the word counter to the blank space.

```
NEXT counter_[, counter]...]
```

You must enter an exclamation point to declare counter a single-precision number. Type

```
!
```

Then press Ctrl-Q Y to delete the rest of the line. Press Enter to move the cursor to the next line, which is blank. You can hide the block's highlight. Do so now by pressing Ctrl-K H. You should have the following portion of the new program:

```
REM** Experiment with FOR...NEXT Statement **
' Learning BASIC, Chapter 3.  File:PBL0202.BAS
REM ** Initialize **
CLS: DEFINT A-Z
FOR counter! = 0 TO 2 STEP 0.1
  PRINT counter!
NEXT counter!
```

Completing a Program

Use your editing skills to break the FOR/NEXT loop away from the initialization portion of the program by inserting a blank line space. Insert the heading Main program as a REM to head the new section. The Initialize and Main program blocks now look like this:

```
REM ** Initialize **
CLS: DEFINT A-Z

REM ** Main program **
FOR counter! = 0 TO 2 STEP 0.1
  PRINT counter!
NEXT counter!
```

Use your knowledge of menus to run the program. A new single-precision number is printed each time through the FOR/NEXT loop. The numbers are displayed vertically, one number on each line (see the following output of code).

```
0
.1
.2
.3
.4
.5
.6
.7
.8000001
.9000001
1
1.1
1.2
1.3
1.4
1.5
1.6
1.7
1.8
1.9
```

Notice that the values for .8 and .9 are not exact. The computer converts the decimal numbers you use in programs to binary numbers that it can understand. Some round-off errors occur in the process.

Changing Display Spacing

When you want to print the numbers one after another on the same line, type a semicolon (;) at the end of the PRINT statement:

```
PRINT counter!;
```

Run the program with this revision. The numbers are printed one after another until no more will fit on one line of the output screen. The rest are printed on the next line (see the following output).

```
0  .1  .2  .3  .4  .5  .6  .7  .8000001  .9000001  1  1.1
1.2  1.3
   1.4  1.5 1.6  1.7  1.8  1.9
```

The number zero (0) and all positive numbers are displayed with a leading blank and a trailing blank. Therefore, two spaces appear between each number.

When you want to print the numbers in 14-character fields, use a comma at the end of the PRINT statement:

```
PRINT counter!,
```

The output is printed in neat fields, as shown in the following output of code:

```
0              .1            .2           .3            .4
.5             .6            .7           .8000001
.9000001
1              1.1           1.2          1.3           1.4
1.5            1.6           1.7          1.8           1.9
```

Let's add a little to the current program. First, press Ctrl-K H to show the marked FOR...NEXT block. Then move the cursor to the end of the NEXT statement and press Enter to move the cursor to the next line. Type:

```
PRINT
```

Press Enter to move the cursor to the next line. Make another copy to the marked block at this position by pressing Ctrl-K C.

Press Ctrl-K C to copy the block to this new position. This time, make the counter start at 2 and stop at 0. Because the start value is greater than the stop value, the value of the increment must be negative. Change these values to read

```
FOR counter! = 2 TO 0 STEP -0.1
```

The rest of the block can remain the same. Hide the highlight of the block with Ctrl-K H. Then move the cursor to the end of the NEXT statement and press Enter. Type

```
END
```

and press Enter. Listing 2.2 is complete. Experiment with the FOR/NEXT statement:

```
REM ** Experiment with FOR...NEXT Statement **
' Learning BASIC, Chapter 2.  File:PBL0202.BAS
```

```
REM ** Initialize **
CLS: DEFINT A-Z

REM ** Main program **
FOR counter! = 0 TO 2 STEP 0.1
  PRINT counter!,
NEXT counter!
PRINT
FOR counter! = 2 TO 0 STEP -0.1
  PRINT counter!,
NEXT counter!
END
```

Run this final version of the program. The output appears in two parts, separated by a blank line. One FOR/NEXT loop counts up, and the other counts down (see the following output).

0	.1	.2	.3	.4
.5	.6	.7	.8000001	.9000001
1	1.1	1.2	1.3	1.4
1.5	1.6	1.7	1.8	1.9
2	1.9	1.8	1.7	1.6
1.5	1.4	1.3	1.2	1.1
.9999998	.8999997	.7999997	.6999997	.5999997
.4999997	.3999997	.2999997	.1999997	9.999969E-2

Summary

You learned how to select menus from the menu bar and browse the File and Run menus. You used the F1 key to access help information about each command in the two menus.

You loaded a program that you saved in Chapter 1 by using the Change directory and Directory commands from the File menu. Then you used the hot key, F7, to step through the program one statement at a time. The Alt-F5 key moved back and forth between the Edit window and the User output screen. You learned to move the cursor within your program by short moves using the arrow keys (left, right, up, and down one character). You used special key combinations to make longer moves (by one word, by one line, from top to bottom, and from bottom to top of the window).

You edited the program, using both Insert and Overwrite editing modes. You used special key combinations to insert and delete program text.

You learned to use Ctrl-Q R to make a very large cursor move to the beginning of your program file, and Ctrl-Q C to make a very large move to the end of the file. You also learned how to use Ctrl-W to scroll the window up one line, Ctrl-Z to scroll the window down one line, Ctrl-C or PgDn to scroll down one screen, and Ctrl-R or PgUp to scroll up one screen.

You can access the Options menu and then use the Autodim command to turn the automatic dimensioning feature for arrays (ten elements) off and on. You also can change the size of the stack, music buffer, com buffer, and tab from commands on the Options menu.

You loaded a previously saved program and explored context-sensitive help. By placing the cursor at keywords in the Edit window and pressing Ctrl-F1, you brought up displays of help information for the keywords REM, CLS, PRINT, DATE$, TIME$, FOR, NEXT, READ, END, and DATA.

You accessed information about a variety of reference material from the main index of the help system. You acquired this help information with these steps:

1. Press F1 to display the index.

2. Select the desired item by using the arrow keys.

3. Press Enter to display help on the selected item.

4. Press F1 to return to the index.

You also learned to copy information from a help screen and paste it into your program with these steps.

1. Type C to display the cursor in the help display.

2. Move the cursor to the beginning of the block to copy and type B.

3. Use the arrow keys to highlight the block.

4. Press Enter to paste the highlighted block into the Edit window at the point where you placed the cursor.

You then modified the general terms of the copied block to make specific names and numbers suitable for your program. You edited the program and added statements and formatted the statements into functional blocks. You inserted REM statements to head the blocks.

Exercises

1. Name the key you use to step through a program when you use the Trace into command on the Run menu.

2. Name the key used to

   a. Move the cursor one character to the right

   b. Move the cursor one character to the left

   c. Move the cursor down one line

   d. Move the cursor up one line

3. The cursor is at the R in REM in the following program line:

   ```
   REM ** Sum and Average Temperatures **
   ```
   You press the Ctrl-F key combination. Where does the cursor move?

4. Use your new editing capabilities to add a print statement to the Print Date, Time, and Temperature Data program (file:PBL0201.BAS). The statement should print your name on the line directly under the time.

5. Suppose that you decide to delete the line you entered in Exercise 4. Describe how you would do it.

6. What is the alternative form of REM?

7. Why should you use a CLS statement before printing information on the User output screen?

8. What is the purpose of the exclamation point (!) following the name of a variable?

9. Describe the purpose of the statement DEFINT A-Z?

Chapter 3

An Introduction to Programming

PowerBASIC is an easy language for programming. You don't need to learn elaborate rules, but you must follow a few simple rules of syntax. It also takes a little time to design your program, but the time spent pays off by making it easier to correct or enhance your program.

Programs are as unique as the individuals writing them. There is not "one correct way" to write a program. However, keep in mind that you write programs to be read and used. Program structures should be clear and straightforward. Programs should consist of functional blocks of code with comments describing the function.

In this chapter, you learn some of the concepts involved in programming. The specific topics discussed in this chapter are

- Variables

- Statements

- Assignment statements

- Loops

- Conditional branches

- The write, test, and debug cycle

- Remarks

Elements of a Program

A program is a series of instructions telling the computer what to do, when to do it, and how to do it. You write a PowerBASIC Lite program with vocabulary (*keywords*) and rules of grammar (*syntax*) that PowerBASIC Lite understands. Some keywords and syntax are described in this chapter to provide you with an introduction to programming.

Variables

The variable is one of the most important concepts used in programming. In mathematical expressions you see variables used in equations such as:

X + Y = 10

Many combinations of values for X and Y can be used to make the equation true (to satisfy or solve the equation). For example:

X = 1 and Y = 9
X = 2 and Y = 8
X = 2.5 and Y = 7.5
X = 3 and Y = 7

Many combinations of values for X and Y satisfy, or solve, the equation. Variables in mathematical expressions usually represent unknown quantities.

Variables have a slightly different meaning when they are used in a computer program. A variable, in a computer program, is a name you give to a memory location that will be used to hold a quantity. Imagine that memory locations are boxes used to store values. A variable is the name given to a box. In the previous example, the variables (names for the number boxes) are X and Y.

X

Y

Different numbers can be stored in the boxes at different times. That's why the names are called variables. For example, at the same time, the memory box named X can hold the value 4, and the memory box named Y can hold 6 (see the following example).

X	4

Y	6

The numbers stored in the boxes may change. For example, if X changes to 7.8 and Y to 3.7, the boxes would look like this:

X	7.8

Y	3.7

A variable, therefore, is the name of a specific memory location. The value of the variable is stored in the memory location that bears its name.

Statements

A *statement* is the simplest building block in a program. A program is a sequence of statements that tells the computer what to do. A program line can contain more than one statement on a line, but you can read your programs more easily if you use only one statement on a line.

Statements that assign a value to a variable are called *assignment statements*. To assign values to the variables X and Y, for example, you would use these two assignment statements:

```
X = 4
Y = 6
```

The statements would assign a memory location to the variables X and Y, and the values in the statements would be stored in the memory locations with the appropriate names (X and Y).

Although the assignment statement looks like a mathematical equation, it works in a slightly different way. The value on the right side of the equal sign is assigned to the memory location named on the left side of the equal sign. Thus a variable can be used to modify itself. For example, if the assignments in the example are made, the memory boxes would hold

X	4

Y	6

You can now modify the values of the variables with the following two assignment statements:

```
X = X + 1
Y = Y + 1
```

When the computer encounters the first assignment statement, it performs the following steps:

1. The expression on the right side of the equal sign (X + 1) is evaluated using the current value of X (4 + 1 = 5).

2. The evaluation of the right side is assigned to the variable (X). This new assignment is stored in the memory location assigned to X.

X	5

Y	6

The same steps are performed when the computer executes the second assignment statement for the variable Y. The values stored in memory are now:

X	5

Y	7

Other statements can direct the computer to perform some specific action, such as clearing the screen with the one-word statement:

```
CLS
```

Most programs contain a CLS statement to clear the screen in preparation for printing some information on the screen. For example,

```
CLS
PRINT X + Y
```

In this case, the first statement (CLS) clears the screen. In executing the PRINT statement, the computer would obtain the values that had been assigned to the variables X and Y, add them together, and print the result on-screen.

You use an END statement to tell the computer when it has reached the end of a program.

A program is a sequence of the previous statements. For example,

```
CLS
X = 4
Y = 6
PRINT X + Y
END
```

In this program, the statements are executed in sequence (from top to bottom). The program contains five executable statements, which are the statements PowerBASIC executes when a program is run.

In addition to executable statements, a program can contain comments. Comments are text that is not executed. Use comments, or remarks, as reminders to tell you what a program does. Here is another program, first with no comments and then with comments added.

```
CLS
PRINT "This is a program."
END

REM ** This program prints a single line of text **
CLS
PRINT "This is a program."
END
```

The PRINT statement tells the computer to print the characters enclosed in the quotation marks. The group of characters enclosed by the quotation marks is called a *string constant*. The first line is a remark and is not executed. The last three statements are executable statements.

This program first clears the screen. Then the string in the PRINT statement is displayed. Last, the program ends. This type of program execution is called *sequential execution* because the three statements are executed in the same order in which they appear.

You can use the apostrophe (') in PowerBASIC Lite as a shortcut for the keyword REM. You can add comments to the end of program lines by using the apostrophe. Here is an example of the previous program with comments added.

```
REM ** This program prints a single line of text **
' It contains comments
CLS                              ' clear the screen
PRINT "This is a program."       ' print text
END                              ' end the program
```

For short programs like this one, comments are not necessary. You can overcomment, even in longer programs. Don't comment on something that's obvious from the written statements.

For longer programs, use comments in appropriate places. Use common sense in the number of comments used and their placement. When you return to a program, you scan the comments to see what task a program accomplishes and where and how it accomplishes that task.

Here is another example of a program that executes in a sequential fashion with one-line statements.

```
CLS
PRINT DATE$, TIME$              ' print date and time
PRINT                          ' print blank line
PRINT "Happy Birthday"
PRINT "    to you"
BEEP                           ' beep the speaker
END
```

The second statement in the program contains two *system variables*: DATE$ and TIME$. Use system variables to name values obtained from the computer system. In the preceding program, the values are the computer's date and time.

Notice the third statement. The PRINT statement does not have an appended string. This PRINT statement prints a blank line.

The last PRINT statement uses blank spaces inside the quotation marks to center its string.

Finally, the BEEP statement makes a short sound on the computer's speaker to let you know when the program ends. This statement also can be used at critical points in a program, such as when the program needs input. The following lines show the program's output.

```
01-12-1992    12:30:15
Happy Birthday
    to you
```

Output

Programs are written to solve some problem or to produce some desired action. Program statements act on the information you provide to produce results, which usually are sent to your display screen, your printer, a communications port, or some other device. You have seen output sent to the display screen by PRINT statements. You can send output to your printer by using LPRINT statements. For example,

```
CLS
LPRINT DATE$, TIME$          ' send date and time to printer
LPRINT                       ' print blank line
LPRINT "Happy Birthday"      ' send string to printer
LPRINT "    to you"          ' send string to printer
BEEP
END
```

Input

Sometimes, you want to interrupt the execution of a program to enter data from the keyboard. The INPUT statement is helpful for this purpose. For example, you might want to print a birthday greeting using a person's name. You can clear the screen and interrupt the computer with these two lines:

```
CLS
INPUT BirthdayName$
```

The first statement clears the screen. Then the INPUT statement interrupts the computer. You see a screen with a question mark and a blinking cursor in the upper-left corner.

```
? _
```

BirthdayName$ is a variable. The dollar sign ($) following the name indicates that this variable is a string-type variable. The name you type from the keyboard is assigned to that variable.

The lone question mark does not indicate what you should enter. You can explain what to enter by adding a string to the INPUT statement. You can change the second line to

```
INPUT "Enter a name"; BirthdayName$
```

When this line is executed, the required data is a little more obvious. It looks like the following line of output:

```
Enter a name? _
```

The following short program uses such an INPUT statement:

```
CLS
INPUT "Enter a name"; BirthdayName$
CLS
PRINT DATE$, TIME$
PRINT
PRINT "Happy Birthday"
PRINT BirthdayName$              ' print the name you entered
BEEP
END
```

The screen is cleared first. Then the INPUT statement interrupts the program, prints its prompt, and waits. You then type the following name:

```
Enter a name? Margaret_
```

When you press Enter, the screen is cleared again. The date and time are printed. Then the birthday message with the name you entered appears. The following output shows the final screen with the date, time, and birthday message. The beep from the computer's speaker signifies the end of the program.

```
01-12-1992    12:30:15
Happy Birthday
Margaret
```

Loops

A helpful control structure is the simple *loop*. It performs a statement or set of statements for a certain number of times or until the loop reaches some specified limit or condition.

PowerBASIC has three different types of loops:

- FOR/NEXT
- WHILE/WEND
- DO/LOOP

The following sections provide a brief look at each type of loop.

FOR/NEXT Loops

You use a FOR/NEXT loop when you want a shortcut for code that will be repeated several times. For example, think of a relay race with four members on each relay team. One at a time, each runner circles the track and passes the baton to the next runner. You can write the directions for the entire team rather than for each member by writing in the form of a FOR/NEXT loop.

```
FOR each runner from the first to the fourth
   run once around the track            ' each runner follows
   pass the baton to the next runner    ' these directions
NEXT runner
```

The FOR/NEXT structure written for the computer is a little more formal. A loop similar to the relay-team analogy can be written to add four numbers.

```
FOR count = 1 TO 4          ' start at 1, end at 4
   Sum = Sum + count        ' add counter to the sum
   PRINT Sum                ' print the current sum
NEXT count                  ' increase the counter by one
```

The loop begins with a FOR statement. It specifies the name of the variable used as a counter, the starting value of the counter, and the ending value of the counter. This line defines how many times the loop will run:

```
FOR count = 1 TO 4               ' start at 1, end at 4
```

The NEXT statement is the last statement, indicating the end of the loop. Each time it is executed, the value of the counting variable is increased by one. The computer then loops back to the FOR statement to see whether the limit of counter has been reached.

```
NEXT count                       ' increase the counter by one
```

Between the FOR statement and the NEXT statement, you write the statements that you want to be executed each time through the loop. These statements are indented so that you can easily see the loop.

```
Sum = Sum + count          ' add counter to the sum
PRINT Sum                  ' print the current sum
```

Here is the formal syntax for a FOR/NEXT loop:

```
FOR counter = start TO stop [STEP increment]
   .
   . {statements}
   .
NEXT [counter]
```

The statements between the FOR statement and the NEXT statement are called the *body* of the loop. In standard programming practice, you indent the body of a loop, to clearly identify a nonsequential structure.

The following program uses a FOR/NEXT loop to print the integers from 1 to 10:

```
REM ** Count from 1 to 10 **
FOR count% = 1 TO 10
  PRINT count%;
NEXT count%
END
```

When the loop is entered, the value of *count%* is set to 1. The body of the loop contains one statement telling the computer to print the value of the counter. Because no STEP value is specified, the NEXT statement increments the counter to 1 when it is executed. The computer returns to the FOR statement with the value of count% now equal to 2. This value is checked against the limit (10) to determine whether another pass through the loop is needed. The execution of the loop continues until the value 10 is printed. At that time the NEXT statement increments the value of count% to 11. Because this value is greater than the limit of the loop counter (10), the END statement is executed, which causes an exit from the loop, ending the program.

In addition to the PowerBASIC keywords in this program, you provide the name of the counter (count%) for the loop. This word is a *variable*, which is the name for a quantity that can change (vary) during the execution of a program. The value of count changes each time the body of the loop is executed from 1 through 10 in incremental steps of 1 (1, 2, 3, 4, 5, 6, 7, 8, 9, 10).

The percent sign (%) designates this variable (count%) as an integer variable. In addition to providing the variable's name, you also provide the starting value (1) and ending value (10) for the variable in the FOR statement (1 TO 10).

The semicolon following the variable (count%) in the PRINT statement tells the computer to keep printing on the same line until the line is full. If you could see the output screen at the end of each pass through the loop, you would see the current value of count% added to the previous values (see table 3.1).

Table 3.1. The output for each loop execution.

Pass Number	Output
1	1
2	1 2
3	1 2 3
4	1 2 3 4
5	1 2 3 4 5
6	1 2 3 4 5 6
7	1 2 3 4 5 6 7
8	1 2 3 4 5 6 7 8
9	1 2 3 4 5 6 7 8 9
10	1 2 3 4 5 6 7 8 9 10

What you actually see is the output at the end of the program with all numbers printed on the same line.

```
1  2  3  4  5  6  7  8  9  10
```

WHILE/WEND Loops

In some programming situations, you cannot anticipate when the value of a variable reaches the maximum value you can allow. Therefore, you cannot predict the final value for a loop counter in a FOR/NEXT loop. In these situations, you use a WHILE/WEND loop that checks for a condition at the beginning of a loop. It executes the statements within the loop while the specified condition exists.

Imagine yourself in a grocery store. You decide to buy a pound of dried banana chips. The chips are stored in a bin containing a scoop. A scale is nearby for weighing the chips. You go through a process similar to a WHILE/WEND loop to select the desired quantity of chips.

```
Initially: scale pointer at zero, no chips on the scale
WHILE the scale pointer is below the one-pound marker
   Fill the scoop with chips
   Empty the scoop in the scale
   Check the scale pointer
Loop back
```

These actions are similar to the WHILE/WEND loop in the following program. This loop increments consecutive integers as long as the total is less than 100:

```
count% = 0
total% = 0
WHILE total% < 100
  INCR count%
  total% = total% + count%
WEND
```

The initial conditions are specified before the loop is entered in the analogy, and in the actual WHILE/WEND loop. In the analogy,

```
Initially: scale pointer at zero, no chips on the scale
In the WHILE/WEND loop:  count% = 0
                         total% = 0
```

The WHILE statement specifies the condition when the exit will be made from the loop. The condition is checked before any of the actions in the body of the loop are carried out. When the condition is false, the rest of the loop is skipped and the statement following the loop is executed. In the analogy,

```
WHILE the scale pointer is below the one-pound marker
In the WHILE/WEND loop: WHILE total% < 100
```

The statements between the WHILE statement and the WEND statement are executed while the condition in the WHILE statement is true. In the analogy,

```
Fill the scoop with chips
            Empty the scoop onto the scale
            Check the scale pointer
In the WHILE/WEND loop: INCR count%
                        total% = total% + count%
```

The WEND statement marks the end of the loop. In the analogy, you check the scale pointer. In the WHILE/WEND loop, the value of total% is checked when control is returned to the WHILE statement by the WEND statement. In the analogy,

```
Loop back
In the WHILE/WEND loop: WEND
```

The following is a short program using the WHILE/WEND loop just described.

```
CLS
count% = 0
total% = 0
WHILE total% < 100
  INCR count%                   ' increase count% by 1
  total% = total% + count%      ' compute running total
WEND
PRINT "count ="; count%, "total ="; total%
END
```

The counter (count%) and sum (total%) are initialized to 0 before entering the loop. Inside the loop, the value of the variable count% increases (INCRements) by 1 from the PowerBASIC statement.

```
INCR count%
```

A running sum (total%) is calculated by adding the value of count% to the previous value of total%.

```
total% = total% + count%
```

This statement is not like a mathematical equation. It is an *assignment statement*. The right side of the assignment statement is calculated and assigned to the variable on the left side of the statement. For example, when the loop begins, the value of total% is 0. The value of count% is 1. Therefore, the right side of the assignment statement (total% + count%) is calculated as $0 + 1 = 1$. This value then is assigned to the variable (total%) on the left side of the assignment statement.

On the second pass through the loop, the new value of total% is 1. Because the value of count% is now 2, the right side of the assignment statement is calculated as $1 + 2 = 3$.

The value of 3 is assigned to total%. This process continues until the condition in the WHILE statement becomes false.

When the value of total% becomes equal to or greater than 100, the WHILE statement detects that the condition is false. So, the rest of the statements in the loop are skipped. The PRINT statement following the loop is executed. The program then ends. Table 3.2 shows the value of count% and total% after each pass through the loop.

Table 3.2. The values for count% and total%.		
Pass Number	**count%**	**total%**
1	1	1
2	2	3
3	3	6
4	4	10
5	5	15
6	6	21
7	7	28
8	8	36
9	9	45
10	10	55
11	11	66
12	12	78
13	13	91
14	14	105

The output goes to the screen through the PRINT statement after exiting from the loop. The statement displays a string (count =), the value of count%, a string (total =), and then the value of total%. The final count and the total are displayed as shown in the following line of output:

```
count = 14    total = 105
```

The FOR/NEXT and WHILE/WEND loops are structures that can perform almost any looping requirements needed. You can satisfy an even wider variety of conditions, however, with DO/LOOP.

DO/LOOP Loops

DO/LOOP is a variation of the WHILE/WEND loop. The body of this loop also is executed while, or until, a specified condition is true. It differs from the WHILE/WEND loop by offering a variety of ways to specify the condition.

The DO/LOOP loop lets you set conditions for looping at either the beginning or end of the loop.

```
DO WHILE condition
   body of loop
LOOP

DO UNTIL condition
   body of loop
LOOP

DO
   body of loop
WHILE condition

DO
   body of loop
UNTIL condition
```

Mixing Structure Types

Programs can contain both sequential and loop structures. You used a program with these structures in Chapter 1, "Getting Started," in listing 1.2. The executable statements of that program follow.

```
CLS
Sum = 0
FOR day = 1 TO 7
   READ temperature
   Sum = Sum + temperature
NEXT day
Ave = Sum / 7
PRINT Sum, Ave
END
```

The program begins with sequential statements, cycles through a loop structure seven times, and ends with more sequential statements.

Conditional Branches

To execute a specified statement or send control to a different part of the program, *conditional branches* may interrupt the normal sequential flow of a program or the execution of a loop. PowerBASIC provides IF and SELECT CASE statements to perform conditional branches.

IF Statements

Many conditional branches can be handled by a simple IF / THEN statement. For example, suppose that you are reading a book and are interrupted by a telephone call. You stop reading and answer the phone. When the phone conversation is finished, you return to the book.

```
For page 1 to last page
  Read a page
  IF telephone rings, then answer the phone and converse
Next page
```

In the following similar IF/THEN programming statement, the conditional branch to the PRINT statement is made only when the value of total is greater than 100. When this condition is true, the count is printed. Then the execution of the loop is continued.

```
FOR count = 1 TO 50
  total = total + count
  IF total > 100 THEN PRINT count
NEXT count
```

As another example, consider a FOR/NEXT loop that counts and sums the values of the counter. You can use a conditional branch to exit from the loop when the total reaches or exceeds a specified value.

```
CLS
total% = 0
FOR count% = 1 TO 50
  total% = total% + count%
  IF total% >= 100 THEN EXIT FOR        ' conditional branch
NEXT count%
PRINT "count ="; count%, "total ="; total%
END
```

While the value of total% is less than 100, the program cycles through the FOR/NEXT loop. When the value of total% is greater than or equal to 100, the condition in the IF statement is true, causing a branch (jump) to the PRINT statement.

The total increases like the loop programs described earlier, and the output is the same as the other kinds of loops.

```
count = 14    total = 105
```

Use the ELSE option in an IF/THEN structure to provide branches for multiple conditions.

```
IF total% >= 100 THEN EXIT FOR ELSE PRINT total%
```

Multiple conditions using the IF/THEN/ELSE structure lead to long and complicated program lines that are hard to read. To avoid this, PowerBASIC Lite offers a multiple-line (or block) version of the IF/THEN/ELSE structure. PowerBASIC Lite produces code that is clearer than single-line IF/THEN ELSE statements. The following program uses the multiple-line IF...END IF structure.

```
total% = 0
FOR count% = 1 TO 50
  total% = total% + count%
  IF total% < 100 THEN
      PRINT "count ="; count%
    ELSE
      PRINT "Finished"
      EXIT FOR
  END IF
NEXT count%
PRINT "count ="; count%, "total ="; total%
END
```

The block IF...END IF structure begins with an IF statement. The last word on this line must be THEN. The block following the IF statement can contain any number of statements. When the condition specified in the IF statement is not true, the block following the ELSE statement is executed. The end of the block structure must be an END IF statement.

When the value of total% is less than 100, the PRINT statement of the IF block is executed. When total% becomes greater than or equal to 100, the two statements following the ELSE statement are executed. The output of this program follows.

```
count = 1
count = 2
count = 3
count = 4
count = 5
count = 6
count = 7
count = 8
count = 9
count = 10
count = 11
count = 12
count = 13
Finished
count = 14     total = 105
```

Learning BASIC

The block IF...END IF structure also can contain intermediate blocks headed by the keyword ELSEIF. This option is described in Chapter 7, "Program Control Structures."

SELECT CASE Structures

In many programs, you have a variety of things to do, all based on the value of some variable. PowerBASIC contains a SELECT CASE *structure* to handle such tasks. A PowerBASIC Lite structure is a series of statements used to perform a function. Consider some food stored in your refrigerator. The actions you might take with a specific food can be shown in the following analogy to a SELECT CASE structure:

```
SELECT case age
  CASE = more than one week
    discard
  CASE one day to one week
    usable, eat with care
  CASE < one day
    fresh, enjoy
END SELECT
```

This short program uses the SELECT CASE structure to classify the number you enter:

```
CLS
INPUT "Enter a positive number"; number
SELECT CASE number
  CASE < 50
    PRINT "Small number"
  CASE 50 TO 100
    PRINT "medium number"
  CASE > 50
     PRINT "big number"
  CASE ELSE
    PRINT "Not a positive number"
END SELECT
END
```

The SELECT CASE structure begins with a SELECT CASE statement that includes the expression to be evaluated. The structure ends with an END SELECT statement. Each possible case that the evaluated expression (number in this example) can assume is listed between the SELECT CASE and END SELECT statements. The last case in this structure should be a CASE ELSE block that is executed when the expression does not satisfy any of the other cases. In this example, the CASE ELSE block prints a message that says you entered a number that was not positive.

Functions

PowerBASIC Lite has many built-in *functions*. Think of a function as a mysterious black box with a button on it. When you press the button, the black box produces a value. PowerBASIC Lite has *numeric functions* and *string functions*. The value produced by a numeric function is a number. The value produced by a string function is a string.

RND is a numeric function used to produce random numbers. For example, the RND function in the following lines of code produces five random numbers. Each number is greater than 0 but less than 1.

```
FOR RandNum = 1 TO 5
  PRINT RND
NEXT RND
```

The printed numbers looks like this:

```
.9686200609430671
.201711411587894
.519515969324857
.1322406628169119
.8741881158202887
```

The INKEY$ function is a string function used to detect a keystroke made while a program is running. In the following example, the program prints your name until you press a key. INKEY$ detects the keystroke, making the WHILE condition false. This action causes an exit from the loop.

```
CLS
INPUT "Enter your name"; yourname$
WHILE INKEY$ = ""
  PRINT yourname$,
WEND
```

A complete list of predefined functions is in Appendix C, "PowerBASIC Lite Components." A description of predefined functions is in Chapter 16, "PowerBASIC Lite Reference."

In addition to the predefined functions, you can write your own functions as described in Chapter 8, "Subroutines, Functions, and Procedures."

The Program-Creation Cycle

To create a working program, you usually go through a three-step cycle:

1. *Write*. Enters the statements into memory or saves to a file (or rewrites to correct errors).

2. *Test*. Compiles and runs the program with test data. Determines whether the program works correctly.

3. *Debug*. Determines the source of the error and how to correct it when a program does not work correctly.

After the debug step is completed and you return to step 1, you rewrite the program and repeat the cycle. In general, the more complex a program, the longer it takes to run successfully.

The following sections describe each step in the cycle. A more thorough discussion of debugging is in Chapter 14, "Dynamic Debugging."

Writing Programs

The more time and care you use in writing your programs, the less time you need to test and debug them. Writing programs is usually an individual task. You write a program to solve a specific problem or to perform a specific task. Yet, when two people write programs to perform the same task, the programs are unique to the individual writing them.

Although there is not one *correct way* to write a program, you should follow the general guidelines in this section.

Study the task you want the program to accomplish, and make a plan for solving the problem. Ask yourself these questions:

1. What is the overall purpose of the program?

2. What kind of input does the program need?

3. How will the program process the input?

4. What kind of output will it produce, where will the output go, and how will it look?

5. How can the program be broken into manageable parts?

6. How will the parts fit into the main program?

7. Can these parts be broken into smaller pieces?

Some programmers draw a graphic diagram to outline the overall problem and break it into a series of small problems. Others use REM statements to form a skeleton outline with headings for each part of the problem.

Regardless of the method you use to outline the problem, you then can write the code to solve one small problem at a time. Write a program segment (such as a procedure) for each small problem. You usually can test each segment as it is completed, to help decrease testing and debugging time.

Complicated problems may require you to break the original program segments into smaller subsidiary pieces. Books often describe this process as *top-down design* because you start with a general description and work toward a more specific one.

Use several remarks in your program so that you can scan them later to see what the program does and how it works. You might know how the program works when you write it, but its function can be elusive when you return to it later.

Use variable names that relate to the variable's function. Single letters such as x, y, and z have little meaning. Instead, use descriptive names such as count, total, and index.

You never finish a program. Continue to study it to see whether you can find a more efficient way to write individual blocks of code. PowerBASIC is a rich language with a variety of tools that provide many different ways to build a program. The easier a program is to read, the easier it is to revise and maintain.

Testing Programs

When you write your program in short, manageable blocks and test each one separately, the time needed to test the completed program may be short. This section discusses testing the final version of a program.

Run the program using simple data. When the program cannot handle simple data, it's time to move on to debugging.

When the program works correctly with simple data, try some difficult data. See how the program handles numeric overflow. Watch variables in the Watch window to see any strange intermediate or end results.

Consider what happens when the user enters an invalid entry. For example, many programmers use a Y/N choice for user input and check for only one or the other input. What happens when the character entered is neither Y nor N?

Examine all subroutines and procedures for incorrect exits.

Put the program aside and wait a few days. Then test the program again.

Give your program to someone else to test. Code you wrote might contain false assumptions. Someone else might not make those assumptions and therefore would be more likely to uncover bugs.

Testing requires some intuition and common sense. Test for any unusual circumstances you can think of.

Debugging Programs

Debugging is the term used for determining why a program doesn't work correctly and fixing the problem (bug) so that the program works correctly. Minimize your debugging tasks by using much time and care in writing and testing the smaller parts of your program. When the smaller parts of your program run correctly, the debugging chores for the complete program are simpler and easier.

The PowerBASIC Lite compiler finds many errors before PowerBASIC Lite attempts to run the program. When the compiler finds the first error, the error is named and numbered. In addition, control returns to the editor with the cursor resting at the offending line. PowerBASIC Lite finds errors even when the program is run. These errors are also named and numbered. The cursor indicates their location. A list of the most common errors, whether discovered at compile time or at run-time, are explained in Appendix D, "PowerBASIC Lite Selected Error Codes."

Other types of errors are more elusive. You learn to look for these elusive bugs in Chapter 14, "Dynamic Debugging." Use PowerBASIC Lite's powerful tools to step through a program, or parts of a program, one instruction at a time. By stepping through your programs and watching the statements execute, you can check the logic of your plan. You also can watch the values of variables change and thus ensure that calculations or assignments are being carried out correctly.

Regardless of the computer language you use and the care you take in using the language, programming errors are common. Remember that each step in the program writing cycle is important. Each step is dependent on the other steps. Debugging can be a time-consuming and detailed chore. The time and care you spend on writing and testing your programs simplifies the debugging step.

Using Remarks in Programs

You saw how the REM statement and its abbreviated form (') can describe what various parts of a program do. The PowerBASIC Lite compiler does not execute or use remarks. You include them to make your source program more readable and understandable.

Developing Programs from Remarks

You use remarks to make an outline of your programs. Then you go back and add executable statements to each item in the outline. You test parts of your program as they are developed. For example, you can make the following outline:

```
REM ** Sales Tax Calculator **
' Learning BASIC, Chapter 6. File: PBL0601.BAS
REM ** Initialize **
REM ** Enter data **
REM ** Calculate tax and total cost **
REM ** Print price, tax, and total cost **
REM ** Do again or End? **
```

With the outline finished, you know how to create the program.

First, complete the initialize block. Assuming that you want to declare all variables to be integers and that the sales-tax rate in your community is 6.5 percent, you can add to the Initialize remark:

```
REM ** Initialize **
CLS: DEFINT A-Z
TaxRate! = .065
```

Because you want the capability of calculating the tax on more than one item, you can use a DO/LOOP loop to enclose the rest of the program. Then you need a way to enter the purchase price. You can use an INPUT statement to request and accept each entry:

```
REM ** Enter data **
DO
  INPUT "What is the price"; price!
```

To calculate the cost, use the variable TaxRate! and assign the value .065 in the Initialize block. Multiply it by the variable price!, used in the INPUT statement. Then add this value to the price:

```
REM ** Calculate tax and total cost **
tax! = TaxRate! * price!
cost! = tax! + price!
```

The calculation serves no purpose unless it is displayed. That is the task for the next block. You used the PRINT statement earlier for displaying data. Use it again to display all three values of interest: the price, the tax, and the total cost. Then print a blank line:

```
REM ** Print price, tax, and total cost **
PRINT "Price:"; price!
PRINT "Sales tax:"; tax!
PRINT "Total cost:"; cost!
PRINT
```

Now, how should you wrap it all up? A simple LOOP statement sends control back to the beginning of the loop. However, you can use an UNTIL or WHILE keyword to exit the loop. The exit condition can be triggered by entering 0 for the price.

```
REM ** Do again or End? **
  LOOP UNTIL price! = 0
END
```

The condition in the LOOP statement tells the computer to cycle back to the top of the loop until the value of the variable price! is 0. When you enter a price of 0, the calculations are all 0. An exit from the loop ends the program.

REM statements, used in this way, force you to think about how to formulate the program. They make programming easier and less likely to have errors in logic. From the original outline, you should have the program in listing 3.1.

Listing 3.1. The sales tax calculator.

```
REM ** Sales Tax Calculator **
' Learning BASIC, Chapter 3. File: PBL0301.BAS

REM ** Initialize **
CLS: DEFINT A-Z
TaxRate! = .065

REM ** Enter data **
DO
  INPUT "What is the price"; price!

  REM ** Calculate tax and total cost **
  tax! = TaxRate! * price!
  cost! = tax! + price!

  REM ** Print price, tax, and total cost **
  PRINT "Price:"; price!
  PRINT "Sales tax:"; tax!
  PRINT "Total cost:"; cost!
  PRINT

  REM ** Do again or End? **
LOOP UNTIL price! = 0
END
```

How the Program Works

When you enter and run this program, you first see the prompt for a price, a question mark, and a blinking cursor on an otherwise blank screen. This is the result of the INPUT statement in the Enter data block. Now you can enter the price of an item.

You enter the price of an item at the cursor's position. Then the computer does the calculations and displays the result. An immediate return to the top of the loop is made, and the program makes a request for another entry.

Whenever you want to quit, enter zero (0) for the price. The following output shows a typical run with three nonzero entries made. A 0 is entered to exit the loop.

```
What is the price? 22.95
Price: 22.95
Sales tax: 1.49175
Total cost: 24.44175

What is the price? 13.45
Price: 13.45
Sales tax: .874249949175
Total cost: 14.32425

What is the price? 17.50
Price: 17.50
Sales tax: 1.1375
Total cost: 18.6375

What is the price? 0
Price: 0
Sales tax: 0
Total cost: 0
```

Notice that the sales tax and total cost do not look like dollars and cents. You learn to format data in a later chapter.

Summary

A program is a series of instructions telling a computer what to do, when to do it, and how to do it. There is not one correct way to write a program. A program is an individual creation. Careful planning and patient development help you write programs that work correctly. Other helpful techniques include

- Outlining the program with REM statements or a graphics diagram.

- Breaking up the program into small parts.

- Using a liberal number of program comments (remarks).

- Using meaningful variable names.

- Testing the program thoroughly with all kinds of data; have others test it too.

- Using the debugging tools of PowerBASIC Lite to help you find errors.

- Studying the completed program and looking for refinements and improvements.

The instructions in a program supply information (input) to the computer or tell it how to get information to use. The instructions also tell how to process the information and where and how to send the results (output) of that processing.

You write a PowerBASIC Lite program with keywords (vocabulary) and rules of grammar (syntax) that PowerBASIC Lite understands. The keywords are classified into three groups: statements, functions, and system variables.

When you create a program, you go through a three-step cycle: write, test, and debug. This cycle is repeated until you think that the program works properly. The first step requires careful planning and writing of the code in short, manageable blocks. Test and debug each block of code before moving on to the next block. PowerBASIC Lite has debugging tools you can use to locate bugs (errors in the program). When all the parts have passed the cycle successfully, you repeat the cycle for the complete program.

Programs can be simple, such as a few sequentially executed lines composed of single statements; or you can use more than one statement on a single line. More complex programs take advantage of PowerBASIC Lite's loop and conditional branch structures: DO/LOOP, FOR/NEXT, and WHILE/WEND loops and IF/THEN, block IF, and SELECT CASE conditional branches. Functional processes can be separated from your main program by using FUNCTION...END FUNCTION and SUB...END SUB procedures.

Many PowerBASIC tools perform similar functions. You choose the tool that best fits your programming task. The choice of tools and the way you use them is what makes each program unique.

Exercises

1. Name the three steps used to create a program.

2. When PowerBASIC Lite finds an error, describe how it indicates the error and the error's location in the program.

3. Show what is displayed on the screen when the following two-line program segment is executed:

```
CLS
INPUT YourName$
```

4. Show what is displayed on the screen when the following two-line program segment is executed.

```
CLS
INPUT "Enter your name"; YourName$
```

5. Show the output of this program segment.

```
CLS
FOR number = 1 TO 15 STEP 3
  PRINT number;
NEXT number
```

6. Show the output of the following program segment.

```
CLS
FOR count% = 1 TO 10
  IF count% < = 5 THEN
      PRINT count%
    ELSE
      PRINT "Finished"
      EXIT FOR
  END IF
NEXT count%
```

7. Write a sequentially executed program segment that prints the current date, the current time, and your name.

8. Write a short program using a FOR/NEXT loop to print the even numbers from 20 to 30 (inclusive).

Chapter 4

Statements, Operators, Expressions, and Functions

As you saw in the first three chapters, statements make up PowerBASIC Lite programs. The statements are executed in sequence unless some statement alters the sequential flow. You used a FOR/NEXT loop in the Sum and Average Temperatures program in Chapter 1, "Getting Started." FOR and NEXT are examples of statements that interrupt the sequential flow of a program until the loop condition is completed. This chapter looks more closely at PowerBASIC Lite statements.

This chapter discusses

- How to use single and multiple statements on a line

- The three types of operators: arithmetic, relational, and logical

- Expressions and how to use them

- How to form statements from expressions and operators

- How to use functions in statements

- How to write programs that use statements, operators, expressions, and functions

Statements

Statements are building blocks you use to create a program. A program is a sequence of lines containing statements, remarks, blank lines, and labels.

Statement lines follow this syntax:

```
[line number] statement [: statement]...[remark]
```

A statement line can begin with a line number. PowerBASIC programs do not require line numbers. Line numbers are retained to maintain compatibility with earlier BASIC versions. You do not use them in this book. Statement lines contain one or more statements and an optional ending remark.

You used statements, remarks, and blank lines in earlier programs. A *label* can appear on a line by itself. A label is a name that marks a specific place in a program. You use it when a program needs to interrupt its normal sequential operation and go to the statement following the label. This book uses labels sparingly. PowerBASIC contains programming structures that allow you to avoid unnecessary jumps from place to place in the program through the use of GOTO statements.

Single Statement per Line

Many program lines contain only one statement; for example:

```
CLS
PRINT
END
```

Some program lines have no executable statements, but do have a REM statement or its apostrophe (') form. REM usually is classified as a statement, but the computer does not execute it. Remarks identify the functions of various parts of a program. When you use plenty of remarks, you can read just the remarks and know exactly what a program does. You saw the following remarks in a previous program.

```
REM ** Main program **
' Print date and time
'Sum and average temperatures
```

You also saw program lines that contain one statement and a closing remark.

```
CLS                     ' Clear the screen
PRINT DATE$             ' Print today's date
PRINT                   ' Print a blank line
```

Multiple Statements per Line

A program line can contain more than one statement per line, with the statements separated by a colon. This feature is another one, like line numbers, that PowerBASIC has retained principally for compatibility with earlier BASIC versions. You can find statements in a program easily when you put only one statement per line. This book occasionally uses multiple statements per line if there is a close functional relationship between two or more statements. For example, initialization chores can be grouped on one line:

```
REM ** Initialize **
CLS: DEFINT A-Z
```

Long Statement Lines

PowerBASIC lines hold a maximum of 248 characters. However, you should avoid writing lines with more than the 77 characters. Extra characters do not show in the Edit window. Printed output also can break lines at inappropriate places when the line is longer than your printer line-width.

In situations in which syntax requires a line longer than 77 characters, you can break the line with an underscore (_) character. Using FIELD statements when you format a data file often requires long lines. The following PRINT statement illustrates how a long line can be broken by an underscore.

```
PRINT "This is a long sentence that goes on for more "_
      "than 77 characters, extending beyond one line."
```

The compiler sees this as one long line, starting with PRINT and ending with line. It does not interpret the underscore character as part of the string to be printed.

Operators

Operators are symbols or words, such as the plus sign (+), that represent arithmetic, relational, or logical operations. *Operands* are the quantities on which operators act. In the numeric expression 5 + 4, the plus sign is the operator, and the integers 5 and 4 are the operands.

Arithmetic Operators

Arithmetic operators perform the normal mathematical operations of addition, subtraction, multiplication, division, negation, and exponentiation.

Arithmetic operators also perform two special integer operations: integer division and MOD. The integer division symbol is the backslash (\). It returns the integer result of the division. The MOD operator returns the integer remainder of the integer division.

Table 4.1 shows PowerBASIC Lite arithmetic operators listed in the order of precedence, when used together in a numeric expression. Operations listed on the same line have the same precedence.

Table 4.1. Arithmetic operations.

Operator	Operation	Example
^	Exponentiation	5 ^ 4
–	Negation	–10
*, /	Multiplication, division	5 * 6, 14 / 3
\	Integer division	21 \ 6
MOD	Modulo	21 MOD 6
+, –	Addition, subtraction	5 + 4, 18 – 8

Study the table. Then look at the program segment that follows. Make a guess at the results of each statement. Load PowerBASIC Lite if you haven't already. Then type and run the program lines to check your guesses.

```
CLS
PRINT 5 + 4 / 3 * 2
PRINT 23 - 2 ^ 3
PRINT 22 \ 6
PRINT 22 MOD 6
END
```

The output of the program shows:

```
7.666667
15
3
4
```

The highest order of precedence in the first example belongs to the division (/) and multiplication (*) operations. These operations are performed from left to right (division first, then multiplication), giving this result:

```
5 + 1.333333 * 2
5 + 2.666667
```

The addition is performed last: 5 + 2.666667 = 7.666667.

Using parentheses is helpful when you write expressions containing multiple operations. For example:

```
PRINT 5 + ((4 / 3) * 2)
PRINT 23 - (2 ^ 3)
```

Usually you don't run a program like this; you use a hand-held calculator. You can use PowerBASIC Lite as a calculator by making use of a feature found on the Debug menu (see figure 4.1).

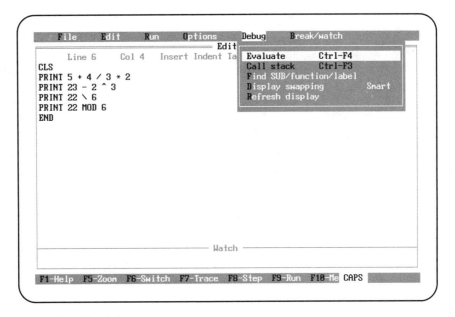

Figure 4.1. The Debug menu.

Press Enter after the Evaluate command is highlighted. A window appears with the cursor blinking in the Evaluate box at the top of the window. You enter arithmetic operators and operands, and the result is displayed in the Result box. In the Evaluate box, type

```
5 + 4 / 3 * 2
```

Press Enter to see the result (see figure 4.2).

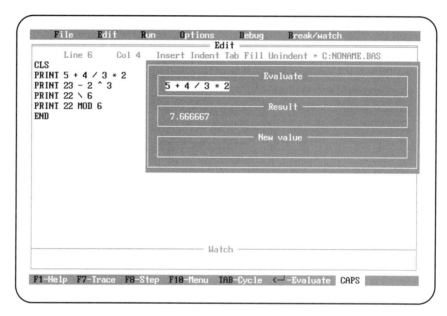

Figure 4.2. The result of evaluation.

According to the order of precedence in which arithmetic operations are performed (see table 4.1), the division (/) operation is performed first, which gives a partial answer of 1.333333, then multiplication (*), which gives a partial answer of 2.666667, and last, the addition, which gives the final result, 7.666667.

Because multiplication and division have the same order of precedence, they are performed from left to right. Division is performed first because the division operator (/) is to the left of the multiplication operator (*).

The exponentiation operation cannot be performed in the evaluate box, but you can evaluate 23 – 2 ^ 3 by using its equivalent form: 23 – 2 * 2 * 2. The result printed is 15.

Also try 22 \ 6 and 22 MOD 6 in the Evaluate box. The integer division result is 3 (the dividend in a pencil-and-paper division), and the MOD operation displays a result of 4 (the remainder of a pencil-and-paper division).

Press Esc to return to the Edit window.

When the arithmetic operators +, –, *, /, \, MOD, and ^ are used, and the operations do not contain parentheses, the order of operations is

1. All exponentiations (^) are first, in left-to-right order.

2. All negations (changing a number to its negative) are next, in left-to-right order.

3. All multiplication (*) and division (/) operations are next, in left-to-right order.

4. All integer divisions (\) operations are next, in left-to-right order.

5. All MOD operations are next, in left-to-right order.

6. Finally, all additions (+) and subtractions (–) are next, in left-to-right order.

You can use parentheses to modify the normal order of operations. Use parentheses to indicate suboperations. In evaluating operations that contain parentheses, the computer uses the following steps:

1. Beginning at the left end of the operations, the computer scans to the right until it finds a right parenthesis.

2. It evaluates the parenthetical suboperations. This evaluation replaces the subexpression, as well as the parentheses for a further evaluation of the operations.

Steps 1 and 2 are repeated until all expressions within parentheses are evaluated. After this, the resulting parentheses-free operations are evaluated. When you nest parentheses, the operations in parentheses are evaluated from the inside parentheses outward.

For example: 3 * (18 / (4 + 5)) is evaluated:

```
1.  3 * (18 / 9)
2.  3 * 2
3.  6
```

Relational Operators

Use *relational operators* to compare two numbers or two strings. The result of the comparison is a *Boolean* result (after George Boole, a 19th century British mathematician). These results have two possible outcomes: TRUE or FALSE. For example, the comparison

```
5 > 6     (5 is greater than 6)
```

is FALSE because 5 is not greater than 6. Of course, computers work with numbers, and PowerBASIC Lite actually returns a value of 0 for FALSE and –1 for TRUE. You have to interpret the result with the proper truth value. Table 4.2 lists the relational operators used by PowerBASIC.

Table 4.2. The relational operators.

Operator	Relation	Example
=	Equality	7 = 7
< >	Inequality	8 < > 7
<	Less than	7 < 8
>	Greater than	8 > 7
< =, = <	Less than or equal to	5 < = 6
> =, = >	Greater than or equal to	6 > = 5

Look at the following program segment, and decide whether the computer will print 0 (for FALSE) or –1 (for TRUE) for each of the numeric relations in the PRINT statements.

```
CLS
PRINT 8 + 1 = 9
PRINT 8 + 2 <> 9 + 1
PRINT 8 + 1 < 9 + 1
PRINT 9 - 2 > 9 + 2
PRINT 9 + 2 <= 9 - 2
PRINT 9 + 2 >= 9 - 2
END
```

After you make your decisions, type and run the program segment. You should see the numbers shown in the column labeled *Result* in table 4.3. The meaning of the resulting numbers and the reason the relation is TRUE or FALSE are shown in the table.

Table 4.3. Interpretation of relational operations.

Relation	Result	Meaning	Reason
8 + 1 = 9	–1	TRUE	9 = 9
8 + 2 <> 9 + 1	0	FALSE	10 = 10
8 + 1 < 9 + 1	–1	TRUE	9 < 10
9 – 2 > 9 + 2	0	FALSE	7 < 11
9 + 2 <= 9 – 2	0	FALSE	11 > 7
9 + 2 >= 9 – 2	–1	TRUE	11 > 7

Relational operators also compare strings of characters that are enclosed in quotation marks, such as: "Cat" > "Dog." That relation is FALSE (0) because the ASCII code for the letter *C* is less than the ASCII code for the letter *D* (see ASCII codes in Appendix B, "ASCII, Extended Key, and Scan Codes"). The ASCII codes of the individual letters in the strings are compared from left to right.

String ordering is based on two criteria:

1. The ASCII code values of the characters the strings contain.

2. The number of characters in the strings.

The comparison ends when a difference is found in the ASCII codes of a letter or when the end of a shorter string is reached. Strings are described in more detail in Chapter 5, "Numbers, Constants, Strings, and Variables," and Chapter 6, "String Manipulation."

Logical Operators

Logical operators perform logical (Boolean) operations on numeric values. Numbers are converted to integers before a logical operation takes place. Logical operators frequently are used with relational operators. In this case, the relational operations are carried out before the logical operation. The logical operations therefore are carried out on TRUE and FALSE operands. Descriptions and examples of each of the logical operators follows.

- AND performs a logical AND on two operands. The operation returns –1 (TRUE) when *both* operands are true. Otherwise, the operation returns 0 (FALSE). Study the examples in table 4.4. Note that only AND operations having both operators TRUE return the value TRUE.

Table 4.4. Examples of AND operations.

Operation	Translation	Value
0 AND 0	FALSE AND FALSE	FALSE
–1 AND 0	TRUE AND FALSE	FALSE
–1 AND –1	TRUE AND TRUE	TRUE
5 < 6 AND 3 < 4	TRUE AND TRUE	TRUE

- OR (sometimes called "inclusive or") operates on two operands and returns –1 (TRUE) when *one or both* operands is true. The OR operation returns 0 (FALSE) only when *both* operands are FALSE. For examples of OR operations, see table 4.5.

111

Table 4.5. Examples of OR operations.

Operation	Translation	Value
–1 OR 0	TRUE OR FALSE	TRUE
0 OR 0	FALSE OR FALSE	FALSE
6 > 5 OR 7 < 8	TRUE OR TRUE	TRUE
5 > 6 OR 8 < 7	FALSE OR FALSE	FALSE

- XOR (exclusive or) operates on two operands and returns a –1 (TRUE) when *the two operands are different* (one TRUE and one FALSE) (see table 4.6). It returns 0 (FALSE) when both operands are the same. Another way to look at it is that XOR returns TRUE when one operand is TRUE, but not both.

Table 4.6. Examples of XOR operations.

Operation	Translation	Value
–1 XOR 0	TRUE XOR FALSE	TRUE
–1 XOR –1	TRUE XOR TRUE	FALSE
6 < 5 XOR 7 < 6	FALSE XOR FALSE	FALSE
6 < 5 XOR 6 < 7	FALSE XOR TRUE	TRUE

- EQV. (equivalence) operates on two operands and returns the opposite value of XOR (see table 4.7). It returns –1 (TRUE) when *the two operands are the same* and 0 (FALSE) when *the two operands are different*.

Table 4.7. Examples of EQV operations.

Operation	Translation	Value
–1 EQV 0	TRUE EQV FALSE	FALSE
–1 EQV –1	TRUE EQV TRUE	TRUE
6 < 5 EQV 7 < 6	FALSE EQV FALSE	TRUE
6 < 5 EQV 6 < 7	FALSE EQV TRUE	FALSE

• IMP (implication) operates on two operands (see table 4.8). It returns 0 (FALSE) only when the first operand is TRUE and the second operand is FALSE. In all other cases it returns –1 (TRUE).

Table 4.8. Examples of IMP operations.

Operation	Translation	Value
–1 IMP –1	TRUE IMP TRUE	TRUE
0 IMP –1	FALSE IMP TRUE	TRUE
0 IMP 0	FALSE IMP FALSE	TRUE
–1 IMP 0	TRUE IMP FALSE	FALSE

These logical operators perform *binary* operations. A binary operation is one in which two operands are combined. Because of the many possible operand combinations, it is easier to refer to a table of truth values to check results of logical operations. Table 4.9 shows such a truth table where x and y are the operands. The letter T stands for TRUE, and the letter F stands for FALSE. To read the table, determine the values of the two operands. When the first is TRUE and the second is FALSE, read the second row of the table. Find the column for the particular operator you are looking up (AND, OR, XOR, EQV, or IMP). The value returned for the operation is in that row and column.

Table 4.9. Truth table for logical operations.

x	y	x AND y	x OR y	x XOR y	x EQV y	x IMP y
T	T	T	T	F	T	T
T	F	F	T	T	F	F
F	T	F	T	T	F	T
F	F	F	F	F	T	T

The following loop demonstrates the use of the block IF structure with relational and logical operations.

```
CLS: RANDOMIZE TIMER
DO
  number% = INT(RND * 100) - 50
  even% = number% MOD 2
  PRINT number%;
  IF (number% > 0 AND even% = 0) THEN
      PRINT "TRUE, positive and even"
    ELSE
      PRINT "FALSE"
  END IF
  DELAY 1
LOOP
```

The loop selects a random integer in the range –50 to 49. The MOD operator is used to determine whether the number is even. Then the number is printed. The final truth of the condition in the IF statement

```
(number% > 0 AND even% = 0)
```

depends on two intermediate truth values:

1. The random integer is positive (number% > 0).

2. The integer is even (number% MOD 2).

When both intermediate values are TRUE, the THEN block is executed. When either, or both, of the intermediate values is FALSE, the ELSE block is executed. The PowerBASIC DELAY statement is used to provide readable output. To end a run, press Esc.

The output of a short run follows:

```
 40 TRUE, positive and even
 19 FALSE
-7 FALSE
-15 FALSE
 45 FALSE
 20 TRUE, positive and even
-11 FALSE
```

Relational and logical operations can be used in a similar way in other PowerBASIC program structures. Here are the same operations used with SELECT CASE.

114

```
CLS: RANDOMIZE TIMER
DO
  number% = INT(RND * 100) - 50
  even% = number% MOD 2
  PRINT number%;
  SELECT CASE (number% > 0 AND even% = 0)
    CASE -1
      PRINT "TRUE, positive and even"
    CASE ELSE
      PRINT "FALSE"
  END SELECT
  Delay 1
LOOP
```

Expressions

An expression is a combination of constants and variables connected by operators. An expression can be as simple as a single numeric value. You form more complex expressions by combining operands with arithmetic, relational, and logical operators.

Simple Expressions

A simple expression can be a single numeric value used in a PRINT statement, such as

```
PRINT 3.141593
```

A simple expression also can be a variable or a string you used in previous programs. For example

- A system variable: PRINT DATE$

- A variable: PRINT counter!

- A string: PRINT "Time"

You saw more complex expressions in the last section when operators and operands were combined.

Complex Expressions

When you combine simple expressions with connecting operators, you create more complex expressions. You used expressions involving arithmetic operators, such as

```
PRINT 5 + 4 / 3 * 2
PRINT 23 - 2 ^ 3
PRINT 22 MOD 6
```

You also experimented with expressions formed with arithmetic and relational operators:

```
PRINT 8 + 2 <> 9 + 1
PRINT 8 + 1 < 9 + 1
PRINT 9 - 2 > 9 + 2
```

You saw how logical operators are used with TRUE (–1) and FALSE (0), and relational values.

-1 AND 0 is FALSE	(0 returned)
-1 AND -1 is TRUE	(–1 returned)
-1 IMP 0 is FALSE	(0 returned)
5 < 6 AND 3 < 4 is TRUE	(–1 returned)
5 < 6 OR 8 < 7 is FALSE	(0 returned)
6 < 5 XOR 7 < 6 is FALSE	(0 returned)
6 < 5 EQV 7 < 6 is TRUE	(–1 returned)

Using Functions in Expressions

PowerBASIC Lite has several helpful *functions* built into its language. Two built-in functions frequently used are INT (the integer function) and RND (the random number function).

You should practice using PowerBASIC's help system by looking up these functions now. You find them by accessing the Functions item on the Help index (see Chapter 2, "Using PowerBASIC Lite"). Briefly, INT converts a numeric expression to an integer. Its syntax is

```
y = INT(numeric expression)
```

As you see, INT requires a numeric expression in parentheses as an *argument*. An argument is a numeric or string expression on which the function operates to produce the result assigned to *variable y*. A variable is a name applied to a numeric or string quantity. You saw two types of variables earlier: DATE$ and counter!. PRINT statements used the system variable DATE$ and the single-precision numeric variable counter!.

```
PRINT DATE$
PRINT counter!
```

The RND function returns a random extended-precision value between 0 and 1. The syntax for RND is

```
y = RND [(numeric expression)]
```

The numeric expression argument is optional. See the help section on the RND function for an explanation. The argument is unnecessary, but can be used for special effects described in the help section.

Use these two functions together to obtain a random integer. You can assign the expression INT(RND * 100) to a variable named amount:

```
amount = INT(RND * 100)
```

Because the value of RND is greater than 0 and less than 1, the value of RND * 100 is greater than 0 and less than 100. The expression returns an integer in the range 0 to 99. The returned value is assigned to the variable named amount. You can use this expression in a program in the following section. Try printing a few values produced with this expression by running the following program segment:

```
FOR number = 1 TO 5
  amount = INT(RND * 100)
  PRINT amount;
NEXT number
```

Typical results would be

```
96  20  51  13  87
```

Program Examples

The next program demonstrates the use of expressions involving arithmetic and relational operators with the AND logical operation. It also uses the INT and RND functions.

117

Before the expression involving the arithmetic, relational, and logical operators is reached, an integer is assigned to a variable named `amount`, as described in the previous section.

The complex expression used in the program is contained in an `IF`/`THEN`/`ELSE` statement. A detailed discussion of this statement is in Chapter 7, "Program Control Structures." The two relational operations in the expression contain different arithmetic operations.

```
amount + 33 > 80
```

and

```
amount / 3 < 50
```

A random integer in the range 0 to 99 has been assigned previously to `amount`. These two relational operations each return TRUE or FALSE, depending on the value of `amount`.

The two relational operations are connected by the AND operator to form an expression:

```
amount + 33 > 80 AND amount / 2 < 40
```

Therefore, when both relational operations are TRUE, the value of the complete expression is TRUE. When either or both of the relational operations is FALSE, the complete expression is FALSE. Therefore, when `amount` is greater than 47 and less than 80, the value of the expression is TRUE.

If you have programmed in BASIC before, you know that IF/THEN/ELSE statements involving long expressions make a program difficult to read. When an expression is too long to fit on one line of the screen, the expression usually is broken at an inappropriate place.

You can use PowerBASIC's underscore continuation character (_), discussed earlier in this chapter, to break a long single-line statement at a logical place. For example, the following long line is broken after the keyword THEN:

```
IF amount + 33 > 80 AND amount / 2 < 40 THEN_
  PRINT "True" ELSE PRINT "False"
```

As an alternative, you can use PowerBASIC's block IF structure.

```
IF amount + 33 > 80 AND amount / 2 < 40 THEN
    PRINT "True"
  ELSE
    PRINT "False"
END IF
```

When the expression in the IF clause is TRUE, the word *True* is printed. When the expression is FALSE, the word *False* is printed.

Listing 4.1 uses this IF statement to classify the ten random integers assigned to the variable amount. Declare the two variables used in the program to be integers in the Initialize block by

```
DEFINT A-Z
```

Listing 4.1. Operations with random numbers.

```
REM ** Operations with Random Numbers **
' Learning BASIC, Chapter 4. File: PBL0401.BAS

REM ** Initialize **
CLS: DEFINT A-Z

REM ** Main Program **
FOR number = 1 to 10
  amount = INT(RND * 100)
  PRINT amount;
  IF amount + 33 > 80 AND amount / 2 < 40 THEN_
    PRINT "True" ELSE PRINT "False"
  PRINT
NEXT number
END
```

Type the program and save it as PBL0401.BAS. Then run the program. The output of listing 4.1 follows.

```
96 False

20 False

51 True

13 False

87 False

 2 False

47 False

95 False

31 False

76 True
```

As you can see on-screen, the first random number is 96. When 96 is added to 33, the result is 129. The result is greater than 80, so the first relational operation is TRUE. When 96 is divided by 2, the result is 48. This result is not less than 40, so the second relational operation is FALSE. Because AND is the logical operation and the operands are not both true, the final truth value is FALSE. Table 4.10 shows the random integer selected, the truth value of each operand, and the truth value of the complete expression for each of the 10 passes through the FOR/NEXT loop.

Table 4.10. Analysis of the output in listing 4.1.

amount	amount + 33 > 80	amount / 2 < 40	Expression
96	T	F	F
20	F	T	F
51	T	T	T
13	F	T	F
87	T	F	F
2	F	T	F
47	F	T	F
95	T	F	F
31	F	T	F
76	T	T	T

Run the program again and you see that the program produces the same set of ten numbers with the same results as the first run.

The random numbers generated by RND are not actually random but the result of an *algorithm* (a special process of solving some type of problem). A start (or *seed*) value determines where to select the beginning number in the chain of "random" numbers, produced by the algorithm. Unless you provide a different seed value, the algorithm selects the same numbers each time a program is run. You can use a RANDOMIZE statement to provide the seed value. The syntax for RANDOMIZE is

```
RANDOMIZE [numeric expression]
```

When you omit the numeric expression, the program is interrupted and you are prompted to enter a number to seed the random number generator. You then must enter a seed number before the program can continue. You can provide a seed number automatically by using the TIMER function as the numeric expression. When you use the TIMER function, the program is not interrupted for the seed number.

The computer keeps track of the seconds that pass after midnight. Access this value by using the TIMER function. TIMER returns a single-precision number equal to the number of seconds since midnight, according to the computer's time.

You use this function as the numeric expression in the RANDOMIZE statement. Because the value of TIMER is always changing, it supplies a seed value that is different for each run of the program.

Insert the RANDOMIZE statement in the Initialize block of the program (refer to listing 4.1). It must be executed before the RND function is used in order to provide a new seed value each time the program runs. The revised Initialize block is

```
REM ** Initialize **
CLS: DEFINT A-Z
RANDOMIZE TIMER
```

Run the program several more times, and see a new set of ten random numbers each time. The following shows a typical output when the program is run with this revision.

```
61 True

85 False

55 True

28 False

99 False

 1 False

68 True

45 False

56 True

92 False
```

If you want new random integers each time you run the program, save the program with the revision.

The program in listing 4.2 uses an OR logical operation on expressions that use relational operators less than (<) and greater than (>) in the operands of the expressions. It also uses numerous assignment statements and arithmetic operations.

121

Listing 4.2. Tally responses.

```
REM ** Tally Responses **
' Learning BASIC, Chapter 4. File: PBL0402.BAS

REM ** Initialize **
CLS: DEFINT A-Z
RANDOMIZE TIMER

REM ** Main Program **
FOR number = 1 to 50
  response = INT(RND * 7)
  IF response < 1 OR response > 5 THEN BEEP
  IF response = 1 THEN INCR Tally1
  IF response = 2 THEN INCR Tally2
  IF response = 3 THEN INCR Tally3
  IF response = 4 THEN INCR Tally4
  IF response = 5 THEN INCR Tally5
NEXT number
PRINT "Number 1 selections:"; Tally1
PRINT "Number 2 selections:"; Tally2
PRINT "Number 3 selections:"; Tally3
PRINT "Number 4 selections:"; Tally4
PRINT "Number 5 selections:"; Tally5
TallyTotal = Tally1 + Tally2 + Tally3 + Tally4 + Tally5
BadVotes = 50 - TallyTotal
PRINT "Valid votes ="; TallyTotal
PRINT "Invalid votes ="; BadVotes
END
```

The program simulates a voter poll with a small sample population (50). Integers 0 through 6 randomly select responses to the poll. Responses of 0 and 6 are invalid. When you hear the computer beep, you know that the program discarded an invalid response. Responses 1 through 5 are tallied. The number of tallies for each valid vote is printed, with the totals of valid and invalid votes. Here is a typical tally of the 50 votes:

```
Number 1 selections: 8
Number 2 selections: 5
Number 3 selections: 9
Number 4 selections: 7
Number 5 selections: 3
Valid votes = 32
Invalid votes = 18
```

Summary

In this chapter, you learned about the components that make up a program. The components include statements, operators, operands, expressions, and functions. Statements are the building blocks of programs. Statement lines can be a single keyword or as long as 248 characters. More than one statement can be written on the same statement line.

You also learned about three kinds of PowerBASIC Lite operations: arithmetic, relational, and logical. You saw the symbols, called operators, used for each operation: arithmetic operators (table 4.1), relational operators (table 4.2), and a truth table for logical operators (table 4.9).

You used the Evaluate box, accessed from the Debug menu, to evaluate some arithmetic operations. You used some short program segments to display the results of arithmetic and relational operations. You saw the results of logical operators used on operands containing relational operations.

Relational operators (=, <>, <, >, <= or =<, and >= or =>) are used to compare two quantities (numbers or strings). The result of the comparison is either TRUE (–1) or FALSE (0).

Logical operators (AND, OR, XOR, EQV, and IMP) perform logical (Boolean) operations on numeric values. When relational and logical operators are used together, the relational operations are carried out before the logical operations.

You used simple and complex expressions of all three types of operations. You were introduced to three functions: INT, RND, and TIMER, as well as the RANDOMIZE statement.

At the close of the chapter, you used a program (listing 4.1), to demonstrate the use of complex expressions. The expressions were in a long IF/THEN/ELSE statement. You used an underscore (_) character to break that statement into two lines so that it was more readable. The final program, listing 4.2, used complex expressions to tally a simulated voter poll.

Exercises

1. Can a program line contain more than one statement?

2. Can a program line contain more than 77 characters?

3. Which of the following three terms applies to the plus sign (+)?

    operand
    operator
    expression

123

4. What is the result of the following expression?

```
3 * 6 - 12 / 2 ^ 2?
```

5. Is the expression 5 <= 6 TRUE or FALSE?

6. Is 14 – 3 >= 9 + 2 TRUE or FALSE?

7. Is the result of the following relational and logical operations TRUE or FALSE?

```
5 < 6 OR 3 > 4
```

8. Name the range of possible values for the variable in the following assignment statement:

```
number = INT(RND * 20)
```

9. When the value of the variable amount is 60, is the following statement TRUE or FALSE?

```
amount + 33 > 80 AND amount / 2 < 40
```

10. What numerical values does the computer use to represent TRUE and FALSE?

11. Describe the purpose of the underscore(_) character.

Chapter 5

Numbers, Constants, Strings, and Variables

As you learned in Chapter 4, "Statements, Operators, Expressions, and Functions," PowerBASIC Lite programs are composed of statements. You read that statements contain expressions formed by numbers, strings, operands, operators, and functions. In this chapter, you see many types of numbers that PowerBASIC Lite can handle; you also learn to use strings, constants, and variables. Here are some topics you will learn about in this chapter:

- Number types: integer, long integer, quad integer, single precision, double precision, extended precision, BCD fixed point, and BCD floating point

- Constants: string, numeric, and named

- Variable types: integer, floating point, and string

- Legal names for variables

- Defining variables by type

- More program examples

Number Types

PowerBASIC Lite provides a variety of number types, supporting eight unique types. You can group these eight types into three classes of numbers: integer, floating point, and binary-coded decimal. This grouping gives you many options and presents the problem of choosing the right type for your programming situation. Usually, simple integers and single-precision number types are suffi-cient. As you study the properties of each number type, you discover reasons for picking one type over another to do specific tasks.

You can designate a number as a specific type by appending a special character (*type indicator*) to the end of the number. You also can specify variables by using a type indicator. For example,

- 23% specifies that the number 23 is an integer.

- number specifies that the variable number is an integer variable.

- 2.35! specifies that the number 2.35 is a single-precision number.

- fcost specifies that the variable cost is a single-precision variable.

The following sections describe each type of number.

Integer Numbers

Integer numbers have no decimal part. This class of numbers contains the counting numbers (1, 2, 3, 4, 5, and so on), zero (0), and the negatives of the counting numbers (–1, –2, –3, –4, –5, and so on). The three subclasses of integers (*integer*, *long integer*, and *quad integer*) differ in the range of values available and the amount of memory they use.

Integers

The simplest and fastest numbers to use in your PowerBASIC Lite programs are integers. Integers have no decimal point. PowerBASIC Lite integers range from –32,768 to 32,767. Although this range sets a limit on the usefulness of integers, it is adequate for many applications. Using integers produces fast and compact program code. Each integer needs only 2 *bytes* of memory storage space. One byte is equal to 8 binary digits. A byte is the space needed to store a single text character.

Notice in the following integer examples that you use no commas with integers containing four or more digits:

```
-235   0   16   -1024   32145   -24
```

The type specifier for integers is the percent (%) sign.

Enter and run the following program segment to see what happens when an integer is larger than the legal range of integers.

```
CLS
FOR number% = 32765 to 32767
  PRINT number%
NEXT number%
```

When you run this program segment, an error message appears on the status line of the Edit window.

```
Error 6: Overflow
```

You may wonder what's going on. The integers in the FOR statement are within the legal values for integers. Look at the User output screen by pressing Alt-F5. You see the values you expected.

```
32765
32766
32767
```

The overflow occurs because of the way a FOR/NEXT loop works. Each time the NEXT statement is executed, the value of the variable number% increases by 1. The values 32765, 32766, and 32767 are printed. Then the variable increases by 1 to 32768 *before* it is tested for the loop limit. This value, which is beyond the range of integers, causes the overflow error even though the loop executes successfully.

Long Integers

When you want to use an integer outside the legal integer range of –32,768 to 32,767, you use PowerBASIC Lite's *long integers*. Long integers span the range from –2,147,483,648 to 2,147,483,647. The price of this extended range is that you need twice as much memory for storage. A long integer requires 4 bytes of memory. Calculations performed with long integers take more time than calculations performed with integers, but are faster than other types of numbers.

Long integers look just like integers, but can have more digits. The type specifier for long integers is the ampersand (&).

Long integers are helpful in intermediate calculations of large sums of money, expressed in cents rather than dollars and cents. Final results can be obtained by dividing the intermediate result by 100 to change the format to dollars and cents. You can express values as large as $21 million.

Imagine having an investment worth $12,345,678.90, or 1,234,567,890 pennies. You acquire a windfall of $9,012.34 (901,234 pennies). You add the windfall to your investment. Using long integers, you can calculate your new invested amount with the following three-line program segment.

```
CLS
Account& = 1234567890 + 901234
PRINT Account&; Account& / 100
```

When you run the program segment, you see the amount printed in pennies and in dollars and cents.

```
1235469124   12354691.24
```

Quad Integers

Quad integers are longer than long integers. Their range is from -2^{63} to $2^{63} - 1$. Calculations using quad integers are carried out to 19 digits, but results are rounded to 18 digits for display purposes. A PRINT statement displays a maximum of 16 digits by default. A quad integer requires 8 bytes of memory space for storage.

The type specifier for quad integers is a double ampersand (&&). Notice that the quad integer number in the following PRINT statement has 19 digits followed by the quad integer type specifier. Enter and run the two-statement program segment.

```
CLS
PRINT 1234567890123456789&&
```

The output is

```
1.234567890123457E+18
```

The quad integer is expressed in *floating-point notation*. Floating-point notation is similar to the scientific notation that mathematicians use.

Floating-point notation: 1.23E+18

Scientific notation: 1.23×10^{18}

Floating-point notation consists of two parts:

1.234567890123457 (called the *mantissa*)

E+18 (the *exponent*)

The mantissa contains the digits of the value being expressed in floating-point notation. The decimal point in the mantissa is always immediately to the right of the first nonzero digit. The exponent is a power of 10. When you multiply the mantissa by the power of 10 specified in the exponent, you have the value in common numeric notation.

To change the number in the previous example to common numeric notation, you multiply the mantissa by 10 raised to the 18th power. In layman's terms, you move the decimal point 18 places to the right to obtain

1,234,567,890,123,457,000

Notice that the 19 places of the number you asked to be printed round off to 16 significant digits when it is printed. The last three places are filled with zeros. You can increase to 18 digits the number of places to be printed by using the STR$ function within a PRINT statement. Add a third line to the program segment so that it reads

```
CLS
PRINT 1234567890123456789&&
PRINT STR$(1234567890123456789&&, 18)
```

This new statement tells the computer to print the quad integer value in string form to 18 places. The STR$ function and strings are described in more detail in the Chapter 6, "String Manipulation."

Run this revised program segment. You see

```
1.234567890123457E+18
1.23456789012345678E+18
```

When the STR$ function is used with the print statement, 18 digits are displayed. Eighteen is the largest number of digits that can be displayed for quad integers.

Floating-Point Numbers

Floating-point numbers can contain decimal points. This number type fills in the gaps between the integers. Between each integer is an infinite number of floating-point values. PowerBASIC Lite offers three kinds of floating-point numbers: *single precision*, *double precision*, and *extended precision*. Like the different types of integers, these floating-point number types differ in range and the amount of memory they use.

Single-Precision Numbers

The type specifier for single-precision numbers is the exclamation mark (!). Single-precision numbers require 4 bytes of memory space for storage. A single-precision number can contain a decimal point and have a range from $-3.37E+38$ to $3.37E+38$. Numbers very close to 0, however, are evaluated as 0.

Figure 5.1 gives a graphical interpretation of single-precision range and the small gap. The range is not drawn to scale because the gap is tiny. You can ignore it for any practical programming purposes.

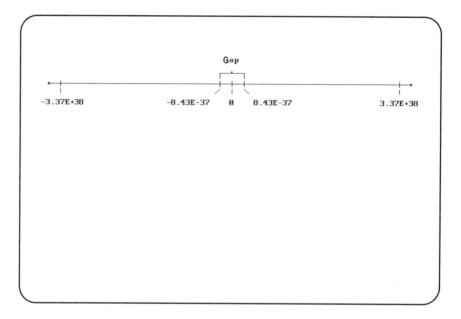

Figure 5.1. The range of single-precision numbers.

Enter the following short program segment and run it.

```
CLS
PRINT -8.43E-38!
PRINT -8.43E-39!
PRINT
PRINT 8.43E-38!
PRINT 8.43E-39!
```

The following output displays the correct value for -8.43E-38! and 8.43E-38! but displays 0 for -8.43E-39! and 8.43E-39!.

```
-8.43E-38
0

8.43E-38
0
```

Double-Precision Numbers

Double-precision numbers require twice as much memory space as single-precision numbers: 8 bytes. Consequently, calculations using double-precision numbers consume more time than those with single-precision numbers.

The type specifier for double-precision is the number, or pound, sign (#). The range of double-precision values extends from

- Approximately 4.19E–307 to 1.67E+308 for positive numbers

- Approximately –1.67E+308 to –4.19E–307 for negative numbers

Values in a small range (– 4.19E–307 to 4.19E–307) are interpreted as 0. This range is tiny and can be ignored for practical purposes. Type the following short program segment and run it.

```
CLS
PRINT -4.19E-308#
PRINT -4.19E-309#
PRINT
PRINT 4.19E-308#
PRINT 4.19E-309#!
```

The correct value for –4.19E–308# and 4.19E–308# is displayed in the following output, but a 0 is displayed for –4.19E–309# and 4.19E–309#.

```
-4.19E-308
0

4.19E-308
0
```

The storage requirement of double-precision values becomes significant when you program with arrays. Double-precision arrays "eat up" memory fast, at 8 bytes per array element.

Extended-Precision Numbers

Extended-precision numbers are used primarily internally by PowerBASIC Lite when necessary. This data type has been provided so that you can take advantage of its extra range and precision. The type specifier for extended precision is a pair of number signs (##).

Extended precision requires 10 bytes of storage and has an approximate range of –1.2E+4932 to 1.2E+4932. Extended-precision values can be displayed up to 18 significant digits.

As with quad integers, PRINT statements display up to 16 digits by default. To print all 18 significant extended-precision digits, you add a STR$ function to the PRINT statement. For example, when you use *number##* as a variable to represent an extended-precision number, use

```
PRINT STR$(number##, 18)
```

Because PowerBASIC uses extended-precision numbers internally, this number type is most efficient. When memory size and speed are more important than the precision of results, however, the use of integer or single-precision numbers is best.

Binary-Coded Decimal Numbers

PowerBASIC also can use two different forms of *binary-coded decimal* (BCD) numbers: fixed point and floating-point. As the name implies, this number type uses a binary code to represent decimal numbers. This is the most accurate way to represent nonintegers. Using the binary-coded decimal format eliminates round-off errors that occur when you use single-precision and other noninteger number types. Calculations performed with this number type, however, are the slowest of all number types.

Type specifiers are the at sign (@) for BCD fixed-point numbers and a pair of at signs (@@) for BCD floating-point numbers. The use of binary-coded number types is for advanced programming and is not discussed further in this tutorial guide. These number types are an excellent choice when you create spreadsheets, accounting packages, or other financial forms. A summary showing type specifiers and memory use for variables (see table 5.3) also applies to number types.

Constants

PowerBASIC Lite programs process two distinct classes of data: *constants* and *variables*. A variable can change its value during a program run, as described in Chapter 3, "An introduction to Programming," and again later in this chapter. A constant's value is fixed at compile time and cannot change during a program run. For example, the value of pi (the ratio of a circle's circumference to its diameter) does not change. When pi is used in a program, its value is specified as a constant in the program.

```
Pi! = 3.141593
```

PowerBASIC supports three types of constants: *string constants*, *numeric constants*, and a special form of integer constant, *named constants*. All three constant types are described in the following sections.

String Constants

String constants are simply groups of characters enclosed in quotation marks. For example, you saw the following string constants in earlier programs. In each case, the string constant is in quotation marks ("Date", "Time", "Sum is", "Average is", "True", and "False").

```
PRINT "Date"
PRINT "Time"
PRINT "Sum is"; Sum
PRINT "Average is"; Ave
IF amount + 33 > 80 AND amount / 2 < 40 THEN_
   PRINT "True" ELSE PRINT "False"
```

When a string constant is the last element on a line, the closing quotation marks are optional. For example,

```
PRINT "Date
PRINT "Time
```

I do not personally recommend omitting the closing quotation marks. Having both opening and closing quotes clearly marks the beginning and end of the string constant.

Numeric Constants

Numeric constants represent numeric values. They consist primarily of the digits 0 through 9 and a decimal point. Use a leading minus (–) sign with a negative constant. A leading plus sign (+) is optional for positive constants but usually is not displayed.

PowerBASIC Lite uses the amount of precision necessary to process the constants you provide. As you saw earlier, PowerBASIC can use all the number types: integer, long integer, quad integer, single precision, double precision, extended precision, binary-coded decimal fixed point, or binary-coded decimal floating point.

You also can force a constant to be stored with a specified precision by following the constant with one of the variable type specifiers (%, &, &&, !, #, ##, @, @@). When a specifier does not follow a numeric constant, PowerBASIC uses the following rules to determine how to store the value.

1. When the value contains no decimal point and is in the range from –32,768 to 32,767, it is stored as an integer.

2. When the value is an integer beyond the range of integers and is in the range -2^{31} to $2^{31} -1$, it is stored as a long integer.

3. Integers beyond the range of long integers are stored as quad integers.

4. When the numeric constant contains a decimal point and has up to six digits, it is stored as single precision.

5. A numeric constant with a decimal point and more than 6 but less than 17 digits is stored as double precision.

6. Integers too large to be stored as quad integers but small enough to fall within the range of double-precision numbers are stored also as double precision. Larger values (with as many as 18 significant digits) are stored as extended precision.

Table 5.1 shows some examples of how PowerBASIC Lite stores numeric constants.

Table 5.1. Numeric constant storage.

Constant	Storage Precision
231	Integer
32855	Long integer
231.3	Single precision
1.205321	Double precision
1234567.890123456	Extended precision

Alternative Number Systems

PowerBASIC enables you to express integers in number systems having a different base than the decimal system (base 10). It is sometimes convenient to express integers in hexadecimal (base 16), octal (base 8), or binary (base 2) notation. You cannot represent long integers and quad integers by an alternative notation.

Data for PowerBASIC Lite programs usually is entered in decimal form. These numbers are converted to binary notation for use by the computer. Results are converted to decimal notation for display.

An understanding of the binary number system is essential if you use one of the alternative number systems. Binary constants contain only the digits 0 and 1, and can be a maximum of 16 digits. A binary number must be preceded by &B. Here are some binary numbers.

```
&B0011        &B0101        &B1100        &B00011110
```

Each place in a binary number is a power of 2. Place values increase from right to left. For example,

```
&B0001 = 2 raised to the power of 0 = 2 ^ 0 = 1
&B0010 = 2 raised to the power of 1 = 2 ^ 1 = 2
&B0100 = 2 raised to the power of 2 = 2 ^ 2 = 4
&B1000 = 2 raised to the power of 3 = 2 ^ 3 = 8
&B10000 = 2 raised to the power of 4 = 2 ^ 4 = 16
```

To convert a binary number to decimal value, add the decimal place values of the binary number that have a value of 1. For example,

```
&B0011 = 2 + 1 = 3
&B0101 = 4 = 1 = 5
&B1100 = 8 + 4 = 12
&B00011110 = 16 + 8 + 4 + 2 = 30
```

Octal constants are rarely used today. The octal number system contains the digits 0 through 7. PowerBASIC Lite can handle octal numbers up to six digits. An octal constant must be preceded by &O, &Q, or &. Here are some examples of octal numbers:

```
&Q031        &Q205        &Q107        &Q1062
```

Each place in an octal number is a power of 8. Place values increase from right to left. For example,

```
&Q0001 = 8 raised to the power of 0 = 8 ^ 0 = 1
&Q0010 = 8 raised to the power of 1 = 8 ^ 1 = 8
&Q0100 = 8 raised to the power of 2 = 8 ^ 2 = 64
&Q1000 = 8 raised to the power of 3 = 8 ^ 3 = 512
&Q10000 = 8 raised to the power of 4 = 8 ^ 4 = 4096
```

To convert an octal number to decimal value, add the products of each place value and the decimal equivalent of the octal number in that place. For example,

```
&Q031 = (3 * 8) + 1 = 25
&Q205 = (2 * 64) + 5 = 133
&Q107 = (1 * 64) + 7 = 71
&Q1062 = (1 * 4096) + (6 * 8) + 2 = 4146
```

Hexadecimal constants are helpful when you use graphics and calculate machine addresses. Hexadecimal constants consist of as many as four characters from the set of digits 0 through 9 and the letters A through F. A hexadecimal number must be preceded by &H. Here are some hexadecimal numbers:

```
&H68      &H2A      &H5D       &H25F
```

Each place in a hexadecimal number is a power of 16. Place values increase from right to left. For example,

```
&H001 = 16 raised to the power of 0 = 16 ^ 0 = 1
&H010 = 16 raised to the power of 1 = 16 ^ 1 = 16
&H100 = 16 raised to the power of 2 = 16 ^ 2 = 256
&H1000 = 16 raised to the power of 3 = 16 ^ 3 = 4096
```

To convert a hexadecimal number to decimal value, add the products of each place value and the decimal equivalent of the hexadecimal number in that place. For example,

```
&H68 = (6 * 16) + 8 = 104
&H2A = (2 * 16) + 10 = 41
&H5D = (5 * 16) +12 = 92
&H25F = (2 * 256) + (5 * 16) + 15 = 607
```

Here are examples of constants, in alternative number systems, that represent the decimal integer 256.

```
&H100    &O400    &400    &B100000000
```

Hexadecimal and binary constants are described in Chapter 12, "Graphics."

Named Constants

PowerBASIC Lite enables you to refer to integer constants by name. Those of you familiar with other languages will recognize that this reference by name is similar to the CONST feature of Pascal or the DEFINE feature of C.

To name an integer constant, precede its identifier (name) with the % sign, and then assign an integer value to it. A common convention capitalizes named constants. Notice the difference in the looks of a named constant and a variable in this example:

```
%COUNT = 0     ' a named constant assigned a value of 0
count% = 5     ' a variable assigned an initial value of 5
PRINT %COUNT; count%   ' they are separate entities
```

The integer constant and the variable look similar except for the placement of the type specifier (% in this example). You've seen variables before. They are discussed in the following section, "Variables."

Named constants are typically defined at the beginning of a program. They are used for constants that appear often in the program so that the value may be easily changed. For example, a program can calculate statistical information for a class of students. The number of students in the class can be assigned to a named constant, such as

```
%NUMKIDS = 35
```

This constant is used in many places in the program.

As the upper for the loop:

```
FOR number% = 1 TO %NUMKIDS
  INPUT score!(number%)
  total! = total! + score!
NEXT number%
```

To calculate the average score:

```
Average! = total! / %NUMKIDS
```

In another loop that calculates a score's deviation from the class average:

```
FOR number% = 1 TO %NUMKIDS
  Deviation! = score!(number%) - Average!
NEXT number%
```

If the number of students changes, you only have to change the value of %NUMKIDS where it is named at the beginning of the program.

The program in listing 5.1 uses two named constants, %START and %STOP. This program uses the %START constant twice after naming it. The program uses the %STOP constant four times after naming it.

Listing 5.1. The Analyze Student Scores program.

```
REM ** Analyze Student Scores **
' Learning BASIC, Chapter 5.  File: PBL0501.BAS

REM ** Initialize **
CLS
%START = 1          ' named constant
%STOP = 10          ' named constant
```

continues

Listing 5.1. (continued)

```
REM ** Read and Total Scores **
FOR count% = %START TO %STOP
  READ score!
  total! = total! + score!
NEXT count%
DATA 95, 80, 75, 85, 80, 70, 90, 85, 80, 85
average! = total! / %STOP
RESTORE

REM ** Analyze Scores **
PRINT "There were"; %STOP; "scores - ";
PRINT "the average was"; average!
PRINT
PRINT "Student"; TAB(15); "Score"; TAB(28); "Deviation"
PRINT
FOR count% = %START TO %STOP
  READ score!
  PRINT TAB(3); count%; TAB(16); score!;
  PRINT TAB(30); score! - average!
NEXT count%
END
```

One block of the program uses both named constants in the FOR statement of a FOR/NEXT loop. This block reads student scores and calculates the average of all scores. This procedure is similar to the program that summed and averaged temperatures in Chapters 1 and 2. There are two differences: the use of the named constants and the use of the RESTORE statement.

While reading each item from the DATA list, an internal pointer moves from item to item. The same DATA items are used also in another block of the program. Rather than duplicate the list of scores, the RESTORE statement is used. It tells the computer to move the data pointer back to the first item in the list so that the values can be reused.

The Analyze Scores block of the program analyzes the data and prints the results in tabular form. This step uses many forms of the PRINT statement that use various combinations of string constants, named constants, variables, and the TAB function. The TAB function, with its argument, enables you to format items as a table. The argument (the value in parentheses) specifies the column number to use when printing the following item. For example,

```
TAB(15)
```

means move to column number 15 before printing.

The output of the Analyze Student Scores program is in table 5.2. At the top is the number of scores and the average. Below this information is the table of scores, including each student's number, score, and deviation from the average score.

Table 5.2. The output from listing 5.1.

There were 10 scores—the average was 82.5

Student	Score	Deviation
1	95	12.5
2	80	–2.5
3	75	–7.5
4	85	2.5
5	80	–2.5
6	70	–12.5
7	90	7.5
8	85	2.5
9	80	–2.5
10	85	2.5

For a different series of scores, the DATA list will change, of course. When the class size changes, just change the values of %START and %STOP in the initialization block and modify the data. Each time the program encounters the named variables, it uses the new values.

Variables

A variable is a name you give to a memory location that holds the value of that variable. Variables represent numeric or string values. Unlike constants, the value of a variable can change during program execution. The memory location named as a variable holds this changing value. Variable names begin with a letter and can have a maximum of 255 letters and digits. For example, you can use the variable count to tally the number of people who attend a meeting. Set count equal to 0 when your meeting hall is opened. As people sign in, increase the count.

```
count% = 0
DO
   INPUT attendee$        ' attendee signs in
   INCR count%            ' increase the count by one
LOOP
```

You can look at the value of count at any time to see what the attendance is.

Variable Types

The variable types supported by PowerBASIC Lite include the eight described in the section titled "Number Types"—integer, long integer, quad integer, single precision, double precision, extended precision, binary-coded decimal (BCD) fixed point, and binary-coded decimal floating point. In addition, PowerBASIC Lite supports *string* and *flex string* types.

You can declare a range of variables to be a specific type by using a DEF*type* statement: DEFINT (integer), DEFLNG (long integer), and so on. You specify the range following the DEF type keyword. For example,

```
DEFINT A-M
```

This statement declares as integers any variable whose name begins with a letter from A through M, inclusive. For more information about defining variable ranges, use the PowerBASIC Lite help system. You can find all types from the Statements item on the Main index list of the help system.

You also can specify the type of a specific variable by appending the appropriate type specifier to the variable name. For example,

```
count!
```

The exclamation mark (!) declares the variable count to be a single-precision variable.

Table 5.3 summarizes the most important features of the variable types that PowerBASIC Lite supports.

Table 5.3. A summary of variable types.

Type	Specifier	Size (bytes)	DEFtype
Integers			
Integer	%	2	DEFINT
Long integer	&	4	DEFLNG
Quad integer	&&	8	DEFQUD
Floating point			
Single precision	!	4	DEFSNG
Double precision	#	8	DEFDBL
Extended precision	##	10	DEFEXT
BCD fixed point	@	8	DEFFIX
BCD floating point	@@	10	DEFBCD

Type	Specifier	Size (bytes)	DEFtype
String*			
String	$	2	DEFSTR
Flex string	$$	2	DEFFLX

* When a string is stored, PowerBASIC uses 2 bytes of memory to locate where the string is stored. The amount of additional memory used to store a string depends on the length of the string.

You often assign variables an initial value, such as the following integer variable:

```
number% = 3
```

The variable's value can change at any time in the program. For example, you can increase its value by 2 with the statement

```
number% = number% + 2
```

Notice that PowerBASIC Lite uses the equal sign (=) to assign a value to a variable. Its meaning is slightly different from its use in a mathematical expression. When an equal sign is used to assign a value to a variable, the computer evaluates the expression on the right side of the equal sign and assigns it to the variable on the left side. Thus, a variable can be used to assign a new value to itself.

PowerBASIC also has an INCR statement that performs the same operation.

```
INCR number%, 2
```

Numeric Variables

Numeric variables represent the number types described earlier in the section called "Number Types" in this chapter. Values assigned to numeric variables have the same ranges and restrictions as the number types of the same section. Here are some examples of each numeric variable type:

Integers	day%, count%, month%, DayOfMonth%
Long integers	DayofCentury&, BigNumber&, Population&
Quad integers	DayofAD&&, BiggerNumber&&, BirthsAD&&
Single precision	amount!, total!, average!, counter!
Double precision	measurement#, logarithm#, HiPi#
Extended precision	SciMeasure##, ExtLog##
BCD fixed point	account@, deposit@, NewAmount@
BCD floating point	AccountFlt@@, DepositFlt@@

String Variables

String variables contain character data of arbitrary length (as many as 32,750 characters). Each string variable uses 2 bytes of memory to hold a *handle number*. The handle number is a value used internally to locate information about a string. The type specifier for strings is the dollar sign ($) or the DEFSTR type definition. Here are some examples of string assignment and DEFSTR statements:

```
Name$ = "Jon Able"
Msg$ = "Press any key to continue."
DEFSTR C-F
```

Strings are described in Chapter 6, "String Manipulation."

Flex String Variables

Flex strings are a PowerBASIC innovation. A pair of dollar signs ($$) or the DEFFLX type definition is used to specify this class of strings. Each flex string takes 2 bytes to store the flex string's handle number. The maximum length of a flex string is 32,750 characters. Flex strings can be thought of as arrays of characters that can be manipulated in ways similar to the ways in which arrays are manipulated. The use of flex strings in advanced applications is beyond the scope of this book.

Variable Names

Variable names must begin with a letter and have as many as 255 characters (letters and digits). Long names, however, are not practical. You can be generous in naming important variables because long variable names don't use extra *run-time* memory. Run-time memory is the memory where PowerBASIC compiles your source program. For example, the variable names EndOfMonth and eom require 4 bytes of run-time memory.

You must remember that cat%, cat&, cat!, and cat# are all distinct variables because each has a different type specifier. You also should use the same uppercase and lowercase letters when you use the same variable in more than one place in your program. Count!, count!, and COUNT! are distinct names to PowerBASIC Lite.

Defining Variables

The default type for variables is single precision. PowerBASIC uses this type when you have not declared a variable using either of the following methods.

1. Specify a specific variable by appending a type declaration character to the variable's name.

2. Using DEF*type* to declare a range of variables to be a specific type such as DEFINT, DEFSNG, or DEFSTR.

You used the following variable names in earlier programs: amount, Ave, average!, BadVotes, day, day%, count%, counter!, number, response, score!, Sum, TallyTotal, temperature, and total!. You also used the DEF*type* declaration: DEFINT A-Z.

Most programs in this book include the general declaration DEFINT A-Z near the beginning of the program. All variables then will be integers unless declared otherwise by a type specifier. Use integers when possible because they save space and time. Using DEFINT A-Z enables you to omit adding the % specifier to each integer variable.

Putting the Parts in Place

You have seen many of the parts that comprise a PowerBASIC Lite program. The program in listing 5.2 shows how different parts fit together to make a complete, finished product. The program is short, but it demonstrates how various types of numbers, strings, constants, and variables work together.

Listing 5.2. Calculating the area and circumference of circles.

```
REM ** Calculate Area and Circumference of Circles **
' Learning BASIC, Chapter 5.  File: PBL0502.BAS

REM ** Initialize **
CLS: DEFINT A-Z    ' DEFtype is integer
%START = 1         ' named constant
%STOP = 5          ' named constant
pi! = 3.14159      ' single-precision variable

REM ** Calculate and print area and circumference **
' Combine the use of named constants, numeric constants,
' string constants, integers, single-precision numbers,
' and variable type specifiers
FOR count = %START TO %STOP
  radius! = 1.315 * count
  PRINT "Radius is:"; radius!
  PRINT "Circle area:"; pi! * radius! ^ 2
  PRINT "Circle circumference:"; 2 * pi! * radius!
  PRINT
```

continues

Listing 5.2. (continued)

```
NEXT count
PRINT "count is now"; count
PRINT "%START is still"; %START
PRINT "%STOP is still"; %STOP
END
```

The User output screen is cleared, and all variables are declared to be integers by a DEFINT statement in the Initialize block. The same block assigns values to the named constants %START and %STOP and the single-precision variable pi!.

The named constants are the beginning and end values for a FOR/NEXT loop that calculates the radius, area, and circumference of a circle. The calculations use several number and variable types. The program makes five passes through the loop.

At the end of the loop, the current values of the variable count and the named constants %START and %STOP are printed. You see the variable values change, but constants stay the same.

Enter and run the program. The user output screen at the end of a run looks like this:

```
Radius is: 1.315
Circle area: 5.432516645281726
Circle circumference: 8.262382

Radius is: 2.63
Circle area: 21.73006658112691
Circle circumference: 16.52476

Radius is: 3.945
Circle area: 48.892649807753554
Circle circumference: 24.78715

Radius is: 5.26
Circle area: 86.92026632450762
Circle circumference: 33.04953

Radius is: 6.575
Circle area: 135.8129161320432
Circle circumference: 41.31191

count is now 6
%START is still 1
%STOP is still 5
```

The three calculations radius, area, and circumference involve mixed number types. Notice how PowerBASIC Lite displays the results.

Observe that the radius is calculated from an integer variable (`count`) value and a single-precision constant (1.315). The result is assigned to a single-precision variable (`radius!`).

```
radius! = 1.315 * count
```

Because the values of count range from 1 to 5, the product of `count` and 1.315 contains no more than four digits. The result, therefore, is classified as a single-precision number and is printed as a single-precision value. As shown in the list in the "Numeric Constants" section of this chapter, a numeric value containing a decimal point and as many as six digits is stored as single precision.

Also note that the area is calculated from a single-precision variable (`pi!`) and another single-precision variable (`radius!`) raised to the power of an integer constant (2):

```
pi! * radius! ^ 2
```

The single-precision value of `radius!` is first raised to the power of the constant (2). This gives an intermediate value containing more than six digits in three passes through the loop. In these cases, the intermediate value is classified as a double-precision number. In the other two cases, the intermediate value is classified as a single-precision number. The intermediate values are multiplied by the single-precision value of the `pi!` variable. In all cases, the result has more than six digits. The final result, therefore, is classified as a double-precision or extended-precision number and is displayed with 16 digits.

The circumference is calculated from an integer constant (2), and two single-precision variables (`pi!` and `radius!`).

```
2 * pi! * radius!
```

The intermediate result of multiplying the constant 2 and the single-precision value of the variable `pi!` is a single-precision value. Multiplied by the single-precision variable `radius!`, the result is also a single-precision value and is displayed with seven digits.

The result printed for the area has 16 digits, which is long. If you want only seven digits to be displayed for this result, you perform the operation and assign it to a single-precision variable. Then print the value of the variable. For example, you can replace the line that calculates and prints the area with the following two lines:

```
area! = pi! * radius! ^ 2
PRINT "Circle area:"; area!
```

Using these two lines, the output is displayed as shown:

```
Radius is: 1.315
Circle area: 5.432517
Circle circumference: 8.262382

Radius is: 2.63
Circle area: 21.73007
Circle circumference: 16.52476

Radius is: 3.945
Circle area: 48.89265
Circle circumference: 24.78715

Radius is: 5.26
Circle area: 86.92027
Circle circumference: 33.04953

Radius is: 6.575
Circle area: 135.8129
Circle circumference: 41.31191

count is now 6
%START is still 1
%STOP is still 5
```

Now you know something about PowerBASIC Lite's number types and how numeric constants and variables are handled. You also learned a little about strings. In Chapter 6, you get a closer look at manipulating strings.

Summary

In this chapter you learned about numbers, constants, expressions, and variables and the way PowerBASIC Lite uses them.

There are eight unique number types: integers, long integers, and quad integers; single-precision, double-precision, and extended-precision numbers; and two types of binary-coded decimal numbers.

Integers are classified by the number of digits they contain, with integers having the least number of digits and quad integers the greatest number of digits. The number of digits in long integers falls between the other two types. Sample program segments giving examples of each type demonstrated the distinct characteristics.

Short program examples demonstrated the ranges of values for single, double, and extended precision. You learned how to display as many as 18 digits for extended-precision results.

Binary-coded decimal numbers are helpful in advanced programming applications such as spreadsheets and accounting program packages.

You learned that characters enclosed in quotation marks are string constants. Numeric constants can represent any of the number types. The value of a constant

146

stays the same throughout the program. You also can use integer constants in hexadecimal, octal, or binary number systems by preceding the constant by the appropriate symbol: &H for hexadecimal, &O, &Q, or & for octal, and &B for binary constants. You also learned to refer to named constants by their name, similar to that of variables.

You learned that variables can represent all types of strings and numeric values. The value of a variable can change during a program. You define a range of variables by a DEF*type* statement (DEFINT, DEFLNG, DEFEXT, and so on). Individual type specifiers can define the type of specific variables. Variable names begin with a letter and contain as many as 255 characters (letters and digits). You should choose variable names long enough to be descriptive, but short enough to be practical.

You used many types of numbers, strings, constants, and variables in two demonstration programs. You saw an analysis of each program and its output.

With the components you learned about in this chapter, you are ready for the exercises that follow. You also can look at ways you can manipulate strings in the next chapter.

Exercises

1. PowerBASIC Lite calculations are performed fastest by which number type?

2. Classify each of the following numbers as integer, long integer, or quad integer.

   a. 32777   c. 2147483641

   b. -354   d. 3147583777

3. Write 3.2158269E+07 in common numeric notation.

4. Write 13,143,215 in floating-point notation.

5. You use a continuation symbol to break a long program line into two or more parts. What character do you use for the line-continuation symbol?

6. Revise listing 5.1 so that it reads and calculates scores for a class of 25 students. Use the data in listing 5.1 and add appropriate scores.

7. Write DEF*type* statements to define all variables A through K as integers, L through P as long integers, Q through W as single precision, and X through Z as double precision.

8. Suppose that you have defined variable ranges as in Exercise 7. You want to add the use of a variable named Money as a single-precision variable. How do you declare Money to be a single-precision variable?

Chapter 6

String Manipulation

$\mathbf{A}$s you learned in Chapter 5, "Numbers, Strings, Constants, and Variables," strings enclosed in quotation marks are called *string constants*. This chapter shows you many ways to manipulate more string constants and string variables to enhance your programs. The following topics are discussed in this chapter:

- Using strings as remarks to explain your programs and to form an outline used for program development

- Using string prompts with INPUT statements to enhance and clarify data entry requests

- Using INPUT$ and INKEY$ to verify a keystroke, and INSTR to check for appropriate range and entry type

- Using string functions and statements such as ROUND, SPACE$, SPC, PRINT USING, and USING to enhance displays of programs

- Viewing and using substrings contained in strings

- Altering strings

Using Remarks in Programs

As you may recall, you can use the REM statement and its abbreviated form (') to describe the different parts of a program. Although remarks are not strings in a technical sense, they can be used in ways that are similar to string constants. Remarks do not execute or print; they just make your program easier to read and understand.

Developing Programs from Remarks

You can use remarks to make an outline of your programs. Then you can add executable statements to each item in the outline. You can test parts of your program as you develop them. For example, you might make the following outline:

```
REM ** Sales Tax Calculator **
' Learning BASIC, Chapter 6.    File: PBL0601.BAS
REM ** Initialize **
REM ** Enter data **
REM ** Calculate tax and total cost **
REM ** Print price, tax, and total cost **
REM ** Do again or End? **
```

The finished outline gives you a clear idea of how to create the program.

First, complete the Initialize block. Assuming that you want to declare all variables to be integers and that the sales tax rate in your community is 6.5 percent, you might add the following to the Initialize remark:

```
REM ** Initialize **
CLS: DEFINT A-Z
TaxRate! = .065
```

Because you want to be able to calculate the tax on more than one item, you might insert a label into the program on the line preceding the line that asks you to enter the purchase price of a specific item. Then you can return to the label after calculating the tax and adding it to the purchase price. A label is followed with a colon and must be on a line by itself. Remember, a label does not execute; it just marks a specific place in the program. (You might use LoopHere as the label.) Then you need a way to enter the purchase price. Use an INPUT statement to request and accept each entry.

```
REM ** Enter data **
LoopHere:
INPUT price!
```

The Calculate Tax and total cost block is easy, given all you now know about numbers and variables. Use the variable TaxRate!, to which you assigned the value of .065 in the Initialize block. Multiply TaxRate! by the variable, price!, used in the INPUT statement. Then add the resulting value to the price. Following is the code for this block:

```
REM ** Calculate tax and total cost **
tax! = TaxRate! * price!
cost! = tax! + price!
```

The calculation serves no purpose unless it is displayed. The next block handles that task. You have already used the PRINT statement for displaying data. To display all three values of interest (the price, the tax, and the total cost) use the PRINT statement again, as follows:

```
REM ** Print price, tax, and total cost **
PRINT "Price:"; price!
PRINT "Sales tax:"; tax!
PRINT "Total cost:"; cost!
```

Now, how should you wrap it all up? When you want to compute the total cost for many items, you don't want to have to run the program several times to get all costs. You want the program to pause so that you can see the result. You also want a way to continue, either back to the label for another item or to end the program.

You can use a special string function, INPUT$, to tell the computer to pause until you press a specified number of keys (one, in this example). Then use an IF/THEN statement to decide whether to go back. Here is one way to do it:

```
REM ** Do again or End? **
PRINT "Press the spacebar for another item.";
PRINT " Press any other key to end."
kbd$ = INPUT$(1)                      ' wait for 1 keypress
IF kbd$ = CHR$(32) THEN GOTO LoopHere
END
```

The PRINT statements display a clue to what you should do. The INPUT$(1) function causes the computer to stop until you press one key. Your keystroke is assigned to the string variable kbd$.

CHR$ is another string function you probably will use often. Used in this IF/ THEN statement, CHR$ says, "If the key you pressed has an ASCII code of 32, then go back to the place in the program where you find a label named LoopHere." A blank space, printed when you press the spacebar, has an ASCII code of 32; therefore, the computer returns to the label when you press the spacebar. When you press any other key, kbd$ has a different value and the THEN clause of the IF/THEN statement does not execute. Instead, the END statement on the next line executes, and the program ends.

REM statements used in this way force you to think about how to formulate a program. They make programming easier and less likely to have errors in logic. From the original outline, you now have the program shown in listing 6.1.

Listing 6.1. Sales tax calculator.

```
REM ** Sales Tax Calculator **
' Learning BASIC, Chapter 6.  File: PBL0601.BAS

REM ** Initialize **
CLS: DEFINT A-Z
TaxRate! = .065

REM ** Enter data **
LoopHere:
INPUT price!

REM ** Calculate tax and total cost **
tax! = TaxRate! * price!
cost! = tax! + price!

REM ** Print price, tax, and total cost **
PRINT "Price:"; price!
PRINT "Sales tax:"; tax!
PRINT "Total cost:"; cost!

REM ** Do again or End? **
PRINT "Press the spacebar for another item.";
PRINT " Press any other key to end."
kbd$ = INPUT$(1)                        ' wait for 1 keypress
IF kbd$ = CHR$(32) THEN GOTO LoopHere
END
```

How the Program Works

If you enter and run this program, a question mark and a blinking cursor display in the upper-left corner of an otherwise blank screen. The INPUT statement in the Enter Data block causes the computer to pause, print a question mark, and wait for you to enter a number. Now it is time for you to enter the price of an item. You will see some other options that you can use with INPUT (more about this in the next section).

After you enter the price of an item at the cursor's position, the computer does its calculations and displays the result. The PRINT statements in the final block of the program remind you how to continue or exit. Press the spacebar to enter another item; press another key to quit. The following shows the output of a typical run. A message describes how to continue or end the program.

```
? 22.95
Price: 22.95
Sales tax: 1.49175
Total cost: 24.44175
Press the spacebar for another item. Press any other key to end.
```

Four keywords (INPUT, GOTO, INPUT\$, and CHR\$) used in this program have not been discussed yet, although you probably recognize them if you have ever programmed in any version of BASIC. If you are unfamiliar with these keywords, access the Help index by pressing F1 from PowerBASIC Lite. To find INPUT and GOTO, use the Help index's Statements item; to find INPUT\$ and CHR\$, use the Functions item.

The syntax for INPUT is

```
INPUT [;] [prompt string {;¦,}] variable list
```

Remember, in syntax format, the information enclosed in square brackets is optional. No optional information is included in listing 6.1; the variable list includes only one item, price!, shown here.

```
INPUT price!
```

When you use the INPUT statement in this format, only the question mark and cursor indicate the need for an entry.

The syntax for GOTO is

```
GOTO {label¦linenumber}
```

The braces indicate that you must use one of the options separated by the ¦ character (a label or a line number). Listing 6.1 uses the label LoopHere:

```
IF kbd$ = CHR$(32) THEN GOTO LoopHere
```

Notice that a colon follows the label in the program's Enter data block, but that no colon is used when the label is referenced in the GOTO statement.

GOTO, an old BASIC statement, is retained for compatibility with earlier versions of BASIC. PowerBASIC Lite has structured statements that work more efficiently. Until you learn about such structures in Chapter 7, "Program Control Structures," you can use GOTO. After this chapter, you never see GOTO again in this book.

You learned enough about loops in Chapter 3, "An Introduction to Programming," to realize that a WHILE/WEND or DO/LOOP can replace the LoopHere and GOTO statement in listing 6.1. For example, the original statements can be replaced with a DO statement. The GOTO in the IF/THEN statement can be replaced with EXIT LOOP, and a LOOP statement would be added just before the end of the program, as shown in the following:

153

```
DO                                        ' label replaced
    .
    .   statements from listing6.1
    .
    IF kbd$ <> CHR$(32) THEN EXIT LOOP    ' GOTO replaced
LOOP                                      ' added statement
END
```

The string function, CHR$, is used with GOTO in the IF / THEN statement. The syntax for CHR$ is

```
s$ = CHR$(integer expression [,integer expression]...)
```

where s$ represents a variable name, and integer expression is an item in the argument list. Each expression in the list must evaluate to an integer between 0 and 255.

In this program, CHR$ has only one integer expression, 32, which represents a space. (The space character has an ASCII code of 32.)

The syntax for the string function, INPUT$, is

```
s$ = INPUT$(n [, [#] filenumber])
```

where s$ represents a variable name and n is the number of characters to read. Use this statement to read characters from a file or from the keyboard. If the file number is included, the characters are read from the specified file.

Because the file number is omitted in the sample program, the computer pauses at the INPUT$ function and waits until you press a key. One character is read from the keyboard. That character is assigned to the variable, kbd$, as follows:

```
kbd$ = INPUT$(1)
```

Use the INPUT$ function when you want program execution to pause until you press a key. PowerBASIC Lite also has an INKEY$ function that detects keystrokes while the program is running. To see how INKEY$ works, enter and run the following program segment:

```
CLS
number% = 1
DO
PRINT number%;
INCR number%
IF INKEY$ = CHR$(32) THEN EXIT LOOP
LOOP
```

When this segment runs, the computer displays its counting capability. Most versions of BASIC increase the value of a variable by a statement like

```
number% = number% + 1
```

in which the expression to the right of the equal sign adds 1 to the value of the variable, number%, and then assigns the new value to the same variable, thus increasing its value. A special PowerBASIC statement

```
INCR number%
```

is used in the program segment to accomplish the task.

You can increment the variable by any other amount by specifying the amount, as in the following example:

```
INCR number%, 5    ' adds 5 to number%
```

To interrupt the stream of integers produced by the program segment, press the spacebar. The computer continues to count until you press the spacebar. When you press the spacebar, the INKEY$ function recognizes the ASCII code (32); the IF condition is true, and the stream of numbers stops.

The question mark, used as a prompt for the INPUT statement in listing 6.1, gives no clue as to what you should enter. You need a better prompt. (And you get one soon, in this chapter's "Input Strings" section.)

The sales tax and total cost displayed earlier in this chapter (as output) have no resemblance to money values. Money should be displayed in dollars-and-cents format. This chapter's "Output Strings" section shows you how to format output information.

Enhancing Programs with Strings

You can use strings to clarify required entries and displayed output. The syntax used by PowerBASIC Lite for input and output (I/O) statements and functions can provide optional information that corrects the starkness of unadorned data. You have already seen the PRINT statement used in this way. The next two sections provide information about using strings for I/O statements.

Input Strings

To add information for the entry of data used in the program in listing 6.1, you can insert a PRINT statement immediately before the INPUT statement, as follows:

```
PRINT "Enter the price";
INPUT price!
```

The semicolon at the end of the PRINT statement causes the cursor to remain on the same line for the entry prompt, which looks like this:

```
Enter the price? _
```

As you may recall, the use of a prompt string is one of the optional features in the syntax for the INPUT statement. If the prompt string is in the INPUT statement

```
INPUT "Enter the price"; price!
```

you don't need the PRINT statement.

To display the prompt and accept the entry at any position on the screen, just make sure that a LOCATE statement with this syntax:

```
LOCATE [row][,[column][,[cursor][,start][,stop]]]
```

precedes the INPUT statement. The *row* option is an integer expression (1-25) specifying the screen row for the cursor. The *column* option is an integer expression (1-80) specifying the cursor's column position. The *cursor* option specifies whether the cursor is visible (1) or invisible (0). If the cursor option is omitted, the cursor remains in its current state (visible or invisible). The cursor is composed of eight rows of pixels, numbered 0 through 7. The shape of the cursor is determined by the value you specify for start (first row of visible pixels) and stop (last row of visible pixels).

For example, suppose that you want to place the cursor at a specific place on the screen (row 2, column 4 in the following example) in preparation for printing or entering some data. You could use the following statements:

```
LOCATE 2, 4
INPUT "Enter an integer (1-5):"
value$ = INPUT$(1)
PRINT value%
```

Because of the LOCATE statement, the string "Enter an integer (1-5):" is printed on row 2 beginning at column 4. The INPUT$(1) function accepts one keystroke and assigns it to the string variable value$. The PRINT statement then prints your entry on the next line (line3) as shown in the following:

```
                             Columns
                       1         2         3
Line          12345678901234567890123456789 0
1
2                  Enter an integer (1-5):
3             4
```

The E of the word Enter appears at row 2, column 4 of the screen because of the LOCATE statement. Because your entry (4 in this example) was assigned to a string variable, it is printed at the beginning (position 1) of the next line (3) by the PRINT statement.

A problem arises when this simple program segment is used in a practical program. What happens if the user enters a number outside the 1-5 range? The computer accepts it. When the value is somewhere else in the program, it produces erroneous or unpredictable results. You can use the INSTR function to reject entries that are not in the specified range. You can check the syntax of this function in the Help index. INSTR searches a string for the first occurrence of a specified character or string. Here is a short program segment that uses this function:

```
DO
  CLS
  LOCATE 2, 4
PRINT "Enter an integer (1-5):"
value$ = INPUT$(1)
IF INSTR(" 1 2 3 4 5", value$) <> 0 THEN EXIT LOOP
LOOP
PRINT value$
END
```

The integer that you enter is assigned in string form to value$ by the INPUT$(1) function. The INSTR function compares the single character assigned to value$ to the characters in the string "12345". If INSTR finds a match, the function returns the position of the match; if no match is found, INSTR returns 0.

For example, enter the number 8; no match is found. Control returns to the top of the DO\LOOP, the screen is cleared, and the message request for another entry is printed. If you enter 5 for the integer, INSTR finds a match at position 5 in the string "12345". It prints the entry on the next line as follows:

```
    Enter an integer (1-5):
5
```

You can use the INSTR function on string entries also. For example, study the following program segment:

```
DO
  CLS
  PRINT "Enter a letter (A-E):"
  letter$ = INPUT$(1)
  IF INSTR("ABCDE", UCASE$(letter$)) <> O THEN EXIT LOOP
LOOP
PRINT letter$
END
```

157

When this program segment runs and you type **E**, you see the following:

```
Enter a letter (A-E)?:
E
```

When you type the letter *E*, it is printed; if you type a lowercase *e*, the function does not accept it. The program returns to the top of the loop, the screen clears, and the message, "Enter a letter (A-E):", appears again.

Sometimes you want to accept string entry regardless of whether it is upper- or lowercase. You can use the UCASE$ function to change all lowercase letters of an entry to uppercase. For example, you can insert UCASE$ in the previous program segment, as follows:

```
DO
  CLS
  PRINT "Enter a letter (A-E):"
  letter$ = INPUT$(1)
  IF INSTR("ABCDE", UCASE$(letter$)) = 0 THEN EXIT LOOP
LOOP
PRINT letter$
END
```

Now, even when you enter a lowercase letter, the INSTR function looks for its uppercase counterpart. Yet, when the function finds a match, the PRINT statement prints the letter just as you entered it. For example, typing the letter *c* produces the following:

```
Enter a letter (A-E)?:"
c
```

The uppercase form (C) is compared to the string "ABCDE" and a match is found in position 3. Because the IF condition is true, the EXIT LOOP statement executes. The letter you entered (c) prints in lowercase, and the program ends.

The UCASE$ function has a companion function, LCASE$, which returns the lowercase characters *a-z*. These functions are helpful when you are trying to match strings or portions of strings without disturbing the case of the original strings.

The LCASE$ function would be used when you wanted to compare an entry with lowercase letters. For example, the previous uppercase example could be modified as follows:

```
DO
  CLS
  PRINT "Enter a letter (a-e):"
  letter$ = INPUT$(1)
  IF INSTR("abcde", LCASE$9LETTER$)) <> O THEN EXIT LOOP
LOOP
PRINT letter$
END
```

In this program segment the LCASE$ function uses the lowercase of your entry to compare with the string (also lowercase). After the comparison, your entry is printed as you entered it. For example, suppose that you entered the uppercase letter B. A match would be found in position 2, and the output would be

```
Enter a letter (a-e):
B
```

Output Strings

You can use several string functions and statements to enhance your output, as well as your input. First, take a look at how the PowerBASIC Lite ROUND function works. This function has the following syntax:

```
x = ROUND(numeric expression, n)
```

The value of *n* is the number of places you want following the decimal point. For example, the tax rate used in listing 6.1 has three places to the right of the decimal point (.065). When you enter a price of 22.95, the sales tax is displayed as a single-precision number (1.49175). You can use the ROUND function to round the sales tax to two places, by changing the calculated value of the tax with this statement:

```
tax! = ROUND(tax!, 2)
```

This value is printed as 1.49, which more closely resembles a money value (dollars and cents). The program in listing 6.2 uses the ROUND function in this way.

Listing 6.2. Sales-tax calculator, version 2.

```
REM ** Sales Tax Calculator Number 2 **
' Learning BASIC, Chapter 6.  File: PBL0602.BAS

REM ** Initialize **
CLS: DEFINT A-Z
TaxRate! = .065

REM ** Enter data **
DO
  INPUT price!

  REM ** Calculate tax and total cost **
  tax! = TaxRate! * price!
  tax! = ROUND(tax!, 2)      ' round tax to 2 decimal places
  cost! = tax! + price!
```

continues

Listing 6.2. (continued)

```
   REM ** Print price, tax, and total cost **
   PRINT "Price: $"; price!
   PRINT "Sales tax: $"; tax!
   PRINT "Total cost: $"; cost!

   REM ** Do again or End? **
   PRINT "Press the spacebar for another item.";
   PRINT "Press any other key to end."
   kbd$ = INPUT$(1)
   IF kbd$ <> CHR$(32) THEN EXIT LOOP
LOOP
END
```

Notice that, this time, the string constants in the PRINT statements, which display the results, contain a dollar sign ($). As you can see in the following output of listing 6.2, the price, sales tax, and total cost now look like dollars and cents:

```
? 22.95
Price: $ 22.95
Sales tax: $ 1.49
Total cost: $ 24.44
Press the spacebar for another item. Press any other key to end.
```

Another way to produce this output is to change all decimal values to long integers for the calculations, and then convert the results to decimal places. You can do this by revising the Calculate tax and total cost block to the following:

```
REM ** Calculate tax and total cost **
NewRate% = TaxRate! * 1000        ' rate as an integer
LongPrice& = price! * 100         ' price in cents
Tax& = NewRate% * LongPrice& / 1000 ' tax in cents
cost! = (tax& + LongPrice&) / 100 ' dollars & cents
```

Also, you must change one line in the Print price, tax, and total cost block. This line changes the tax to dollars and cents:

```
PRINT "Sales tax: $"; tax& / 100
```

When you run the program with these revisions, the output looks exactly like the preceding output.

You can use PowerBASIC Lite's PRINT USING statement in several ways to format output. The next program (listing 6.3) uses a string to provide the format:

```
format$ = "$###.##"
```

The string constant assigned to format$ specifies that a dollar sign be printed. Each number sign (#) holds a place in the result for one digit. This technique is in listing 6.3, the third version of the Sales-tax Calculator program.

Listing 6.3. Sales-tax Calculator, version 3.

```
REM ** Sales Tax Calculator Number 3 **
' Learning BASIC, Chapter 6.  File: PBL0603.BAS

REM ** Initialize **
CLS: DEFINT A-Z
TaxRate! = .065

REM ** Enter data **
DO
  INPUT price!

  REM ** Calculate tax and total cost **
  tax! = TaxRate! * price!
  cost! = tax! + price!

  REM ** Print price, tax, and total cost **
  format$ = "$###.##"
  PRINT "Price:      ";: PRINT USING format$; price!
  PRINT "Sales tax:  ";: PRINT USING format$; tax!
  PRINT "Total cost: ";: PRINT USING format$; cost!

  REM ** Do again or End? **
  PRINT "Press the spacebar for another item.";
  PRINT " Press any other key to end."
  kbd$ = INPUT$(1)                      ' wait for 1 keypress
  IF kbd$ <> CHR$(32) THEN EXIT LOOP
LOOP
END
```

This time a string is printed to identify the result. On the same line, a PRINT USING statement provides the format and the variable whose value is to be printed. Blank spaces in the string constants that identify each result align the numeric results in neat columns, as follows:

```
? 22.95
Price:      $ 22.95
Sales tax:  $  1.49
Total cost: $ 24.44
```

Another form of the Print price, tax, and total cost block produces the same output. This form assigns to string variables some strings that describe the value being printed, and then the string variables are used in PRINT USING statements. Here is the alternate form:

161

```
REM ** Print price, tax, and total cost **
pstring$ = "Price:" + SPACE$(5)
tstring$ = "Sales tax: "
cstring$ = "Total cost:"
PRINT USING "& $###.##"; pstring$; price!
PRINT USING "& $###.##"; tstring$; tax!
PRINT USING "& $###.##"; cstring$; cost!
```

The SPACE$ function returns a string of a specified number of spaces. As used in the assignment to pstring$, SPACE$(5) *catenates* (joins) five spaces to the string "Price:". This assignment

```
pstring$ = "Price:" + SPACE$(5)
```

produces the same result as

```
pstring$ = "Price:        "
```

Do not confuse the SPACE$ function with the SPC function, which causes blank spaces to be printed. SPC can be used only in PRINT statements.

When the display is made, the specified string replaces the ampersand (&) in the string of the PRINT USING statement. When you print the price, for example, the value of the variable pstring$ replaces the ampersand. The value of the variable price! is formatted according to the format in the format string ($###.##).

One more alternative to the block that prints the same final results exists. This one, which uses the PowerBASIC Lite USING$ function, has the following syntax:

```
x$ = USING$(fs$, expression)
```

where *fs$* is a format string and *expression* is the numeric or string expression you want to format. To format the price in the same way PRINT USING formatted it, for example, you use the following:

```
USING$("$###.##", price!)=
```

To produce the same output shown previously with USING$, the block that prints the results is

```
REM ** Print price, tax, and total cost **
pstring$ = "Price:" + SPACE$(6) + USING("$###.##", price!)
tstring$ = "Sales tax:  " + USING("$###.##", tax!)
cstring$ = "Total cost: " + USING("$###.##", cost!)
PRINT pstring$
PRINT tstring$
PRINT cstring$
```

Printing can be done in many ways. Experiment, trying several ways, and then choose the best method for the specific programming situation.

Viewing and Altering Strings

PowerBASIC Lite has many functions and statements for viewing and altering the characters in strings. Usually, three string functions (LEFT$, RIGHT$, and MID$) are used to extract a substring from a string. A substring is a group of successive characters contained in another string. For example

"in" is a substring occupying positions 2 and 3 in the string "win".

"234" is a substring occupying positions 3, 4, and 5 of the string "012345".

"245" is not a substring of the string "012345" because 2, 4, and 5 are not successive characters in "012345".

You use LEFT$ to extract a substring from the left end of a string, and RIGHT$ to extract a substring from the right end. Use the MID$ function to extract a substring of specified length from any specified position in a string.

In the following PRINT statement, LEFT$ is used to extract seven characters from the left of the string "you can win":

```
PRINT LEFT$("you can win", 7)
```

Executing this statement prints the following substring:

```
you can
```

The extracted string consists of seven characters (c, a, and n, one blank space, and w, i, and n).

The string function, RIGHT$, is used in the next statement to extract seven characters from the right of the string "you can win":

```
PRINT RIGHT$("you can win", 7)
```

When this statement is executed, the following substring prints:

```
can win
```

You can use the MID$ function to achieve the same result as LEFT$ or RIGHT$. MID$ specifies the original string, the position at which extraction is to begin, and the number of characters to extract:

163

```
PRINT MID$("you can win", 4, 3)
```

This statement starts at position 4 in the original string, and extracts the 3 characters can.

MID$ can be used also as a statement on an assignment's left. As a statement, MID$ replaces characters in one string with characters from another. For example, to replace a portion of the string variable, Original$, with the string constant "two", use the following four lines:

```
Original$ = "string one"
PRINT Original$
MID$(Original$, 8) = "two"
PRINT Original$
```

The first and second printings of the string variable, Original$, show that the word two replaces three characters at the end of the original string, beginning at position 8:

```
string one
string two
```

The following program segment replaces four letters of an eight-character string beginning at the second position of the original string "opinions".

```
CLS
Original$ = "opinions"
PRINT original$
MID$(original$, 2, 4) = "ctag"
PRINT Original$
```

When you run this segment, the following output shows the replacement of "pini" of the original word "opinions" with the four letters "ctag" results in the string "octagons".

```
opinions
octagons
```

You can use many other PowerBASIC Lite functions to view or alter string information. Characters or substrings within a string can tally, remove, verify, replace, and extract. The program in listing 6.4 shows many ways to view and manipulate string data.

Listing 6.4. String-manipulator program.

```
REM ** String Manipulator **
' Learning BASIC, Chapter 6.  File: PBL0604.BAS

REM ** Initialize **
CLS
' Original string and duplicate
Original$ = "This mad dog bites each cat it sees."
Duplicate$ = Original$

REM ** Manipulate the string **
' Tally "i", "t", and "it"
PRINT "Original: "; TAB (30); Original$
PRINT "i and t: "; TAB (29); TALLY(Original$, ANY "it")
PRINT "it: "; TAB (29); TALLY(Original$, "it")

' Remove mad and verify
TakeOut$ = "mad "
NoMad$ = REMOVE$(Original$, TakeOut$)
PRINT "mad is gone: "; TAB (30); NoMad$
WhereDiffer = VERIFY(Original$, NoMad$)
PRINT "Strings differ at position: "; TAB (29); WhereDiffer

' Remove all vowels
PRINT "No vowels: "; TAB (30); REMOVE$(Original$, ANY "aeiou")

' Switch cat and dog
REPLACE "cat " WITH "animal " IN Duplicate$
REPLACE "dog " WITH "cat " IN Duplicate$
REPLACE "animal " WITH "dog " IN Duplicate$
PRINT "Switch animals: "; TAB (30); Duplicate$

' Extract substrings
sub1$ = EXTRACT$(Original$, " se") + "."
PRINT "sees is out: "; TAB (30); sub1$
sub2$ = EXTRACT$(sub1$, " each") + "."
PRINT "each cat it is out: "; TAB (30); sub2$
PRINT "Biggest of The, dog, cat: ";
PRINT TAB(30); MAX$("The", "dog", "cat")
PRINT "Biggest of The, Dog, Cat: ";
PRINT TAB(30); MAX$("The", "Dog", "Cat")
PRINT "Smallest of the, dog, cat: ";
PRINT TAB(30); MIN$("the", "dog", "cat")
PRINT "Three in a row: "; TAB(30); REPEAT$(3, "cats ")
END
```

When you enter and run the program, you should see the following output:

```
Original:                    This mad dog bites each cat it sees.
i and t:                     6
it:                          2
mad is gone:                 This dog bites each cat it sees.
Strings differ at position:  6
No vowels                    Ths md dg bts ch ct t ss.
Switch animals:              This mad cat bites each dog it sees.
sees is out:                 This mad dog bites each cat it.
each cat it is out:          This mad dog bites.
Biggest of The, dog, cat:    dog
Biggest of The, Dog, Cat:    The
Smallest of the, dog, cat:   cat
Three in a row:              cats cats cats
```

The following sections discuss the new string functions and statements used in the program in listing 6.5. Remember—use the Help system to get more information on any of the functions or statements.

TALLY Function

The original string, "This mad dog bites each cat it sees." prints first. Then the TALLY function is used. The keyword, ANY, in the second argument, specifies that all occurrences of the lowercase letters *i* and *t* are to be counted.

```
TALLY(Original$, ANY "it")
```

After this value prints, the same function is used again, this time without the keyword ANY, causing the tally only where the lowercase *i* and *t* occur together.

```
TALLY(Original$, "it")
```

When the ANY option is omitted, the string ("it") is treated as an entity. The letters "i" and "t" must occur together in the specified order to be tallied. When the ANY option is used (ANY "it"), the letters "i" and "t" are treated as unique characters. Each occurrence of "i" or "t" is tallied.

REMOVE$ and VERIFY Functions

A REMOVE$ function removes four characters—the word mad and the space following it—from the Original$ string. The remaining substring is assigned to the string variable NoMad$:

```
TakeOut$ = "mad "
NoMad$ = REMOVE$(Original$, TakeOut$)
```

Then the VERIFY function compares the strings Original$ and NoMad$, returning the first position in which the strings differ:

```
WhereDiffer = VERIFY(Original$, NoMad$)
```

The REMOVE$ function is used again, this time with the keyword, ANY, included in the second argument. Any vowels (a, e, i, o, u) are removed from the string, leaving only the consonants:

```
REMOVE$(Original$, ANY "aeiou")
```

REPLACE Statement

REPLACE statements are used to switch the words cat and dog in the string Duplicate$ (a duplicate of the string named Original$). The statement is used three times.

The string "animal" is used as a temporary substitution (or placeholder), so the words "cat" and "dog" can be replaced in separate steps. The two replacements cannot be made in a single step by the REPLACE statement (see the following).

```
REPLACE "cat " WITH "animal " IN Duplicate$
REPLACE "dog " WITH "cat " IN Duplicate$
REPLACE "animal " WITH "dog " IN Duplicate$
```

EXTRACT$ Function

The EXTRACT$ function returns a substring made up of all characters in the original string, up to the first occurrence of a specified character or string. The EXTRACTS function is used twice. The first use

```
sub1$ = EXTRACT$(Original$, " se") + "."
```

returns the whole string, up to the space before the word "sees," by extracting (from the original string) the blank, the word "sees," and the period. Then it catenates a period to the substring that is returned.

167

The second use of the function

```
sub2$ = EXTRACT$(sub1$, " each") + "."
```

extracts everything before the blank space, the word "each," and the period from the first substring (sub1$). EXTRACT$ then puts the period back on the returned substring.

MAX$ and MIN$ Functions

The MAX$ function scans its argument list and returns the largest (maximum) value. The MIN$ function scans its argument list and returns the smallest (minimum) value. The value of string arguments is determined from the ASCII codes in the argument's characters. Remember, lowercase letters have higher values than uppercase letters. For example, the ASCII code for *a* is 97; for *A*, it is 65. The MAX$ function is used twice to show how lower- and uppercase letters are considered when sizes are being compared.

```
PRINT MAX$("The", "dog", "cat")
PRINT MAX$("The", "Dog", "Cat")
```

In the first case, *d* is higher than *c* (alphabetically and in ASCII codes) and higher than *T* (in ASCII code). In the second case, in which all the words begin with an uppercase letter, *T* has the highest value (both alphabetically and in ASCII code).

The MIN$ function finds the smallest of the three lowercase words.

```
PRINT MIN$("the", "dog", "cat")
```

REPEAT$ Function

REPEAT$, the last function in the program, repeats a string the specified number of times.

```
REPEAT$(3, "cats ")
```

Experiment with all the functions and statements in listing 6.4. Use them in various ways. Study their syntax and descriptions in the Help system and see whether you can find other statements and functions there that alter strings. If possible, experiment by using statements and functions on strings of your own.

String Functions Used with Numbers

Numeric values can be converted to string form and acted on by string functions. Remember that numeric values are printed with one leading and one trailing blank. It is often convenient to change the number with the STR$ function and remove the blank spaces with LTRIM$ and RTRIM$. Enter and run the following program segment:

```
CLS
num1% = 12: num2% = 130
PRINT "123456789"
PRINT num1%; num2%
```

When you run this segment, the first PRINT statement prints a string of numbers showing the numbers assigned to num1% and num2%. The output looks like the following:

```
123456789
 12  130
```

Each numeric value is printed with a leading blank space and a trailing blank space. To demonstrate the use of the STR$ function, add two more lines to the program segment so that you have

```
CLS
num1% = 12: num2% = 130
PRINT "123456789"
PRINT num1%; num2%
a$ = STR$(num1%): b$ = STR$(num2%)    ' convert to strings
PRINT a$; b%
```

The numbers are printed as before. Then the STR$ function converts the numbers to string format (a$ and B$) for printing by the last PRINT statement. The output looks like the following:

```
123456789
 12  130
 12  130
```

Notice that the values printed in string format no longer have a trailing blank. The leading blank can be removed by using the LTRIM$ function. Do this by adding another line to the previous program segment to obtain

```
CLS
num1% = 12: num2% = 130
PRINT "123456789"
PRINT num1%; num2%
a$ = STR$(num1%): b$ = STR$(num2%)    ' convert to strings
PRINT a$; b$
PRINT LTRIM$(a$); LTRIM$(b$)          ' trim leading blank
```

Run this program to see the blank spaces removed by the LTRIM$ function in the last line.

```
123456789
 12   130
 12 130
12130
```

Another string function (LEN) returns the length of a string (the number of characters in the string). Add another line to the previous program segment to measure the length of a$ and b$.

```
CLS
num1% = 12: num2% = 130
PRINT "123456789"
PRINT num1%; num2%
a$ = STR$(num1%): b$ = STR$(num2%)    ' convert to strings
PRINT a$; b$
PRINT LTRIM$(a$); LTRIM$(b$)          ' trim leading blank
PRINT LEN(a$); LEN(b$)                ' print length
```

When you run this revised segment, the last line displays the length of the numbers when they are converted to strings.

```
123456789
 12   130
 12 130
12130
 3   4
```

You can see that a$ is three characters long and b$ is four characters long because they have a leading blank. Also notice that the LEN function returns the values in numeric format with a leading blank space and a trailing blank space.

Summary

This chapter showed you how to begin creating a program by writing an outline with REM statements, each of which describes a specific task in the program. You then saw how to write statements to make a complete block for each REM in the outline.

You used INPUT statements to permit entry of data, and the INPUT$ function to interrupt the program until you pressed a key. You used INKEY$ to check for a keystroke without interrupting a program. You used CHR$(32) to see whether the ASCII code of the key pressed was that of the spacebar; if it was, a GOTO statement returned control to an INPUT for another entry. The syntax for each of these statements was shown.

You also learned to provide input prompts to clarify the desired entry. You used the LOCATE statement to place information on the screen at a specific row and column, the INSTR function to ensure appropriate entry values, and you learned how to trim leading or trailing spaces from a string with LTRIM$ and RTRIM$.

You used functions such as ROUND, PRINT USING, SPACE$, SPC, and USING to enhance program output.

The chapter closed with discussions and demonstrations of many ways to view and alter string data. These included the following statements and functions:

- LEFT$, RIGHT$, and MID$, to return portions of strings

- REMOVE$, to remove characters from a string, and VERIFY, to verify the first position at which two strings differ

- REPLACE, to replace substrings in a string, and EXTRACT$, to extract a substring from a string

- MAX$, to return the largest value from a list of strings, and MIN$, to return the smallest value from a list of strings

- REPEAT, to repeat a string a specified number of times

Do the exercises in the following section, to see how well you remember this wealth of information. You now should know many of the details needed to use the program-control structures in Chapter 7, "Program-Control Structures."

Exercises

1. Describe the purpose of a label in a PowerBASIC Lite program.

2. Describe the difference between the actions caused by the following statements:

```
kbd$ = INPUT$(1)
kbd$ = INPUT$(2)
```

3. The following statement checks for a keystroke:

```
IF kbd$ = CHR$(32) THEN GOTO LoopHere
```

Tell what happens when you

a. press the spacebar.

b. press Enter.

4. Write one INPUT statement, that produces the same result, to replace the following two statements:

```
PRINT "Enter an integer (1-10)";
INPUT number%
```

5. Write a LOCATE statement to place the cursor at column 3, row 5.

6. Describe the difference between the LTRIM$ and the RTRIMS$ functions.

7. A variable, named value!, has a value of 23.26438. The following statements are executed:

```
number! = ROUND(value!, 3)
PRINT number!
```

What is printed?

8. The value of cost! calculates as 123.7849. The following statements are executed:

```
format$ = "$###.##": PRINT USING format$; cost!
```

What is printed?

9. What is the value of MID$("original", 2, 3)?

10. What is the string that results from the following?

```
REPLACE "large" WITH "small" IN "Some dogs are large."
```

Chapter 7

Program Control Structures

Y ou should classify control structures into three types: sequential, loops, and conditional branches. Most of the earlier programs in this book are sequential, with statements executing in the order entered. Some of the earlier programs include FOR/NEXT loops and IF/THEN conditional branches. In this chapter, you'll take a close look at loop and conditional branch structures.

Topics in this chapter include the following:

- The three varieties of loops: FOR/NEXT, WHILE/WEND, and DO/LOOP

- Demonstrations of FOR/NEXT loops, which are best for executing a group of statements a specific number of times or using a fixed-increment step value, and WHILE/WEND loops, which enable the loop to execute while a specific condition exists

- Discussions and demonstrations of the many forms of the DO/LOOP, the most flexible, all-purpose loop structure

- The two types of conditional branches: IF/THEN block and SELECT CASE structures

- Demonstrations of the way the IF/THEN block structure extends the power of the IF/THEN statement of previous BASIC versions. The SELECT CASE structure enables different groups of statements to be executed, depending on the expression's value

Loops

The most helpful program control structure is a simple loop. Loops enable you to repeat a block of one or more statements. PowerBASIC Lite has three kinds of

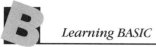

loops: FOR/NEXT, WHILE/WEND, and DO/LOOP. You have seen the FOR/NEXT loop in earlier chapters. Each kind of loop is discussed in detail in this chapter.

FOR/NEXT Loops

The statements FOR and NEXT enclose statements you want repeated a specified number of times. The illustration in figure 7.1 names the components of a FOR statement. The FOR statement tells the computer

- What variable to use for the limits of the loop

- What variable value to use for the beginning of the loop

- What variable value to use for the end of the loop

- Optionally, the increment to add to the variable each time the execution of the loop is completed (STEP)

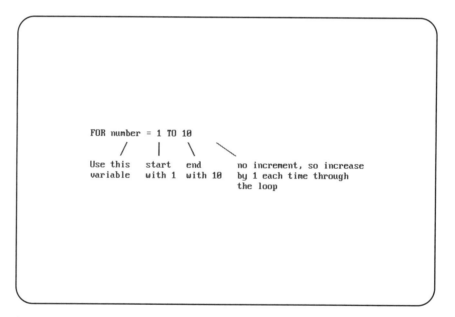

Figure 7.1. Components of a FOR statement.

You used STEP values of 0.1 and −0.1 to count by increments of one-tenth (see Chapter 2, "Using PowerBASIC Lite). Here is a short program segment demonstrating the use of the STEP keyword to increase or decrease the frequency of a sound:

```
FOR note% = 800 TO  900 STEP 10
   SOUND note%, 5
NEXT note%
FOR note% = 890 TO 800 STEP -10
  SOUND note%, 5
NEXT note%
```

Enter and run this program segment. The frequency of the sound increases in steps of 10 in the first loop and decreases by 10 in the second loop. Therefore, the sound rises and then falls.

The SOUND statement generates a tone of specified frequency and duration. The duration is measured in *clock ticks*, 18.2 of which occur per second. The tones in this example last for 5 clock ticks (about one-third of a second).

The NEXT statement indicates the end of the loop. The use of the variable (note%) to control the number of executions is optional in the NEXT statement. (This book always includes the variable for clarity.)

In Chapter 5, "Numbers, Strings, Constants, and Variables," you used the following FOR/NEXT loop in listing 5.1:

```
%START = 1
%STOP = 10
FOR count% = %START TO %STOP
  READ score!
  total% = total% + score!
NEXT count%
```

On the first pass through the loop, the value of count% is 1. Each time the NEXT statement is executed, count% is increased by 1. This value is compared to the upper limit (%STOP = 10) in the FOR statement. As long as the value is not greater than 10, the loop is repeated. On the tenth pass, the NEXT statement increases the value of count% to 11. This value exceeds the upper limit in the FOR statement, and the program exits the loop. Execution continues at the statement following NEXT.

By using some of the string functions you learned in the last chapter in a FOR/NEXT loop, you can draw a "window" on the screen. You can use such a window to display an important message, a menu, or other needed information. The following short program segment uses FOR/NEXT, LOCATE, STRING$, and CHR$.

```
LOCATE 10, 28: PRINT STRING$(25, 219)
LOCATE 14, 28: PRINT STRING$(25, 219)
FOR row = 11 TO 13
  LOCATE row, 28: PRINT CHR$(219);
  LOCATE row, 52: PRINT CHR$(219)
NEXT row
```

When you enter and run this program segment, a rectangle is drawn on the screen with broad brush strokes (see figure 7.2).

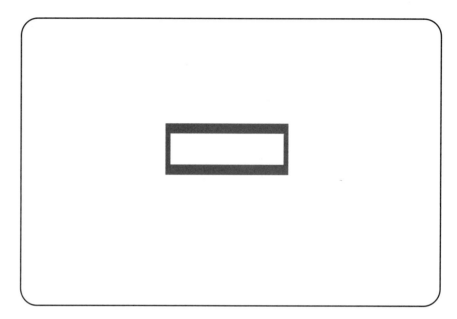

Figure 7.2. Rectangle drawn by string functions.

You saw the CHR$ function used in the last chapter. This time the function prints the character assigned to an ASCII code of 219. This character is a solid block, the size of a text-character space.

The STRING$ function may be new to you. It prints a string consisting of the specified number (25, in this example) of characters having a specified ASCII code (here, 219).

Nested FOR/NEXT Loops

Nested loops are formed by placing one loop inside another. The outside loop controls the large aspect of the task. For each single interaction of the outside loop, an inside loop completely executes, controlling a small aspect of the task. Clearly, the inside loop runs more times than the outside one.

For example, you might specify a changing position on the screen by controlling the outside loop with a row variable and the inside loop with a column variable. Enter and run the following program segment:

```
FOR row = 11 TO 13
  COLOR row
  FOR column = 29 TO 51
    LOCATE row, column: PRINT CHR$(219);
  NEXT column
NEXT row
COLOR 7
```

The nested loops create a rectangle with three different color bars. On the first pass through the outside loop, the foreground color is set (by the COLOR statement) to the same value as row (11). The inner loop then prints a solid block of that color at each column 29 through 51 in row 11. When the NEXT statement of the inner loop increases the value of column to 52, the program exits the inner loop. The NEXT statement of the outer loop then increases the value of row to 12. The COLOR statement changes the foreground color to 12, and the inner loop creates a new row of blocks in the new color. When the value of column reaches 52 again, an exit is made from the inner loop. The NEXT statement in the outer loop increases the value of row to 13. The color is again changed, and a new row of blocks is printed in the new color. When the exit is made from the inner loop, the NEXT statement of the outer loop increases the value of row to 14. The FOR statement of the outer loop detects that its upper limit is exceeded, and the program exits the outer loop.

The foreground color is changed back to its default value (7). You should restore the default color so that future output appears in normal colors. Figure 7.3 shows the output of the previous program segment.

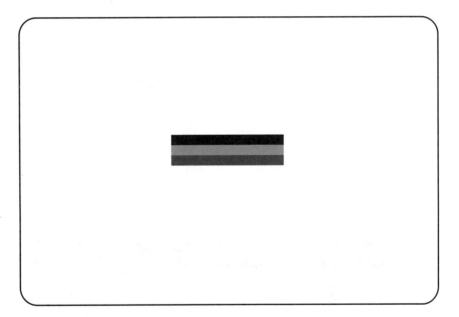

Figure 7.3. Rectangle of color bars.

Table 7.1 lists the foreground colors for Color Graphics Adapters (CGAs) using text mode. Enhanced Graphics Adapters (EGAs) and Video Graphics Array Adapters (VGAs) can display more colors than CGAs.

Table 7.1. Foreground colors for the CGA.

Number	Color
0	Black
1	Blue
2	Green
3	Cyan
4	Red
5	Magenta
6	Brown
7	White
8	Gray
9	Light blue
10	Light green
11	Light cyan
12	Light red
13	Light magenta
14	Yellow
15	High-intensity white

The program in listing 7.1 uses one unnested and two nested FOR/NEXT loops to draw an outline of a rectangle (see figure 7.2) and color bars (see figure 7.3) inside the outline. In addition, the program shows how to print a message inside the rectangle.

Listing 7.1. The message center program.

```
REM ** Message Center **
' Learning BASIC, Chapter 7.  File: PBL0701.BAS

REM ** Initialize **
CLS: DEFINT A-Z

REM ** Main program **
' Outline rectangle
LOCATE 10, 28: PRINT STRING$(25, 219)
LOCATE 14, 28: PRINT STRING$(25, 219)
FOR row = 11 TO 13
  LOCATE row, 28: PRINT CHR$(219);
```

```
   LOCATE row, 52: PRINT CHR$(219)
NEXT row
' Fill center of rectangle
FOR row = 11 TO 13
  COLOR row
  FOR column = 29 TO 51
    LOCATE row, column: PRINT CHR$(219);
  NEXT column
NEXT row
' Print message
COLOR 15, 12
LOCATE 12, 29: PRINT "  Leave your message      ";
COLOR 7, 0
END
```

Enter listing 7.1 and run the program. The colored rectangle and message shown in figure 7.4 are displayed.

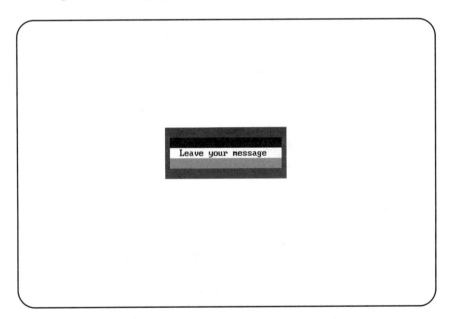

Figure 7.4. Output of the message center program.

Notice that COLOR is used with two parameters to print the message. In text mode, the COLOR statement can specify a foreground color, a background color, and a border color:

```
COLOR [foreground][,background][,border]
```

The border color is not in the program statement:

```
COLOR 15, 12
```

This statement changes the foreground to color number 15 and the background to color number 12 for printing the message. Before the program ends, the foreground and background colors change back to their default values (white and black, respectively):

```
COLOR 7, 0
```

The default color for the screen's border is black. For most applications it can remain unchanged. Some users find a different color border distracting.

Leaving FOR/NEXT Loops Early

Suppose that you want to add the sequence of positive even integers, but want to stop when the total exceeds 5,000. PowerBASIC has an EXIT FOR statement that leaves a FOR/NEXT loop prematurely when a given condition exists. To leave the loop at a desired point, you can use this statement:

```
IF total > 5000 THEN EXIT FOR
```

Here is a short program segment that uses EXIT FOR to leave the loop when the total exceeds 5,000:

```
CLS: DEFINT A-Z
FOR even = 2 TO 1000 STEP 2
  total = total + even
  IF total > 5000 THEN EXIT FOR
  LOCATE 12, 37: PRINT even
  LOCATE 13, 38: PRINT total
NEXT even
```

The starting value for the loop is 2; the STEP value also is 2. The loop's upper limit is 1,000 (but the loop doesn't reach that value).

Enter and run the program segment. As the program runs, the even number and total change rapidly. When the total exceeds 5,000, the program exits the loop. Because the total is tested before the value of the current integer and total are printed, the values displayed when the program ends are the values before the exit value is reached. The last values printed are 140 for the integer and 4970 for the total.

WHILE/WEND Loops

Sometimes you want to use a loop but don't know the exact number of times you want it to execute. FOR/NEXT loops need a starting value and an ending value for the loop counter. A WHILE/WEND loop checks for a specific condition in its WHILE statement, then performs the instructions within the loop while that condition exists. The WEND statement marks the end of the loop.

```
WHILE condition
   block of statements
WEND
```

The *condition* is an integer expression, usually a relational or logical expression. If the expression is TRUE (evaluates to a nonzero value) all the statements between WHILE and WEND are executed. Then the program returns to the WHILE statement and repeats the test. If the expression is still TRUE, the enclosed statements are executed again. The process is repeated until the expression evaluates to zero. The program then executes the statement following WEND.

If the condition evaluates to FALSE (zero) on the first pass, the statements between WHILE and WEND are not executed. Consider the following WHILE/WEND loop:

```
CLS
WHILE Shares% <> 0
   INPUT "Number of shares "; Shares%
   INPUT "Price per share  "; Price!
   Worth# = Worth# + Shares% * Price!
   PRINT
WEND
PRINT USING "$##,###.##"; Worth#
END
```

If this program segment executes with no initial value set for the variable, Shares%, the WHILE/WEND loop does not execute and the value of Worth# does not change. When the value of Worth# is not set, the PRINT statement following the loop prints the value as zero dollars. Otherwise, the last value of Worth# prints.

You can avoid this by setting (before the loop is encountered) a value for Shares%. This value is not used except to make the initial condition for the statement TRUE so that the loop is executed at least once. For example, you can insert the assignment on the same line as the CLS statement, as follows:

```
CLS: Shares% = 1
```

The value (1) is not used in calculating the value of Worth# because (1) is replaced by the value you enter inside the WHILE/WEND loop. The following shows some typical entries and results when the loop is entered with a value of one (1) assigned to the Shares% variable:

```
Number of shares ? 500
Price per share  ? 12.125

Number of shares ? 400
Price per share  ? 16.5

Number of shares ? 0
Price per share  ? 10

$12,662.50
```

To leave the loop, enter a value of zero (0) for the number of shares. At this point, what you enter for the price per share does not matter. When the price per share is multiplied by zero, nothing is added to the last value of Worth#. Therefore, you get the correct result.

To make an early exit from a WHILE/WEND loop, insert an EXIT LOOP statement at an appropriate place in the loop. For example, you can add an EXIT LOOP statement to the preceding program segment just after entering the number of shares, as follows:

```
CLS: Shares% = 1
WHILE Shares% <> 0
  INPUT "Number of shares "; Shares%
  IF Shares% = 0 THEN EXIT LOOP
```

When you run the program segment with this change and enter 0 (zero) for Shares%, the program does not request the price. The total value of the previous entries is printed immediately following the zero (0) entry.

The DO loop, discussed next, is similar to the WHILE/WEND loop but more versatile in the way it uses the condition that controls execution of the loop.

DO Loops

The simplest form of a DO/LOOP has no exit and runs until the computer is interrupted, as follows:

```
DO
  PRINT "Press Ctrl-Break to stop me "
LOOP
```

The string in the PRINT statement repeats until you press Ctrl-Break or the program is interrupted in some other way.

You can provide an EXIT LOOP statement inside the loop to check whether a key has been pressed. The INKEY\$ function

```
DO
   PRINT "Press ESC to stop me "
   IF INKEY$ = CHR$(27) THEN EXIT LOOP
LOOP
```

works fine. When this program segment runs, the message prints repeatedly until you press Esc (ASCII code 27). You can use this type of loop as a time delay, as follows:

```
start! = TIMER
DO
   LOCATE 12, 30
   PRINT "Wait until the loop ends"
   IF TIMER > start! + .75 THEN EXIT LOOP
LOOP
CLS
```

This program segment reads the computer's timer. Then the loop is executed (printing the string at the specified location) until .75 seconds have passed. Then the program exits the loop and the screen is cleared.

The DO/LOOP offers several ways to specify how to exit the loop.

DO Loops that Use WHILE

Adding a WHILE statement to the DO statement causes the DO loop to perform in the same manner as a WHILE/WEND loop. The following DO WHILE/LOOP produces the same result as the WHILE/WEND loop shown previously:

```
CLS: Shares% = 1
DO WHILE Shares% <> 0
   INPUT "Number of shares "; Shares%
   INPUT "Price per share   "; Price!
   Worth# = Worth# + Shares% * Price!
   PRINT
LOOP
PRINT USING "$##,###.##"; Worth#
END
```

Also, you can place the WHILE statement at the end of the loop, thus guaranteeing that the DO/LOOP executes at least once. In this case, the Shares = 1 statement preceding the loop is unnecessary.

When the WHILE statement is placed at the end of the loop, the test for the condition is made after the loop has been executed. If the condition is TRUE, control returns to the DO statement and the loop executes again. If the condition is FALSE, the statement following the WHILE statement is executed.

Following is a program segment using WHILE at the end of the loop:

```
CLS
DO
  INPUT "Number of shares "; Shares%
  INPUT "Price per share  "; Price!
  Worth# = Worth# + Shares% * Price!
  PRINT
LOOP WHILE Shares% <> 0
PRINT USING "$##,###.##"; Worth#
END
```

DO Loops that Use UNTIL

You can add even more variety to the DO/LOOP by using an UNTIL statement, which can be attached to either the DO or the LOOP statement. When you use the UNTIL statement with DO, the loop operates the same as a DO WHILE/LOOP or a WHILE/WEND loop, except that you must use the opposite condition. The following statements are equivalent:

- DO WHILE Shares% <> 0

- DO UNTIL Shares% = 0

Here is the preceding example, written as a DO UNTIL/LOOP:

```
CLS: Shares% = 1
DO UNTIL Shares% = 0
  INPUT "Number of shares "; Shares%
  INPUT "Price per share  "; Price!
  Worth# = Worth# + Shares% * Price!
  PRINT
LOOP
PRINT USING "$##,###.##"; Worth#
END
```

The UNTIL statement also can be at the end of the loop, thus ensuring at least one execution of the loop. The result is the same as a DO/LOOP WHILE, except that UNTIL uses the opposite condition. The following statements are equivalent:

- LOOP WHILE Shares% <> 0

- LOOP UNTIL Shares% = 0

184

Here is the loop with the UNTIL statement used at the end of the loop:

```
CLS
DO
  INPUT "Number of shares "; Shares%
  INPUT "Price per share  "; Price!
  Worth# = Worth# + Shares% * Price!
  PRINT
LOOP UNTIL Shares% = 0
PRINT USING "$##,###.##"; Worth#
END
```

The DO/LOOP may contain an EXIT condition also. You can write the previous examples with an EXIT LOOP statement following the first entry, as in this example of the DO loop:

```
CLS
DO
  INPUT "Number of shares "; Shares%
  IF Shares% = 0 THEN EXIT LOOP
  INPUT "Price per share  "; Price!
  Worth# = Worth# + Shares% * Price!
  PRINT
LOOP
PRINT USING "$##,###.##"; Worth#
END
```

In this example, the exit occurs when you enter a zero (0) for the number of shares. The output is printed as follows:

```
Number of shares ? 500
Price per share  ? 12.125

Number of shares ? 400
Price per share  ? 16.5

Number of shares ? 0
$12,662.50
```

None of the previous examples is the "right way" to write the loop. The form you choose depends on what you want your program to do. When you want the loop to be executed at least one time, place the condition in a WHILE or UNTIL statement at the end of the loop. There might be times when you do not want the loop to execute unless the specified condition is TRUE. In this case, place the condition at the beginning of the loop. Remembering the differences between the loops is important; otherwise, the results of executing a loop might surprise you.

Conditional Branches

Conditional branches are structures that interrupt the sequential execution of a program when a specified condition exists. You already have seen IF/THEN statements, the simplest kind of conditional branch. This section describes the block IF and SELECT CASE conditional branches. Both structures provide multiline blocks of statements that execute when specific conditions are satisfied.

Block IF Conditional Branch

You saw the following IF/THEN statement:

```
IF Shares% = 0 THEN EXIT LOOP
```

in the preceding program segment.

In Chapter 4, "Statements, Operators, Expressions, and Functions," you saw that statements often become long and need to be broken into two or more parts, such as the following PRINT statement.

```
PRINT "This is a long sentence that goes on for more "_
      "than 77 characters, extending beyond one line."_
```

IF/THEN statements also can be quite long, especially when they contain *complex expressions,* such as the following:

```
IF y MOD 4 = 0 AND y MOD 100 <> 0 OR y MOD 400 = 0
   THEN PRINT "Leap year"
```

With the addition of ELSE clauses, IF/THEN statements can be not only long but also difficult to read and understand.

PowerBASIC provides a block-structured version of IF/THEN statements. This multiline structure lists separate actions in blocks of individual statement lines. The block structure is easier to read than a single line IF/THEN statement.

Use the block IF structure to test for certain conditions specified by the structure's IF and ELSEIF clauses. When the condition of the first block is true, that particular block of the structure is executed. When the condition is not true, that clause is not executed. Then the block examines and treats the next conditional clause the same way. This process continues until the IF block reaches the ELSE block. If none of the conditions in the IF or ELSEIF blocks is true, the ELSE block is executed.

Here is the syntax used for the block IF structure.

```
IF integer expression [,] THEN
    {block of statements}
  ELSEIF integer expression [,] THEN
    {block of statements}
    .
    .
    .
  ELSE
    {block of statements}
END IF
```

The following block IF structure has one long block of statements that execute when a simulated temperature controller reads a temperature below 18 degrees. This program segment has no ELSEIF or ELSE blocks.

```
IF Temp! < 18 THEN                                'Heat it up
  LOCATE 12, 35: PRINT "Heater ON"
  DO WHILE Temp! < 20
    SOUND 900, .3
    Temp! = Temp! + .1
    HeatOn! = TIMER
    DO WHILE TIMER < HeatOn! + .2: LOOP
  LOOP
  LOCATE 12, 35: PRINT SPACE$(9)
END IF
```

Notice the first line of the block IF structure. Nothing must follow the THEN keyword. That's how the PowerBASIC Lite compiler distinguishes block IF from a conventional IF statement. (Notice also that THEN is the last keyword on an ELSEIF line. I'll get to that later.) And notice the last statement. A block IF structure always ends with an END IF statement. END IF requires a space; ELSEIF does not. It is conventional to indent the blocks in the same way the body of a loop structure is indented.

When the temperature falls below 18 degrees, this block executes. The Heater On message prints. The temperature increases by increments of one-tenth of a degree until the temperature reaches 20 degrees. Then the message is erased and the end of the block is executed.

You can use a similar structure to lower the temperature when it is more than 22 degrees. The simulated temperature controller keeps the temperature in the approximate range of 18-22 degrees.

Listing 7.2 uses the described block IF structure with IF, ELSEIF, and, ELSE clauses to simulate such a temperature controller.

Listing 7.2. Temperature-control program.

```
REM ** Temperature Control Simulation **
'Learning BASIC, Chapter 7.  File: PBL0702.BAS
'Uses block IF for heater and cooler

REM ** Initialize **
CLS: DEFINT A-Z: RANDOMIZE TIMER
Temp! = 20

REM ** Draw rectangle for display **
LOCATE 10, 32: PRINT STRING$(16, 219)
LOCATE 15, 32: PRINT STRING$(16, 219)
FOR row = 11 TO 14
  LOCATE row, 32: PRINT CHR$(219)
  LOCATE row, 47: PRINT CHR$(219)
NEXT row
COLOR 4
FOR row = 11 TO 14
  FOR column = 33 TO 46
    LOCATE row, column: PRINT CHR$(219);
  NEXT column
NEXT row

REM ** Main Program - Control Temperatures **
COLOR 7, 0
LOCATE 18, 28: PRINT "Press Ctrl-Break to quit"
DO
  IF Temp! < 18 THEN                          ' heat it up
      LOCATE 13, 35: PRINT "Heater ON";
      DO WHILE Temp! < 20
        SOUND 900, .3
        Temp! = Temp! + .1
        HeatOn! = TIMER
        DO WHILE TIMER < HeatOn! + .2: LOOP   ' an inside loop
        LOCATE 12, 35: PRINT Temp!;
      LOOP
      LOCATE 13, 35: PRINT SPACE$(9);
    ELSEIF Temp! > 22 THEN                    ' cool it off
      LOCATE 13, 35: PRINT "Cooler ON";
      DO WHILE Temp! > 20
        SOUND 200, .8
        Temp! = Temp! - .1
        ColdOn! = TIMER
        DO WHILE TIMER < ColdOn! + .2: LOOP   ' an inside loop
        LOCATE 12, 35: PRINT Temp!;
      LOOP
      LOCATE 13, 35: PRINT SPACE$(9);
    ELSE                                      ' random changes
      DO WHILE Temp! <= 22 AND Temp! >= 18
        Change! = RND - .5                    ' random change
```

```
            Temp! = Temp! + Change!
            Start! = TIMER                    ' wait awhile
            DO WHILE TIMER < Start! + .2: LOOP
            COLOR 7, 4
            LOCATE 12, 35: PRINT Temp!;        ' print temperature
         LOOP
    END IF
 LOOP
 COLOR 7, 0
 END
```

The temperature is set at 20 degrees in the Initialization block. Then a rectangle filled with color, similar to the one discussed earlier, is drawn.

The Main program block turns on the heater when the temperature falls below 18 degrees, turns on the cooler when the temperature rises above 22 degrees, and produces random temperature changes. Each action takes place in its own block of the block IF structure headed by the following lines:

```
IF Temp! < 18 THEN                  ' heat it up
ELSEIF Temp! > 22 THEN              ' cool it off
ELSE                                ' random changes
```

Because the original temperature is 20 degrees, the IF block and ELSEIF block do not execute immediately. The ELSE block produces random changes in the temperature. When the temperature rises above 22 degrees, the program exits the ELSE block, the ELSEIF block turns on the cooler until the temperature falls back to 20 degrees, and control goes to the ELSE block. When the random changes produce a temperature less than 18 degrees, the IF block turns on the heater until the temperature rises to 20 degrees.

Enter and run the program. Sit back and relax. Watch the temperature changes on the screen. Let the program run until you have seen the heater and the cooler in action. Figure 7.5 shows an interrupted display with the heater on.

Use single line IF/THEN statements for actions that can be written in a statement or two, but use the block IF structure when more than a few statements are to be executed.

An IF/THEN block structure can include any number of ELSEIF conditions and actions that take place when the condition is true. Use the last block, ELSE, to provide actions when the condition does not satisfy any of the IF or ELSEIF conditions. Remember, nothing must share the same line as the ELSE keyword.

189

Figure 7.5. Temperature controller display.

SELECT CASE Conditional Branch

In many programs, a computer might make one of several actions depending on the value of a variable. The SELECT CASE structure enables the computer to make the selection from a list of multiple-choice actions. The structure begins with a SELECT CASE statement that contains an expression, like

```
SELECT CASE expression
```

The action taken by the computer is selected from a list of "CASES" depending on the value of **expression**. Each CASE (choice of action) contains a block of statements that are executed when the CASE's condition is TRUE. Here is the syntax for the SELECT CASE structure.

```
SELECT CASE expression
  CASE condition 1
    block of statements
  [CASE condition 2
    block of statements]
  [CASE condition 3
    block of statements]
  [CASE ELSE
    block of statements]
END SELECT
```

The conditions of the CASE clauses include equality, inequality, greater than, less than, and range (from-to).

As an example, suppose that you press a key and want to determine the ASCII code of the character. Consider the following three possibilities and the CASE conditions that head a block of statements to provide the desired result.

1. The character is an uppercase letter. Its ASCII code is in the range of 65-90.

   ```
   CASE 65 TO 90
   ```

2. The character is a lowercase letter. Its ASCII code is in the range of 97-122.

   ```
   CASE 97 TO 122
   ```

3. Press some other character. The ASCII code is in neither range 65-90 nor range 97-122.

   ```
   CASE ELSE
   ```

The program in listing 7.3 uses a SELECT CASE structure with these three cases to make the selection and print information about the entries you make. You enter a five-letter word. The MID$ function selects one letter at a time. The ASC function provides the letter's ASCII code.

Listing 7.3. ASCII codes for words program.

```
REM ** ASCII Codes for Words **
'Learning BASIC, Chapter 7.  File: PBL0703.BAS
'Uses SELECT CASE

REM ** Initialize **
CLS: DEFINT A-Z

REM ** Get word **
DO
  INPUT "Enter a 5-letter word, please: ", word$
  ' Find ASCII code of each letter
  FOR place = 1 TO 5
    code = ASC(MID$(word$, place, 1))
    SELECT CASE code
      CASE 65 TO 90
        PRINT "Letter"; place; "has ASCII code"; code
        PRINT "ASCII code for lower case is"; code + 32
        PRINT
      CASE 97 TO 122
        PRINT "Letter"; place; "has ASCII code"; code
        PRINT "ASCII code for upper case is"; code - 32
        PRINT
      CASE ELSE
```

continues

Listing 7.3. (continued)

```
        PRINT "Character"; place; "is not a letter"
        PRINT "Its ASCII code is"; code
        PRINT
    END SELECT
  NEXT place
  LOCATE 18, 5: PRINT "Press ESC to quit";
  PRINT " - any other key for another word"
  kbd$ = INPUT$(1)
  CLS
LOOP UNTIL kbd$ = CHR$(27)
END
```

Enter and run the program. Type in five-character words, mixing upper- and lowercase letters. Try entering numbers and other printable characters. The following output shows a sample display of a word analysis:

```
Enter a 5-letter word, please? Abe1%
Letter 1 has ASCII code 65
ASCII code for lowercase is 97

Letter 2 has ASCII code 98
ASCII code for upper case is 66

Letter 3 has ASCII code 101
ASCII code for upper case is 69

Character 4 is not a letter
Its ASCII code is 49
Character 5 is not a letter
Its ASCII code is 37




    Press ESC to quit - any other key for another word
```

You used one version of a temperature-control simulation in listing 7.2. The listing contained a block IF structure to provide for three different actions based on the value of the temperature, as follows:

- Temp! < 18—Turn heater on

- Temp! > 22—Turn cooler on

- Temp! 18 to 22—Plot random temperature changes

Use a SELECT CASE structure with the following CASES in place of the block IF structure of the program in listing 7.2.

```
CASE < 18
CASE > 22
CASE ELSE or CASE 18 TO 22
```

Listing 7.4 demonstrates the use of SELECT CASE with these three CASE clauses.

Listing 7.4. Temperature-control simulation, program 2.

```
REM ** Temperature Control Simulation Number 2 **
'Learning BASIC, Chapter 7.  File: PBL0704.BAS
'Uses SELECT CASE for heater and cooler

REM ** Initialize **
CLS: DEFINT A-Z: RANDOMIZE TIMER
Temp! = 20

REM ** Draw rectangle for display **
LOCATE 10, 32: PRINT STRING$(16, 219)
LOCATE 15, 32: PRINT STRING$(16, 219)
FOR row = 11 TO 14
  LOCATE row, 32: PRINT CHR$(219)
  LOCATE row, 47: PRINT CHR$(219)
NEXT row
  COLOR 4
  FOR row = 11 TO 14
  FOR column = 33 TO 46
    LOCATE row, column: PRINT CHR$(219);
  NEXT column
NEXT row

REM ** Main Program - Control Temperatures **
COLOR 7, 0
LOCATE 18, 28: PRINT "Press Ctrl-Break to quit"
DO
  SELECT CASE Temp!
    CASE < 18                              ' heat it up
      LOCATE 13, 35: PRINT "Heater ON";
      DO WHILE Temp! < 20
        SOUND 900, .3
        Temp! = Temp! + .1
        HeatOn! = TIMER
        DO WHILE TIMER < HeatOn! + .2: LOOP
        LOCATE 12, 35: PRINT Temp!;
      LOOP
      LOCATE 13, 35: PRINT SPACE$(9);
    CASE > 22                              ' cool it off
      LOCATE 13, 35: PRINT "Cooler ON";
      DO WHILE Temp! > 20
        SOUND 200, .8
        Temp! = Temp! - .1
```

continues

193

Listing 7.4. (continued)

```
        ColdOn! = TIMER
        DO WHILE TIMER < ColdOn! + .2: LOOP
        LOCATE 12, 35: PRINT Temp!;
      LOOP
      LOCATE 13, 35: PRINT SPACE$(9);
    CASE ELSE
      DO WHILE Temp! <= 22 AND Temp! >= 18
        Change! = RND - .5              ' random change
        Temp! = Temp! + Change!
        Start! = TIMER                  ' wait awhile
        DO WHILE TIMER < Start! + .2: LOOP
        COLOR 7, 4
        LOCATE 12, 35: PRINT Temp!;     ' print temperature
      LOOP
  END SELECT
LOOP
COLOR 7, 0
END
```

The CASE ELSE statement also can be written as

```
CASE 18 TO 22
```

It is always a good idea to include a CASE ELSE block as the last block in a SELECT CASE structure to catch any entries that don't fit other cases. Then if you forget to provide for a unique case, your program is not interrupted with an error message or some unexpected action.

The output of the program in listing 7.4 is similar to the output shown in figure 7.5.

Summary

This chapter described three kinds of loops—FOR/NEXT, WHILE/WEND, and DO/LOOP—as well as two kinds of branch structures—block IF and SELECT CASE. Each kind of loop was demonstrated in at least one program.

You saw how to use FOR/NEXT loops to execute a block of statements a specific number of times, or to increment the controlling variable by a fixed amount. You learned about using an EXIT FOR statement to make an early exit from a FOR/NEXT loop. You learned also that loops can be nested.

WHILE/WEND loops are used when you cannot determine the exact number of times a loop is executed or when no fixed increment can be used for a controlling variable. You can use an EXIT LOOP statement to exit from a WHILE/WEND loop before the condition in the WHILE statement is satisfied.

DO loops add flexibility to the exit condition of a WHILE/WEND loop. You can use four forms to express the condition:

- DO WHILE *condition*...LOOP

- DO UNTIL *condition*...LOOP

- DO...LOOP WHILE *condition*

- DO...LOOP UNTIL *condition*

You can also use a DO loop with no condition. You can exit a DO loop prematurely by using an EXIT LOOP statement.

The block IF structure extends the single-line IF/THEN statement so that IF, ELSEIF, and ELSE blocks can contain multiple statements.

The SELECT CASE structure provides a choice of cases that contain blocks of statements. Execution of a particular case depends on the value of a specified conditional expression.

The control structures discussed in this chapter give you a variety of ways to control the flow in your programs. The next chapter discusses two structures even more powerful than the ones in this chapter. Try the exercises before going on to the next chapter.

Exercises

1. Scan this FOR/NEXT loop.

    ```
    FOR number% = 1 TO 10
        PRINT number% ^ 2
    NEXT number%
    ```

    After the loop executes, what is the value of the variable number%?

2. What numbers are printed in the following nested loops?

    ```
    FOR row% = 1 TO 3
        FOR column% = 1 TO 2
            PRINT row%, column%
        NEXT column%
    NEXT row%
    ```

3. You are using the following WHILE/WEND loop in a program:

```
WHILE number% < 100
   SquareValue% = number% ^ 2
   PRINT number%, SquareValue%
   number% = number% + 1
WEND
```

You want to exit the loop when the value of SquareValue% exceeds 5000. You want to print only the values before the limit is exceeded. What statement do you insert in the loop, and where do you insert the statement to satisfy these conditions?

4. Study this program segment:

```
CLS: amount! = 0.1
DO WHILE amount! <> 0
   INPUT "amount"; amount!
   Total! = Total! + amount!
LOOP
PRINT Total!
```

Rewrite this segment, using each of the following forms:

a. DO UNTIL...LOOP
b. DO...LOOP UNTIL
c. DO...LOOP WHILE

5. Write a program using a block IF structure to tabulate age of respondents to a reading poll. Tabulate ages below 40 in the first block, ages 40-65 in the second block, and ages over 65 in a third block. Use an INPUT statement to enter the responses to the poll.

6. Write the program of exercise 5, using a SELECT CASE structure.

Chapter 8

Subroutines, Functions, and Procedures

Simple programs are usually short, sequential in execution, and may contain loops and conditional branches. As programs become more complex, the number of blocks of code increases; some blocks may be repeated. This chapter shows some ways to write such repeated blocks of code as *subroutines*, *functions*, or *procedures*. In this chapter, you will learn about the following topics:

- Subroutines, a labeled set of instructions that execute when a GOSUB statement executes.

- Three types of functions: those that are built in to PowerBASIC Lite; user-defined functions; and "true" functions. Given certain information, called *arguments*, functions calculate and return a value.

- Procedures (also called *subprograms*) that perform a series of statements called from the main program block.

- The use of subroutines, functions, and procedures to separate a program into structures, with each structure performing its own task. By sectioning a complex program into short, simple structures, you make your programs easier to read and understand.

Subroutines

Earlier versions of BASIC use subroutines to organize programs into logical blocks. Although PowerBASIC has more efficient methods for organizing programs, it retains the subroutine structure. Because subroutines are somewhat obsolete, this discussion is brief.

A PowerBASIC subroutine begins with a line label or a line number. A line label must stand alone on a line. When a GOSUB statement executes, it calls a subroutine. The subroutine contains a RETURN statement that returns control to the statement immediately following the GOSUB statement that called the subroutine, as in the following example:

```
GOSUB HeatOn                    ' call subroutine
PRINT temperature!
  .
  .                             ' other main program statements
  .
REM ** SUBROUTINE: HeatOn **
HeatOn:                         'Start subroutine
  .
  .                             'Other statements
  .
RETURN                          'Return to main program
```

The program in listing 8.1 shows how to call a subroutine to print a date/time stamp on the printed output of the program.

Listing 8.1. Print date and time stamp in subroutine.

```
REM ** Sum and Average Temperatures, Add Date/Time **
' Learning BASIC, Chapter 8.  File: PBL0801.BAS

REM ** Initialize **
CLS: DEFINT A-Z
Sum! = 0

REM ** Main program block **
FOR day = 1 to 7
  READ temperature!
  Sum! = Sum! + temperature!
NEXT day
Average! = Sum! / 7
GOSUB DateTime                          ' go to subroutine
PRINT                                   ' back from subroutine
PRINT "The average temperature was ";
PRINT USING "##.##"; Average!
END
```

```
DATA 72.5, 69.3, 72.1, 75.7, 74.8, 73.2, 71.1

REM ** SUBROUTINE: DateTime
DateTime:                           ' label marks beginning
PRINT DATE$, TIME$
PRINT
RETURN                              ' to main program
```

The program sums daily temperatures for a week and calculates the weekly average temperature. It then uses the subroutine to stamp the date and time of the calculations. When the RETURN statement in the subroutine is executed, control passes back to the main program where the average temperature is printed. The program's output looks like this:

```
12-16-1991      14:58:37


The average temperature was 72.67
```

Notice that the subroutine is beyond the main program block, separated from the main program by the END statement. Because of this separation, the subroutine executes *only* when called by the GOSUB statement. If you omit the END statement, execution of the program continues into the subroutine a second time, and a RETURN without GOSUB message displays.

Subroutines are an old-fashioned method of organizing BASIC programs into logical parts. The use of GOSUB provides an opportunity for misuse. For example, GOSUB provides for the following poor programming techniques: jumping into the middle of a subroutine, multiple RETURN statements in the subroutine, and unintentional clashes between variables of the same name used in a subroutine and in the Main program.

PowerBASIC implements subroutines to provide compatibility with earlier versions of BASIC. PowerBASIC has function and procedure structures to handle situations previously performed by subroutines.

If you insist on using subroutines, use a single entry and exit point. Then the only way into a subroutine is its first line; the only exit is the single RETURN statement on the last line of the subroutine.

Functions

As described in Chapter 3, "Introduction to Programming," you can think of a function as a mysterious black box. You can access the black box by executing its name. The box performs its task and returns a value (result). The returned value is then used in your program. Functions can be used with string or numeric data.

Some functions require arguments (such as INT and SQR). The function uses the argument to produce the value it returns; others (such as RND and TIMER) require no argument. (They use a value produced by the computer.)

Functions provide a convenient and efficient way to act on certain types of data and produce results quickly. This section describes two types of functions. The simplest to use are the predefined functions built into PowerBASIC. Use these functions in a statement line to accomplish common computing tasks. The second type of function is a one-line or multiple line definition you create to perform a certain task. Both types return a value (result).

Predefined Functions

PowerBASIC provides many predefined functions to perform common computing tasks. Many of these perform mathematical feats and some operate on strings. Here are some examples:

- ABS(*expression*) returns the absolute value of a numeric expression

- COS(*expression*) returns the trigonometric cosine of a numeric expression (usually an angle in radians)

- INT(*expression*) converts a numeric expression to an integer

- RND[(*expression*)] returns a random number

- SGN(*expression*) returns the sign (+1 or –1) of a numeric expression

- SQR(*expression*) returns the square root of a numeric expression

- INPUT$(*number*) reads a specified number of characters from the keyboard

- LCASE$(*expression*) returns a string expression as all lowercase letters

- UCASE$(*expression*) returns a string expression as all uppercase letters

- TIMER returns the number of seconds since midnight (used in time delays and to seed the random-number generator)

You already have used many of these functions. All of them, and other helpful predefined functions, are in PowerBASIC's Help system.

Single-Line User-Defined Functions

A single-line function, in its simplest form, contains the words DEF FN, followed by the function's name, an equal sign, and the expression defining the function. In the following example

```
DEF FNCelToFahr! = 1.8 * Celsius! + 32
```

The function name is `FNCelToFahr!` and the expression definition is 18 * Celsius! + 32.

Variables that appear in a single-line function are global by default. Their values are shared with the rest of the program. In this example, the value of Celsius! is assigned or calculated elsewhere in the program.

Single-line functions are particularly useful for short expressions used more than once in a program. Although the position of the definition in a program is not important, grouping the function definitions together is good programming practice. In this book, single-line user-defined functions are placed near the beginning of a program.

The preceding example can be used in scientific programs in which temperatures must be converted (for display purposes) from degrees Celsius (used within the program) to degrees Fahrenheit. Listing 8.2 shows such a conversion and display.

Listing 8.2. Temperature conversion program.

```
REM ** Temperature Conversion **
' Learning BASIC, Chapter 8.  File: PBL0802.BAS
' Reads Celsius temperatures & Prints Fahrenheit

REM ** Initialize **
CLS: DEFINT A-Z

REM ** Define function **
DEF FNCelToFahr! = 1.8 * Celsius! + 32

REM ** Read data, convert, print, and end **
FOR number = 1 to 10
  READ Celsius!
  LOCATE number + 8, 15
  PRINT Celsius!; "Celsius ="; FNCelToFahr!; "Fahrenheit"
NEXT number
END

REM ** Celsius DATA **
DATA 13.2, 13.9, 14.4, 14.6, 14.6
DATA 14.4, 14.1, 13.8, 12.2, 12.9
```

The definition of the conversion function is in the Define function block. Notice that the function name includes the single-precision symbol to match the data type used. To access (*call*) the function, use the function name with the letters FN to distinguish it from a variable name. The function is called in the PRINT statement of the next block, as follows:

```
PRINT Celsius!; "Celsius ="; FNCelToFahr!; "Fahrenheit"
```

Celsius is the value the function reads; FNCelToFahr! is the Fahrenheit value returned from the function.

When the program ends, you can read the data from the output screen. Then press a key to return to the Edit window. Remember, you can toggle between the Edit window and the Output screen by pressing Alt-F5. Here is the program output:

```
13.2 Celsius = 55.76 Fahrenheit
13.9 Celsius = 57.02 Fahrenheit
14.4 Celsius = 57.92 Fahrenheit
14.6 Celsius = 58.28 Fahrenheit
14.6 Celsius = 58.28 Fahrenheit
14.4 Celsius = 57.92 Fahrenheit
13.8 Celsius = 56.84 Fahrenheit
12.2 Celsius = 53.96 Fahrenheit
12.9 Celsius = 55.22 Fahrenheit
```

Now here is a function that converts Fahrenheit to degrees Celsius:

```
DEF FNFahrToCel! = (Fahr! - 32) * 5 / 9
```

You can use this function in a program that accepts data in degrees Fahrenheit and then converts the data to Celsius for use in the program. Then use the previous function to convert results back to Fahrenheit for output. Thus, Celsius temperatures are used in the program, but data is input and output in degrees Fahrenheit.

You can define many business-oriented relationships by functions. For example, the amount of money accumulated over a period of years using simple interest can be defined as follows:

```
DEF FNSimpAmount = Principal * (1 + rate * years)
```

In this function, Principal is the invested amount, rate is the interest percent divided by 100, and years is the number of years the investment is held.

The amount of money accumulated over a period of years using compound interest is

```
DEF FNCompAmount = Prin * (1 + rate / n) ^ (years * n)
```

In this function, `Prin` is the invested amount, `n` is number of times per year the interest compounds, `rate` is the interest percent divided by 100, and `years` is the number of years the investment is held.

You can write most relationships in algebra, geometry, and other math courses as function definitions. Consider a triangle with sides A, B, and C (see figure 8.1).

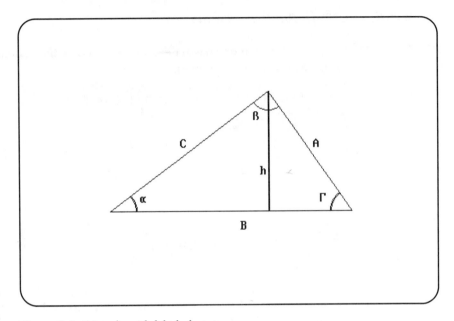

Figure 8.1. Triangle with labeled parts.

In the figure, the base of the triangle is side B. The height is h. Alpha (α) is the angle opposite side A, Beta (ß) is the angle opposite side B, and Gamma (Γ) is the angle opposite side C.

The following are some function definitions you can use to solve the triangle's perimeter and area:

Perimeter:

```
DEF FNSideSum = A + B + C
```

Area:

```
DEF FNAreaOne = (B * h) / 2
DEF FNAreaTwo = (A * B * SIN(Gamma)) / 2
DEF FNAreaThree = SQR(S * (S - A) * (S - B) * (S -C))
```

where S = FNSideSum 12.

You can use single-line functions to define many other relationships between parts of a triangle. Relationships in other geometric shapes also can be used as expressions in a single-line function.

Multiline User-Defined Functions

Use a multiline function when you need more than one line to define a function. Here is the syntax for a multiline function.

```
DEF FNIdentifier [(argument list)] [SHARED]
   [LOCAL variable list]
   [STATIC variable list]
   [SHARED variable list]
      .
      .  (statements)
      .
   [EXIT DEF]
      .
      .

      .
   [FNIdentifier = expression]
END DEF
```

The first statement of DEF FN names the function with *Identifier*. This name must be unique; no other variable, function, procedure, subroutine, or label can share the name. *argument list* is an optional sequence of variables that serve only to define the function; they have no relationship to other variables outside of the function with the same name. The variables serve as placeholders for values that are passed to the function.

By default, variables appearing within DEF FN function definitions are SHARED with (global to) the rest of the program. This default is subject to change, so you would make an effort to explicitly declare every SHARED variable used in a DEF FN function. You can do this with a SHARED variable list within the function or by including the SHARED keyword in the DEF FN block header.

Variables that you want to be local to the DEF FN function are declared in the optional LOCAL variable list. The optional STATIC variable list is specified when it is important that a variable retain its value between invocations of (calls to) the function yet be alterable only within the function.

You can use an EXIT DEF statement to return from a DEF FN function before reaching its END DEF statement.

A multiline DEF FN function definition usually includes an assignment statement to the *function identifier* and is terminated with an END DEF statement.

The body of a multiline function contains one or more statements. The position of DEF FN function definitions within your source code is immaterial, although clarity is served by grouping them together in a single area of the program. Function definitions cannot be nested.

Here is an example of a multiline user-defined function:

```
DEF FNCount%(StringCon$)
  words = 0
  FOR number = 1 TO LEN(StringCon$)
    char$ = MID$(StringCon$, number, 1)
    IF char$ = " " THEN INCR words
  NEXT number
  FNcount = words + 1
END DEF
```

The function counts the spaces in the string you enter. This is an easy way to get an approximate word count, and demonstrates how to use a multiline DEF FN. To use this example, you would assign a variable name to a string. The string is passed to the function definition by using the variable name (Astring$ in this example) as an argument in the function name, as

```
PRINT FNcount%(Astring$)
```

After all the spaces are counted, a value of one is added; the final count is assigned to the function's name just before the end of the function.

```
FNcount = words + 1
```

The value of this assignment is returned by DEF FN for use in the program.

The upper limit of the FOR/NEXT loop is defined by the LEN function, which was discussed in Chapter 6, "String Manipulation." The upper limit is the number of characters in the string you enter and pass to the function.

```
FOR number = 1 TO LEN(StringCons)
```

The string you enter is assigned to Astring$ in the main program and passed to DEF FN by the following lines (listing 8.3).

```
LINE INPUT Astring$
PRINT "The word count is "; FN(Astring$)
```

The reference to FN(Astring$) passes the string to the function and receives the returned value that is printed.

Listing 8.3. Count words in strings.

```
REM ** Count Words in Strings **
' Learning BASIC, Chapter 8.  File:PBL0803.BAS
' Uses multiline DEF FN

REM ** Initialize **
CLS: DEFINT A-Z

REM ** Define multiline function **
DEF FNCount%(StringCon$)
  LOCAL words, number, char$
  words = 0
  FOR number = 1 TO LEN(StringCon$)
    char$ = MID$(StringCon$, number, 1)
    IF char$ = " " THEN INCR words
  NEXT number
  FNcount = words + 1
END DEF

REM ** Use the definition **
LOCATE 25, 10: PRINT "Enter quit as a string to quit";
LOCATE 1,1
DO
  PRINT "Type a string on the next line"
  LINE INPUT Astring$
  IF UCASE$(Astring$) = "QUIT" THEN EXIT LOOP
  PRINT "The word count is "; FNCount%(Astring$)
  PRINT
LOOP
CLS
END
```

A LINE INPUT statement reads the string you enter. The statement reads an entire line from the keyboard into a string variable (Astring$ in this program). Commas and semicolons, which are usually treated as delimiters, are accepted as part of the string. The statement accepts keystrokes until you press Enter, thereby terminating the string and making the assignment to the specified string variable. LINE INPUT can read as many as 255 characters into a string variable.

To end the program, type **quit** as a string (in response to the Enter quit as a string to quit prompt at the bottom of the screen).

```
IF UCASE$(Astring$) = "QUIT" THEN EXIT LOOP
```

As you can see, the UCASE$ function (discussed in Chapter 6, "String Manipulation") is used here so that you can exit the loop by using the word *quit* in any combination of upper- or lowercase letters.

The following shows the word-count output for three strings:

```
Type a string on the next line
This is my first string.
The word count is  5

Type a string on the next line
This string is longer than the first one.
The word count is  8

Type a string on the next line
I'll quit after typing this string.
The word count is  6

Type a string on the next line
quit
```

Multiline DEF FN functions enable a function to spread over many program lines. You can use them like subroutines; unlike subroutines, however, they can be placed anywhere in a program. They return a single value to the statement that called them.

By default, variables used within a DEF FN function are shared with other parts of the program. You can declare variables *local* to the function, however, by using a LOCAL statement, as follows:

```
LOCAL words, number, char$
```

Local variables are temporary variables available and visible only in the structure in which they are used. Because the variables words, number, and char$ are declared local, you can use them elsewhere in the program without affecting the values in the function. With local variables, you can use the same name for variables like "number" and "count", the most popular ones. Local variables are initialized to zero whenever the function or procedure is called by a DEF FN, FUNCTION, or SUB procedure.

As described at the beginning of this section, a variable can be declared to be STATIC. Static variables, like local variables, are visible only in a function or procedure. But static variables are not initialized to zero every time the function or procedure is called. These variables keep their value when you exit the function or procedure. They initialize to zero only when the program begins.

Only simple variables can be passed to a DEF FN multiline function. Array variables (discussed in Chapter 9, "Arrays") cannot be passed to DEF FN multiline functions.

FUNCTION Structure

PowerBASIC supports "true functions", with the FUNCTION...END FUNCTION program structure. Compared to the DEF FN structure, the FUNCTION...END FUNCTION structure has several advantages. Some of the most important advantages follow:

- FUNCTION can pass an entire array as a single parameter. Arrays are discussed in Chapter 9, "Arrays".

- You can specify the default variable type in a FUNCTION to be SHARED, STATIC, or LOCAL.

- Variables are LOCAL in a FUNCTION unless you specify SHARED or STATIC as the default variable type, or unless you specify a particular variable's attribute with the SHARED or STATIC statement.

The syntax for a PowerBASIC Lite FUNCTION is

```
FUNCTION name [(parameter list)][LOCAL¦STATIC¦SHARED]
  [LOCAL variable list]
  [STATIC variable list]
  [SHARED variable list]
  ( statements )
  [name = return value]
  ( statements )
  [EXIT FUNCTION]
  ( statements )
END FUNCTION
```

name is the name of the function. The name must be unique; no other variable, function, procedure, subroutine, or label can share it. *parameter list* is a list of variables (separated by commas) passed to the function. *return value* is the value returned by the function.

Here is a short example that shows how a FUNCTION is used.

```
REM ** Main program **
CLS: DEFINT A-Z           ' value to be passed
Temp = 85
PRINT Temp
PRINT "From FUNCTION, Temp is now"; HeatOn(Temp)
PRINT "To the main program, Change ="; Change
END
REM ** Change temperature FUNCTION **
FUNCTION HeatOn(Change)
  FOR number = 1 TO 4
    Change = Change + number
  Next number
  HeatOn = Change
END FUNCTION
```

The value of `Temp` is printed and then passed to the function when the FUNCTION name (HeatOn) is referenced in the `PRINT` statement.

```
PRINT "From FUNCTION, Temp is now"; HeatOn(Temp)
```

This statement calls the function and prints the value returned by the function.

The value to `Temp` (85) is passed to the function. This value is assigned to the variable `Change` for use inside the function.

```
FUNCTION HeatOn(Change)
```

`Change` is local to the function by default. It has meaning only inside the function. The `FOR/NEXT` loop of the function increases the value of `Change` to 86, then 88, then 91, and finally 95. The value is then returned to the function by assigning it to the name of the function in the statement.

```
HeatOn = Change
```

The output shows the initial value of `Temp` and the final values of `Temp` and `Change` as seen by the main program.

```
85
From FUNCTION, Temp is now 95
To the main program, Change = 0
```

Notice that the value of `Temp` is now 95. The value of `Change` printed by the main program is zero because `Change` is local to the function.

Although variables in a `FUNCTION` are local by default, declaring variables local, static, or shared helps to make a program clear and readable. When you come back to a program later, you can see what kinds of variables are used by looking for the keywords: `LOCAL`, `STATIC`, and `SHARED`.

The program in listing 8.5 uses one `FUNCTION` structure. It remove spaces from a string that you enter.

Listing 8.4. Triangle and circle calculations.

```
REM ** Removing Spaces from a String **
' Learning BASIC, Chapter 8.  File:PBL0805.BAS
' Uses FUNCTION structures

REM ** Initialize
CLS

REM ** Main program **
DO
```

continues

Listing 8.4. (continued)

```
   PRINT "Type a string at the prompt, then press Enter."
   PRINT "To quit, press Enter without typing anything.
   LINE INPUT "> "; strng$
   IF strng$ = "" THEN EXIT LOOP
   ' Call RemoveSpaces$ function
   PRINT: PRINT RemoveSpaces$(strng$)
   PRINT
LOOP
END

REM ** RemoveSpaces$ FUNCTION **
FUNCTION RemoveSpaces$(FullString$)
  Rebuild$ = ""
  FOR position = 1 TO LEN(FullString$)
    char$ = MID$(FullString$, position, 1)
    IF char$ <> " " THEN Rebuild$ = Rebuild$ + char$
  NEXT position
  RemoveSpaces$ = Rebuild$
END FUNCTION
```

You can place FUNCTION structures anywhere in a program. In this book, they are placed after the main program as in this example. The main program enables you to enter a string. Your entry is assigned to a variable (strng$) and passed to the RemoveSpaces$ FUNCTION by the following PRINT statement:

```
PRINT RemoveSpaces$(strng$)
```

The FUNCTION removes all spaces from the string and returns the result to the main program so that it can be printed by the preceding PRINT statement.

The string, when passed, is called FullString$ locally in the FUNCTION. The function initializes the variable Rebuild$ to a null (empty) string. The LEN function (with FullString$ as its argument) is used as the upper limit of a FOR/NEXT loop. Each character of FullString$ (from left to right) is examined by the MID$ function. When the examined character is a space, it is ignored (not catenated to Rebuild$). When the examined character is a character, it is catenated to Rebuild$. Thus, a string is created with no spaces. When the FOR/NEXT loop is complete, the value of Rebuild$ is returned by assigning this value to the FUNCTION name, RemoveSpace$ by this statement:

```
RemoveSpace$ = Rebuild$
```

Enter and run the program in listing 8.5. An example of the output follows.

```
Type a string at the prompt, then press Enter.
To quit, press Enter without typing anything.
> Please remove the spaces from this sentence.

Pleaseremovethespacesfromthissentence.

Type a string at the prompt, then press Enter.
To quit, press Enter without typing anything.
> 1218 Exchange Street

1218ExchangeStreet

Type a string at the prompt, then press Enter.
To quit, press Enter without typing anything.
>
```

Write and experiment with some FUNCTION structures of your own. Doing so will help you understand how this structure works and will also help you to understand the procedure structure in the next section.

Procedures

The most obvious difference between a FUNCTION and a SUB procedure is that the procedure does not return a value. SUB procedures also cannot be called from within an expression, don't have a type, and don't include an assignment to the procedure name.

Procedures are invoked with a CALL statement, as in the following example:

```
CALL HeatOn(Temp!)
```

In this example, HeatOn is the name of the procedure; the value of Temp! is passed to the procedure. A procedure has the following syntax:

```
SUB name [(parameter list)][STATIC¦SHARED¦LOCAL]
  [LOCAL variable list]
  [STATIC variable list]
  [SHARED variable list]
  .
  . statements
  .
  [EXIT SUB]
  .
  .
  .
END SUB
```

211

The parameter list of a SUB procedure, a FUNCTION, or a DEF FN is limited to a maximum of 16 parameters. The default variable type for a SUB is local unless declared to be shared or static in the procedure header or in a variable list.

Arrays (discussed in Chapter 9, "Arrays") can be passed to a FUNCTION or to a SUB procedure, but not to a DEF FN.

The program in listing 8.5 uses a procedure to count the words in a string and squeeze out all spaces. This may not sound very helpful, but you can expand the program to keep track of the location from which the spaces were removed. Later, the string can be restored to its original form.

Listing 8.5. Count words and squeeze strings.

```
REM ** Count Words and Squeeze Strings **
' Learning BASIC, Chapter 8.  File:PBL0805.BAS
' Uses SUB procedure

REM ** Initialize **
CLS: DEFINT A-Z

REM ** Main program **
LOCATE 25, 10: PRINT "Enter quit as a string to quit";
LOCATE 1,1
DO
  PRINT "Type a string on the next line."
  LINE INPUT StringCon$
  IF UCASE$(StringCon$) = "QUIT" THEN EXIT LOOP
  CALL SqueezeCount(StringCon$)                    ' call SUB
  PRINT "The word count is "; words
  PRINT Squeeze$
  PRINT
LOOP
CLS
END

SUB SqueezeCount(StringCon$)
  SHARED words, Squeeze$
  words = 1: Squeeze$ = ""
  FOR number = 1 TO LEN(StringCon$)
    char$ = MID$(StringCon$, number, 1)
    IF char$ = " " THEN
        INCR words
      ELSE
        Squeeze$ = Squeeze$ + char$
    END IF
  NEXT number
END SUB
```

This program is similar to listing 8.4. A SUB procedure counts the words and squeezes the spaces from the string. The procedure, which is called from the main program, passes the string the user enters.

```
CALL SqueezeCount(StringCon$)
```

The procedure shares the word count and the squeezed string with a SHARED statement.

```
SHARED words, Squeeze$
```

The SHARED statement can be omitted if you use the CALL statement and SUB procedure header to pass the shared variables back and forth between the main program and the procedure.

The CALL statement would be

```
CALL SqueezeCount(StringCon$, words, Squeeze$)
```

The SUB header would be

```
SUB SqueezeCount(StringCon$, Words, Squeeze$)
```

The procedure examines each character of the string. When the character is a space, a word is counted. When the character is not a space, the character is added to an accumulating string containing no spaces.

```
IF char$ = " " THEN
    INCR words
  ELSE
    Squeeze$ = Squeeze$ + char$
END IF
```

The following is a typical output:

```
Type a string on the next line.
This is my first string.
The word count is  5
Thisismyfirststring.

Type a string on the next line.
This string is a little longer.
The word count is  6
Thisstringisalittlelonger

Type a string on the next line.
This is the last string, followed by quit.
The word count is  8
Thisisthelaststring,followedbyquit

Type a string on the next line.
quit
```

213

As you have seen, the FUNCTION and SUB structures provide more control over the use of variable types (LOCAL, STATIC, and SHARED). Primarily, functions perform frequently used calculations. Procedures are better suited to blocks of statements that perform some related, logical actions you want to exclude from the main program block. Your main program becomes the director of program flow, with details performed elsewhere.

As you will see in Chapter 9, "Arrays," arrays can be passed to a FUNCTION or a SUB procedure. If such arrays are altered in any way, the revised array can be shared with other parts of the program by using a SHARED statement.

Summary

In this chapter, you learned about the similarities and differences between subroutines, functions, and procedures. GOSUB and RETURN are implemented in PowerBASIC to retain compatibility with earlier versions of BASIC. You use the PowerBASIC structures, FUNCTION and SUB, in place of the older subroutine structure.

Use the subroutine structure (GOSUB...RETURN) only if you write the program to ensure a single entry point and a single RETURN statement as the last line in the subroutine.

In addition to using predefined functions such as INT, RND, LCASE$, and others, you can define your own functions in PowerBASIC. You can define functions with a single-line DEF FN, as in previous versions of BASIC. For longer definitions, PowerBASIC provides a multiline definition structure, DEF FN...END DEF. Such single- or multiline definitions are called by referencing the name of a function in an assignment statement or in a PRINT statement. Only simple variables (not arrays) can be passed to a DEF FN, whether it is single- or multiline.

The FUNCTION structure can be passed simple variables or entire arrays. You can specify whether the variables used in a FUNCTION are LOCAL, STATIC, or SHARED. Variables are local by default. Local variables are invisible outside the FUNCTION; they are initialized to zero each time the FUNCTION is called. Static variables are invisible outside the FUNCTION but are initialized to zero only when the program begins. Shared variables are shared with other parts of the program. A FUNCTION is called in the same way as single- or multiline functions.

The SUB procedure structure also can be passed simple variables and arrays. Variables in this structure also are local by default, but you can use the LOCAL, STATIC, or SHARED keywords to change the default type or to override the default type for specified variables. A CALL statement calls a procedure.

This chapter demonstrated each structure type in one or more programs. In Chapter 9, "Arrays," you will learn about arrays and how to use the FUNCTION and SUB structures with statements that manipulate elements of an array.

Exercises

1. Explain what happens when the following program segment is run:

   ```
   GOSUB DateTime
   FOR number = 1 TO 7
     PRINT number
   NEXT number

   DateTime:
   PRINT DATE$, TIME$
   PRINT
   RETURN
   ```

2. PowerBASIC supports subroutines to maintain compatibility with earlier BASICs. What statement is used to call a subroutine?

3. In listing 8.3, a cubic equation is

   ```
   DEF FNCubic = (x ^ 3) + (4 * x ^ 2) - (10 * x) -30
   ```

   A value of –26 is returned when the value of x is 2. What value is returned when the value of x is –2?

4. A variable (A$) is assigned to the following string:

   ```
   A$ = "a string"
   ```

   What does the following statement print?

   ```
   PRINT LEN(A$)
   ```

5. A multiline DEF FN is named HeatOff. It passes only one variable (Temp!). Write the first and last lines of the function.

6. The following two sentence entry is made in listing 8.6. There are two spaces between the period of the first sentence and the first word of the second sentence. What word count will be printed?

   ```
   Count my words.  Guess how many words.
   ```

7. Here is a partially completed variation of listing 8.1. Write a SUB procedure to calculate the sum and average of the seven temperatures. Write a second SUB to print the date and time. Format the output to look like that shown in figure 8.1.

   ```
   CLS: DEFINT A-Z
   CALL DateTime
   CALL SumAve
   END
   ```

Chapter 9

Arrays

Earlier chapters of this book showed you many types of variables. A *simple* variable, for example, has no relationship to other variables. Examples of this type of variable are

```
count%    score!    Original$    Worth#    HeatOn!
```

Sometimes there is such a close relationship between a group of variables that it is helpful to treat them as an *array*. An array is a group of string or numeric data sharing the same variable name, such as

```
Score%(1)    Score%(2)    Score%(3)    Score%(4)    Score%(5)
```

The individual variables, or values, that make up the array are *elements*. You can use an element of an array in a statement or expression in the same way you use a simple variable. In other words, each element of an array is a variable.

An array has a certain size, or number of elements, determined either before the program runs or dynamically, when running the program. The process of specifying the number of elements is called *dimensioning* the array. Dimensioning gives each element a number, or *subscript*, so that that particular element of the array can be accessed. The subscripts are in order, beginning with 0 and progressing for the number of elements in the array by default. However, PowerBASIC enables you to set the upper and lower subscripts.

The type of array is specified by an identifying character appended to the array name. For example,

count%() — % specifies the array elements are integer, and 2 bytes of memory are used to store each element.

amount&() — & specifies the array elements are long integer, and bytes of memory are used to store each element.

Array types use the same identifiers (identifying character) as the number types they represent.

In this chapter you will learn how to define arrays, how to use them in programs, and how to view and modify their contents. Here is a list of topics covered in the chapter:

- Types of arrays

- How to define arrays

- How to dimension arrays

- Using upper and lower bounds on arrays

- Using arrays in programs

- How to scan, erase, and sort arrays

- How to insert an element into and delete an element from an array

Array Types

Because array elements are variables, an array and its elements have different types just as simple variables have different types. There are numeric arrays and string arrays. Numeric arrays can have elements that are integers, long integers, quad integers, single-precision, double-precision, extended-precision, BCD fixed, or BCD floating type. (All elements of one array must be of the same type.) String arrays can be simple-string or flex-string type.

Defining Arrays

An array is defined by a *dimension statement*. Individual elements of an array are defined by their subscripts. An array has a *lower bound* (its lowest subscript) and an *upper bound* (its highest subscript). The methods used to specify these attributes of an array are described in the following sections.

Subscripts

An entire array is referenced by empty parentheses, as Item%(). Individual elements of an array are differentiated by a subscript, enclosed in parentheses, that follows the array name. For example, Item%(1) and Item%(4) are two distinct elements of the array Item. You can think of variable values as stored in boxes inside the computer (see figure 9.1).

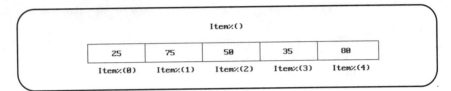

Figure 9.1. A five-element array named Item%.

By default, the first element in an array has a subscript of zero. To change this subscript, you use either a DIM statement or an OPTION BASE statement. Both statements are described in the next section, "Dimensioning an Array."

An array subscript just identifies a particular element with the given array name. The array name, together with the subscript, is used to locate the value of the array element in memory. In figure 9.1, for example, the value 50 is in box number 2; therefore, Item%(2) equals 50.

As you will see, arrays can have more than one dimension. Think of one-dimensional arrays as lists made up of rows of numbers. You can visualize two-dimensional arrays as tables made up of rows and columns.

Declaring the name and type of an array, as well as the number and organization of its elements, is done by dimensioning the array.

Dimensioning an Array

You specify the number of elements in an array along with the array's name and type in a DIM statement. For example, you can name, type, and dimension the one-dimensional array in figure 9.1 by the following statement:

```
DIM Item%(4)
```

This statement specifies the name of the array as Item, its type as integer, and the maximum subscript as 4. The array has five elements: Item%(0), Item%(1), Item%(2), Item%(3), and Item%(4).

219

By default, the lowest numbered subscript is zero (0). You can change this number to 1 by using an OPTION BASE statement

```
OPTION BASE 1
```

If this OPTION BASE statement were used before the dimension statement, the array would not have an element Item(0). The array would have four elements.

```
Item%(1), Item%(2), Item%(3), and Item%(4).
```

The OPTION BASE statement is included for compatibility with programs from an earlier version of BASIC. PowerBASIC offers a more powerful method of controlling subscripts. It uses an alternative form of the DIM statement to specify the lowest and highest subscripts. For example, the statement

```
DIM Item%(1:5)
```

specifies 1 as the lowest subscript and 5 as the highest subscript. This form of DIM makes the OPTION BASE statement unnecessary.

The program in listing 9.1 uses a single-precision array to hold the temperatures for a given week. SUB procedures do most of the detailed work. The main program block just calls the procedures and prints the average temperature for the week.

Listing 9.1. Weekly Temperatures.

```
REM ** Weekly Temperatures **
' Learning BASIC, Chapter 9.  File:PBL0901.BAS

REM ** Initialize **
CLS: DEFINT A-Z
DIM day!(1:7)                              ' dimension array

REM ** Main program **
CALL DateTime
CALL Temperature(Average!, day!())
PRINT: PRINT "The average temperature was ";
PRINT USING "##.##"; Average!
END

DATA 71.8, 75.3, 80.2, 79.6, 75.4, 74.9, 76.2

SUB DateTime
  PRINT DATE$, TIME$
  PRINT
END SUB
```

```
SUB Temperature(Average!, day!())
  FOR number = 1 TO 7
    READ day!(number)                    ' fill the array
    PRINT "Day"; number; day!(number) ' print temperature data
    Sum! = Sum! + day!(number)
  NEXT number
  Average! = Sum! / 7
END SUB
```

The output, which follows, displays the date and time of the program run, the average temperature for the week, the number of the day, and the day's temperature:

```
05-20-1991    22:53:28

Day 1  71.8
Day 2  75.3
Day 3  80.2
Day 4  79.6
Day 5  75.4
Day 6  74.9
Day 7  76.2

The average temperature was 76.20
```

You also can use a range of values to dimension an array with elements whose subscripts do not begin with 0 or 1. For example, you could use this dimension statement:

```
DIM Population%(1800:1899)
```

to define an array that holds a city's population for each year from 1800 through 1899. The element number (subscript) corresponds to the year of the stored data. Anything you do to make the names of variables more meaningful helps anyone who uses your programs.

The program in listing 9.2 dimensions an array in a similar way. An element's subscript identifies the year of the data contained in the element.

Listing 9.2. Population Growth of Micity.

```
REM ** Population Growth of Micity **
' Learning BASIC, Chapter 9.   File:PBL0902.BAS

REM ** Initialize **
CLS: DEFINT A-Z
DIM PopMicity(1980:1990)              ' dimension array

REM ** Main program **
FOR year = 1980 TO 1990
  READ PopMicity(year)                ' fill the array
NEXT year
CALL PrintIt(PopMicity())
END

DATA 16452, 16524, 16611, 16703, 16814, 16950
DATA 17240, 17333, 17428, 17519, 17633

SUB PrintIt(PopMicity())
  FOR year = 1980 TO 1990
    IF year <> 1980 THEN
      growth = PopMicity(year) - PopMicity(year - 1)
    END IF
    TotalPop& = TotalPop& + PopMicity(year)
    TotalGrow = TotalGrow + growth
    PRINT year; PopMicity(year); growth
  NEXT year
  Average! = TotalPop& / 11
  PRINT: PRINT "The average population was"; Average!
  PRINT "The average growth was"; TotalGrow / 10; "per year"
END SUB
```

The DIM statement sets the upper and lower limits for the subscripts of the PopMicity array as 1980 and 1990.

```
DIM PopMicity(1980:1990)              ' dimension array
```

These upper and lower bounds are used in the FOR/NEXT statement to read the values for the elements in the PopMicity array.

```
FOR year = 1980 TO 1990
  READ PopMicity(year)                ' fill the array
NEXT year
```

Because the array's total grows quite large, the variable `TotalPop&` is specified as a long integer. If a simple integer were used, an overflow would occur when adding the elements of the array.

```
TotalPop& = TotalPop& + PopMicity(year)
```

The growth of the population is calculated by subtracting the population of successive years. Because 11 years are involved, the array has 11 elements. Although the average population is based on all 11 years, the growth is based on 10 comparisons. Therefore, the calculations for average population and average growth use different divisors.

- Average population equals `TotalPop& / 11`

- Average growth equals `TotalGrow / 10`

Enter and run the program. The output, which follows, shows the year (first column), the population for that year (second column), and the growth in population for that year from the previous year (third column).

```
1980    16452    0
1981    16524    72
1982    16611    87
1983    16703    92
1984    16814    111
1985    16950    136
1986    17240    290
1987    17333    93
1988    17428    95
1989    17519    91
1990    17633    114

The average population was 17018.82
The average growth was 118.1 per year
```

Lower and Upper Bounds

Two PowerBASIC functions return the values of an array's lower and upper boundaries (subscripts). The `LBOUND` function returns the lower bound (the smallest possible subscript) of an array's specified dimensions; the `UBOUND` function returns the upper bound (the largest possible subscript). After an array has been dimensioned, you can access the bounds by using one of these functions with the proper syntax, as follows:

```
Lower = LBOUND(array(dimension))
Upper = UBOUND(array(dimension))
```

In this syntax, *array* is the array's name and *dimension* is the number of dimensions in the array. You can use these functions also in an expression such as that used in a FOR statement. The following statement opens a loop in a dimensioned array:

```
INPUT "How many strings (1-5)"; limit
DIM Strng$(1:limit)
FOR str = LBOUND(Strng$(1)) TO UBOUND(Strng$(1))
```

In this example, you can enter the number of strings you want. The DIM statement uses this value as the upper limit for the subscripts of the array (Strng$). Then the lower and upper bounds of the one-dimensional string array (Strng$) are used to control the beginning and end values of the loop. Remember, the value in parentheses (1) following the array name refers to the number of dimensions of the array, not an element number.

The statements in the example are used in the program in listing 9.3. Notice that the limit must be entered before the DIM statement is executed. The use of a variable in the DIM statement forces a *dynamic* dimensioning of the array. Dynamic dimensioning sets aside memory for the array during the program's execution rather than when the program is compiled. When you know the limits of an array and express them as constants, memory can be set aside when the program is compiled. This is called *static* dimensioning. Because static dimensioning is done before the program runs, it produces faster execution times than dynamic dimensioning.

Listing 9.3. Count words and squeeze strings, version 2.

```
REM ** Count Words and Squeeze Strings, version 2 ** '
' Learning BASIC, Chapter 9. File:PBL0903.BAS

REM ** Initialize **
CLS: DEFINT A-Z

REM ** Main program **
INPUT "How many strings (1-5)"; limit
DIM Strng$(1:limit) 'dimension the array
FOR str = LBOUND(Strng$(1)) TO UBOUND(Strng$(1))
  LINE INPUT "String: "; Strng$(str) 'fill the array
  CALL Count(Strng$(), str, Squeeze$, total)
  PRINT Squeeze$
  PRINT
NEXT str
```

```
PRINT "Total number of words:"; total
END

SUB Count(Strng$(), str, Squeeze$, total)
  STATIC words
  Squeeze$ = " "
  FOR number = 1 TO LEN(Strng$(str))
    char$ = MID$(Strng$(str), number, 1)
    IF char$ = " " THEN
        INCR words
      ELSE
        Squeeze$ = Squeeze$ + char$
    END IF
  NEXT number
  total = words + str
END SUB
```

When you run this program, you enter the number of strings you want. The program suggests a range of 1 to 5 strings but does not check to ensure that you honor the suggestion. The number of strings is assigned to the variable, limit, used in the DIM statement.

A LINE INPUT statement accepts your strings. LINE INPUT accepts a maximum of 255 characters for a string entry.

Each time you enter a string, the SUB procedure is called by

```
CALL Count(Strng$(), str, Squeeze$, total)
```

The values of the variables passed back and forth between the main program and the SUB are listed in parentheses in the CALL statement and again in the SUB header.

```
SUB Count(strng$(), str, Squeeze$, total)
```

In this program, the word count accumulates for all the strings you enter. Therefore, the variable (words) used to count the spaces is declared to be static by the STATIC statement.

```
STATIC words
```

Because of the STATIC statement, the value of words is initialized when the program begins but is not initialized each time the procedure is called. Therefore, words accumulates the spaces in all strings.

After the spaces in a string are counted, a variable (total) is assigned the number of spaces in the string plus the number of the string being entered.

```
total = words + str
```

Because the program cannot predict how many strings you will enter, this statement is used to provide the total number of words, no matter how many strings are entered. To compile the word count, the program actually counts spaces. Because there is one more word following the last space in each string, the word count must be increased by one for each string that is entered. If one string is entered, 1 is added to the number of spaces to get the total word count. If two strings are entered, 2 is added to the number of spaces, and so on. Thus, the value of `total` includes all spaces in the strings you enter plus the number of strings entered.

A typical output of the program follows:

```
How many strings (1-5)? 3
String: This string has five words.
 Thisstringhasfivewords.

String: This string will have six words.
 Thisstringwillhavesixwords.

String: This is a longer string made up of many words.
 Thisisalongerstringmadeupofmanywords.

Total number of words: 21
```

In this example, three strings were entered. The words are counted and each string is squeezed. Each squeezed string is printed inside the FOR/NEXT loop of the main program. When the loop completes, the number of words is printed.

Arrays with Multiple Dimensions

Arrays can have one or more dimensions. PowerBASIC has a maximum of eight dimensions. A one-dimensional array is similar to a list of items. You can think of a two-dimensional array as a table or matrix of items, with rows and columns. Figure 9.2 illustrates one way to visualize a two-dimensional array of five rows, with two columns in each row.

The program in listing 9.4 reads items into a five-row, two-column array and displays the array in rows and columns.

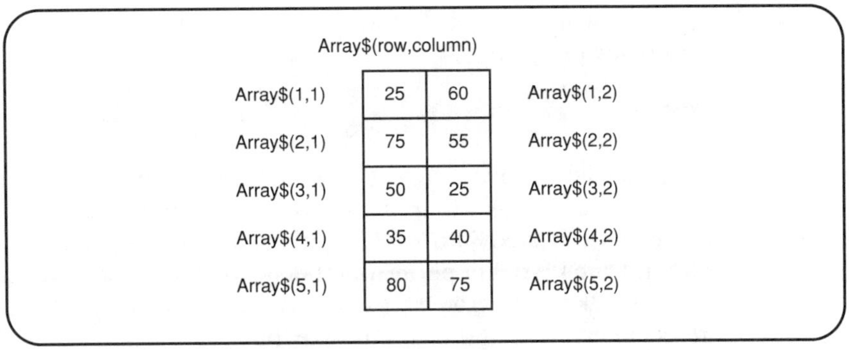

Array$(row,column)

Array$(1,1)	25	60	Array$(1,2)
Array$(2,1)	75	55	Array$(2,2)
Array$(3,1)	50	25	Array$(3,2)
Array$(4,1)	35	40	Array$(4,2)
Array$(5,1)	80	75	Array$(5,2)

Figure 9.2. Array with five rows and two columns.

Listing 9.4. A two-dimensional phone-number array program.

```
REM ** Two-Dimensional Phone Array **
' Learning BASIC, Chapter 9.  File:PBL0904.BAS

REM ** Initialize **
CLS: DEFINT A-Z
DIM PhoneArray$(1:5, 1:2)

REM ** Main program **
' Enter array
FOR row = 1 TO 5
  FOR column = 1 TO 2
    READ PhoneArray$(row, column)
  NEXT column
NEXT row
LOCATE 12, 5: PRINT "Press a key to view the array"
kbd$ = INPUT$(1)
' View the array
CLS
FOR row = 1 TO 5
  PRINT ">"; TAB(5); PhoneArray$(row, 1);
  PRINT TAB(20); PhoneArray$(row, 2)
NEXT row
END

DATA John Able, 999-1111, Phil Candy, 999-1314
DATA Mary Evers, 999-4187, Tim Henry, 997-7135
DATA Sheri West, 995-1234
```

The two-dimensional array (PhoneArray$) is dimensioned in the Initialize block of the program.

```
DIM PhoneArray$(1:5, 1:2)
```

The dimensions for the rows (1:5) and the columns (1:2) are separated by a comma. The strings entered as elements in the array are read from DATA statements in nested FOR/NEXT loops. In each row, a person's name is read into column 1 and his or her phone number into column 2. Then a prompt asking you to Press a key to view the array is printed. When you press a key, the array prints in neat rows and columns, like this:

```
>    John Able     999-1111
>    Phil Candy    999-1314
>    Mary Evers    999-4187
>    Tim Henry     997-7135
>    Sheri West    995-1234
```

The TAB function provides spacing between the columns for each row, as follows:

```
PRINT ">"; TAB(5); PhoneArray$(row, 1);
PRINT TAB(20); PhoneArray$(row, 2)
```

Arrays with dimensions greater than two or three are hard to visualize, but you can use them.

Modifying Arrays

PowerBASIC provides several statements that perform operations on the array. Such operations include

- Erasing dynamic arrays to reclaim memory space
- Resetting static arrays to zero or null string
- Inserting an element into an array
- Deleting an element from an array
- Sorting the elements of an array in ascending or descending order

All of these statements are discussed in the following sections.

Erasing an Array

The ERASE statement deallocates dynamic arrays, resets static numeric-array elements to zero, or resets static string-array elements to null (empty) strings.

The program in listing 9.2 uses a static numeric array, PopMicity, to store the population for the years 1980-1990. After using the array, you can reset all elements in the array to zero by inserting the following ERASE statement:

```
ERASE PopMicity
```

just before the program's END statement.

Then you can insert the following loop to verify that the values of the elements are zero:

```
FOR year = 1980 TO 1990
  PRINT PopMicity(year);
NEXT year
```

When you add these lines of code, you see this information first:

```
1980   16452   0
1981   16524   72
1982   16611   87
1983   16703   92
1984   16814   111
1985   16950   136
1986   17240   290
1987   17333   93
1988   17428   95
1989   17519   91
1990   17633   114

The average population was 17018.82
The average growth was 118.1 per year
```

Then the array is erased, and you see that the elements in the array have been set to zero by the string of zeros printed by the PRINT statement of the FOR/NEXT loop in the added lines of code.

```
0  0  0  0  0  0  0  0  0  0  0
```

All elements have been initialized to zero, and you can reuse the array.

The program in listing 9.3 contains a dynamically dimensioned string array, String$(). You can test the ERASE statement in that program by inserting the following lines of code just before the END statement in the main program block.

```
PRINT: PRINT "bytes available:"; FRE(-1)
ERASE Strng$
PRINT "bytes after erase:"; FRE(-1)
```

The FRE function returns the amount of free memory available for your program. FRE(-1) returns the number of bytes left in memory for data. FRE(-2) returns the number of bytes left on the stack. FRE in a string argument (or a numeric argument of zero) returns the number of bytes available for allocation to a string.

After making this addition and executing the program, you see a display similar to the one shown when the original program was run, but you also see that the ERASE statement has freed some memory space. Using the same entries you made earlier with the revised program causes the following information to be printed:

```
How many strings (1-5)? 3
String: This string has five words.
 Thisstringhasfivewords.

String: This string will have six words.
 Thisstringwillhavesixwords.

String: This is a longer string made up of many words.
 Thisisalongerstringmadeupofmanywords.

Total number of words: 21

bytes available: 65424
bytes after erase: 65472
```

The amount of memory freed may not seem like much. If you are using large arrays, however, the extra memory may be significant.

As one last experiment with the ERASE statement, wrap a FOR/NEXT loop around the last FOR/NEXT loop in the program shown in listing 9.4. This program prints an array of names and phone numbers. The last section (with additions) should be revised as follows:

```
FOR number = 1 TO 2                        ' added line
  FOR row = 1 TO 5
    PRINT ">"; TAB(5); PhoneArray$(row, 1);
    PRINT TAB(20); PhoneArray$(row, 2)
  NEXT row
  IF number = 1 THEN ERASE PhoneArray$     ' added line
NEXT number                                ' added line
```

After you make this revision, the original array is printed on the first pass through the inside loop. Then the array is erased. On the second pass through the inside loop, blank lines appear, headed only by the prompt symbol (>).

```
>    John Able      999-1111
>    Phil Candy     999-1314
>    Mary Evers     999-4187
>    Tim Henry      997-7136
>    Sheri West     995-1234
>
>
>
>
>
```

The elements have been reset to null strings.

Scanning an Array

You can scan an array to find the first element of the array that satisfies a specified relation for a specified expression. Use the relational operators (=, <, >, <>, >=, and, <=) to create a condition for the scan, as in the following example:

```
ARRAY SCAN PopMicity(), > 17000, TO Over%
```

The statement in this example scans the numeric array PopMicity, looking for the first element whose value is greater than 17000. The number of that element is assigned to the integer variable, Over%.

The syntax for ARRAY SCAN differs slightly for numeric and string arrays. For more details, use the PowerBASIC Lite Help system.

Scanning Numeric Arrays

You can see a demonstration of two variations of ARRAY SCAN for numeric arrays by inserting the following lines in the program in listing 9.2. Insert the lines just ahead of the END statement in the main program block.

```
ARRAY SCAN PopMicity(), > 17000, TO Over
PRINT "First element > 17000:"; Over
ARRAY SCAN PopMicity(1984) FOR 4, > 17000, TO Over
PRINT "First element from 1984 > 17000:"; Over
```

Run the revised program. The previous results appear first, followed by the scanned information.

```
1980   16452   0
1981   16524   72
1982   16611   87
1983   16703   92
1984   16814   111
1985   16950   136
1986   17240   290
1987   17333   93
1988   17428   95
1989   17519   91
1990   17633   114

The average population was 17018.82
The average growth was 118.1 per year
First element > 17000: 7
First element from 1984 > 17000: 3
```

The first ARRAY SCAN returns a value of 7 (beginning at element 1;1980). This indicates that the seventh element, PopMicity(1986), is the first year the population was greater than 17000. You can see this is true from the printed population list.

The second ARRAY SCAN returns a value of 3. This indicates that the third element, PopMicity(1986), is the first element greater than 17000 when the scan starts with the year 1984 (the fifth element).

Both forms locate the element PopMicity(1986), but they do so in different ways. The first ARRAY SCAN statement scans the entire array because of the open parentheses following the array name.

```
ARRAY SCAN PopMicity(),...
```

Thus, the first scan starts with the first element, PopMicity(1980).

The second scan begins with the fifth element because that element (1984) is enclosed in parentheses following the array name. The second scan is made on only 4 elements (1984, 1985, 1986, and 1987) because of the FOR 4 option.

```
ARRAY SCAN PopMicity(1984) FOR 4,...
```

Scanning String Arrays

Use the program in listing 9.4 to scan a string array. The array, PhoneArray$(), is two-dimensional, with five rows and two columns. When you use ARRAY SCAN with this two-dimensional array, the scan is made as though the array elements are one list. The list starts with row 1, column 1, proceeds to the next row in that column, then starts on row 1, column 2, and so on.

(1,1), (2,1), (3,1), (4,1), (5,1), (1,2), (2,2), (3,2), (4,2), and (5,2).

Insert the following lines in listing 9.4, just ahead of the END statement. Notice the use of the continuation character (_) to break the lines so that they are not too long.

```
ARRAY SCAN PhoneArray$(1, 1) FOR 5, = "Mary Evers",_
  TO Same
PRINT Same; PhoneArray$(Same, 1); SPC(3);_
  PhoneArray$(Same, 2)
ARRAY SCAN PhoneArray$(), FROM 1 TO 3, COLLATE UCASE,_
  = "TIM", TO Same
PRINT Same; PhoneArray$(Same, 1); SPC(3);_
  PhoneArray$(Same, 2)
ARRAY SCAN PhoneArray$(), FROM 1 TO 8, = "995-1234",_
  TO Same
PRINT Same; PhoneArray$(Same - 5, 1); SPC(3);_
  PhoneArray$(Same - 5, 2)
```

Run the revised program. The output of the program follows:

```
>    John Able      999-1111
>    Phil Candy     999-1314
>    Mary Evers     999-4187
>    Tim Henry      997-7135
>    Sheri West     995-1234
  3 Mary Evers 999-4187
  4 Tim Henry 997-7135
 10 Sheri West 995-1234
```

Keep in mind that the scan considers the elements of the array to be in the order shown in table 9.1.

Table 9.1. Scan order of array elements.

Scan Order	Element	Value
1	(1,1)	John Able
2	(2,1)	Phil Candy
3	(3,1)	Mary Evers
4	(4,1)	Tim Henry
5	(5,1)	Sheri West
6	(1,2)	999-1111 (phone number of John Able)
7	(2,2)	999-1314 (phone number of Phil Candy)
8	(3,2)	999-4187 (phone number of Mary Evers)
9	(4,2)	997-7135 (phone number of Tim Henry)
10	(5,2)	995-1234 (phone number of Sheri West)

233

The first ARRAY SCAN statement starts a scan for the string, "Mary Evers", at position (1, 1) and scans five consecutive elements (because of the FOR 5 option). Because the string equals the value of the third element, a match is found. The value (3) of the variable, Same, is returned. This value is printed with the name and the associated phone number, which verify the scan.

The second ARRAY SCAN scans the complete array until it finds a match and then uses a different option, FROM 1 TO 3. This option says to examine only the first three characters of each element. That is enough to search for the string "TIM". Because the COLLATE UCASE option treats all lowercase letters as uppercase during the scan, the first three letters of Tim Henry are TIM. A value of 4 is returned to the variable, Same, as the string is found in the fourth element. Again, the value (4) of Same is returned. This value and both elements of row 4—(Same, 1) and (Same, 2)— are printed.

The final ARRAY SCAN scans the entire array until it finds a match. The first 8 characters in each element are scanned to match the string "995-1234." The scan finds the match and returns a value of 10 to the variable, Same, which prints. This element is really (5,2), the phone number of Sheri West.

The scan order and the row value for the elements containing the names are the same (see table 9.1). However, the scan order and the row values for the elements containing the phone numbers are different.

When a scan is made on a phone number, calculate the correct element number for printing by subtracting 5 from the scan order number when a match is found. For example, if a phone number match is found at Same = 8 (Mary Evers' phone number), the correct row is found by Same −5 = 3. So, Array(3,1) = "Mary Evers" and Array(3,2) = "999-4187."

To convert the 10 to the correct row in the two-dimensional array, 5 (the upper bound of the row dimension) is subtracted in the PRINT statement, as follows:

```
PRINT Same%; PhoneArray$(Same - 5); SPC(3);_
   PhoneArray$(Same - 5)
```

Experiment with other variations of the ARRAY SCAN statement, using programs with arrays you have already tested. Then take a look at other array statements in the following sections.

Inserting and Deleting Elements

When information changes, you want to be able to insert new information into an array and delete obsolete information fom the array. Inserting and deleting elements is different from changing the contents of an element. You can delete obsolete elements from an array with an ARRAY DELETE statement. Here are two examples to use when you delete an element, move other elements, and insert new data.

This statement

```
ARRAY DELETE PopMicity() FOR 11, 17650
```

deletes the first element in the array PopMicity(1980), moves all other elements up one position (one subscript smaller), and inserts the value 17650 as the 11th element (subscript 1990). Another example is

```
ARRAY DELETE PopMicity(1988), 17531
```

This statement deletes the value in the element whose subscript is 1988, moves the values in elements following 1988 (1989 and 1990) to elements 1988 and 1989, and places the value 17531 in the vacant element whose subscript is 1990.

Both of these statements are in the program shown in listing 9.5.

Listing 9.5. Population growth with DELETE.

```
REM ** Population Growth with DELETE **
' Learning BASIC, Chapter 9.  File:PBL0905.BAS

REM ** Initialize **
CLS: DEFINT A-Z
DIM PopMicity(1980:1990)               ' dimension array

REM ** Main program **
FOR year = 1980 TO 1990
  READ PopMicity(year)                 ' fill the array
NEXT year
CALL PrintIt(PopMicity())
ARRAY DELETE PopMicity() FOR 11, 17650
ARRAY DELETE PopMicity(1988), 17531
PRINT: PRINT "Press a key to see new array"
kbd$ = INPUT$(1)
CALL PrintIt(PopMicity())
END

DATA 16452, 16524, 16611, 16703, 16814, 16950
DATA 17240, 17333, 17428, 17519, 17633

SUB PrintIt (PopMicity())
  CLS
  FOR year = 1980 TO 1990
    IF year <> 1980 THEN
      growth = PopMicity(year)- PopMicity(year - 1)
    END IF
    TotalPop& = TotalPop& + PopMicity(year)
    TotalGrow = TotalGrow + growth
```

continues

235

Listing 9.5. (continued)

```
    PRINT year; PopMicity(year); growth
  NEXT year
  Average! = TotalPop& / 11
  PRINT: PRINT "The average population was"; Average!
  PRINT "The average growth was"; TotalGrow / 10; "per year"
END SUB
```

Although this program is similar to the "Population Growth of Micity," used as listing 9.2, the two ARRAY DELETE statements are added after the original array is printed. The PrintIt procedure is called a second time to print the revised array.

```
CALL PrintIt                              ' print original array
ARRAY DELETE PopMicity() FOR 11, 17650
ARRAY DELETE PopMicity(1988), 17531
PRINT: PRINT "Press a key to see new array"
kbd$ = INPUT$(1)
CALL PrintIt                              ' print revised array
```

The original array displays the following output:

```
1980   16452   0
1981   16524   72
1982   16611   87
1983   16703   92
1984   16814   111
1985   16950   136
1986   17240   290
1987   17333   93
1988   17428   95
1989   17519   91
1990   17633   114

The average population was 17018.82
The average growth was 118.1 per year
```

After the revision, the array, average population, and average growth change, as you can see from the following output:

```
1980   16524   0
1981   16611   87
1982   16703   92
1983   16814   111
1984   16950   136
1985   17240   290
1986   17333   93
1987   17428   95
1988   17633   205
1989   17650   17
1990   175310-119

The average population was 17128.82
The average growth was 100.7 per year
```

The first ARRAY DELETE statement deletes the value of the first element of the original array (16452). All the values of the original array move from their original places to the element with the next smallest subscript, and the value 17650 moves into the last element (year 1990). The second ARRAY DELETE statement deletes the value whose subscript is 1988 (the value 17519); the values in 1989 and 1990 are moved to 1988 and 1989. Then the value 17531 is placed in element 1990. Table 9.2 shows the values in each element before and after each deletion.

Table 9.2. Elements of PopMicity array.

Element	Original	After First Change	After Second Change
1980	16452	16524	16524
1981	16524	16611	16611
1982	16611	16703	16703
1983	16703	16814	16814
1984	16814	16950	16950
1985	16950	17240	17240
1986	17240	17333	17333
1987	17333	17428	17428
1988	17428	17519	17633
1989	17519	17633	17650
1990	17633	17650	17531

The ARRAY INSERT statement works in a similar way. For example, to insert a new name and phone number in the two-dimensional array, you use the following pair of statements:

```
ARRAY INSERT PhoneArray$(5, 1) FOR 2, "Carmen Opra"
ARRAY INSERT PhoneArray$(5, 2), "999-4321"
```

These statements insert the name Carmen Opra and the phone number 999-4321 into the fifth row of the array. This moves the values that were in row 5 to row 6, with new subscripts. The DIM statement that dimensions the array must have an upper bound large enough to accommodate the new elements.

These two ARRAY INSERT statements are used in the program in listing 9.6.

Listing 9.6. Insert for phone array.

```
REM ** Insert for Phone Array **
' Learning BASIC, Chapter 9.  File:PBL0906.BAS

REM ** Initialize **
CLS: DEFINT A-Z
DIM PhoneArray$(1:6, 1:2)

REM ** Main program **
' Enter array
FOR row = 1 to 5
  FOR column = 1 TO 2
    READ PhoneArray$(row, column)
  NEXT column
NEXT row
LOCATE 12, 5: PRINT "Press a key to view the array"
kbd$ = INPUT$(1)
' View the array
NumNames = 5
CALL PrintIt (PhoneArray$(), NumNames)
ARRAY INSERT PhoneArray$(5, 1) FOR 2, "Carmen Opra"
ARRAY INSERT PhoneArray$(5, 2), "999-4321"
PRINT: PRINT TAB(5); "Press a key to see new array"
kbd$ = INPUT$(1)
NumNames = 6
CALL PrintIt (PhoneArray$(), NumNames)
END

DATA John Able, 999-1111, Phil Candy, 999-1314
DATA Mary Evers, 999-4187, Tim Henry, 997-7135
DATA Sheri West, 995-1234
```

```
SUB PrintIt (PhoneArray$(), NumNames)
  CLS
  FOR row = 1 TO NumNames
    PRINT ">"; TAB(5); PhoneArray$(row, 1);
    PRINT TAB(20); PhoneArray$(row, 2)
  NEXT row
END SUB
```

Notice that the array's row dimension is increased (to 6) to accomodate the inserted data. Printing moves to a SUB procedure that is called twice. First, the original array is printed, displaying the information shown earlier.

```
>    John Able      999-1111
>    Phil Candy     999-1314
>    Mary Evers     999-4187
>    Tim Henry      997-7135
>    Sheri West     995-1234
```

The second time, the revised array is printed, with the information inserted correctly.

```
>    John Able      999-1111
>    Phil Candy     999-1314
>    Mary Evers     999-4187
>    Tim Henry      997-7135
>    Carmen Opra    999-4321
>    Sheri West     995-1234
```

Sorting an Array

You may find that the ARRAY SORT statement is the most helpful of PowerBASIC Lite's array-manipulating features. Using it, you can sort (in either ascending or descending order) a complete array or a section of consecutive elements in an array.

You also can specify a *tag array* that keeps related items together. For example, the two-dimensional PhoneArray$ can separate into two single-dimensional arrays: Person$, containing names, and Phone$, containing phone numbers. You can sort on the Person$ array. When the value in any element of the Person$ array changes to a different element, the value in the Phone$ array "tags along" to the element of that array that has the same subscript. In this way, the names and phone numbers are always paired in like elements of different arrays.

The program in listing 9.7 uses this technique. The PhoneArray$ is separated into two arrays: the Person$ array is sorted and the Phone$ array is the tag array.

Listing 9.7. Sort an array with tag-along.

```
REM ** Sort an Array with Tag Along **
' Learning BASIC, Chapter 9.  File:PBL0907.BAS

REM ** Initialize **
CLS: DEFINT A-Z

REM ** Main program **
DIM Person$(1:6), Phone$(1:6)
' Enter array
FOR element = 1 to 6
   READ Person$(element), Phone$(element)
NEXT element
LOCATE 12, 5: PRINT "Press a key to view the array"
kbd$ = INPUT$(1)
' View the array
NumNames = 6
CALL PrintIt(Person$(), Phone$(), NumNames)
ARRAY SORT Person$(), COLLATE UCASE,_
  TAGARRAY Phone$(), DESCEND
PRINT: PRINT "Press a key to see sorted array"
kbd$ = INPUT$(1)
CALL PrintIt(Person$(), Phone$(), NumNames)
END

DATA "Candy,Phil", 999-1314, "Opra, Carmen", 999-4321
DATA "West, Sheri", 995-1234, "Able, John", 999-1111
DATA "Henry, Tim", 997-7135, "Evers, Mary", 999-4187

SUB PrintIt(Person$(), Phone$(), NumNames)
  CLS
  FOR element = 1 TO NumNames
    PRINT ">"; TAB(5); Person$(element);
    PRINT TAB(20); Phone$(element)
  NEXT element
END SUB
```

Notice that the names in the Person$ array are listed in reverse order (last name first) in the DATA statement so that the array sort is made on the last names, and the names are not in alphabetical order.

The PrintIt procedure is called twice. The first time, the original arrays are printed.

```
>    Candy, Phil    999-1314
>    Opra, Carmen   999-4321
>    West, Sheri    995-1234
>    Able, John     999-1111
>    Henry, Tim     997-7135
>    Evers, Mary    999-4187

Press a key to see sorted array
```

After the original arrays print, the sort is performed by the following lines:

```
ARRAY SORT Person$(), COLLATE UCASE,_
    TAGARRAY Phone$(), DESCEND
```

The COLLATE UCASE option considers the values in the Person$ array in their uppercase form when making the sort. The Phone$ array is specified as the tag array, and the sort is made in descending order. When the PrintIt procedure is called the second time, the sorted array is printed, as follows:

```
>    West, Sheri    995-1234
>    Opra, Carmen   999-4321
>    Henry, Tim     997-7135
>    Evers, Mary    999-4187
>    Candy, Phil    999-1314
>    Able, John     999-1111
```

The study of arrays is good preparation for the use of data files, a more practical way to save data that will be used later. Sequential data files are discussed in Chapter 10, "Sequential Files." For more information about random-access data files, see Chapter 11, "Random-Access Files."

Summary

Arrays group related variables together under a single name. You define a variable by a name, a type specifier, and a dimension. The elements within the array are defined by subscripts, with a distinct subscript for each element.

The information you put in a DIM statement enables you to use the LBOUND (smallest available subscript) and UBOUND (largest available subscript) functions to access the limits of the subscripts that define the arrays' elements. Arrays can be passed to FUNCTION and SUB procedures.

Arrays may have as many as eight dimensions, although more than two or three are hard to visualize. You can think of one-dimensional arrays as lists, and two-dimensional arrays as tables consisting of rows and columns.

You can modify existing arrays by using the following special array statements:

- ERASE deallocates dynamic arrays; it resets elements of static numerical arrays to zero and elements of static string arrays to null (empty).

- ARRAY SCAN scans an array for the first element that matches a specified relational condition.

- ARRAY DELETE deletes a specified single element from an array.

- ARRAY INSERT inserts a new element into an array at a specified position.

- ARRAY SORT sorts all or a group of consecutive elements into ascending or descending order.

A good foundation in the use of arrays leads to a good understanding of the files discussed in the next two chapters. Try the following exercises before moving on to the study of sequential files.

Exercises

1. List the subscripts available for arrays dimensioned by

   a. DIM LowScores(3)
   b. DIM HighScores(3:6)

2. Listing 9.1 averaged the temperatures for one week. How do you change the program to average the temperatures for a complete month (January, for example)?

3. Rewrite the Temperature SUB procedure of listing 9.1 so that the data is formatted in the following way:

   ```
   Day      Temperature
    1          71.8
    2          75.3
    3          80.2
    4          79.6
    5          75.4
    6          74.9
    7          76.2
   ```

4. Explain the difference in entries that can be made by the following statements:

a. `INPUT "String: "; Strng$(str)`
b. `LINE INPUT "String: "; Strng$(str)`

5. What is the maximum number of dimensions an array can have?

6. How many dimensions does an array with the following statement have?

```
DIM PaperFile$(1:20, 1:8, 1:2)
```

7. A one-dimensional array contains the following elements: `Product(1) = 45`, `Product(2) = 98`, `Product(3) = 50`. The following statement is executed:

```
ARRAY INSERT Product(2), 35
```

List the values in the three elements after this change.

8. A one-dimensional array contains the following elements: `Sales(1) = 123`, `Sales(2) = 35`, `Sales(3) = 98`. The following statement is executed:

```
ARRAY SORT Sales() FOR 3, ASCEND
```

List the values in the three elements after the change.

Chapter 10

Sequential Files

So far, you have created, compiled, run, and saved PowerBASIC program files composed of statement lines. All statements were formatted to satisfy the syntax of the PowerBASIC language. PowerBASIC programs can create and save to disk another kind of file: *a data file*.

The traditional programming nomenclature subdivides data files into individual *records*. Each record consists of one or more *fields*. Figure 10.1 illustrates one record of a data file divided into three fields.

John Able	102 Evers Rd.	999-1111	one record
field 1	field 2	field 3	

Figure 10.1. One record divided into three fields.

For example, in a mailing program, each record in an associated data file represents one person. Within each record is one or more fields containing information about that person. The data file can contain many records.

In this chapter, you learn the basics of using one kind of data file, a *sequential file*. The discussion of sequential data files is divided according to two kinds of data files:

1. Unstructured sequential data files, which are composed of records with only one field.

2. Structured sequential data files, which are composed of records with two or more fields.

The topics covered in this chapter are

- Naming and creating unstructured sequential data files

- Reading unstructured sequential data files

- Printing unstructured sequential data files

- Appending to unstructured sequential data files

- Naming and creating structured sequential data files

- Reading structured sequential data files

- Printing structured sequential data files

- Appending to structured sequential data files

Sequential files are stored as ASCII text files. As you enter text from the keyboard, a carriage return/line feed character (which is inserted by pressing the Enter key) separates the text into records. Because of the way in which sequential files are created and read, these files are portable to other programs, programming languages, and computers.

Sequential files are the common denominator for data processing. They can be read by word processing programs and editors (such as PowerBASIC's editor), used by other MS-DOS applications (such as database managers), and sent through serial ports to other computers.

Unstructured Sequential Files

An *unstructured sequential file* consists of records that have one field. Each record is composed of one string of variable length. You write a record to an unstructured sequential file as though you are writing to the display screen. You read a record from the file as though the data is coming from a DATA statement or from the keyboard.

Naming and Creating a File

Because you save data files to disk, you name the disks using a format that conforms to MS-DOS file-naming conventions. You should limit file names to eight characters plus a three-letter extension. For example, the name of the unstructured data file created later in this section contains eight characters and a three-letter extension.

```
REMINDER.SEQ
```

The three-letter extension (SEQ) is an arbitrary indication that this is a sequential file. Any three letters can be used. You can enter the name as `Reminder.Seq`. MS-DOS considers both names to be the same. When possible, you should select names that reflect the contents of the file. This file contains notes to remind you of things to do. Here are some other names you can use.

```
NOTES.SEQ        MindJog.USQ      DoSoon.SQL
NotePad.SQL      ToDo.SEQ         DoLater.USQ
Reminder.TXT     WhenTime.TXT     DONE.TXT
```

The data shown in Table 10.1 is an example of information you can place in an unstructured sequential file.

Table 10.1. Data for an unstructured sequential file.

Record	Note
1	This is my reminder file.
2	It is an unstructured sequential file.
3	One reminder is in each record.
4	Appointment 1/13 10 AM, Dr. Webb.
5	Meet with Bob 1/15 1 PM.
6	1/22, royalty due.
7	1/26, Chapter 10 due.
8	1/31, pay rent.

Create a sequential file by using the following steps:

1. OPEN the file. You have two options to prepare the file for outputing data to disk.

   - OPEN FOR OUTPUT. If no file exists with the name you use, a new file is created. If a file exists with the name you use, that file's contents are erased and the file is treated as a new file.

   - OPEN FOR APPEND. If a file by the same name already exists, the data is appended to the end of the existing file. If a file by the name you use does not exist, a new file is opened.

2. Output data to the file using WRITE #, PRINT #, or PRINT # USING.

3. CLOSE the file. The CLOSE statement closes a file after the program completes all I/O (input/output) operations.

In your first file-creation program, you use the following key statements and options:

```
OPEN FOR OUTPUT
LINE INPUT
WRITE #
CLOSE
```

The OPEN Statement

You must enter an OPEN statement before you can write to a file or read from a file. You also must declare the kind of access for which the file is opened in the OPEN statement. When you open a file, you assign the file a number. This file number is used to access or write to the file. For example

```
OPEN "REMINDER.SEQ" FOR OUTPUT AS #1
```

REMINDER.SEQ is the file name, FOR OUTPUT declares the kind of access, and the file number is specified by AS #1. If you want the file to be written to a disk drive that is different from the current default disk drive, specify that drive in the file name. For example, to write the file to a disk in drive B when you are working from drive C, use

```
OPEN "B:REMINDER.SEQ" FOR OUTPUT AS #1
```

Sequential files can be opened for output or for input, but not for output and input at the same time. Sequential files also can be opened for append rather than output. You also can open more than one file at a time, provided that each open file has a different file number.

The LINE INPUT Statement

LINE INPUT is excellent for entering records in an unstructured sequential file because it accepts a single string (up to 255 characters). Another advantage of using LINE INPUT is that it accepts punctuation marks as part of the string. For example, you can enter a string with a comma or a semicolon, as

```
Note: To end the file, just press Enter.
```

     LINE INPUT accepts all the characters you type (up to 255) until you press the Enter key.

     You also can include a prompt in the statement to indicate that the computer is waiting for a record to be entered. For example

```
LINE INPUT "Note: "; Note$
```

     When you see the prompt (Note:), you type a record and press the Enter key. The record is written to the file by a WRITE # statement. Because the notes are entered within a DO LOOP, a prompt for another note then appears.

The WRITE # Statement

Use the WRITE # statement to write information to an open file. Specify the number of the file you are writing to in the WRITE # statement, along with one or more expressions. In this example, the one expression is the variable, Note$. To use the statement, a file must be open and data must be available to write to the open file, as in these three lines:

```
OPEN "B:REMINDER.SEQ" FOR OUTPUT AS #1
LINE INPUT "Note: "; Note$
WRITE #1, Note$
```

     The WRITE # statement inserts commas between each expression, puts string data inside double quotation marks, and does not output a space before positive numbers. For example, a WRITE # statement writes the note in the previous example as

```
"To end the file, just press Enter."
```

     The quotes are sent to the file with the expression.

     WRITE # is the preferred way to write to a sequential file, because it formats the output with quotation marks and commas.

The CLOSE Statement

When a program no longer needs a file, it is closed. Once a file is closed, you can no longer write to it or read from it. You must open the file again before you can use it. When a file is closed, a new file can be opened and given the number of the closed file. However, two files with the same number cannot be opened at the same time.

To close all open files, use

```
CLOSE
```

You also can close an individual file by appending the file's number to the CLOSE statement. For example

```
CLOSE #1, #3
```

This statement closes the files with the numbers 1 and 3. Open files with other numbers remain open.

A Program Application

The program in Listing 10.1 uses the previously described statements to open an unstructured data file. You can enter notes and reminders from the keyboard. The program displays near the bottom of the screen directions for entering data.

Listing 10.1. Creating an unstructured sequential file.

```
REM ** Create an Unstructured Sequential File **
' Learning BASIC, Chapter 10. File: PBL1001.BAS

REM ** Initialize **
CLS: DEFINT A-Z
DIM Direct$(22:24)
' Enter directions into array
Direct$(22) = "Put data disk in drive A."
Direct$(23) = "At the prompt, type a note and press Enter."
Direct$(24) = "To end the file, just press Enter."

REM ** Main Program **
' Print directions
FOR row = 22 TO 24
  LOCATE row, 3: PRINT Direct$(row);
NEXT row
CALL MakeFile
PRINT "File complete and closed."
END

SUB MakeFile
    ' Create file
    OPEN "A:REMINDER.SEQ" FOR OUTPUT AS #1    ' open file
    LOCATE 1, 1
    DO
```

```
        LINE INPUT "Note: "; Note$
        IF Note$ = "" THEN EXIT LOOP
        WRITE #1, Note$
     LOOP
     CLOSE #1
END SUB
```

Enter the program and run it. Enter the data from Table 10.1 at the prompts provided by the LINE INPUT statement. The following output shows three notes entered and the prompt for the fourth note.

```
Note: This is my reminder file.
Note: It is an unstructured sequential file.
Note: One reminder is in each record.
Note:
```

After entering all notes, press Enter at the prompt without typing a string. The program exits from the DO/LOOP and prints the message, "File complete and closed." The program ends.

Reading and Printing a File

Now that you have the file on disk, you can read it later. To create a program that reads the unstructured data file, use the following key statements and option:

```
OPEN...FOR INPUT...
INPUT #,
PRINT
CLOSE
```

To read a file, open it, just as you do when you create files, use OPEN to open a file. Use FOR INPUT, rather than FOR OUTPUT, so the data can be input from the file. Again, you need a file number to identify the file.

```
OPEN "A:REMINDER.SEQ" FOR INPUT AS #1
```

The file name must match the name under which the file was output to disk. Include the disk drive specification if the file is not on the disk in the default drive. You can use any file number that is not already in use. You do not have to use the number that was used to create the file.

Use INPUT # to access the records from the sequential file named in the OPEN statement. The program reads one record at a time and assigns that record to the

251

specified variable. The variable type must match the type of data in the record. In this program, strings are used, so the variable Note$ is a string variable. If you want to see the record, you must print the record to the screen or to your printer.

```
INPUT #1, Note$
PRINT Note$
```

You can enclose these statements in a loop so that all file records can be read and printed.

Use a CLOSE statement to close the file. A file number is optional in this statement. If no file number is used, all open files are closed.

```
CLOSE #1
```

A program that reads the REMINDER.SEQ file created in Listing 10.1 is shown in Listing 10.2. Notice that the two programs are similar.

Listing 10.2. A program that reads an unstructured sequential file.

```
REM ** Read an Unstructured Sequential File **
' Learning BASIC, Chapter 10. File: PBL11002.BAS

REM ** Initialize **
CLS: DEFINT A-Z
DIM Direct$(22:23)
  Direct$(22) = "Put data disk in drive A."
  Direct$(23) = "Press Enter to see next record."

REM ** Main Program **
  ' Enter directions
  FOR row = 22 TO 23
    LOCATE row, 3: PRINT Direct$(row);
  NEXT row
CALL ReadFile
LOCATE 22, 3: PRINT SPACE$(40)
PRINT "File complete and closed."; SPC(8); BEEP
END

SUB ReadFile
  OPEN "A:REMINDER.SEQ" FOR INPUT AS #1    ' open file
  LOCATE 1, 1: kbd$ = INPUT$(1)
  DO UNTIL EOF(1)
    INPUT #1, Note$
    PRINT Note$
    kbd$ = INPUT$(1)
  LOOP
  CLOSE #1
END SUB
```

Enter and run the program. Directions appear at the bottom of the screen.

```
Put data disk in drive A.
Press Enter to see next record.
```

Use a different drive designation in the program if you are not using drive A for reading the file.

Each time you press Enter (or any other key), a record appears on the screen until you reach the end of the file. The DO LOOP uses a condition that looks for the *end-of-file marker* (*EOF*) inserted automatically at the end of the file when it is created.

```
DO UNTIL EOF(1)
```

The number in parentheses, (1), indicates the end-of-file marker for file number 1.

When you reach the end of the file, the program exits from the loop, closes the file, erases the directions, displays a message, and sounds a beep to let you know that file reading is complete. The program ends.

```
LOCATE 22, 3: PRINT SPACE$(40)
PRINT "File complete and closed."; SPC(8);
BEEP
END
```

The following output shows the screen after the file has been read and closed.

```
This is my reminder file.
It is an unstructured sequential file.
One reminder is in each record.
Appointment 1/13 10 AM, Dr. Webb.
Meet with BOB 1/15 1 PM.
1/22, royalty due.
1/26, Chapter 10 due.
1/31, pay rent.




File complete and closed.
```

253

Appending to a File

The use of FOR APPEND in place of FOR OUTPUT in the OPEN statement is the only difference between the OPEN statement when it is used to append to a file and when it is used to create a file.

```
OPEN "A:REMINDER.SEQ" FOR APPEND AS #1
```

When you use FOR APPEND and name a file that does not exist, the program opens a new file just as if you were creating a new file. If the file name exists, data that you enter is appended to the end of the file. The existing data remains intact. In the next program, FOR APPEND either creates a new file or appends to an existing file.

Listing 10.3 combines the capabilities of creating, appending, or reading and printing a file. A menu is used to select the desired operation. The operations are performed in SUB procedures. The program is longer than previous programs, but each functional part is short and simple. You have already seen all the statements that are used.

Listing 10.3. Manipulating files.

```
REM ** Manipulating Files **
' Learning BASIC, Chapter 10. File: PBL1003.BAS

REM ** Initialize **
CLS: DEFINT A-Z
DIM Direct$(22:24)

REM ** Main Program **
CALL Menu
PRINT "File is closed."
END

SUB Menu
  DO UNTIL choice$ = "Q"
    CLS
    LOCATE 5, 25: PRINT STRING$(24, 219)
    LOCATE 12, 25: PRINT STRING$(24, 219)
    FOR row = 6 TO 11
      LOCATE row, 25
      PRINT CHR$(219); SPC(22); CHR$(219)
    NEXT row
    LOCATE 7, 29: PRINT "Create a File";
    LOCATE 8, 29: PRINT "Append to a File";
    LOCATE 9, 29: PRINT "Read a File";
    LOCATE 10, 29: PRINT "Quit";
    LOCATE 14, 19
    PRINT "Enter the first letter of your choice."
```

```
      choice$ = UCASE$(INPUT$(1))
      SELECT CASE choice$
        CASE "C", "A"
          CALL MakeFile
        CASE "R"
          CALL ReadFile
        CASE "Q"
          CLOSE
        CASE ELSE
          BEEP
      END SELECT
    LOOP
END SUB

SUB MakeFile
SHARED FileName$, Direct$()
  CLS
  INPUT "Enter file location (such as A:)"; path$
  INPUT "File name with extension"; FileName$
  CLS
  ' Enter directions
  Direct$(22) = "Put data disk in drive and press Enter."
  Direct$(23) = "At the prompt, type a note and press Enter."
  Direct$(24) = "To end the file, just press Enter."
  FOR row = 22 TO 24
    LOCATE row, 3: PRINT Direct$(row);
  NEXT row
  ' Create file
  FileName$ = path$ + FileName$
DO
  kbd$ = INPUT$(1)
LOOP UNTIL kdb$ = CHR$(13)
  OPEN FileName$ FOR APPEND AS #1
  'both new and existing files will work
  LOCATE 1, 1
  DO
    LINE INPUT "Note: "; Note$
    If Note$=""Then EXIT LOOP
    WRITE #1, Note$
  LOOP
  CLOSE #1
END SUB

SUB ReadFile
SHARED Direct$(), FileName$
  CLS
  INPUT "Enter file location (such as A:)"; path$
  INPUT "Enter file name with extension"; FileName$
  CLS
  ' Enter directions
  Direct$(22) = "Put data disk in drive A and press Enter."
```

continues

255

Listing 10.3. (continued)

```
  Direct$(23) = "Press Enter to see next record."
  FOR row = 22 TO 23
    LOCATE row, 3: PRINT Direct$(row);
  NEXT row
  ' Read file
  FileName$ = path$ + FileName$
DO
  kbd$ = INPUT$(1)
LOOP UNTIL kbd$ = CHR$(13)
  OPEN FileName$ FOR INPUT AS #1
  LOCATE 1, 1
  DO UNTIL EOF(1)
    INPUT #1, Note$
    PRINT Note$
DO
    kbd$ = INPUT$(1)
LOOP UNTIL kbd$ = CHR$(13)
  LOOP
  CLOSE #1
END SUB
```

As in previous programs, the disk drive and filename are catenated (joined) by the plus sign (+).

```
FileName$ = path$ + FileName$
```

After executing the initialization block, the main program calls the menu SUB procedure and ends the program when you select Quit from the menu. The Menu SUB procedure prints the menu and uses the SELECT CASE structure to call other SUB procedures. You select your choice from the menu items by entering the first letter of the desired item. Figure 10.2 shows the menu.

The MakeFile procedure creates or appends to a file. This procedure is similar to the procedure (MakeFile) used in Listing 10.1. Another procedure, named ReadFile, is used to read and print the file. This ReadFile procedure is similar to the procedure (ReadFile) used in Listing 10.2. However, to enter the disk drive and filename of the file created and read, use the procedures in Listing 10.3, as follows:

```
INPUT "Enter file location (such as A:)"; path$
INPUT "Enter file name with extension"; FileName$
```

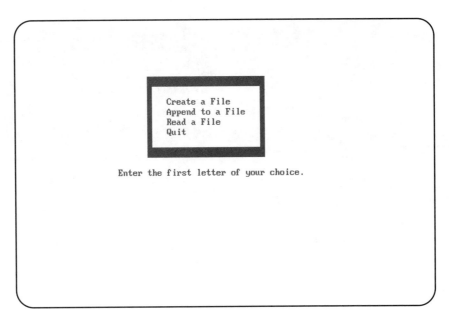

Figure 10.2. The menu of Listing 10.3.

If you want to use the default drive for writing to or reading from the file, press the Enter key without entering a disk drive at the first prompt. Include the file name and extension at the second input prompt. For example

```
Enter file location (such as A:)? A:
Enter file name with extension? Reminder.Seq
```

The program provides on-screen directions for creating or appending to a file. The following output shows a file being created with the MakeFile procedure.

```
Note: File names in OPEN statements are string expressions.
Note: Your program can write or read files on another drive.
Note: The OPEN statement can contain a disk drive (path)
specification.
Note: An OPEN statement FOR OUTPUT is used to create a new
file.
Note:
```

When all entries have been made, press the Enter key without typing anything. The file closes, and the menu is displayed. The natural choice is to read and print the file to verify that it has been entered correctly. Enter the letter R from the menu to read and print the file. The following output shows the complete file printed by the ReadFile procedure. The next keypress clears the screen and displays the menu again.

```
File names in OPEN statements are string expressions.
Your program can write or read files on another drive.
The OPEN statement can contain a disk drive (path) specification.
An OPEN statement FOR OUTPUT is used to create a new file.
An OPEN statement FOR APPEND can create a new file or append
records to an existing file.
An existing file is read by using FOR INPUT in the OPEN statement.
CLOSE frees the file number for use by another OPEN statement.
```

Structured Sequential Files

Records in *structured sequential files* contain two or more fields separated (delimited) by special characters (usually commas). You can compare a structured sequential file to a two-dimensional array. Each record is like an array row, and each field is like an array column.

Naming and Creating a File

You name a structured sequential file the same way you name an unstructured sequential file. File names must conform to the MS-DOS file-naming conventions. For example

```
A:FoneFile.SSQ
```

Where A: is the drive, FoneFile is the file name, and SSQ is a three-letter extension representing structured sequential. This file might hold names in one field and phone numbers associated with those names in a second field. The records in the file might be organized as shown in Table 10.2.

Table 10.2. Data for a structured sequential file.

Record	Field 1	Field 2
1	Able, John	999 1111
2	Candy, Phil	999 1314
3	Evers, Mary	999 4187
4	Henry, Tim	997 7135
5	Henry, Sara	997 7135
6	Opra, Carmen	999 4321
7	West, Sheri	995 1234

A structured sequential file is created the same way as an unstructured sequential file. Use the following steps:

1. OPEN the file either FOR OUTPUT or FOR APPEND.

2. Enter the records from the keyboard, from DATA statements, or from some other source.

3. Write records to the file using WRITE #, PRINT #, or PRINT # USING.

4. CLOSE the file.

Creating a Structured Sequential File Application

The program in Listing 10.4 uses the data from Table 10.2 to create a structured sequential file with seven records and two fields per record. The file is similar in structure to the PhoneArray array used in Chapter 8, "Subroutines, Functions and Procedures."

Listing 10.4. Create a structured sequential file.

```
REM ** Create a Structured Sequential File **
' Learning BASIC, Chapter 10. File: PBL1004.BAS

REM ** Initialize **
CLS: DEFINT A-Z
DIM Direct$(2:3)
  Direct$(2) = "Put data disk in drive A."
  Direct$(3) = "Then, press Enter."

REM ** Main Program **
  ' Read directions
  FOR row = 2 TO 3
    LOCATE row, 3: PRINT Direct$(row);
  NEXT row
DO
  kbd$ = INPUT$(1)
LOOP UNTIL kbd$ = CHR$(13)
  ' Make the file
CALL MakeFile
CLS: BEEP
PRINT "File complete and closed."
END

SUB MakeFile
  OPEN "A:FONEFILE.SSQ" FOR OUTPUT AS #1    ' open file
  FOR record = 1 TO 7
```

continues

Listing 10.4. (continued)

```
    READ person$, phone$              ' read from DATA below
    WRITE #1, person$, phone$         ' write 2 records to file
  NEXT record
  CLOSE #1
END SUB

DATA "Able, John", 999 1111, "Candy, Phil", 999 1314
DATA "Evers, Mary", 999 4187, "Henry, Tim", 997 7135
DATA "Henry, Sara", 997 7135, "Opra, Carmen", 999 4321
DATA "West, Sheri", 995 1234
```

Enter and run the program. This time you do not see the data as it is entered. The records are read from DATA statements and immediately are written to the file. You can add a PRINT statement after the READ statement if you want to see the records as they are entered. After the program reads each record, a WRITE # statement writes that record to the file.

Because the data in sequential files are in ASCII text, you can read them directly from MS-DOS. After you run the program, exit from PowerBASIC Lite and go to MS-DOS to view the file. At the DOS prompt, type

```
C:\>TYPE A:FONEFILE.SSQ
```

and press Enter.

The following output file appears on your screen.

```
C> Type A: FONEFILE.SSQ
"Able, John","999 1111"
"Candy, Phil","999 1314"
"Evers, Mary","999 4187"
"Henry, Tim","997 9135"
"Henry, Sara","997 7135"
"Opra, Carmen","999 4321"
"West, Sheri","999 1234"

C>
```

This is the way the WRITE # statement writes records to the file. Note that each field is in quotation marks, adjacent fields are separated by a comma, and records are on separate lines.

For an experiment, load PowerBASIC Lite again with Listing 10.4. Change the WRITE # statement in the MakeFile SUB procedure to

```
PRINT #1, person$, phone$
```

Run the program again. Exit from PowerBASIC Lite and go back to DOS. Use the TYPE command to print the file with this revision. This time the file should list the following output:

```
Able, John     999 1111
Candy, Phil    999 1314
Evers, Mary    999 4187
Henry, Tim     997 7135
Henry, Sara    997 7135
Opra, Carmen   999 4321
West, Sheri    999 1234
```

The PRINT # statement stores the data just like it was read from the data statements. There are no quotation marks, each record is written to the file as it would be printed on the screen, and each field is in a separate print field (14 characters wide).

The difference in the way WRITE # and PRINT # write data to a file is significant, as you will see when data is read from the file in the next program.

Reading and Printing a Structured Sequential File

Reading a structured sequential file is similar to reading an unstructured sequential file. An OPEN FOR INPUT statement opens the specified file. Use an INPUT # or a LINE INPUT # statement to read records. Your choice depends on the statement used to write the data to the file you are going to read. You will see that WRITE # and INPUT # go well together, as do PRINT # and LINE INPUT #.

Listing 10.5 reads and prints the file created by Listing 10.4. Listing 10.5 uses an INPUT # statement to read the records as individual fields. This way of reading assumes that WRITE # is used to write the records in Listing 10.4.

Listing 10.5. Reading a structured sequential file.

```
REM ** Read a Structured Sequential File **
' Learning BASIC, Chapter 10. File: PBL1005.BAS

REM ** Initialize **
CLS: DEFINT A-Z
DIM Direct$(22:23)
  Direct$(22) = "Put data disk in drive A."
  Direct$(23) = "Press Enter to see next record."
```

continues

261

Listing 10.5. (continued)

```
REM ** Main Program **
  ' Enter directions
  FOR row = 22 TO 23
    LOCATE row, 3: PRINT Direct$(row);
  NEXT row
  ' Read the file
CALL ReadFile
LOCATE 22, 3: PRINT SPACE$(40)
PRINT "File complete and closed."; SPC(8); BEEP
END

SUB ReadFile
OPEN "A:FONEFILE.SSQ" FOR INPUT AS #1     ' open file
  LOCATE 1, 1
DO
  kbd$ = INPUT$(1)
LOOP UNTIL kbd$ = CHR$(13)
  DO UNTIL EOF(1)
    INPUT #1, person$, phone$
    PRINT person$, phone$
DO
    kbd$ = INPUT$(1)
LOOP UNTIL kbd$ = CHR$(13)
  LOOP
  CLOSE #1
END SUB
```

INPUT # reads records and PRINT prints two separate fields in FONEFILE.SSQ.

```
INPUT #1, person$, phone$
PRINT person$, phone$
```

The program outputs the following:

```
Able, John     999 1111
Candy, Phil    999 1314
Evers, Mary    999 4187
Henry, Tim     997 7135
Henry, Sara    997 7135
Opra, Carmen   999 4321
West, Sheri    995 1234
```

If a PRINT # statement was used to write records to FONEFILE.SSQ, the comma following the person's last name would be interpreted as a field delimiter (or separator). For example, the first three records would be printed as

```
Able         John      999 1111
Candy        Phil      999 1314
Evers        Mary      999 4187
```

Each time `person$` is read, the comma after the last name is interpreted as a delimiter. The last name is assigned to the variable `person$`. Because there are no more delimiters in the record, the rest of the record is interpreted as the phone number.

When you use `PRINT #` to write a record, you should use `LINE INPUT #` to read the record. `LINE INPUT #` reads a complete line from a sequential file and assigns it to a string variable. For example, the read and print lines in Listing 10.5 could be

```
LINE INPUT #1, strng$           ' read entire record
PRINT strng$                    ' prints entire record
```

Provided you used `PRINT #` to write records to the file, these two statements would print to the screen just as when INPUT #1 and WRITE #1 were used (see output following listing 10.5).

If you use a `WRITE #` statement to write records to the file and you use `LINE INPUT #` to read a record, the record is read and printed just as it appears in the file. For example, the three previous records would be printed as

```
"Able, John"."999 1111"
"Candy, Phil","999 1314"
"Evers, Mary", 999 4187"
```

Quotation marks and the comma delimiter are printed, along with both fields.

Remember, use `LINE INPUT #` to read a sequential file when a `PRINT #` statement writes it. Use `INPUT #` to read a sequential file when a `WRITE #` statement writes its records. `LINE INPUT #` reads a complete record. `INPUT #` reads each field.

Appending to a Structured Sequential File

You know you can open a file to append records to an existing file. The original file created by Listing 10.4 enters records in ascending order of the last names in the `person$` field. When you append records to the file, the names you enter are appended to the end of the file. Chances are high that the file with the appended records will no longer be in order. Now's your chance to use some of the array modifications from Chapter 9, "Arrays."

You can use the program in Listing 10.6 to append records to an existing file. This program reads the file to make sure the new records have been appended. While the program reads the file, it also creates two arrays: one that holds the names and one that holds the phone numbers. The array holding names is sorted with the array holding phone numbers, "tagging along" as discussed in Chapter 9, "Arrays." The sorted arrays are written to a file of the same name opened FOR OUTPUT. Writing to the file FOR OUTPUT erases the old file and creates a new file with records in ascending order of the names.

Listing 10.6. Appending, sorting, and rewriting a file.

```
REM ** Append, Sort, and Rewrite a File **
' Learning BASIC, Chapter 10. File: PBL1006.BAS

REM ** Initialize **
CLS: DEFINT A-Z
DIM Direct$(2:3), PersonArray$(1:25), PhoneArray$(1:25)

REM ** Main Program **
CALL AppendFile(Direct$())
CLS: BEEP
LOCATE 1, 3: PRINT "File complete and closed."
CALL ReadFile(Direct$(), PersonArray$(), PhoneArray$(), number)
CLS
ARRAY SORT PersonArray$() FOR number,_
  COLLATE UCASE, TAGARRAY PhoneArray$()
CALL ReWrite (PersonArray$(), PhoneArray$(), number)
CALL ReadFile (Direct$(), PersonArray$(), PhoneArray$(), number)
END

SUB AppendFile(Direct$())
  ' Enter directions
  Direct$(2) = "Put data disk in drive A."
  Direct$(3) = "At the prompt, press Enter."
  FOR row = 2 TO 3
    LOCATE row, 3: PRINT Direct$(row);
  NEXT row
DO
  kbd$ = INPUT$(1)
LOOP UNTIL kbd$ = CHR$(13)
  ' Create file
  CLS
  OPEN "A:FONEFILE.SSQ" FOR APPEND AS #1
  DO
    LINE INPUT "Enter name (Last, First): "; person$
    IF person$ = "" THEN EXIT LOOP
    LINE INPUT "Phone number: "; phone$
    WRITE #1, person$, phone$
  LOOP
  CLOSE #1
END SUB
```

```
SUB ReadFile (Direct$(), PersonArray$(), PhoneArray$(), number)
  ' Enter directions
  Direct$(2) = "Put data disk in drive A."
  Direct$(3) = "Press Enter to read a record."
  FOR row = 2 TO 3
    LOCATE row, 3: PRINT Direct$(row);
  NEXT row
  ' Read file
  OPEN "A:FONEFILE.SSQ" FOR INPUT AS #1    ' open file
  LOCATE 1, 1
DO
  kbd$ = INPUT$(1)
LOOP UNTIL kbd$ = CHR$(13)
  CLS: number = 0
  DO UNTIL EOF(1)
    number = number + 1
    INPUT #1, person$, phone$
    PersonArray$(number) = person$
    PhoneArray$(number) = phone$
    PRINT person$, phone$
    DO
      kbd$ = INPUT$(1)
    LOOP UNTIL kbd$=CHR$(13)
  LOOP
  CLOSE #1
END SUB

SUB ReWrite(PersonArray$(), PhoneArray$(), number)
  OPEN "A:FONEFILE.SSQ" FOR OUTPUT AS #1
  FOR record = 1 TO number
    WRITE #1, PersonArray$(record), PhoneArray$(record)
  NEXT record
  CLOSE #1
END SUB
```

Enter the program. Before you run it, you should run the program in Listing 10.4 to be sure the original array is in FONEFILE.SSQ. Then run the program in Listing 10.6.

Call the AppendFile procedure first so that you can append new records to the file. Provide separate prompts and entries for the name (entered *last name, first name*) and phone numbers. The following output shows two appended files. Pressing Enter at the name prompt without entering a name ends the append section and closes the file.

The AppendFile procedure is called first so that you can append new records to the file. Separate prompts and entries are provided for the name (entered last name, first name) and the phone numbers. The following output shows two files being appended. Pressing the Enter key at the name prompt without entering a name ends the append section and closes the file.

265

```
Enter name (Last, First): Barfly, Bill
Phone number: 998 9176
Enter name (Last, First): Jones, Zeke
Phone number: 997 3947
Enter name (Last, First): _
```

The ReadFile procedure is then called. An INPUT # statement reads the records in individual fields. The data in each field is assigned to a variable (an array element) and also is printed. After the INPUT # statement completely reads the file, it is closed. In the following output, you can see that the names are no longer in ascending order:

```
Able, John      999 1111
Candy, Phil     999 1314
Evers, Mary     999 4187
Henry, Tim      997 7135
Henry, Sara     997 7135
Opra, Carmen    999 4321
West, Sheri     995 1234
Barfly, Bill    998 9176
Jones, Zeke     997 3947
```

Then an ARRAY SORT statement in the main program block sorts the array in ascending order of the names in PersonArray$, with PhoneArray$ as the tag-along array. When sorted, the Rewrite procedure is called to open a file.

```
OPEN "A:FONEFILE.SSQ" FOR OUTPUT AS #1
```

Because the file opens FOR OUTPUT, the old file with the same name is erased. A new file is created. The array is written to the new file.

When the program returns to the main program block, the ReadFile is called again to verify that the records are now in the desired order. The result is shown in the following output:

```
Able, John      999 1111
Barfly, Bill    998 9176
Candy, Phil     999 1314
Evers, Mary     999 4187
Henry, Sara     997 7135
Henry, Tim      997 7135
Jones, Zeke     997 3947
Opra, Carmen    999 4321
West, Sheri     995 1234
```

You can write a program with a menu to incorporate creating, appending, reading, sorting, and rewriting in a similar manner to Listing 10.3. The program is quite long; however, you can break it into small, simple parts with SUB procedures.

Uses of Sequential Files

Sequential files are best for applications that perform sequential processing, such as mailing lists and phone lists. You also can use sequential files in situations where all the data being processed can be held in memory simultaneously. Then you can read in the entire file, manipulate the information, and write the file back at the end. Sequential files lend themselves to use with databases, in which the length of individual records is variable.

Sequential files have a major drawback. To access an individual record, you must start at the first record and access each record in order until you have the desired record. With *random-access files,* which are discussed in Chapter 11, you can access an individual record immediately.

Table 10.3 lists the PowerBASIC statements and functions that control sequential file input/output operations. Use the help system for more detailed information about these commands.

Table 10.3. Sequential file I/O commands.

Statement/Function	Operation
CLOSE	Terminates operations on a file
EOF	Returns a signal when the end of a file is reached
INPUT #	Reads data from a sequential file
INPUT$	Reads a specified number of characters from a sequential file into a string variable
LINE INPUT #	Reads an entire line from a sequential file into a string variable
LOC	Returns the number of 128-byte blocks written or read since opening the file
LOF	Returns the length of a disk file
OPEN	Opens a file for INPUT, OUTPUT, or APPEND mode and gives it a number
PRINT #	Prints to the file with preset spacing and columns
PRINT # USING	Prints to the file with user-defined formatting
WRITE #	Writes comma-delimited data to a file

Summary

Sequential data files are stored as ASCII text files. The files are composed of records. A record can consist of only one field (unstructured), or it can be subdivided into two or more fields (structured). Sequential files are named according to MS-DOS conventions: File names have a maximum of eight characters and a three-letter extension. Fields in a record of a sequential file can vary in length.

To write to a sequential file, open the file FOR OUTPUT or FOR APPEND. Use FOR OUTPUT to create a new file. Use FOR APPEND to create a new file or to append to an existing file. Use WRITE # or PRINT # to write a record to a file.

To read from a sequential file, you open the file FOR INPUT. Use INPUT # or LINE INPUT # to read records from a sequential file. WRITE and INPUT # work well together, as do PRINT # and LINE INPUT.

When you are finished working with a sequential file, you close it with a CLOSE statement.

In this chapter, you learned to create, read, and append to unstructured and structured sequential files. You saw the difference in the way WRITE # and PRINT # handle data. You learned how to use a menu to select the desired method of operating on the data in sequential files. You also learned to apply PowerBASIC's array-sorting capabilities to an appended file. Try the following exercises before moving to Chapter 11, "Random-Access Files."

Exercises

1. If you want to create a new unstructured sequential file, the file can be opened by which of the following: FOR INPUT, FOR OUTPUT, or FOR APPEND?

2. How is a record terminated when you are entering records to an unstructured sequential file from the keyboard?

3. Why would you use LINE INPUT instead of INPUT to accept data to be read into a record of an unstructured sequential file?

4. Listing 10.1 uses a WRITE # statement to write records to the REMINDER.SEQ file. What statement do you use to read records from the REMINDER.SEQ file?

5. If you want to add records to an existing unstructured sequential file, the file must open with which of the following: FOR INPUT, FOR OUTPUT, or FOR APPEND?

6. What is the purpose of the EOF function?

7. Revise the program in Listing 10.6 so that it displays a menu from which you can create a file, append to an existing file, sort records, rewrite the sorted file, or quit the program.

Chapter 11

Random-Access Files

So far, you have used program files (composed of statement lines) and sequential files (composed of records of data). PowerBASIC also can create, manipulate, and save *random-access* data files. Random-access files are data files you can access in any sequence.

The name "random-access files" implies their major benefit: Every record is always available. When you want to access the 999th record in a 1,000-record file, you can. With a sequential file, you must access each record from 1 to 999 to access the 999th record.

Random-access files can waste disk space because space is allocated according to the longest record in the file. Each record must be the same length. Most records and many fields, therefore, contain several blank spaces.

In this chapter, you learn the basics of using random-access data files. This chapter covers the following topics:

- Distinguishing between random-access files and sequential data files

- Creating random-access data files

- Reading random-access data files

- Changing records in random-access data files

- Sorting records in random-access data files

Noting Differences Between Data File Types

Records in a sequential file vary in length. Each record holds the necessary data with no wasted space. Random-access records all must be the same length. Otherwise, blank spaces fill out short records. You can waste precious space with blanks.

Sequential files are stored as ASCII text files. Each character in the data takes up one memory location. Random-access files store string data in the same way that sequential files do, but spaces are added to fill out the field. Random-access files store numbers by *IEEE* standard floating-point conventions. The IEEE standard floating-point format is the way numbers are stored in the computer's memory. All numbers of the same type occupy the same amount of memory space and the same amount of disk space. For example, each of the following single-precision values require four bytes (the same space they occupy in memory).

```
0 1.734912E-27 18001.3 482 435000000
```

By contrast, numbers in a sequential file require as many bytes as they have ASCII characters, plus one for the delimiting comma if WRITE # was used to write the number to a file. The integer 13592, for example, has five ASCII characters and requires six bytes in a sequential file. The same integer used in a random-access file and stored in IEEE format requires only two bytes of file space. If records are consistent in length and contain mostly numbers, random files save space over the equivalent sequential form.

Because of the way sequential files are created and read, they are portable to other programs, programming languages, and computers. Word processing programs and editors (such as PowerBASIC's editor) can read these files. Other MS-DOS applications (such as database managers) can use sequential files. You also can send them through serial ports to other computers. Random-access files are not necessarily transportable. You can't peek inside them with an editor.

When you use random-access files, you must specify the record and field lengths before storing information in the file. Therefore, you need to have knowledge about the information that will be put in the file. You should allow extra record length for data of an unknown size that might be added later. The structure of a random-access file means that you need more time and planning to set it up than you need to set up a corresponding sequential file.

After you create a data file, random-access files are manipulated more easily than sequential files. Individual records in sequential files are not as easy to access and modify as are records in a random-access file.

Creating a Random-Access File

Planning the creation of a random-access file requires you to examine the lengths needed for each field in the file. As an example, international direct-dial phone numbers require a country code, a city code, and the local telephone number. To simplify your first look at a random file, let's use a random-access file that holds only the names of the countries and their international country codes.

The file's records have two fields. The first field holds the name of a specific country. The second field holds the country's international phone code. The file's record length is specified when you open the file. Therefore, you must find the longest name. Records for phone codes should all be the same length.

In the example, the longest name is Hong Kong, which has nine characters. You can add countries with longer names later, however. A maximum of 14 characters, therefore, is set for the country name field. The phone codes should be converted by the MKI$ function and stored as a 2-byte (2 character) string. The length of each character is therefore 14 + 2 or 16 characters. The record length is specified in the OPEN statement for the file.

Creating a File

You can create and write random-access files using the following steps:

1. Open the file for random-access, assign a file number, and specify the length of each record.

```
OPEN FileName$ FOR RANDOM AS #1 LEN = 16
```

If you don't specify the record length for the file, a default value of 128 is used. You don't have to specify whether you are opening the file for input or output. The FOR RANDOM specification enables you to use the file for input and output while the file is open.

2. After you open a file, you execute a FIELD or MAP statement to define a mapping between a series of string variables and the *file buffer*. A file buffer is an area of memory used to store data temporarily when reading or writing to a file. The FIELD statement is the traditional way to create a map (a matching of lengths).

```
FIELD #1, 14 AS Fcountry$, 2 AS Fcode$
```

This statement sets the format for the records as 14 characters for the field named Fcountry$ and three characters for the field named Fcode$. When this statement is executed, Fcountry$ and Fcode$ become a special kind of variable known as a *field* variable. Do not use field variables on the left side of an assignment statement except when they are preceded by LSET or RSET.

PowerBASIC also provides a MAP statement, a more modern and efficient way to create a map between flex string variables and file buffers.

```
MAP #1, 14 AS country$$, 3 AS code$$
```

Notice the type specifier for flex strings is the double dollar sign ($$). When using flex strings, you can use the variables (country$$ and code$$) as regular variables without the restrictions of the field variables used with FIELD. In addition, you do not need to use the LSET operation that is required when FIELD is used with regular strings. Therefore, when using flex strings and MAP, you can omit the LSET or RSET keywords in step 3 of this series.

3. All data is stored in PowerBASIC Lite random-access files as strings. Numbers must first be converted to string form with the appropriate function (such as MKI$ for integers). Then load the field variables with data, using LSET or RSET.

```
LSET Fcountry$ = country$
LSET Fcode$ = MKI$(code)
```

The "F" in Fcountry$ and Fcode$ is a visual indicator for field variables.

4. Use PUT to write the record to the file.

```
PUT #1, Record%
```

5. Close the file unless you want to read records while the file is open.

Random-access files are formally structured. You must follow that structure carefully. Table 11.1 lists random-access commands.

Table 11.1. Random-access file I/O commands.

Statement or Function	Operation
CLOSE	Closes a file.
CVI, CVL, CVQ, CVS,	Converts field variables into the CVD, CVE, CVF, CVB the corresponding numeric type.
CVMD, CVMS	Converts Microsoft-format numeric fields into PowerBASIC single-precision and double-precision values.

Statement or Function	Operation
FIELD	Defines field variables.
GET	Reads a record from a random-access file.
LOC	Determines the last record number read.
LOF	Returns the length of a file.
LSET, RSET	Moves string data into the random-access file buffer, either left- or right-justified format.
MAP	Defines field variables (flex strings only.)
MKI$, MKL$, MKQ$, MKS$	Converts specific numeric types into a form that can be assigned to a field variable MKD$, MKE$, MKF$, MKB$
MKMS$, MKMD$	Converts PowerBASIC single and double-precision values into Microsoft-format strings.
OPEN	Opens a file in random-access mode.
PUT	Writes a record to a random-access file.

Note: The CV-, CVM-, MK-$, and MKM-$ functions used in Table 11.1 refer to the following number types:

I = integer

L = long integer

Q = quad integer

S = single-precision

D = double-precision

E = extended-precision

F = fixed binary-coded decimal

B = floating-point binary-coded decimal

This chapter does not discuss all these commands. Remember, you can get more information about the commands by using PowerBASIC's help system.

Creating a Demonstration File

The demonstration program in Listing 11.1 clarifies the process of creating a random-access file.

Listing 11.1. A random-access file of country phone codes.

```
REM ** Random Access File of Country Phone Codes **
' Learning BASIC, Chapter 11.  File:PBL1101.BAS

REM ** Initialize **
CLS: DEFINT A-Z

REM ** Set up and write records **
INPUT "Disk drive: "; drive$
INPUT "File name with extension: "; FileName$
FileName$ = drive$ + FileName$
OPEN FileName$ FOR RANDOM AS #1 LEN = 16
FIELD #1, 14 AS Fcountry$, 2 AS Fcode$
FOR record = 1 TO 5
  READ country$, code
  LSET Fcountry$ = country$
  LSET Fcode$ = MKI$(code)
  PUT #1, record
NEXT record
PRINT "LOF for "; FileName$; " is"; LOF(1)
CLOSE #1
PRINT: PRINT "File is created and closed."
PRINT "Press a key"
END

DATA China, 86,  Hong Kong, 852,  Japan, 81
DATA Korea, 82,  Taiwan, 886
```

The data and format used in this listing are intentionally simple so that you can focus on the process of creating the file. Each of the five records has two fields: a field for the country's name and a field for the international direct-dial country code. The data might be part of the database of a company that does business in the places listed in the DATA statements.

Use INPUT statements to acquire the drive and file name you want to use for the file.

```
INPUT "Disk drive: "; drive$
INPUT "File name with extension: "; FileName$
FileName$ = drive$ + FileName$
```

Then the file is opened for random access.

```
OPEN FileName$ FOR RANDOM AS #1 LEN = 16
```

The length of the file is specified as 16, with 14 characters for the country name and two characters for the largest number of characters in the country codes. The FIELD statement specifies the format.

```
FIELD #1, 14 AS Fcountry$, 2 AS Fcode$
```

A FOR/NEXT loop reads the data from DATA statements and uses LSET to left-justify the data in the field variables Fcountry$ and Fcode$. Because the codes are numeric data, the MKI$ function is used to change the data from integer format to string format. Then the record is loaded into the file numbered 1 by the PUT statement.

```
FOR record = 1 TO 5
   READ country$, code          ' read data for 2 fields
   LSET Fcountry$ = country$
   LSET Fcode$ = MKI$(code)
   PUT #1, record               ' write record to file
NEXT record
```

If you want to use MAP in place of FIELD, the FOR/NEXT loop is simplified because the LSET statements are unnecessary. Replace the FIELD statement and the FOR/NEXT loop with the following lines:

```
MAP #1, 14 AS country$$, 2 AS code$$
FOR record = 1 TO 5
   READ country$$, code
   code$$ = MKI$(code)
   PUT #1, record
NEXT record
```

Don't confuse the PUT statement used for random-access files with the PUT statement used for graphics. Each has a separate format that allows PowerBASIC to distinguish between the two. The graphics PUT statement is discussed in Chapter 12.

After the file has been created, its length (in bytes) is printed, using the LOF function.

```
PRINT "LOF for "; FileName$; " is "; LOF(1)
```

The file is closed, and appropriate messages are displayed. The following is the program's output:

```
Disk drive: ? a:
File name with extension: ? fonecode.rdm
LOF for a:fonecode.rdm is 80

File is created and closed.
Press a key
```

277

The length of the file (LOF) is 80 bytes because there are five records, each of which is 16 bytes long.

Reading a Random-Access File

A file can be read when you create it, provided the file is left open. The operations of creating the file and reading the file are separated in these examples so that you can concentrate on a single operation. If you enter the same file name used in Listing 11.1, the program in Listing 11.2 reads that file. The programs use identical OPEN and FIELD statements.

Listing 11.2. Reading the random-access phone file.

```
REM ** Read Random Access Phone File **
' Learning BASIC, Chapter 11.  File:PBL1102.BAS

REM ** Initialize **
CLS: DEFINT A-Z

REM ** Set up and write records **
INPUT "Disk drive: "; drive$
INPUT "File name with extension: "; FileName$
FileName$ = drive$ + FileName$
OPEN FileName$ FOR RANDOM AS #1 LEN = 16
FIELD #1, 14 AS Fcountry$, 2 AS Fcode$
PRINT: PRINT "The data in the file is:": PRINT
FOR record = 1 TO 5
  GET #1, record
  PRINT Fcountry$; CVI(Fcode$)
NEXT record
CLOSE #1
PRINT: PRINT "File is closed."
END
```

After the OPEN and FIELD statements are executed, the file records are read from disk, one at a time, by a GET statement. Each record is printed using the field variables Fcountry$ and Fcode$. Notice that the data in Fcode$ is converted back to integer form by the CVI function in the PRINT statement.

```
GET #1, record
PRINT Fcountry$; CVI(Fcode$)
```

If you use a MAP statement to create the file, you should use the same statement when reading the file. To do this, replace the FIELD statement and the FOR / NEXT loop with

```
MAP #1, 14 AS country$$, 2 AS code$$

FOR record = 1 TO 5
  GET #1, record
  PRINT country$$; CVI(code$$)
NEXT record
```

After all the records are printed, the file is closed. An appropriate message is printed. The following output shows the data in the file. The output is the same whether you use the FIELD format or the MAP format.

```
Disk drive: ? a:
File name with extension: ? fonecode.rdm

The data in the file is:

China          86
HongKong       852
Japan          81
Korea          82
Taiwan         886

File is closed.
```

The FIELD statement is used in the programs in the rest of this chapter. Feel free to use the MAP statement and flex strings if you want.

Changing Records in a Random-Access File

Data in some files are changed frequently. You can add records to a sequential file by appending records to the end of the file. However, you cannot readily access and alter individual records in a sequential file.

Each record in a random-access file has its own number. You can retrieve individual records by specifying the record's number. While a random-access file is open, you can alter or retrieve individual records and display them.

To add or alter an individual record of the FONECODE.RDM file, the following series of statements can be executed.

```
INPUT "Record number: "; RecNum        ' record number desired
INPUT "Country: "; country$            ' new country name
INPUT "Code: "; code                   ' new code
LSET Fcountry$ = country$              ' format and load name
LSET Fcode$ = MKI$(code)               ' format and load code
PUT #1, RecNum                         ' write record to file
```

Suppose that your company opens some accounts in Australia and New Zealand and ceases to do business in Hong Kong. You probably would want to replace the Hong Kong data with that of one of the new countries and add a record of data for the other new country.

Listing 11.3 allows you to change data in the phone code file. The block of statements in the previous example is used to change the records. It is assumed that you previously created the random-access file of countries and their phone codes, as in Listing 11.1.

Listing 11.3. Changing a random-access file.

```
REM ** Changing a Random Access File **
' Learning BASIC, Chapter 11.  File:PBL1103.BAS

REM ** Initialize **
CLS: DEFINT A-Z
REM ** Main Program **
CALL GetName(FileName$)
CALL ChangeFile(FileName$, NumFiles)
PRINT: PRINT "Press a key to see the file."
kbd$ = INPUT$(1)
CALL PrintFile(NumFiles)
CLOSE #1: PRINT: PRINT "The file is closed."
PRINT "Press a key."
END

SUB GetName (FileName$)
  ' Get file name and give directions
  INPUT "Disk drive: "; drive$
  INPUT "File name with extension: "; FileName$
  FileName$ = drive$ + FileName$
  PRINT: PRINT "Enter records from the keyboard."
  PRINT "To quit, enter a zero (0) as the record number."
END SUB

SUB ChangeFile(FileName$, NumFiles)
  SHARED Fcountry$, Fcode$
  ' Open file and accept records
  OPEN FileName$ FOR RANDOM AS #1 LEN = 16
  FIELD #1, 14 AS Fcountry$, 2 AS Fcode$
  PRINT "The file is open."
```

```
  DO
    INPUT "Record number: "; RecNum
    IF RecNum = 0 THEN EXIT LOOP
    INPUT "Country: "; country$
    INPUT "Code: "; code
    LSET Fcountry$ = country$
    LSET Fcode$ = MKI$(code)
    PUT #1, RecNum
  LOOP
  PRINT "LOF for "; FileName$; " is now"; LOF(1)
NumFiles = LOF(1) \ 16
END SUB

SUB PrintFile(NumFiles)
SHARED Fcountry$, Fcode$
  CLS
  PRINT "Records in the file:": PRINT
  FOR RecNum = 1 TO Numfiles
    GET #1, RecNum
    PRINT Fcountry$; CVI(Fcode$)
  NEXT RecNum
END SUB
```

As your programs grow, you should break them into structures that perform specific functions. The procedures used in Listing 11.3 make the program flow easier to follow and understand. The main program block in this listing directs the traffic by calling procedures and printing directions. The procedures perform the detailed tasks.

The GetName procedure is called by the main program block after the Initialize block has been executed. The GetName procedure allows you to input the drive name and file name. For example:

```
Disk drive: ? a:
File name with extension: ? FoneCode.RDM
```

Again, if you want to use the default disk drive, at the disk drive prompt, press the Enter key without entering a drive designation.

When the file name is entered, the Main program calls the ChangeFile procedure. With this procedure, you can enter the number of the record you want to change or add. You then enter the necessary data.

The following output shows the entries that replace the Hong Kong data in record number 2 with data for Australia and add data in record number 6 for New Zealand. It also shows that entering zero (0) for the record number completes the change file portion of the program.

```
Disk drive: ? a:
File name with extension: ? fonecode.rdm

Enter records from the keyboard.
To quit, enter a zero (0) as the record number.
The file is open.
Record number: ? 2
Country: ? Australia
Code: ? 61
Record number: ? 6
Country: ? New Zealand
Code: ? 64
Record number: ? 0
LOF for a:fonecode.rdm is now 96

Press a key to see the file.
```

As you see, the length of the file is printed after the changes are completed. A prompt also is displayed, which tells how to print the revised file. When you press a key at this prompt, the revised file is displayed by the PrintFile procedure. The following data is the output.

```
Records in the file:

China          86
Australia      61
Japan          81
Korea          82
Taiwan         886
New Zealand    64

The revised file is closed.
Press a key
```

The data for Australia replaces the Hong Kong data. A record containing the New Zealand data is added.

Sorting a Random-Access File

When you sort a random-access file, a typical sequence is to get two records, compare them, and switch their positions in the file if they are out of order. Because of the way that random-access records are formatted, the process seems complex. Rather than present the sorting procedure as a complete unit, this section first describes the switching procedure. The next section, "Switching Records," demonstrates how to switch the positions of two records in a random-access file.

Switching Records

You access a record from the file with a GET statement. Each field is assigned a new name for the switching process. The following block of statements gets two successive records from a random-access file and assigns their fields to different names.

```
GET #1, RecNum                  ' first record
CountryTemp$ = Fcountry$        ' record 1, field 1
CodeTemp$ = Fcode$              ' record 1, field 2
GET #1, RecNum + 1             ' second record
CountryRec$ = Fcountry$        ' record 2, field 1
CodeRec$ = Fcode$              ' record 2, field 2
```

After you retrieve the two records and assign their fields to separate names, you can put them back in the file in reverse order. Thus, you switch their respective places. For example, you can follow the statements in the previous example with

```
LSET Fcountry$ = CountryRec$    ' fields from second
LSET Fcode$ = CodeRec$          '    record
PUT #1, RecNum                  ' put in first record
LSET Fcountry$ = CountryTemp$   ' fields from first
LSET Fcode$ = CodeTemp$         '    record
PUT #1, RecNum + 1             ' put in second record
```

Listing 11.4 shows you how to switch the positions of adjacent records in an existing random-access file until the records are in the order you desire. You can use this simple method to sort a short file. However, it is not practical for use with a long file. The method is included to demonstrate the switching process that takes place in a more complex sorting program.

Listing 11.4. Switching records in a random-access file.

```
REM ** Switching Records in a Random Access File **
' Learning BASIC, Chapter 11.   File:PBL1104.BAS

REM ** Initialize **
CLS: DEFINT A-Z
REM ** Main program **
CALL GetName(FileName$)
CALL SwitchFile(FileName$)
CLOSE #1: PRINT: PRINT "The file is closed."
PRINT "Press a key."
END

SUB GetName (FileName$)
   ' Get file name and give directions
```

continues

283

Listing 11.4. (continued)

```
    INPUT "Disk drive: "; drive$
    INPUT "File name with extension: "; FileName$
    FileName$ = drive$ + FileName$
END SUB

SUB SwitchFile (FileName$)
  ' Open file and accept records
  SHARED Fcountry$, Fcode$
  OPEN FileName$ FOR RANDOM AS #1 LEN = 16
  FIELD #1, 14 AS Fcountry$, 2 AS Fcode$
  PRINT "The file is open."
  DO
    PRINT: PRINT "Switches records first and first + 1."
    PRINT "To quit, enter zero (0) as the record number."
    INPUT "Record number: "; RecNum
    IF RecNum = 0 THEN EXIT LOOP
    GET #1, RecNum
    CountryTemp$ = Fcountry$
    CodeTemp$ = Fcode$
    GET #1, RecNum + 1
    CountryRec$ = Fcountry$
    CodeRec$ = Fcode$
    LSET Fcountry$ = CountryRec$
    LSET Fcode$ = CodeRec$
    PUT #1, RecNum
    LSET Fcountry$ = CountryTemp$
    LSET Fcode$ = CodeTemp$
    PUT #1, RecNum + 1
    CALL PrintFile
  LOOP
END SUB

SUB PrintFile
  SHARED Fcountry$, Fcode$
  CLS
  PRINT "Records in the file: " PRINT
  FOR RecNum = 1 TO LOF(1) \ 16
    GET #1, RecNum
    PRINT Fcountry$; CVI(Fcode$)
  NEXT RecNum
END SUB
```

The modified FoneCode.RDM file now contains the names and phone codes shown previously: China, Australia, Japan, Korea, Taiwan, and New Zealand. Using this modified file, enter and run the program in Listing 11.4. The program first calls the GetName procedure, which, as it did before, requests and assigns the disk drive and name of the file. When the drive and name have been entered, the program calls the ChangeFile procedure. It opens the file, prints some directions, and requests the record number of the first record you want to switch. For example, the following output shows the screen after the FONECODE.RDM file is opened.

```
Disk drive: ? a:
File name with extension: ? fonecode.rdm
The file is open.

Switches records first and first + 1.
To quit, enter a zero (0) as the record number.
Record number: ?
```

The program displays notification that the file is open. Simple directions for switching records are given. The program prompts you to enter the number of the first record you want to switch. It switches the data in this record with the data in the record with the next highest number.

In this example, the record number entered is 1. When the value is entered, the screen is cleared. The revised file is printed as shown here:

```
Records in the file:

Australia      61
China          86
Japan          81
Korea          82
Taiwan         886
New Zealand    64

Switches records first and first + 1.
To quit, enter a zero (0) as the record number.
Record number: ?
```

Notice that records number 1 and 2 have been switched. The Australia data was switched from record 2 to record 1, and the China data was switched from record 1 to record 2. Directions and a prompt for another switch are displayed below the revised file.

To switch the records back, you enter the number 1 again. To switch records 2 and 3, you enter a 2. To switch records 3 and 4, you enter a 3. To switch records 4 and 5, you enter a 4. You would not enter a 5, because there is no record 6 to use in a switch.

Switching Records Automatically

As another step in the transition to sorting the file, run the program in Listing 11.1 again to obtain the original five-record file. This time, use the filename

PHONCODE.RDM to create a new file. Then enter and run the program in Listing 11.5. This program shows how a record can be "bubbled" from the bottom to the top of the file.

Listing 11.5. Switching a record from bottom to top.

```
REM ** Switching a Record from Bottom to Top **
' Learning BASIC, Chapter 11.  File:PBL1105.BAS

REM ** Initialize **
CLS: DEFINT A-Z

REM ** Main program **
CALL GetName(FileName$)
CALL SwitchFile(FileName$)
CLOSE #1: PRINT: PRINT "The file is closed."
PRINT "Press a key"
END

SUB GetName (FileName$)
  ' Get file name and give directions
  INPUT "Disk drive: "; drive$
  INPUT "File name with extension: "; FileName$
  FileName$ = drive$ + FileName$
END SUB

SUB SwitchFile (FileName$)
  ' Open file and accept records
  SHARED Fcountry$, Fcode$
  OPEN FileName$ FOR RANDOM AS #1 LEN =  16
  FIELD #1, 14 AS Fcountry$, 2 AS Fcode$
  PRINT "The file is open."
  CALL PrintFile
  FOR RecNum = 5 TO 2 STEP -1
    GET #1, RecNum
    CountryTemp$ = Fcountry$
    CodeTemp$ = Fcode$
    GET #1, RecNum - 1
    CountryRec$ = Fcountry$
    CodeRec$ = Fcode$
    LSET Fcountry$ = CountryRec$
    LSET Fcode$ = CodeRec$
    PUT #1, RecNum
    LSET Fcountry$ = CountryTemp$
    LSET Fcode$ = CodeTemp$
    PUT #1, RecNum - 1
    CALL PrintFile
  NEXT RecNum
END SUB
```

```
SUB PrintFile
  SHARED Fcountry$, Fcode$
  PRINT "Records in the file: " PRINT
  FOR Record = 1 TO 5
    GET #1, Record
    PRINT Fcountry$; CVI(Fcode$)
  NEXT Record
  PRINT "Press a key to bubble"
  kbd$ = INPUT$(1): PRINT
END SUB
```

When you run this program, the original file is printed (see the following output).

```
Disk drive: ? a:
File name with extension: ? PHONCODE.RDM
The file . is open.
Records in the file:

China           86
HongKong        852
Japan           81
Korea           82
Taiwan          886
Press a key to bubble
```

Then the first switch occurs. The fifth record (Taiwan 886) is switched with the fourth record (Korea 82). The file is printed again to show the switch. When you press a key, the fourth record (now Taiwan 886) is switched with the third record (Japan 81). This process continues until the second and first records are switched. The final order of records in the file is shown at the bottom of the following output.

```
Press a key to bubble

Records in the file:

China           86
Taiwan          886
HongKong        852
Japan           81
Korea           82
Press a key to bubble

Records in the file:

Taiwan          886
China           86
```

287

```
HongKong          852
Japan             81
Korea             82
Press a key to bubble


The file is closed.
Press a key.
```

Table 11.2 shows the position of the countries in the file originally and after each shift. The codes are shifted with the names of the countries. Notice that the record for Taiwan moves up one position for each switch.

Table 11.2. Positions of the records as they are switched.

Original	Switch 1	Switch 2	Switch 3	Switch 4
China	China	China	China	Taiwan
Hong Kong	Hong Kong	Hong Kong	Taiwan	China
Japan	Japan	Taiwan	Hong Kong	Hong Kong
Korea	Taiwan	Japan	Japan	Japan
Taiwan	Korea	Korea	Korea	Korea

The process demonstrated in this last listing is used in the next section within a more complex sorting process. Position switching takes place only when the country or city name is not in alphabetical order.

Using the Switching Process to Sort

The next program uses the switching process discussed in the previous section, but with a variation. The program compares a record with the record that has the next *lower* number.

Records in the file have been expanded to include the country and city names in the first field, the international country phone code in the second field, and the international city phone code in the third field. The number of records is increased to 13. To save you the trouble of entering the information from the keyboard, the data is contained in DATA statements.

With the added information, the length of the records has increased to 24 and the FIELD statement is changed.

```
OPEN FileName$ FOR RANDOM AS #1 LEN = 24
FIELD #1, 20 AS FLocation$, 2 AS FCoCode$, 2 AS FCicode$
```

There are now three fields to format before writing a record to the file. The first field contains the country and the city separated by a comma. Because a comma is used in the field, quotation marks must be placed around the data the program reads into the first field. For example

```
"Japan, Hiroshima"
```

The second and third fields contain integers for the country and city codes, respectively. The data for a complete record is read in from a DATA statement. For example, the location, country code, and city code

```
"Japan, Hiroshima", 81, 82
```

is read from the DATA statement by

```
READ location$, Cocode, Cicode
```

The main program of Listing 11.6 acts as the program director, calling procedures and printing directions.

Listing 11.6. Creating and sorting a random-access file.

```
REM ** Creating and Sorting a Random Access File **
' Learning BASIC, Chapter 11.  File:PBL1106.BAS

REM ** Initialize **
CLS: DEFINT A-Z

REM ** Main program **
CALL GetName(FileName$)
CALL CreateFile(FileName$)
PRINT: PRINT "Press a key to see the file.": kbd$ = INPUT$(1)
CALL PrintFile
PRINT: PRINT "Press a key to sort the file."
kbd$ = INPUT$(1)
CALL SortFile
PRINT : PRINT "Press a key to see the file.": kbd$ = INPUT$(1)
CALL PrintFile
CLOSE #1: PRINT: PRINT "The file is closed."
PRINT "Press a key"
END
```

continues

289

Listing 11.6. (continued)

```
DATA "Japan, Hiroshima", 81, 82, "Japan, Tokyo", 81, 3
DATA "Korea, Pusan", 82, 51, "Japan, Yokohama", 81, 45
DATA "China, Peking", 86, 1, "China, Shanghai", 86, 21
DATA "Hong Kong, Sha Tin", 852, 0, "China, Canton", 86, 20
DATA "Korea, Seoul", 82, 2, "Taiwan, Taipei", 886, 2
DATA "Taiwan, Kohsiung", 886, 7, "Hong Kong, Kowloon", 852, 3
DATA "Hong Kong, Hong Kong", 852, 5

SUB GetName (FileName$)
  ' Get file name and give directions
  INPUT "Disk drive: "; drive$
  INPUT "File name with extension: "; FileName$
  FileName$ = drive$ + FileName$
  PRINT
END SUB

SUB CreateFile (FileName$)
  ' Open file and accept records
  SHARED FLocation$, FCoCode$, FCiCode$
  OPEN FileName$ FOR RANDOM AS #1 LEN = 24
  FIELD #1, 20 AS FLocation$, 2 AS FCoCode$, 2 AS FCicode$
  PRINT "The file is open."
  FOR record = 1 TO 13
    READ location$, Cocode, Cicode
    LSET FLocation$ = location$
    LSET FCocode$ = MKI$(CoCode)
    LSET FCiCode$ = MKI$(CiCode)
    PUT #1, record
  NEXT record
END SUB

SUB PrintFile
  SHARED FLocation$, FCoCode$, FCiCode$
  CLS
  PRINT "Record in the file: " PRINT
  FOR record = 1 TO 13
    GET #1, record
    PRINT FLocation$; CVI(FCoCode$); CVI(FCiCode$)
  NEXT record
END SUB

SUB SortFile
  SHARED FLocation$, FCoCode$, FCiCode$
  top = 1
  DO WHILE top < 13
    FOR pointer = 13 TO top + 1 STEP -1
      GET #1, pointer
```

```
        LocationTemp$ = FLocation$
        CoCodeTemp$ = FCoCode$
        CiCodeTemp$ = FCiCode$
        GET #1, pointer - 1
        LocationRec$ = FLocation$
        CoCodeRec$ = FCoCode$
        CiCodeRec$ = FCiCode$
        IF LocationTemp$ < LocationRec$ THEN
          LSET FLocation$ = LocationRec$
          LSET FCoCode$ = CoCodeRec$
          LSET FCiCode$ = CiCodeRec$
          PUT #1, pointer
          LSET FLocation$ = LocationTemp$
          LSET FCoCode$ = CoCodeTemp$
          LSET FCiCode$ = CiCodeTemp$
          PUT #1, pointer - 1
        END IF
      NEXT pointer
      top = top + 1
    LOOP
END SUB
```

The program is long, but you have used everything before except the sorting routine in the `SortFile` procedure. The sort is known as a *bubble sort,* which is one of the best-known of all sorting routines. It is simple and has a descriptive name. A bubble sort compares two values (`LocationTemp$` and `LocationRec$` in Listing 11.6) and exchanges their positions when the values are not in alphabetical order. The records in the file seem to bubble their way to the correct level in the ordering process.

In Listing 11.6, an exchange of two records (all three fields) is made when the value of `LocationTemp$` (a field in the record with the lower number) is less than `LocationRec$` (a field in the record with the lower number).

A bubble sort is not efficient, but it is simple to program and easy to understand. A detailed discussion of the many types of sorting routines is beyond the scope of this book.

The program opens with a request for the disk drive and the name of the file. The file is then opened, and you are prompted to press a key to see what is in the drive. This sequence is shown in the following output:

```
Disk drive: ? a:
File opened name with extension: ? codes.rdm

The file is open.

Press a key to see the file.
```

When you press a key, the file (as read from the DATA statements) is displayed with a prompt to press a key to sort the file. As you see in the following output, the records are not in alphabetical order. When you press a key, the file is sorted. The sorted file is not displayed immediately. Instead, another prompt appears, telling you to press a key to see the file.

```
Records in the file:

Japan, Hiroshima       81   82
Japan, Tokyo           81   3
Korea, Pusan           82   51
Japan, Yokohama        81   45
China, Peking          86   1
China, Shanghai        86   21
Hong Kong, Sha Tin     852  0
China, Canton          86   20
Korea, Seoul           82   2
Taiwan, Taipei         886  2
Taiwan, Kohsiung       886  7
Hong Kong, Kowloon     852  3
Hong Kong, Hong Kong   852  5

Press a key to sort the file.

Press a key to see the file.
```

When you press Press a key, the screen is cleared. The sorted file appears as shown in the following output:

```
Records in the file:

China, Canton          86   20
China, Peking          86   1
China, Shanghai        86   21
Hong Kong, Hong Kong   852  5
Hong Kong, Kowloon     852  3
Hong Kong, Sha Tin     852  0
Japan, Hiroshima       81   82
Japan, Tokyo           81   3
Japan, Yokohama        81   45
Korea, Pusan           82   51
Korea, Seoul           82   2
Taiwan, Kohsiung       886  7
Taiwan, Taipei         886  2

The file is closed.
Press a key
```

As you can see, the file is sorted according to the first field (country and city) in ascending alphabetical order. China appears as the first country. The cities also are subordered in ascending alphabetical order. The phone codes have moved along with the country and city names.

Summary

Random-access files store string data as ASCII text. However, numeric data is stored in IEEE format. Records have fixed lengths. Each record is subdivided into fields, the formats of which are specified in a FIELD statement. When you specify the lengths of the fields, they are fixed at that length. When data for a field has fewer characters than the specified field length, the field is padded with blank spaces.

A random-access file is opened by an OPEN statement, which specifies the record length to be used in the file. The record length is the sum of the lengths of all fields. While a file is open, you can write to the file and read from the file.

You use LSET and RSET to load the variables specified in the FIELD statement (field variables) with data. A PUT statement then writes the records to the file. Here are sample statements used to create a random-access file:

```
OPEN FileName$ FOR RANDOM AS #1 LEN = 16
FIELD #1, 14 AS Fcountry$, 2 AS Fcode$
LSET Fcountry$ = country$
LSET Fcode$ = MKI$(code)
PUT #1, record
```

The process of reading records from a random-access file is simpler than the process of writing records. The record is read from the file with a GET statement. You can retrieve, replace, or alter individual records in a random-access file. You also can add records to a random-access file. Records in a random-access file lend themselves to easier manipulation (which includes sorting) than sequential files.

You also can print the records. Any numeric data can be converted from the file's string format to numeric format in the PRINT statement. For example

```
GET #1, record
PRINT Fcountry$; CVI(Fcode$)
```

Use the knowledge you acquired in this chapter to solve the exercises that follow.

Exercises

1. What is the difference between the way string data and numeric data are stored in random-access files?

2. Which type of file (sequential or random-access) is the most portable?

3. Is it necessary to specify a random-access file's record length in the statement that opens the file?

4. Load Listing 11.1 and delete the length of the record so that the OPEN statement reads

   ```
   OPEN FileName$ FOR RANDOM AS #1
   ```

   Before you run the revised program, guess the value that is printed by

   ```
   PRINT "LOF for "; FileName$; " is "; LOF(1)
   ```

   After you've guessed, run the program to see whether your guess is correct.

5. If an open random-access file has five records containing names in field one and numbers in field two, write one statement to retrieve the fourth record in the file. Write a second statement to print the record. Use the field variables FName$ and FPhone$.

6. Modify Listing 11.4 so that you can enter the record numbers of any two files and exchange the records.

7. Modify the SwitchFile SUB procedure in Listing 11.5 so that China and its phone code are switched from the top of the file to the bottom, one step at a time. Use Listing 11.1 to load the original file.

Chapter 12

Graphics

You have seen that a limited kind of graphics can be used in the text mode to draw borders around messages or to make an attractive menu. This chapter discusses other screen modes devoted to producing graphics.

You can create a variety of patterns, colors, and shapes with PowerBASIC Lite graphics statements and functions. Graphics add a new dimension to text-oriented programs, whether they are games, educational tools, math and science applications, or business applications.

This chapter covers the following topics:

- Graphics cards and adapters

- Graphics screen modes

- Locating a graphics position on the screen

- Using basic graphics tools, such as points, lines, and circles

- Coloring the interior of a figure

- Plotting graphs

- Saving and using graphics images

Graphics Cards and Adapters

To run the graphics programs in this book, your computer must have a graphics adapter, such as a Color Graphics Adapter (CGA), an Extended Graphics Adapter (EGA), or a Video Graphics Adapter (VGA). To reach the largest possible number of readers, most of the demonstrations in this book are limited to graphics screen modes 1 and 2, which are common to all the graphics adapters mentioned in the preceding list. Programs written using screen modes 1 and 2 can be altered for other screen modes if your adapter can handle them.

To change to a different screen mode, change the screen mode number in the SCREEN statements used in the program. Change SCREEN *n* to the appropriate number (*n*). All other graphics statements must conform to the screen coordinates and colors available as described in this chapter.

A PowerBASIC Lite program can display text and complex, colorful graphics on the screen. However, the program must work within the constraints of the display hardware available to it. PowerBASIC Lite supports the following classes of video interfaces:

- Monochrome Display Adapter (monochrome text only).

- Color Graphics Adapter (CGA) or Enhanced Graphics Adapter (EGA). Both produce text and graphics in color and in black and white.

- Multicolor Graphics Array Adapter (MCGA), which runs on IBM's Personal System/2 Models 25 and 30.

- Video Graphics Array Adapter (VGA).

- Hercules Graphics Adapter (monochrome graphics and text).

Table 12.1 shows the screen modes, text format, available colors, and pixel resolution for various graphics adapters.

Table 12.1. Graphics adapter characteristics.

Adapter	Mode	Text Format	Colors	Resolution
Monochrome	0	80 col	16	80 × 25
CGA	0	40/80 col	16	80 × 25
	1	40 col	4	320 × 200
	2	80 col	2	640 × 200
EGA	0	40/80 col	16	80 × 25
	1	40 col	4	320 × 200
	2	80 col	2	640 × 200
	7	40 col	16	320 × 200
	8	80 col	16	640 × 200
	9	80 col	4/16	640 × 350
	10	80 col	mono	640 × 350

Adapter	Mode	Text Format	Colors	Resolution
MCGA	0	40/80 col	16	80×25
	1	40 col	4	320×200
	2	80 col	2	640×200
	11	80×30	mono	640×480
VGA	0	40/80 col	16	80×25
	1	40 col	4	320×200
	2	80 col	2	640×200
	7	40 col	16	320×200
	8	80 col	16	640×200
	9	80 col	4/16	640×350
	10	80 col	mono	640×350
	11	80×30	mono	640×480
	12	80×30	16	640×480
Hercules	0	80 col	3	80×25
	2	80 col	2	720×350
	3	80 col	2	720×350

Note: PowerBASIC Lite uses the SCREEN and WIDTH statements to select particular modes. Of course, the video adapter in your computer must support the selected mode. Consult your computer and monitor manuals to see what type of adapter you have.

Graphics Screen Modes

In the past, most software was designed to work within the constraints of the CGA display modes so that the software could be sold to a wider market. Today, the use of VGA and extended VGA graphics hardware is more prevalent. With its superior resolution and color selection, support for VGA is increasing.

In the preceding chapters, programs used screen mode 0 (the text mode), which is the default screen mode. Most adapters can utilize screen modes 1 and 2. Therefore, the discussions in this chapter therefore emphasize those modes. However, screen mode 7 (EGA or VGA) and screen mode 12 (VGA) also are used.

The greatest difference between graphics modes is the number of colors available and the *pixel* resolution. A pixel is a picture element: It is the smallest unit on the screen that can be turned on, turned off, or colored. For example, screen mode 1 has a resolution of 320 columns and 200 rows of pixels that can be displayed, which results in 64,000 different pixel positions. In contrast, 25 rows of 80 characters provides 2,000 different character positions in the text mode.

The pixel positions of a graphics screen are numbered, by default, from the upper-left corner of the screen. Counting begins with zero (0). Thus, the pixel in the upper-left corner of the screen is labeled (0,0), by its column and row position. The pixels in each corner of the display for screen mode 1 are

Upper-left corner: (0,0)   Upper-right corner: (319,0)

Lower-left corner: (0,199)   Lower-right corner: (319,199)

The maximum values for the column and row pixels are greater for graphics screen modes that have greater resolution.

Setting up a Graphics Screen

PowerBASIC Lite provides statements that define the graphics screen before drawing begins. These "set-up" statements define screen characteristics such as the coordinate system, the background color on which drawings are made, and the foreground colors used for text and drawing. The set-up statements are discussed as they are introduced. Set-up statements include

| CLS | COLOR | PALETTE | PALETTE USING |
| SCREEN | VIEW | WIDTH | WINDOW |

As shown in Table 12.1, the resolution (pixel size) varies for different screen modes. The table also shows that the number of available colors varies from mode to mode. The set colors that can be used are called the color *palette.* Just as an artist paints from the colors on his palette, the computer draws in colors from the palette that is defined by set-up statements.

Drawing Tools

When the screen is set up, several graphics statements provide tools for drawing. All graphics figures are composed of points, lines, curves (parts of circles), and circles, or a combination of these basic components. Table 12.3 lists the graphic drawing tools and their functions.

Table 12.2. Drawing tools.

Statement	Function
CIRCLE	Draws all or part of a circle.
DRAW	A mini drawing-language interpreter.
GET	Loads an image from the screen to a pixel-based image array.
LINE	Draws a line or a box, when given two positions.
PAINT	Fills an enclosed area with a solid color or pattern.
PMAP	Performs mapping between physical and world coordinates.
POINT	Returns information about a point.
PRESET	Plots a point (default = attribute 0).
PSET	Plots a point (default = maximum attribute for the current screen mode).
PUT	Copies a pixel-based image array to the screen.

Setting the Screen and Using Some Tools

Let's begin with SCREEN 1 and create a simple program that draws a point within a circle, all of which is within a rectangle. This process uses all the basic drawing statements: PSET, CIRCLE, and LINE. The background color and the set of colors (palette) in screen mode 1 is specified by the COLOR statement which has the following syntax for screen mode 1.

```
COLOR [Background][, Palette]
```

The value of Background is an integer in the range 0-15. Colors available in screen mode 1 are the same as those shown in Table 7.1 of Chapter 7, "Program Control Structures."

The value used for Palette is either 0 or 1. Table 12.3 shows the colors available for each palette. The color assigned to color number zero (0) should be the color specified by Background in the COLOR statement.

Table 12.3. The color values for screen mode 1.

Color	Palette 0	Palette 1
0	Background	Background
1	Green	Cyan
2	Red	Magenta
3	Brown	White

The colors in Table 12.4 are foreground colors, used in graphics statements such as CIRCLE and LINE to draw shapes on the background colored screen. Of course, only color numbers 1, 2, and 3 are visible on the background color. Foreground color 0 can be used to erase a shape drawn previously in colors 1, 2, or 3.

The drawings in Listing 12.1 are first made using the colors of palette 0 as selected by

```
COLOR 0, 0              ' black background (0), palette 0
```

The PSET, CIRCLE, and LINE statements are executed in a FOR/NEXT loop of the UseTools SUB with the foreground color being changed for each pass through the loop. A 1.5-second time delay occurs between color changes. When each color has been used, the palette is changed to one (1) by

```
COLOR 0, 1              ' black background(0), palette 1
```

The UseTools SUB is called again to execute the graphics statements in each of the colors of palette 1.

Listing 12.1. Demonstrating SCREEN 1 colors.

```
REM ** Demonstrate SCREEN 1 Colors **
' Learning BASIC, Chapter 12.  File: PBL1201.BAS

REM ** Initialize **
SCREEN 1
COLOR 0, 0

REM ** Main program **
CALL UseTools
COLOR 0, 1
CALL UseTools
LOCATE 18, 3
```

```
PRINT "Press a key"
END

SUB UseTools
  FOR num = 1 TO 3
    PSET(40 + 60 * num, 100), num
    CIRCLE(40 + 60 * num, 100), 15, num
    LINE(20 + 60 * num, 80)-(60 + 60 * num, 120), num, B
    DELAY 1.5
  NEXT num
  CLS
END SUB
```

Screen mode 1 is selected in the Initialize block. The background color is set to black (0) and the palette is set to (0) by a COLOR statement.

```
SCREEN 1 COLOR (0, 0)
```

The main program block calls the UseTools procedure next. A FOR/NEXT loop sets the color attributes used for the drawing: first 1, then 2, and then 3. A point is set. Then a circle is drawn with that point as its center and a radius of 15. A rectangle enclosing both the circle and the point is then drawn. PowerBASIC's DELAY statement is then used to allow you 1.5 seconds to see the color change.

The DELAY statement suspends program execution for a specified number of seconds. The number of seconds can be specified in either integer arguments or floating-point arguments. Fractional delays are accepted. The time resolution is approximately .054 seconds. Most other languages require an empty DO loop and the TIMER function to time a delay loop such as

```
start! = TIMER
DO WHILE TIMER < start + 1.5
LOOP
```

The DELAY statement is much quicker and easier to write.

The syntax for each of the drawing tools used in the program follows:

```
PSET [STEP](column, row)[, color]
CIRCLE [STEP](column, row), radius [,color_
       [, start, end[aspect]]]
LINE [STEP][column1, row1)]-[STEP](column2, row2)_
     [,[color][, B[F]][, pattern]]
```

The STEP option is not used in any of the statements in this program. Neither are the *start*, *end*, nor *aspect* options in the CIRCLE statement nor the *F* or *pattern* options in the LINE statement. You can access the PSET, CIRCLE, and LINE statements from the Help system to read about the function of these options.

The important thing to notice is that graphics pixel positions are referenced by column and row, in that order. This is the reverse from the order of row and column character positions in a text statement such as LOCATE. In addition, the column and row values are enclosed in parentheses in graphics statements.

```
LOCATE row, column        ' text statement
PSET(column, row)         ' graphics statement
```

The *column* and *row* values can be numeric expressions, as in the *column* value of the following PSET statement, which is used in Listing 12.1:

```
PSET(40 + 60 * num, 100)
```

When *num* equals 1, the *column* value is 100. When *num* equals 2, the *column* value is 160. When *num* equals 3, the *column* value is 220. Therefore, each set of drawings is placed at a different horizontal position on the screen. Figure 12.1 shows the three sets of drawings on the screen.

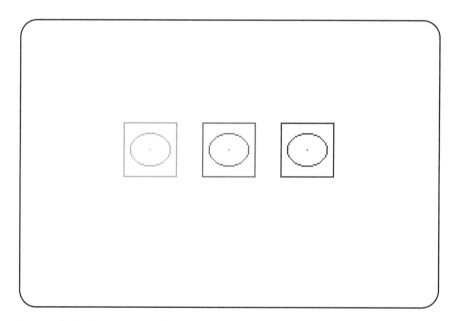

Figure 12.1. The output of Listing 12.1.

After all three sets have been drawn, the main program uses a COLOR statement to change the palette number to 1.

```
COLOR 0, 1
```

The `UseTools` procedure is called again, and you see a new set of colors used. The drawings are the same as those shown in Figure 12.1, except that the colors are different.

Locating Graphics Positions

Because the maximum values for graphics screen coordinates vary from one screen mode to another, the relative position of a figure on display can become confusing.

For example, in screen mode 1, the coordinates (160, 100) are at the approximate center of the screen. In screen mode 2, however, the same coordinates (160, 100) are at the approximate midpoint of the left half of the screen. The approximate center of screen mode 2 is (320, 100). In addition, you often work with graphs of data that have dimensions which do not reasonably match the dimensions of the screen. Therefore, you must scale each coordinate to fit the display properly. Another problem with the default screen numbering is that data to be plotted may need a zero reference near the middle of the screen rather than in the upper-left corner.

You can eliminate these positioning and scaling problems in many cases with one PowerBASIC Lite statement: `WINDOW`. The `WINDOW` statement has the following syntax:

```
WINDOW [[SCREEN](column1, row1)-(column2, row2)]
```

If you use the SCREEN option, (`column1, row1`) defines the upper-left corner of the screen and (`column2, row2`) defines the lower-right corner of the screen.

If you don't use the SCREEN option, (`column1, row1`) defines the lower-left corner of the screen and (`column2, row2`) defines the upper-right corner of the screen.

You can choose the values of column1, row1, column2, and row2. Therefore, you can use the `WINDOW` statement to position your drawing. You scale the screen to fit your drawing's dimensions instead of scaling each drawing to fit the screen's dimensions.

Suppose you want to graph the trigonometric sine function. This function is never larger than 1 or smaller than –1. The `WINDOW` statement can easily scale the screen to fit the graph of the function. The following lines of code define an appropriate window to graph two cycles of PowerBASIC Lite's `SIN` function.

```
SCREEN 1: CLS: pi = 3.141593
WINDOW(-2 * pi, -2)-(2 * pi, 2)
LINE(-2 * pi, 0)-(2 * pi, 0): LINE(0, -2)-(0, 2)
FOR column = -2 * pi TO 2 * pi STEP .025
  PSET(column, SIN(column)), 2
NEXT column
```

303

The graph drawn by these lines is shown in Figure 12.2. The graph fits neatly within the screen's boundaries, which are defined by the WINDOW statement.

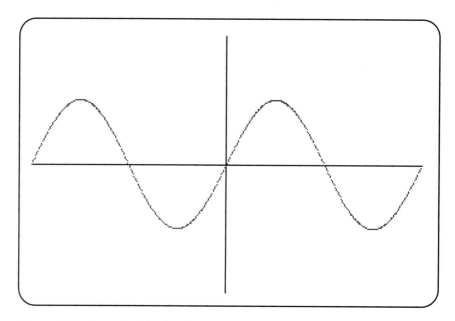

Figure 12.2. A graph of the SIN function.

The lower-left corner of the screen is (–2 * pi, –2), and the upper-right corner of the screen is (2 * pi, 2). In addition to fitting well when SCREEN 1 is used, the graph is displayed in the same relative position when the same WINDOW statement is used in any other screen mode.

Correlating Text and Graphics Positions

You will often create graphics displays that need some added textual information. For instance, when you create a bar graph, you need labels to indicate what the bars represent and a scale to indicate the magnitude of the bars. You also will want to add a title to the graph.

In screen mode 2, coordinates for locating text characters for an 80-character line begin at row 1, column 1 (the upper-left corner of the screen) and end at row 25, column 80 (the lower-right corner of the screen). It is difficult to coordinate these text positions with graphics coordinates that begin with (0, 0) in the upper-left corner of the screen and end at (639, 199) in the lower-right corner of the screen.

You can't change the positioning of the text characters, but you can define a graphics screen to match the text coordinates by using an appropriate WINDOW statement. For example,

```
WINDOW SCREEN(1, 1)-(80, 25)
```

Because the SCREEN option is used in this WINDOW statement, the first pair of coordinates is interpreted as the upper-left corner of the graphics screen and the second pair is interpreted as the lower-right corner of the graphics screen. The statement matches graphics positions with the text positions in an 80-by-25-pixel screen. The program in Listing 12.2 shows how the statement places a rectangle around a text menu in screen mode 2, which is a two-color graphics mode.

Listing 12.2. Menu window number 1.

```
REM ** Menu Window Number 1 **
' Learning BASIC, Chapter 12.  File: PBL1202.BAS

REM ** Initialize **
SCREEN 2: CLS
DEFINT A-Z
WINDOW SCREEN(1, 1)-(80, 25)

REM ** Main program **
CALL Menu
END

SUB Menu
  DO
    LOCATE 10, 30: PRINT "1. Draw a Circle"
    LOCATE 11, 30: PRINT "2. Draw a Rectangle"
    LOCATE 12, 30: PRINT "3. Quit"
    LINE(28, 9)-(50, 13),, B
    LOCATE 15, 24: PRINT "Press the number of your choice."
    kbd$ = INPUT$(1)
    SELECT CASE kbd$
      CASE "1"
        CALL CircleDraw
      CASE "2"
        CALL RectDraw
      CASE "3"
        EXIT LOOP
      CASE ELSE
        CALL Message
    END SELECT
  LOOP
END SUB
```

continues

Listing 12.2. (continued)

```
SUB CircleDraw
  CLS: CIRCLE(40, 13), 5
  LOCATE 20, 34: PRINT "Wait patiently"
  DELAY 4: CLS
END SUB

SUB RectDraw
  CLS: LINE(25, 8)-(55, 18) , , B
  LOCATE 20, 34: PRINT "Wait patiently"
  DELAY 4: CLS
END SUB

SUB Message
  LOCATE 20, 27: PRINT "Wrong keypress, try again"
END SUB
```

The screen coordinates are defined in the Initialize block. The Main program block then calls the Menu procedure. Three menu choices are displayed on lines 10, 11, and 12 of the screen.

```
LOCATE 10, 30: PRINT "1. Draw a Circle"
LOCATE 11, 30: PRINT "2. Draw a Rectangle"
LOCATE 12, 30: PRINT "3. Quit"
```

Because the top line of text is at row 10, you can place the upper side of the rectangle at row 9. The last line of the menu is at row 12, so you can place the lower side of the rectangle at row 13. All text lines begin at column 30. The longest text line is 19 characters. The sides of the rectangles can be placed at column 28 (two character positions left of the text starting the column) and at column 50 (two character positions to the right of the last character of the longest text line). The LINE statement performs the job of drawing the rectangle.

```
LINE(28, 9)-(50, 13),, B
```

Notice that even though no color value is given in this statement, the statement uses two commas to indicate that the default color is to be used. If the extra comma is omitted, the letter *B* is interpreted as a variable having a value that is the color number to be used for drawing.

Directions for using the menu are placed on line 15 just below the menu rectangle. Figure 12.3 shows the menu on-screen.

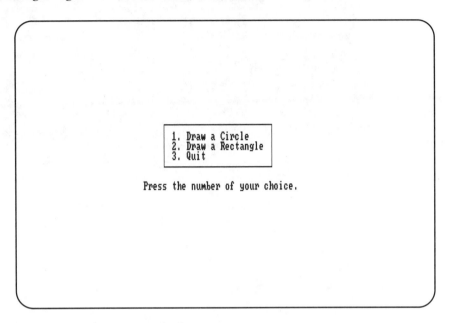

Figure 12.3. The menu on display.

The SELECT CASE structure is used to call appropriate procedures to match your menu choices. One of these procedures (Message) displays an appropriate message if you make an incorrect keypress. Two of the procedures draw figures and provide a four-second time delay. When you select menu choice 3, the called procedure contains an EXIT LOOP statement that leads to the end of the program.

Graphing Temperatures

In Chapter 7, "Program Control Structures," you used two programs that simulated a temperature controller. In those programs, the changing temperatures were printed on the screen in a colored rectangle. The program in Listing 12.3 is another version of those programs. This time a plot of the changing temperatures is graphed.

Listing 12.3. Temperature-control simulation number 3.

```
REM ** Temperature Control Simulation Number 3 **
' Learning BASIC, Chapter 12.  File: PBL1203.BAS

REM ** Initialize **
SCREEN 2: CLS: DEFINT A-Z
WINDOW(0, 10)-(100, 30)
RANDOMIZE TIMER: temp! = 20

REM ** Main program **
DO
  CLS: column = 4
  LINE(2, 18)-(98, 18): LINE(2, 22)-(98, 22)
  PSET(column, temp!)
  DO
    DO WHILE temp! < 22 AND temp! > 18
      change! = RND - .5
      temp! = temp! + change!
      DELAY .2
      LINE -(column, temp!): INCR column
      IF column > 98 THEN EXIT LOOP
    LOOP
    IF column > 98 THEN
        EXIT LOOP
      ELSEIF temp! < 18 THEN
        CALL HeatOn (temp!, column)
      ELSE
        CALL ColdOn (temp!, column)
    END IF
  LOOP
  'Quit or continue
  LOCATE 20, 2
  PRINT "Press Q to quit; any other key to continue";
  kbd$ = UCASE$(INPUT$(1))
  IF kbd$ = "Q" THEN EXIT LOOP
LOOP
END

SUB HeatOn(temp!, column)
  LOCATE 2, 2: PRINT "Heater On"
  DO WHILE temp! < 20
    SOUND 900, .3
    temp! = temp! + .5
    DELAY .2
    LINE -(column, temp!): INCR column
  LOOP
  LOCATE 2, 2: PRINT SPACE$(9)
END SUB
```

```
SUB ColdOn(temp!, column)
  LOCATE 2, 2: PRINT "Cooler On"
  DO WHILE temp! > 20
    SOUND 200, .8
    temp! = temp! - .5
    DELAY .2
    LINE -(column, temp!): INCR column
  LOOP
  LOCATE 2, 2: PRINT SPACE$(9)
END SUB
```

A WINDOW statement in the Initialize block sets the screen coordinates to reasonable boundaries for graphing the temperatures. The coordinate of the lower-left corner of the screen is (0, 10), whereas the coordinate of the upper-right corner of the screen is (100, 30).

```
WINDOW(0, 10)-(100, 30)
```

Boundaries for the normal temperatures are drawn by LINE statements.

```
LINE(2, 18)-(98, 18): LINE(2, 22)-(98, 22)
```

A PSET statement is used to "turn on" the first temperature value.

```
PSET(column, temp!)
```

An abbreviated form of the LINE statement connects each succeeding point until it reaches the right side of the screen.

```
LINE -(column, temp!): INCR column
IF column > 98 THEN EXIT LOOP
```

This form of the LINE statement tells the computer to draw a line from the last point that was referenced to the specified point. The column value is then incremented by 1 in preparation for connecting the next temperature value. A test is made to see whether the right side of the screen has been reached.

When the plot reaches the right side of the screen, you have a choice of quitting the program or continuing. If you continue, the screen is erased and a new plot begins. If you press the letter **Q**, the screen is cleared and the program ends. Figure 12.4 shows a graph of one complete plot across the screen.

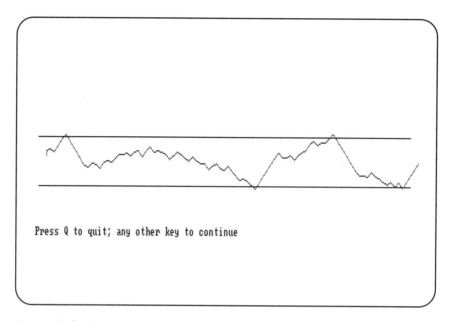

Press Q to quit; any other key to continue

Figure 12.4. The temperature plot from Listing 12.3.

Using the POINT Function

You can determine the characteristics of any point on the graphics screen with the POINT function. Table 12.4 shows various formats of the function and the result of using each format.

Table 12.4. POINT function formats.

Format	Result
x = POINT(0)	Returns the column screen coordinate of the last referenced point.
y = POINT(1)	Returns the row screen coordinate of the last referenced point.
x = POINT(2)	Returns the column world coordinate (WINDOW definition) of the last referenced point.
y = POINT(3)	Returns the row world coordinate (WINDOW definition) of the last referenced point.
kolor = POINT(x,y)	Returns the attribute value (color) of the pixel at (x,y).

Three forms of the POINT function are used in Listing 12.4. Two hundred points of random colors are placed on the screen at random positions. Then the function calls a procedure to seek the locations and colors of the points. The program uses two statements containing POINT functions. The first is

```
IF POINT(column, row) <> 0 THEN
```

This form of the POINT function determines the color number of the point at (*column*, *row*). The second statement containing a POINT function is

```
x = POINT(0): y = POINT(1)
```

These statements detect the coordinates of the point at the current screen position (*x*, *y*).

The program in Listing 12.4 sets random colored points on the screen in an area near the center of the screen. A procedure then is called to detect where the points are and what their color is.

Listing 12.4. POINT demonstration number 1.

```
REM ** POINT Demonstration Number 1 **
' Learning BASIC, Chapter 12.  File: PBL1204.BAS

REM ** Initialize **
SCREEN 1: CLS
DEFINT A-Z: RANDOMIZE TIMER

REM ** Main program **
FOR number = 1 TO 200
   column = RND * 40 + 140
   row = RND * 40 + 80
   kolor = RND * 3 + 1
   PSET(column, row), kolor
NEXT number
LOCATE 22, 2: PRINT "Press Spacebar to find points."
DO
kbd$ = INPUT$(1)
LOOP UNTIL kbd$ = CHR$(32)
CALL FindPoints
END

SUB FindPoints
   LOCATE 22, 2: PRINT "Press Spacebar to end"; SPACE$(9);
   DO UNTIL INKEY$ = CHR$(32)
      column = RND * 40 + 140
      row = RND * 40 + 80
      IF POINT(column, row) <> 0 THEN
         kolor = POINT(column, row)
```

continues

311

Listing 12.4. (continued)

```
        PRESET(column, row)
        x = POINT(0): y = POINT(1)
        LOCATE 2, 2: PRINT x; y; kolor
        SOUND 200 * kolor, .25
        DELAY .25
      END IF
  LOOP
END SUB
```

Figure 12.5 shows the points as they are placed on the screen by a run of the program. The message at the bottom of the screen is displayed after all 200 points are placed. An INPUT$(1) function keeps the display static until you press a key.

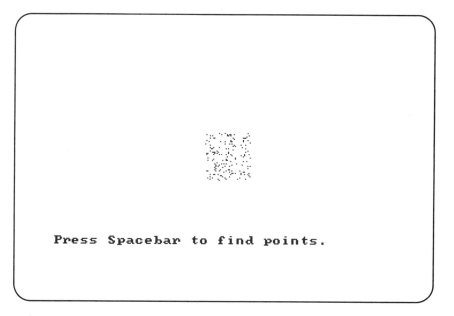

Figure 12.5. The original distribution of colored points.

The FindPoints procedure searches the random points. If the selected point is the same color as the background, the block IF structure is not executed. If the point is not the same color as the background, a series of actions takes place.

- A POINT statement detects the color of a point. Because color is a PowerBASIC reserved word (keyword), it cannot be used as a variable name.

```
kolor = POINT(column, row)=
```

- The point is turned off by a PRESET statement.

```
PRESET(column, row)
```

- POINT functions detect the location of the point.

```
x = POINT(0): y = POINT(1)
```

- The location and color of the point are printed in the upper-left corner of the screen.

```
LOCATE 2, 2: PRINT x; y; kolor
```

- The program makes a sound, the frequency of which depends on the point's color.

```
SOUND 200 * kolor, .25
```

- The program is interrupted for .25 seconds.

```
DELAY .25
```

Therefore, the number of points left on the screen gradually decreases until there are none. Each time a point is removed, its location is printed and a sound is made. Because the area containing the points is small, the search does not take long. Figure 12.6 shows the screen after the number of points has been reduced.

For those who like more colorful points, the program in Listing 12.5 uses screen mode 12 to provide 15 colors in addition to the background color. This program is similar to the one in Listing 12.4. However, the size of the rectangular area in which the points are placed is larger. There is no limit to the number of points placed on the screen.

```
  147   96   2




                                        ·: ··:
                                      ·.   ·· ·:
                                       ·. · ··:
                                        : ·.:·
                                      ·  : ··
                                       ·.: ·.


   Press Spacebar to end
```

Figure 12.6. The screen with some points removed.

Listing 12.5. POINT demonstration number 2.

```
REM ** POINT Demonstration Number 2 **
' Learning BASIC, Chapter 12.  File: PBL1205.BAS

REM ** Initialize **
SCREEN 12: CLS
DEFINT A-Z: RANDOMIZE TIMER

REM ** Main program **
LOCATE 22, 2: PRINT "Press Spacebar to end"
DO UNTIL INKEY$ = CHR$(32)
  column = RND * 80 + 280
  row = RND * 80 + 200
  kolor = RND * 15 + 1
  pcolor = POINT(column, row)
  IF pcolor = 0 THEN
    PSET(column, row), kolor
    SOUND 50 * kolor + 50, .025
  END IF
LOOP
END
```

Random values are selected for column, row, and color. Then the program can detect the color of the point at the selected column and row.

```
pcolor = POINT(column, row)
```

If the point is the same color as the background, it is set to a different color and a sound is made. If the point has a different color than the background, it retains that color.

If screen mode 12 is unavailable to you, you can modify the program for another screen. For example, screen mode 1 requires the following changes:

```
SCREEN 1: CLS
column = RND * 80 + 120
row = RND * 80 + 60
kolor = RND * 3 + 1
```

Enter the program and run it. As each new point is set, the program makes a sound. The frequency of the sound depends on the color selected for the point. Let the program run for some time. When the rectangular area is nearly filled with colored points, you will notice that the time between sounds increases. This time increases because the computer must look at several points before it finds one that needs to be colored.

Using a Painting Tool: The PAINT Statement

Another graphics tool you can use to make your programs more colorful is the PAINT statement.

```
PAINT(column, row), kolor, boundary
```

In this statement, painting begins at the point indicated by (column, row) with the specified color (kolor) and continues until reaching the color specified by boundary. You must be sure that the figure being painted is completely closed and that the starting point is within the enclosed figure. Otherwise, paint spills all over the screen.

The following block of code draws a rectangle, using color 15 in screen mode 12. The LINE statement uses the B option, which specifies that the coordinates be used as opposite corners for drawing a rectangle (box) rather than end points for a line. The interior of the rectangle is painted in 15 other colors, with a 1.5 second time delay separating each painting.

```
SCREEN 12: CLS: DEFINT A-Z
LINE(260, 180)-(380, 300), 15, B
FOR kolor = 0 TO 14
  PAINT(320, 240), kolor, 15
  DELAY 1.5
NEXT kolor
CLS: END
```

If you cannot use screen mode 12, appropriate changes must be made for SCREEN, LINE, PAINT, and the upper limit of the FOR/NEXT loop. For example, the following block shows the necessary changes when you want to use screen mode 1. The screen number is changed, the coordinates for the LINE and PAINT statements are changed to conform with the screen mode limits, and the color number range for kolor is decreased due to the limits of screen mode 1.

```
SCREEN 1: CLS: DEFINT A-Z
LINE (130, 90)-(190, 150), 3, B
FOR kolor = 0 TO 2
  PAINT (160, 120), kolor, 3
  DELAY 1.5
NEXT kolor
CLS: END
```

Enter the program segment, run it, and sit back and enjoy the color changes. You can use the PAINT statement to provide different background colors for text, such as on menus.

Image Movement: GET and PUT

The image of a graphics figure drawn on the screen can be saved in an array by a graphics GET statement. You can then place the image anywhere on the screen with a graphics PUT statement.

The syntax for a GET statement is

```
GET(column1, row1)-(column2, row2), ArrayName
```

The upper-left corner of a rectangle that includes the image is defined by the coordinates (column1, row1). The lower-right corner of the same rectangle is defined by the coordinates (column2, row2). The array's name is placed at the end of the statement.

Because the image is to be stored in an array, you must dimension the array before it can be used. This requires some arithmetic to calculate the number of elements in the array. You start by calculating the number of bytes needed for the image. This is defined by the following equation:

```
Bytes = 4 + height * INT((width * BPP + 7) / 8)
```

where *BPP* is bits per pixel, height is the number of vertical pixels (rows) in the image, and width is the number of horizontal pixels (columns) in the image.

Table 12.5 lists the number of bits per pixel for each screen mode.

Table 12.5. Values for calculating bytes in an array.

Screen Mode	Bits Per Pixel
1	2
2	1
3	1
7	4
8	4
9	4
10	2
11	1
12	4

Let's use a rectangle defined by the following statement as an example.

```
LINE(12, 12)-(28, 20), 2, BF
```

The F added to the B option in the LINE statement tells the computer to fill the rectangle with the same color with which it was drawn (color 2 in this example).

The *width* of this rectangle is 17 ($28 - 12 + 1$). The *height* is 9 ($20 - 12 + 1$). The number of vertical pixels (height) includes rows 12 through 20 inclusive (rows 12, 13, 14, 15, 16, 17, 18, 19, and 20 = 9 rows). Therefore, you must add 1 to the difference $20 - 12$. The same is true for the number of horizontal pixels (columns 12-28 inclusive is 17 columns). The values for *planes* and *BPP* depend on the screen mode used. For screen mode 1, the number of planes is 1 and *BPP* is 2. Therefore, the calculation is

```
Bytes = 4 + height * planes * INT((width * BPP + 7) / 8)
Bytes = 4 + 9 * 1 * INT((17 * 2 + 7) / 8)
      = 4 + 9 * INT(41 / 8)
      = 4 + 9 * 5
      = 49
```

An integer array uses two bytes for each element. Therefore, the number of elements in the array are $49/2 = 25$ elements (rounded upward). You can use a larger dimension than the one calculated. To ensure that all elements will fit, the array in this example is dimensioned for a maximum subscript of 26.

```
DIM rectangle(26)
```

Calculating the dimensions of the image array is the hardest part of creating and moving a graphics figure. The rest is easy. To create and save the array from the previous example, you need only these three statements:

```
DIM box(26)                   ' box is the array's name
LINE(12, 12)-(28, 20), 2, BF  ' draw the color-filled box
GET(12, 12)-(28, 20), box     ' save the array
```

Now comes the fun. You can place the image, which is saved in the array, at any place on the screen with a graphics PUT statement. For example, to place the image near the center of the screen, you use

```
PUT(152, 96), box
```

The column and row values (152, 96) used in the PUT statement define where to place the upper-left corner of the rectangle. You do not need to specify the lower-right corner in this statement.

One good thing about the PUT statement is that it has an option (XOR) which you can use to erase a previously placed image. For example, if you place an image on the screen with the previous PUT statement, you can erase the image by using a second statement with the same coordinates and the XOR option.

```
PUT(152, 96), box, XOR
```

In this manner, you can create the illusion of a moving object by placing an image, erasing it, placing it in a new place, erasing it, placing in it another new place, and so on. The PUT statement has other options: PSET, PRSET, OR, and AND. See the Help system for information on these options.

The program in Listing 12.6 uses the statements discussed in this section to move a rectangle (filled with color) back and forth through a maze that is displayed on the screen.

Listing 12.6. Moving a box about.

```
REM ** Move a Box about **
' Learning BASIC, Chapter 12.  File: PBL1206.BAS

REM ** Initialize **
SCREEN 1: CLS
DEFINT A-Z
DIM box(26)

REM ** Main program **
' Draw box and save in array
LINE(12, 12)-(28, 20), 2, BF
GET(12, 11)-(28, 20), box
CLS
' Draw Maze
LINE(12, 12)-(318, 12)
FOR row = 22 to 162 STEP 20
  LINE(12, row)-(302, row)
  LINE(29, row + 10)-(318, row + 10)
NEXT row
LINE(12, 182)-(302, 182)
LINE(12, 192)-(318, 192)
LINE(12, 22)-(12, 182)
LINE(318, 12)-(318, 192)
row = 12
' Move the box through the maze
DO UNTIL row > 182
  FOR column = 12 to 302 STEP 5
    PUT(column, row), box
    DELAY .05
    PUT(column, row), box, XOR
  NEXT column
  row = row + 10
  FOR column = 302 to 12 STEP -5
    PUT(column, row), box
    DELAY .05
    PUT(column, row), box, XOR
  NEXT column
  row = row + 10
LOOP
END
```

The program begins with the rectangle in the upper-left corner of the maze. As the rectangle reaches the end of one line of the maze, it drops to the next row and travels in the opposite direction. The rectangle works its way from the top to the bottom of the screen. The rectangle in Figure 12.7 is near the midway point of the maze.

319

Figure 12.7. The rectangle midway through the maze.

If you are patient, the rectangle eventually reaches the bottom row and leaves the maze at the bottom-left of the screen. The rectangle is shown near the end of the maze in Figure 12.8.

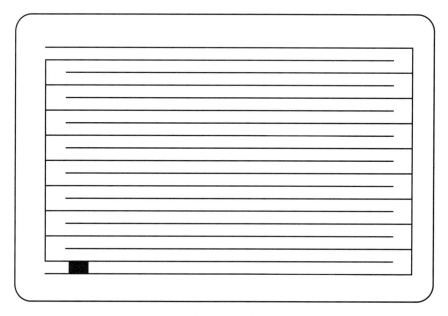

Figure 12.8. The rectangle is near the end of the maze.

You can use the WINDOW statement with GET and PUT, but the calculation for the dimensions of the array must use the default screen coordinates of the current graphics mode. Because the calculation must be made using screen coordinates, the program uses the same coordinate system to avoid confusion.

You also must be sure that the execution of a PUT statement places the image in a position that is entirely within the screen boundaries. PUT images are not clipped like other graphic figures. An error message occurs when a part of the image lies outside the screen's boundaries, and your program is interrupted.

A Menu Window

The GET and PUT statements are also useful for displaying and removing menus. In addition to saving graphics images, you can save text on a graphics screen. The program in Listing 12.7 uses this method instead of erasing the menu and redrawing it each time it is needed.

Listing 12.7. Menu window number 2.

```
REM ** Menu Window Number 2 **
' Learning BASIC, Chapter 12.   File: PBL1207.BAS

REM ** Initialize **
SCREEN 7: CLS
DEFINT A-Z: RANDOMIZE TIMER
DIM AMenu(1704): flag = 0

REM ** Main program **
' Draw and GET menu
COLOR 7, 1
LOCATE 10, 11: PRINT "1. Draw Circles";
LOCATE 11, 11: PRINT "2. Draw Rectangles";
LOCATE 12, 11: PRINT "3. Quit"
LINE(60, 64)-(240, 100), 7, B
FOR column = 61 TO 239
  FOR row = 65 TO 99
    IF POINT(column, row) = 0 THEN
      PSET(column, row), 4
    END IF
  NEXT row
NEXT column
GET(60, 64)-(240, 100), AMenu          ' menu on screen
' Choose from menu
DO
  LOCATE 15, 2: PRINT "Press the number of your choice."
```

continues

321

Listing 12.7. (continued)

```
  kbd$ = INPUT$(1)
  PUT(60, 64), AMenu, XOR                ' menu off
  LOCATE 15, 2: PRINT SPACE$(32)         ' erase message
  CALL Choose(kbd$, flag)
  PUT(60, 64), AMenu, XOR                ' menu on
  IF flag = 1 THEN EXIT LOOP
LOOP
END

SUB Choose (kbd$, flag)
  SELECT CASE kbd$
    CASE "1"
      CALL CircleDraw
    CASE "2"
      CALL RectDraw
    CASE "3"
      flag = 1
    CASE ELSE
      CALL Message
  END SELECT
END SUB

SUB CircleDraw
  num = RND * 15 + 1
  FOR looper = 1 TO num
    radius = RND * 5 + 5
    column = RND * 260 + 40
    row = RND * 25 + 20
    CIRCLE(column, row), radius, num
    DELAY .5
  NEXT looper
END SUB

SUB RectDraw
  num = RND * 15 + 1
  FOR looper = 1 TO num
    s = RND * 30 + 10
    column = RND * 260 + 20
    row = RND * 30 + 150
    LINE(column, row)-(column + s, row + s / 4), num, B
    DELAY .5
  NEXT looper
END SUB

SUB Message
  LOCATE 11, 6: PRINT "Wrong keypress, wait a second";
  DELAY 2: LOCATE 11, 6: PRINT SPACE$(29);
END SUB
```

Items on the menu are printed in the Main program block. A rectangle is drawn to enclose the menu items. Then the interior of the rectangle is colored red by the following nested FOR/NEXT loops:

```
FOR column = 61 TO 239
  FOR row = 65 TO 99
    IF POINT(column, row) = 0 THEN
      PSET(column, row), 4
    END IF
  NEXT row
NEXT column
```

The POINT function detects the color of each point within the rectangle. If the point has the background color (0), the point is changed to red (color 4). The text pixels of the text characters are not colored. Therefore, the background inside the rectangle is changed to red. You could use a PAINT statement to do the background coloring, but the enclosed areas in some letters (D, a, and e) would not be colored. When the background coloring is complete, a GET statement saves the rectangle and the menu in an array named AMenu.

While the menu is on the screen, a message (below the menu) requests you to press the number of your choice. The INPUT$ function reads your keypress. When you press a key, a PUT statement (with the XOR option) removes the menu. The program calls the Choose procedure, and one of four actions takes place. When the appropriate action is completed, another PUT statement places the menu back on the screen for another choice.

```
PUT(60, 64), AMenu, XOR        ' menu off
LOCATE 15, 2: PRINT SPACE$(32) ' erase message
CALL Choose(kbd$, flag)
PUT(60, 64), AMenu, XOR        ' menu on
```

A SELECT CASE structure is used in the Choose procedure to select the appropriate action using four cases.

```
CASE "1"
  CALL CircleDraw
CASE "2"
  CALL RectDraw
CASE "3"
  flag = 1
CASE ELSE
  CALL Message
```

The CircleDraw procedure draws circles of random number, size, and color. The RectDraw procedure draws rectangles of random number, size, and color. Pressing the 3 key ends the program. If you press an incorrect key, CASE ELSE calls the Message procedure to print an error message that stays on the screen for two seconds. Figure 12.9 shows a typical run in progress.

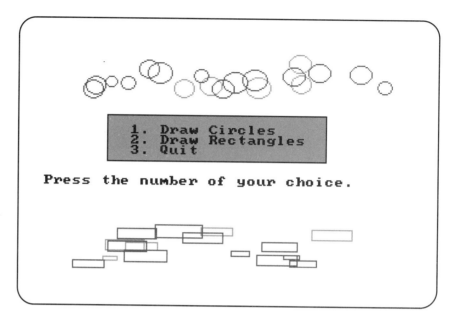

Figure 12.9. A menu with circles and rectangles.

We have only touched on the graphics capabilities of PowerBASIC Lite. A separate book on graphics would be required to do the subject justice. The demonstrations of this chapter form a base from which you can begin explorations on your own. The best way to learn is to experiment.

Summary

The extent to which you can use PowerBASIC Lite's graphics capabilities depends on your computer system's hardware. Some types of graphics adapters and display monitors can display more colors and have a higher resolution (more pixels per screen) than others. A list of adapters and the screen characteristics they can handle is in Table 12.1.

The default numbering scheme for graphics screens begins with row 0 and column 0 in the upper-left corner of the screen. In this scheme, column numbers increase as you move right, and row numbers increase as you move down. The maximum values for columns and rows depend on the graphics screen mode you are using.

Table 12.2 lists statements used to set up a graphics screen in preparation for drawing. Table 12.3 lists statements used as tools for drawing. You used most of the set-up and graphics tool statements in demonstration programs. This chapter used graphics screen modes 1, 2, 7, and 12.

You used the WINDOW statement to set your own limits for screen coordinates so that your application fits neatly within the screen's boundaries. This chapter had demonstrations of menu and temperature graphing applications.

You examined the characteristics of points on the screen with the POINT function and modified the color of points to satisfy specific characteristics. You learned how to calculate the number of bytes and the number of elements needed to dimension a graphics array. You saved graphics arrays with GET statements, and placed the array image at specified locations with PUT statements. Final demonstration programs show how to achieve animation of an image and how a menu can be placed, removed, and replaced.

By this time you should have a pretty good feel for the fundamental capabilities of PowerBASIC. Try the exercises that follow before going on to the discussion of the graphics mini-language in Chapter 13.

Exercises

1. What are the coordinates of the upper-left corner of a graphics screen for the default screen numbering system?

2. If the following statements are used to set up a graphics screen, what is the background color and which palette is used?

```
SCREEN 1: COLOR 0, 1: CLS
```

3. Name the column and row specified by each of the following statements:

   a. LOCATE 12, 5

   b. PSET(14, 30)

4. Describe the difference in the location of the coordinates specified in the following two statements:

   a. WINDOW(0, 0)-(100, 10)

   b. WINDOW SCREEN(0, 0)-(100, 10)

5. Describe the difference in the drawings made by the following statements:

   a. LINE(10, 10)-(100, 40), 3

   b. LINE(10, 10)-(100, 40), 3, B

   c. LINE(10, 10)-(100, 40), 3, BF

6. Describe the difference between the drawings made by the LINE statement of exercise 6a and the combination of the LINE and PAINT statements of exercise 6b.

   a. `LINE(10, 10)-(100, 40), 3, BF`

   b. `LINE(10, 10)-(100, 40), 3, B`
      `PAINT(20, 20), 1, 3`

7. Calculate the value needed to dimension an array in screen mode 1 for the following statement. Then write an appropriate DIM statement.

```
GET(16, 16)-(64, 24), box
```

8. Modify Listing 12.6 so that the box moves down the screen five rows at a time in the leftmost column until it is near the bottom of the screen. Then it moves 20 columns to the right and up five rows at a time until it is near the top of the screen. Continue this sequence until the box reaches the top-right corner of the screen. You can omit drawing the maze.

Chapter 13

A Mini-Language for Drawing

You saw many tools you can use to draw graphics in Chapter 12, "Graphics." PowerBASIC Lite also includes a mini-language with short commands to make drawings. You can use these commands within a DRAW statement to make figures on the screen, using specific lengths and directions. You can change drawing colors and paint the interior of a figure, such as a rectangle or circle.

This chapter explores the commands of the DRAW statement, which can perform most of the functions of other graphics statements. The following topics are discussed in this chapter:

- The basic drawing commands: U, L, R, D, E, F, G, and H

- Supplemental drawing commands: B, C, P, N, A, and T

- A Drawing Utility program incorporating the basic commands of the DRAW statement

- Creating a figure and saving its image as an array

- Moving a figure about the screen with PUT statements

- Saving the image of graphics figures in a file with BSAVE

- Retrieving a graphics figure from a file with BLOAD

Basic DRAW Commands

A DRAW statement's commands are enclosed in quotation marks. The following DRAW statement, for example, draws a rectangle:

```
DRAW "U20 R40 D20 L40"
```

The command tells the computer to draw up 20 pixels (U20) from the cursor's current position, then right 40 pixels (R40), down 20 pixels (D20), and left 40 pixels (L40). This puts the cursor back at the original position after drawing a 40-by-20-pixel rectangle. Notice that all these commands were made relative to the cursor's last position, a point called the *last referenced position*.

When a program begins, the last referenced position is considered, by default, to be the center of the screen. Therefore, drawing the rectangle in the example begins with the last referenced point at the center of the screen. When the line is drawn up 20 pixels, the end of that line becomes the last referenced position for the next command. Therefore, the last referenced position is the position at which the cursor resides after a drawing command is executed.

Table 13.1 lists the basic drawing commands with an explanation of their actions.

Table 13.1. Basic drawing commands.

Command	Action
U*n*	Move up *n* pixels
D*n*	Move down *n* pixels
L*n*	Move left *n* pixels
R*n*	Move right *n* pixels
E*n*	Move diagonally up and right *n* pixels (45-degree angle, clockwise from North)
F*n*	Move diagonally down and right *n* pixels (135-degree angle, clockwise from North)
G*n*	Move diagonally down and left *n* pixels (225-degree angle, clockwise from North)
H*n*	Move diagonally up and left *n* pixels (315-degree angle, clockwise from North)

You can use the *b* and *n* minicommands as a prefix to any of the basic drawing commands.

- The letter *B* doesn't draw as the move occurs (like lifting a pen from the paper, moving the pen to a new position, and lowering the pen).

- The letter *N* retains the last referenced position (like moving the pen, then lifting the pen and moving back to the point at which the movement began).

Drawing with the Basic Commands

The following lines of code demonstrate some of the basic drawing commands. Enter all four lines and then run the program.

```
SCREEN 1: CLS
DRAW "U50 R100 D50 L100": DELAY .5
DRAW "BE10 U30 R80 D30 L80": DELAY .5
DRAW "BR40 BU15 NU10 NR20 ND10 NL20"
```

The result should be that shown in figure 13.1.

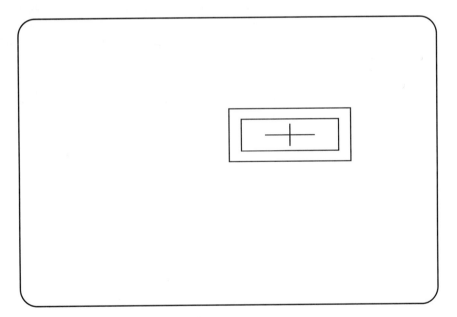

Figure 13.1. Demonstration lines by DRAW statement.

The first DRAW statement draws the largest rectangle. The BE10 command in the second DRAW statement moves the reference point in the direction E10 without drawing. This places the rectangle drawn by the second DRAW statement inside the first rectangle. Two nondrawing moves (BR40 BU15) position the reference point in the third DRAW statement, where it draws the crossed lines.

The commands E, F, G, and H cause diagonal movements. They draw a line similar to the hypotenuse of an isosceles right triangle. For example, imagine a triangle with sides drawn by

```
DRAW "R25 U25"
```

The last referenced point resulting from drawing these two lines would be connected to the original point by the following statement:

```
DRAW "G25"
```

Draw the triangle by entering and running the following lines of code:

```
SCREEN 1: CLS
DRAW "R25 U25": DELAY .5
DRAW "G25"
```

The last line draws the hypotenuse of the triangle, which is longer than either side of the triangle even though the same value is specified for the number of pixels. The G25 command is like a shortcut to draw a straight line that would start and end at the same place as a combination of L25 and D25. However, the line is drawn diagonally, as shown in figure 13.2.

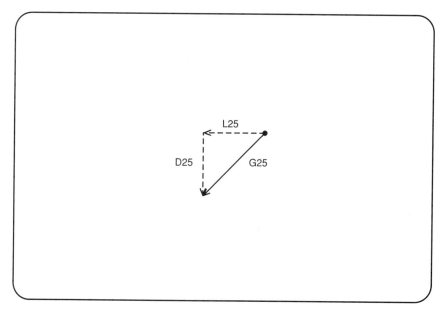

Figure 13.2. A diagonal line drawn with the G25 command.

Figure 13.3 shows the way drawings are made for the commands U5, L5, D5, and R5 from a centered common reference point, and for the commands E5, F5, G5, and H5 from another common reference point.

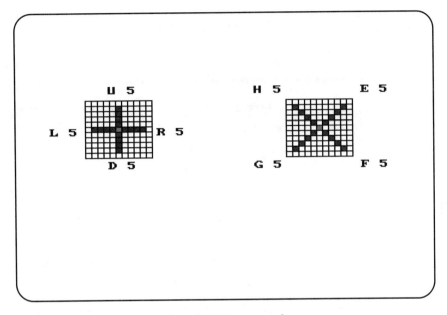

Figure 13.3. Lines drawn by basic DRAW commands.

Moving Without Drawing

By default, the last referenced point is the center of the screen. You won't want every drawing made from this point. To move the invisible drawing cursor to a different point, you precede the command with the letter *B*. For example, to move the cursor up 10 pixels from the last reference point, you use this command:

```
DRAW "BU10"
```

You can make successive moves without drawing a line. For example, you can use any of several ways to move from the center of the screen (160, 100) to the screen coordinates (40, 80) without drawing a line. Here are three equivalent moves:

```
DRAW "BL120 BU20"
DRAW "BU20 BL120"
DRAW "BH20 BL100"
```

331

These statements all define a new last referenced point (40, 80). After any of the statements, the invisible cursor resides at that point.

A Utility Program of Basic Commands

The program in listing 13.1 sets up a program that lets you experiment with the basic drawing commands: D, U, L, R, E, F, G, H, and B.

Listing 13.1. Quick-draw program, number 1.

```
REM ** Quick Draw Program Number 1 **
' Learning BASIC, Chapter 13.  File: PBL1301.BAS

REM ** Initialize **
SCREEN 1: CLS
DEFINT A-Z

REM ** Main Program **
DO
  CALL DrawIt
  LOCATE 23, 1
  PRINT "Press Esc to quit, "
  PRINT "another key for new drawing"; SPC(4)
  kbd$ = INPUT$(1)
  IF kbd$ <> CHR$(27) THEN
      CLS
    ELSE
      EXIT LOOP
  END IF
LOOP
END

SUB DrawIt
  LOCATE 24, 1: PRINT "Commands: D U L R E F G H B Esc";
  DO
      ' Get command
      Letter$ = "Z": Add$ = ""
      WHILE INSTR("DdUuLlRrEeFfGgHhBb", Letter$) = 0
        LOCATE 1, 1: PRINT SPACE$(80): LOCATE 1, 1
        PRINT "What command ? ";
        Letter$ = INPUT$(1)
        IF Letter$ = CHR$(27) THEN EXIT LOOP
        IF UCASE$(Letter$) = "B" THEN
          PRINT Letter$;: Add$ = INPUT$(1)
        END IF
```

```
      WEND
      ' Get number and draw
      IF Letter$ = CHR$(27) THEN EXIT LOOP
      Letter$ = Letter$ + Add$
      LOCATE 1, 1: PRINT "What command ? "; Letter$;
      LOCATE 2, 1: INPUT "Number "; Number$
      Move$ = Letter$ + Number$
      DRAW Move$
    LOOP
END SUB
```

The drawing commands you can use in this program, along with the Esc command used when your drawing is finished, are at the bottom of the screen. When you type a single-letter command (D, U, L, R, E, F, G, or H), another prompt requests the number (of pixels) you want to move. Then the program makes the drawing. When you type **B**, the command prints and the computer waits (on the same line) for the second letter (D, U, L, R, E, F, G, or H). When you type the second letter, another prompt requests the number (of pixels) you want to move.

Enter the program and run it. Try executing the commands listed in table 13.2.

Table 13.2. Experimental commands for listing 13.1.

Drawing Number	Command Sequence
1	B U 80
2	B L 150
3	D 40
4	R 30
5	U 20
6	L 10
7	D 6
8	R 3
9	B R 70
10	B D 50
11	U 20

Figure 13.4 shows the result of these commands.

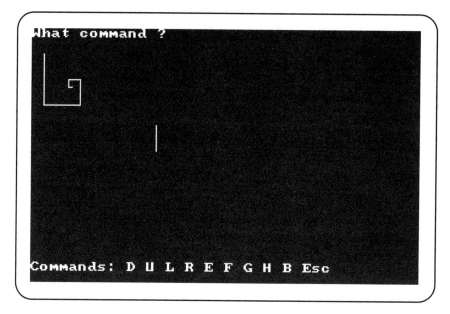

Figure 13.4. Result of DRAW commands in table 13.2.

Enter the commands you want after completing drawing command 11 in table 13.2. When you finish with a drawing, press Esc. Then you can quit the program or clear the screen and start a new drawing with a fresh slate. It may help to make a sketch on paper before using the program to make the drawing.

Other DRAW Commands

The M command is a dual-purpose command. You can use it to specify either absolute or relative coordinates. Suppose, for example, that the last referenced point is (160, 100). You can use the M command to move to the coordinates (220, 80) either of two ways:

```
DRAW "M220, 80"      ' absolute coordinates
```

or

```
DRAW "M+60, -20"     ' relative coordinates
```

The first statement makes a move from (160, 100) to the *absolute screen coordinates* (220, 80), the last referenced point. Absolute coordinates are those which the screen has defined by default.

The second statement makes a move from (160, 100) right 60 pixels and up 20 pixels. The last referenced point of this move is also at screen position (220, 80), calculated from (160 + 60, 100 – 20). Thus, both commands end with the same reference points. The moves in the second statement are made using *relative* coordinates. Relative coordinates are relative to the last referenced point.

Keep in mind that all DRAW commands use the Screen coordinates system discussed in Chapter 12, "Graphics." The WINDOW statement (also discussed in Chapter 12) has no effect on the coordinates used for DRAW statements.

You also should remember that unless the B command precedes the M command, M draws a line as the move is made.

A plus (+) or minus (–) sign before the column coordinates signals to the computer that the specified values are relative coordinates. The last referenced point in both cases has the screen coordinates (220, 80), and both statements accomplish the same thing.

To move the last reference point back to (160, 100), you can use the following relative move:

```
DRAW "BM -60, 20"          ' Relative coordinates
```

You can move the reference point back to (160, 100) also with a BM command, using absolute coordinates.

```
DRAW "BM160, 100"          ' Absolute coordinates
```

Other supplementary commands in table 13.3 do not move the drawing pen. Most of them affect the way the next line is drawn.

Table 13.3. Supplementary DRAW commands.

Command	Action
Cn	Draw with color number n
Pn,m	Paint with color n to boundary color m
An	Set angle n (n = 0, 1, 2, or 3)
TAn	Turn angle n (degrees)
Sn	Scale drawing by factor n

The C and P Commands

The C command determines the drawing color used when a drawing move command is executed. The graphics mode used determines which colors are available. The default color is the highest legal attribute for the current graphics mode. Once a color changes, the change stays in effect until the program ends or until you give another C command. Enter and run the following program segment to see how the C command works:

```
SCREEN 1: CLS
DRAW "U60 R60 D60 L60"              ' default color 3
DRAW "BE5 C1 U50 R50 D50 L50"       ' color 1
DRAW "BE5 U40 R40 D40 L40"          ' still color 1
DRAW "BE5 C2 U30 R30 D30 L30"       ' color 2
```

This program uses the default color (number 3) to draw the outside rectangle. The next two rectangles are drawn by color 1; the small, inner rectangle, by color 2. The final drawing is shown in figure 13.5.

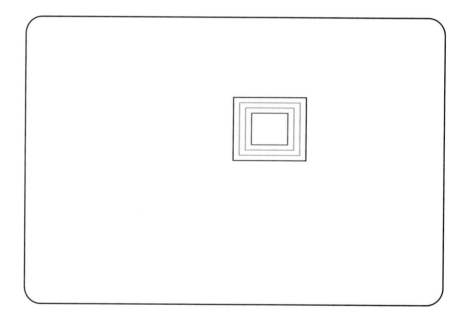

Figure 13.5. C command demonstration.

The P command is similar to the PAINT graphics command. The painting color and boundary color are appended to the P command. To paint a figure, you must move the pen into the interior of an enclosed figure before executing the paint command.

Enter and execute the following block of code to see how the C and P commands work.

```
SCREEN 1: CLS
DRAW "BM 100, 40 C1 F50 L100 E50"
DELAY .5: DRAW "BD10 P2, 1": DELAY .5
DRAW "BM +20, -10 C2 R100 G50 H50"
DELAY .5: DRAW "BR10 BD 5 P1, 2"
```

This program draws and paints two triangles (see figure 13.6).

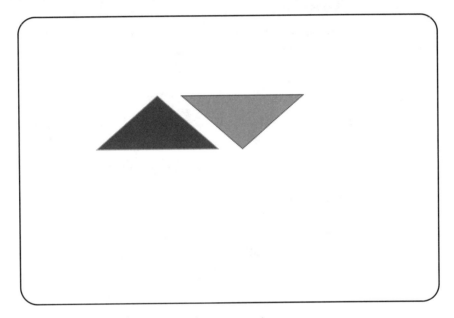

Figure 13.6. C and P commands demonstrated.

The first DRAW statement draws the triangle on the left, using color 1 (C1). To move the reference point inside the triangle, the second DRAW statement makes a move without drawing (BD10). Then the triangle is painted with color 2 (P2, 1). The second value (1) specifies the boundary color of the triangle: "paint with color 2 from boundary (color 1) to boundary." The inverted triangle on the right is drawn with color 2 (C2) and painted with color 1 (P1, 2). The BR10 BD5 commands move the pen in the second triangle before painting.

The A, TA, and S Commands

The A command causes ensuing direction commands (U D L R E F G H) to rotate counterclockwise by a multiple of 90 degrees.

$$0 = 0 * 90$$

$$1 = 1 * 90$$

$$2 = 2 * 90$$

$$3 = 3 * 90$$

You can visualize the effect of the A command as rotating the reference axis 90 degrees. For example, each of the following statements draws a 20-pixel line from the last referenced point toward the top of the screen (up):

```
DRAW "A0 U20"        ' rotate 0 degrees
DRAW "A1 R20"        ' rotate 90 degrees counterclockwise
DRAW "A2 D20"        ' rotate 180 degrees counterclockwise
DRAW "A3 L20"        ' rotate 270 degrees counterclockwise
```

The A command acts in the same manner on the direction commands E, F, G, and H.

You can draw a rectangle using each of the A commands with the same direction command, as in the following example:

```
DRAW "A0 L20 A1 L20 A2 L20 A3 L20"
```

You can use the A commands in a string array named Angles$. To draw the same rectangle using the array, use a FOR/NEXT loop, as follows:

```
Angle$(0) = "A0": Angle$(1) = "A1"
Angle$(2) = "A2": Angle$(3) = "A3"
FOR n = 0 to 3
  DRAW Angle$(n) + "L20": DELAY .5
NEXT n
```

Enter and run this example. The direction command "L20" is catenated to the A command inside the loop. Because of a short time delay, you can see one line drawn each time the loop is executed.

The TA command is more helpful than the A command because it can rotate a direction command by a specified number of degrees in either a clockwise or counterclockwise direction. The range in degrees is –360 to 360. When the value is positive, the line is rotated counterclockwise; if negative, the line is rotated clockwise. For example, the following statements are equivalent:

```
DRAW "TA-45 U10"
DRAW "TA45 L10"
DRAW "E10"
```

Numeric variables can be used in DRAW statements. However, because DRAW statements are strings, numeric variables require special handling when used within a DRAW string. You must specify where to find the numeric variable, and you must convert the value returned to string form. Finding and converting the numeric value is done by

1. appending an equal (=) sign to the command

2. catenating the VARPTR$ function (with the variable as an argument).

For example, executing DRAW "TA 20" is equivalent to the combination of the following statements.

```
degrees = 20
DRAW "TA+" + VARPTR$(degrees)
```

The VARPTR$ function returns a pointer to a variable in string form. The function's primary use is in PLAY and DRAW statements to include numeric variables within command strings.

Enter and run the following lines of code to draw an approximation of a circle.

```
SCREEN 1: CLS: DEFINT A-Z
FOR degrees = -360 TO 0 STEP 10
  DRAW "TA=" + VARPTR$(degrees) + "U5"
NEXT degrees
```

Because the lines, drawn by the DRAW statement, connect end-to-end and each is rotated 10 degrees from the previous line, they form an approximation of a circle. You can make a closer approximation by using STEP with smaller values and shorter lines.

The previous example, with a small change, draws the radii of a circle, spaced 10 degrees apart.

```
SCREEN 1: CLS: DEFINT A-Z
FOR degrees = -360 TO 0 STEP 10
  DRAW "TA=" + VARPTR$(degrees) + "NU30"
NEXT degrees
```

The N command preceding the U command causes the reference point to stay the same. The original reference point acts as the center of a circle. The radii are drawn at intervals of 10 degrees.

The S*n* command sets a scale factor for drawing a line. The specified value (*n*) can range from 1 to 255. The value of *n*, divided by 4, is used as a scale factor in ensuing drawing commands. For example, each of the following statements draws a line 12 units long to the right:

```
DRAW "S1 R48"        ' 1/4 of 48 = 12
DRAW "S2 R24"        ' 2/4 of 24 = 12
DRAW "S3 R16"        ' 3/4 of 16 = 12
DRAW "S4 R12"        ' 4/4 of 12 = 12
DRAW "S5 R10         ' 5/4 of 10 = 12.5
DRAW "S6 R8"         ' 6/4 of  8 = 12
```

Notice that 5/4 of 10 is 12.5, a noninteger. Because scale factors containing decimal parts are converted to integers, 12.5 is converted to 12 for drawing the line.

The program in listing 13.2 uses an increasing scale factor, changing colors, and the rotation of angles to draw rectangles. The scale (S), color (C), and turn angle (TA) commands all use variables. After each rectangle is drawn, the scale is set to S4 (4/4 = 1) and the turn angle to TA0. Then the reference point is moved, in preparation for drawing the next rectangle.

Listing 13.2. Scale, color, and rotate rectangles.

```
REM ** Scale, Color, and Rotate Rectangles **
' Learning BASIC, Chapter 13.  File: PBL1302.BAS

REM ** Initialize **
SCREEN 1: CLS: DEFINT A-Z
scaler = 1: kolor = 0
DRAW "BM 20, 190"

REM ** Draw rectangles **
FOR degrees = 0 TO 270 STEP 45
  kolor = kolor + 1
  IF kolor = 4 THEN kolor = 1
  DRAW "S=" + VARPTR$(scaler) + "C=" + VARPTR$(kolor)
  DRAW "TA=" + VARPTR$(degrees)
  DRAW "R12 D12 L12 U12"
  DRAW "S4 TA0 BR36 BU24"
  scaler = scaler + 1
NEXT degrees
kbd$ = INPUT$(1)
END
```

Because a given scale factor remains in effect until the program ends or a new scale factor is given, the scale is changed to S4 (4/4) to move the last referenced point to a position for drawing a new rectangle. The turn angle must be set to A0 so that the B moves (BR36 BU24) are made with no rotation of direction. The color number (kolor variable) and scale (scaler) increase by one each time through the loop (see figure 13.7).

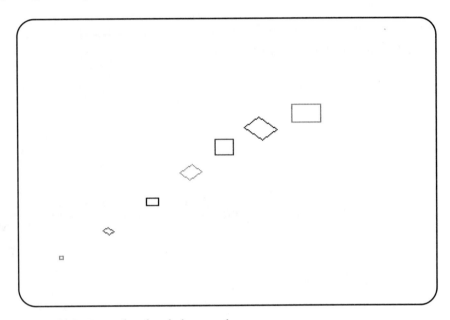

Figure 13.7. Rotated and scaled rectangles.

The smallest rectangle (S = 1) is drawn in the screen's lower left. Each successive rectangle increases in size, rotates 45 degrees, changes color, and is placed up and to the right of the preceding one.

Using DRAW to Make Images

You can make small images quickly with DRAW statements, and save them in numeric arrays. For example, the following DRAW statement draws an arrow with a head and tail:

```
DRAW "NH2 NE2 D8 NH3 NE3"
```

This down-pointing arrow can be enclosed in a rectangle 7 pixels wide and 11 pixels high. A similar arrow, drawn pointing up, can be enclosed in a rectangle of the same dimensions. After assigning the images to arrays, you can save the arrays to disk with PowerBASIC Lite's BSAVE statement. Then, with a BLOAD statement, the images can be loaded into any program that uses the same screen mode. BSAVE and BLOAD are faster than other methods of saving and loading numeric arrays.

Saving Array Images with BSAVE

The BSAVE statement saves the image as a byte-for-byte copy of the data in memory. The statement also includes control information that is used by the BLOAD statement when the file is reloaded.

The program in listing 13.3 creates two images: a down-pointing arrow (PtDn) and an up-pointing arrow (PtUp). The images are saved to the disk drive with the names specified in the program.

Listing 13.3. Create and save images.

```
REM ** Create and Save Images **
' Learning BASIC, Chapter 13.  File:PBL1303.BAS

REM ** Initialize **
SCREEN 1: CLS
DEFINT A-Z
DIM PtUp(0:13), PtDn(0:13)

REM ** Main program **
' Create Images
DRAW "BM10,10 NH2 NE2 D8 NH3 NE3": DELAY 3
GET(7, 8)-(13, 18), PtDn
CLS
DRAW "BM10,10 NG3 NF3 D8 NG2 NF2": DELAY 3
GET(7, 10)-(13, 20), PtUp
CLS
' Save Images
CALL GetName(Naym$,1)
DEF SEG = VARSEG(PtDn(0))
BSAVE Naym$, VARPTR(PtDn(0)), 26
CALL GetName(Naym$,2)
DEF SEG = VARSEG(PtUp(0))
BSAVE Naym$, VARPTR(PtUp(0)), 26
DEF SEG
END
```

```
SUB GetName(N$, number)
  PRINT "Image number"; number
  INPUT "Disk drive (A:, B:, etc.)"; drive$
  INPUT "File name with extension"; Naym$
  N$ = drive$ + Naym$
END SUB
```

The program creates two images and dimensions an array for each image. To find the dimensions of the arrays, you can use the formula discussed in Chapter 12, "Graphics." Each image can be contained in a rectangle 11 pixels high and 7 pixels wide. With the values inserted, the number of elements needed is calculated for screen mode 1 in the following way:

```
Bytes = 4 + 11 * 1 * INT((7 * 2 + 7) / 8)
      = 4 + 11 * INT(21 / 8)
      = 4 + 11 * 2
      = 26
```

Use the calculated value in the BSAVE statements to save the required number of bytes in the image file. The number of elements needed to dimension the arrays is

$$\text{Elements} = \text{Bytes} / 2$$
$$= 26 / 2$$
$$= 13$$

One image is an arrow that points down; the other is an arrow that points up. The arrowhead extends three pixels on each side of the arrow shaft. The tail extends two pixels on each side of the shaft.

As you can see from the following block of code, each image is drawn by a DRAW statement and saved as an array by a GET statement. The screen is cleared after each image is saved.

```
' Create Images
DRAW "BM10,10 NH2 NE2 D8 NH3 NE3"    ' down pointing arrow
GET(7, 8)-(13, 18), PtDn
CLS
DRAW "BM10,10 NG3 NF3 D8 NG2 NF2"    ' up pointing arrow
GET(7, 10)-(13, 20), PtUp
CLS
```

The GetName SUB procedure gets the disk drive where the image file is to be saved and the name of the file. If you are using the default drive to save the files, just press Enter at the request for the drive. If you are using a different drive, type the drive letter followed by a colon. Then type the name of the file (with its extension) in which to save the image. The sequence of prompts and entries is

```
Image number 1
Disk drive (A:, B:, etc.)? A:
File name with extension? DOWN.DAT
```

```
Image number 1
Disk drive (A:, B:, etc.)? A:
File name with extension? DOWN.DAT█
```

Figure 13.8. Entries for one image file.

Remember the name of the files used to save the images. These names are used in another program to retrieve the images from the files.

To save the array image, PtDn, as a file, you first need to specify where the array is stored in memory. Computer memory is organized in blocks of 64K segments. To directly access a location in memory, you must specify the memory address in two portions: the segment and the offset within that segment. The address segment is specified by a DEF SEG statement. In this program, the statement is

```
DEF SEG = VARSEG (PtDn(0))
```

The argument for the VARSEG function gives the name of the array and the array's first element number (PtDn(0)). The VARSEG function returns the segment portion of the address of a variable (the first element of the PtDn array in this case).

You must also specify the location (offset) within the address segment. The offset within the segment is specified by the VARPTR function in a BSAVE statement.

```
BSAVE Naym$, VARPTR(PtDn(0)), 26
```

Naym$ is the disk drive and file name used for saving. The VARPTR function returns the offset portion of the memory address. The value 26 is the number of bytes needed to store the array.

Thus, the complete address in memory is provided by the VARSEG and VARPTR functions, as follows:

```
DEF SEG = VARSEG(PtDn(0))
BSAVE Naym$, VARPTR(PtDn(0)), 26
```

DEF SEG sets the segment address to the value returned by VARSEG(PtDn(0)), the first byte of the PtDn array. Naym$ is the variable that holds the name under which the file is to be saved. VARPTR(PtDn(0)) is the offset of the variable in the specified segment. The value, 26, is the number of bytes to be saved.

The PtUp array is saved in a similar manner. Be sure to enter a different file name for PtUp than you did for the PtDn array (see figure 13.9).

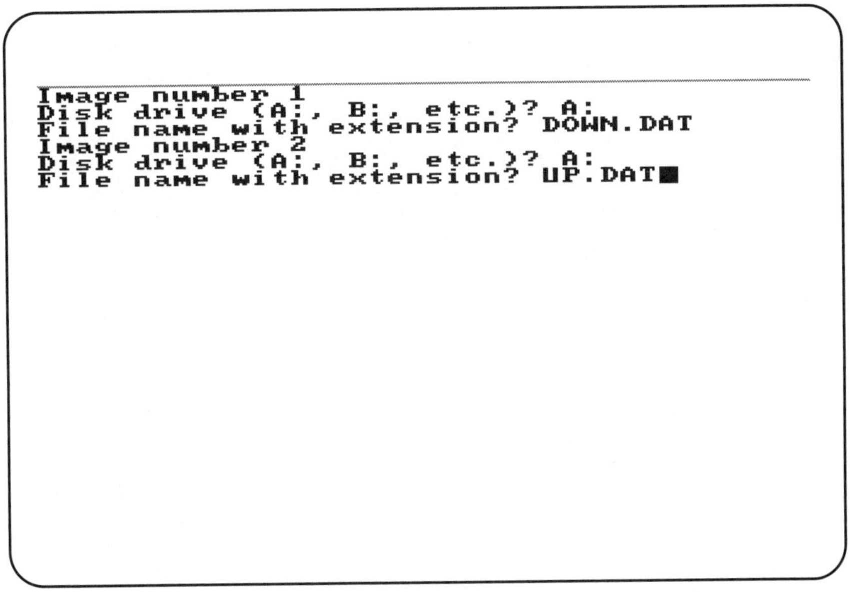

```
Image number 1
Disk drive (A:, B:, etc.)? A:
File name with extension? DOWN.DAT
Image number 2
Disk drive (A:, B:, etc.)? A:
File name with extension? UP.DAT█
```

Figure 13.9. Entries for both image files.

> **Note:** Because different screen modes use memory differently, do not load graphic images in a screen mode other than the one used to create and save the images.

After saving the file, you must restore the BASIC segment with the statement

```
DEF SEG
```

When used alone, DEF SEG resets the segment value to its default value, which is PowerBASIC's main data segment.

Enter listing 13.3 (if you have not done so already) and run the program. Use whatever file names you want. The program ends with the names of your files displayed. You may want to jot down the names so that you know which file to load later to retrieve the images.

After each arrow is drawn, a three-second time delay is provided for your convenience so that you can see the size and shape of the arrows. The delays serve no other purpose. You can delete them if you wish.

Loading Array Images with BLOAD

The BLOAD statement loads into memory a file created with the BSAVE statement. The file is loaded into memory at the address specified by a DEF SEG statement, with the offset specified in the BSAVE statement. For example, you load the file DOWN.DAT that was saved in listing 13.3 as follows:

```
DEF SEG = VARSEG(PtDn(0))
BLOAD Naym$, VARPTR(PtDn(0))
```

The segment address is set to the value returned by VARSEG(PtDn(0)), the address of the first byte of the PtDn array. Naym$ is the variable that holds the name of the file saved by BSAVE. VARPTR(PtDn(0)) is the offset of the array within the specified segment. There is no need to specify the number of bytes to load.

The PtUp array is loaded from its file in the same way, with its own DEF SEG and BLOAD statements. After you load the arrays, reset the default segment with

```
DEF SEG
```

The program in listing 13.4 loads the two arrow images saved in listing 13.3. It then uses the images to indicate where random points have been placed on the screen; it also displays the column and row numbers of each point.

Listing 13.4. Load and use Images.

```
REM ** Load and Use Images **
' Learning BASIC, Chapter 13.   File:PBL1304.BAS

REM ** Initialize **
SCREEN 1: CLS
DEFINT A-Z: RANDOMIZE TIMER
DIM PtUp(0:13), PtDn(0:13)

REM ** Main program **
' Load Images
CALL GetName(Naym$,1)
DEF SEG = VARSEG(PtDn(0))
BLOAD Naym$, VARPTR(PtDn(0))
CALL GetName(Naym$,2)
DEF SEG = VARSEG(PtUp(0))
BLOAD Naym$, VARPTR(PtUp(0))
DEF SEG
CLS
CALL PutPoints(PtDn(), PtUp())
CLS
END

SUB GetName(N$, number)
  PRINT "Image number"; number
  INPUT "Disk drive (A:, B:, etc.)"; drive$
  INPUT "File name with extension"; Naym$
  N$ = drive$ + Naym$
END SUB

SUB PutPoints(PtDn(), PtUp())
LOCATE 23,1: PRINT "Press Esc to Quit";
  DO
    column = RND * 308 + 5
    row = RND * 185 + 10
    PSET(column, row)
    IF row < 100 THEN
        PUT(column - 3, row + 2), PtUp, XOR
        head$ = "Up"
      ELSE
        PUT (column - 3, row - 12), PtDn, XOR
        head$ = "Dn"
    END IF
    LOCATE 1, 2: PRINT column, row;
    kbd$ = INPUT$(1)
    IF head$ = "Up" THEN
        PUT(column - 3, row + 2), PtUp, XOR
      ELSE
        PUT(column - 3, row - 12), PtDn, XOR END IF
        LOCATE 1, 2: PRINT SPACE$(10);
  LOOP UNTIL kbd$ = CHR$(27)
END SUB
```

347

The arrays are dimensioned in the same way as in listing 13.3.

```
DIM PtUp(0:13), PtDn(0:13)
```

The GetName procedure is used to enter the names of the files from which the arrays are retrieved. For example, the procedure is called for the first file as follows:

```
CALL GetName(Naym$,1)
```

The GetName procedure is the same as in listing 13.3. A number for each file is specified, but the order in which you enter the numbers is not critical. Just be sure to use the same file names you used to save the arrays.

When both arrays have been retrieved, the screen is cleared and the SUB procedure, PutPoints, is called. Both arrays are passed to the procedure, as follows:

```
CLS
CALL PutPoints(PtDn(), PtUp())
```

A point is turned on by a PSET statement using random values for column and row.

```
column = RND * 308 + 5
row = RND * 185 + 10
PSET(column, row)
```

Individual points are so small that they are hard to see on a blank screen. The arrows indicate the location of the points as they are displayed.

If the row selected is less than 100, the up-pointing arrow indicates the point's location; otherwise, the down-pointing arrow is used.

```
IF row < 100 THEN
    PUT(column - 3, row + 2), PtUp, XOR
    head$ = "Up"
  ELSE
    PUT (column - 3, row -12), PtDn, XOR
    head$ = "Dn"
END IF
```

Press any key (except Esc) to see the next point.

Because the array holding the arrow is rectangular and the shaft of the arrow is midway in the rectangle, offsets are used for column and row in the PUT statements, to align the arrow with the point displayed (see figure 13.10).

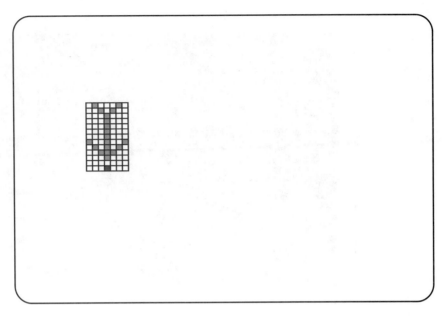

Figure 13.10. Arrow placement.

The XOR option is used so that if a previously set point is covered by the arrow, it is restored when the arrow is removed.

The location (column and row) is displayed in the upper left corner of the screen. Then the INPUT$(1) statement causes the program to wait for you to press a key before continuing. When you press a key (other than Esc), the arrow currently displayed is erased.

```
LOCATE 1, 2: PRINT column, row;
kbd$ = INPUT$(1)
IF head$ = "Up" THEN
    PUT(column - 3, row + 2), PtUp, XOR
 ELSE
    PUT(column - 3, row - 12), PtDn, XOR
END IF
```

Press Esc to exit the loop and return to the main program, where the program ends. When you press any other key a new randomly placed point is set and the cycle repeats. Figure 13.11 shows the screen after many points have been displayed.

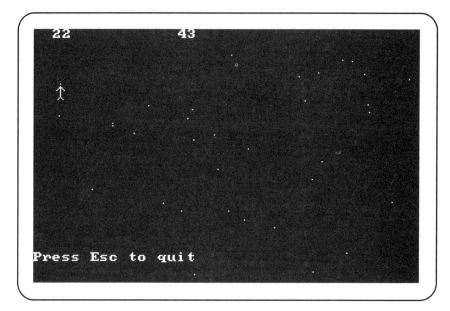

Figure 13.11. Output of listing 13.4.

Using a Cursor Array to Color Text

When you use graphics mode 1, text is printed in the default color (3) of the palette selected in the last COLOR statement. If no COLOR statement has been executed, the default palette 1 (black background), of graphics mode 1, is used; therefore, text is printed as white on black.

You can use some of your newly acquired graphics techniques to change the color of text. You can write a program to create a rectangular cursor array, move it to a specific character, and change the color of the pixels in the cursor.

The program in listing 13.5 creates the cursor and some text, and enables you to use the arrow keys to move the cursor to any character. Then you can change the color of that character by pressing a number (1, 2, or 3) to select a color.

Listing 13.5. Using a cursor array to color text.

```
REM ** Using a Cursor Array to Color Text **
' Learning BASIC, Chapter 13.  File: PBL1305.BAS
```

```
REM ** Initialize **
SCREEN 1: CLS
DEFINT A-Z: DIM kursor(1:11)

REM ** Create cursor and print text **
' Cursor
DRAW "BM0,0 C1 R7 D7 L7 U7"
GET (0, 0)-(7, 7), kursor
CLS
' Text
LOCATE 2, 2: PRINT "Press an arrow key to move the cursor"
PRINT " from letter to letter."
LOCATE 5, 2: PRINT "Press a number: 1, 2, or 3 to change"
PRINT " the color of the character."
LOCATE 8, 2: PRINT "Press the Esc key to quit."

REM ** Put Cursor and Make Changes **
column = 2: row = 2
col = column * 8 - 8: lyne = row * 8 - 8
PUT (col, lyne), kursor, XOR
DO
  DO
    kbd$ = INKEY$
  LOOP WHILE kbd$ = ""
  PUT (col, lyne), kursor, XOR            ' turn off cursor
  IF kbd$ = CHR$(0) + "M" THEN
      col = col + 8                       ' move cursor
      IF col > 312 THEN CALL Adjust1(col%, lyne%)
      PUT (col, lyne), kursor, XOR        ' turn on cursor
    ELSEIF kbd$ = CHR$(0) + "K" THEN
      col = col - 8                       ' move
      IF col < 8 THEN CALL Adjust2(col%, lyne%)
      PUT (col, lyne), kursor, XOR        ' turn on
    ELSEIF kbd$ = CHR$(0) + "P" THEN
      lyne = lyne + 8                     ' move
      IF lyne > 192 THEN CALL Adjust1(col%, lyne%)
       PUT (col, lyne), kursor, XOR       ' turn on
    ELSEIF kbd$ = CHR$(0) + "H" THEN
      lyne = lyne - 8                     ' move
      IF lyne < 8 THEN CALL Adjust2(col%, lyne%)
      PUT (col, lyne), kursor, XOR        ' turn on
    ELSEIF kbd$ > "0" AND kbd$ <= "3" THEN
      kolor = VAL(kbd$)
      FOR poynt = col TO col + 8          ' color text
        FOR tier = lyne TO lyne + 7
          IF POINT(poynt, tier) <> 0 THEN
            PSET (poynt, tier), kolor
          END IF
        NEXT tier
      NEXT poynt
      PUT (col, lyne), kursor, XOR        ' turn on
```

continues

351

Listing 13.5. (continued)

```
    ELSE
      PUT (col, lyne), kursor, XOR          ' turn on
  END IF
LOOP WHILE kbd$ <> CHR$(27)
PUT (col, lyne), kursor, XOR
kbd$ = INPUT$(1):CLS
END

SUB Adjust1 (col%, lyne%)
  IF col > 312 THEN
    col = 8
    lyne = lyne + 8
  END IF
  IF lyne > 192 THEN lyne = 8
END SUB

SUB Adjust2 (col%, lyne%)
  IF col < 8 THEN
    col = 312
    lyne = lyne - 8
  END IF
  IF lyne < 8 THEN lyne = 192
END SUB
```

A DRAW statement is used to create a cyan-colored cursor (C1), which is saved in an array named cursor. Then the screen is cleared.

```
DRAW "BM0,0 C1 R7 D7 L7 U7"
GET (0, 0)-(7, 7), kursor
CLS
```

Using the Program

You can use the left- and right-arrow keys to move the cursor along a line of text; the up- and down-arrow keys to move the cursor from line to line. If the cursor reaches the end of the line while you are pressing the left- or right-arrow key, it moves (up or down) to the beginning of the next line.

To change the color of the character contained in the cursor, press 1, 2, or 3. Pressing 1 changes the color to cyan; 2, to magenta; 3, to white. If you change your mind about a color, you can move the cursor back to a character and press a key for a new color.

When you finish coloring the characters, press Esc to remove the cursor from the screen so that you can examine the result. Then press any key to end the program.

Analysis of the Program

The Put Cursor and Make Changes block does most of the work. When this block is entered, the cursor is positioned at the leftmost character in the first line of text. Text positions are converted to graphics positions to place the cursor where you want it on the screen.

```
column = 2: row = 2                    ' text values
col = column * 8 -8: lyne = row * 8 - 8   ' graphics values
PUT (col, lyne), kursor, XOR
```

The rest of the block consists of one long DO...LOOP that contains a block IF structure with the necessary options for moving the cursor (right, left, down, up) or coloring a character.

When you press a key, a PUT statement with XOR turns off the cursor. If you press one of the arrow keys, the cursor moves in the appropriate direction and another PUT statement turns on the cursor at the new position. When the movement moves the cursor off the screen, an appropriate adjustment is made by calling either the Adjust1 or the Adjust2 procedure.

The Adjust1 procedure is called when the graphics column (col) is greater than 312 or when the graphics line calculation (lyne) is greater than 192. The procedure adjusts the appropriate value. When col is greater than 312, it is set to 8 (the first graphics position) and the value of lyne is adjusted appropriately. Another adjustment is made if the change in lyne will go beyond the bottom of the screen.

```
IF col > 312 THEN
  col = 8
  lyne = lyne + 8
END IF
IF lyne > 192 THEN lyne = 8
```

The Adjust2 procedure is called when the graphics column (col) is less than 8 or when the graphics line (lyne) is less than 8. Adjust2 works like Adjust1. Adjustments are made in this procedure to move the cursor to the right side or bottom of the screen, as appropriate.

After a number key (1, 2, or 3) is pressed, a PSET statement is used in a FOR/NEXT loop to set all the pixels of the appropriate character to the selected color.

```
kolor = VAL(kbd$)
FOR poynt = col TO col + 8                    ' color text
  FOR tier = lyne TO lyne + 7
    IF POINT(poynt, tier) <> 0 THEN
      PSET (poynt, tier), kolor
    END IF
  NEXT tier
NEXT poynt
```

The key to changing only the colors in the letter is the IF POINT statement. Because the background color is 0, the condition in the IF clause of this statement is true only when the pixel's color is different from the background color. When the condition is true, the color of the pixel is set by the PSET statement. Otherwise, nothing changes.

If you press a key other than an arrow or number key (1, 2, or 3), the final ELSE clause of the block IF structure turns the cursor on again.

```
ELSE
PUT (col, lyne), kursor, XOR               ' turn on
```

The pointer does not move and the color of the character does not change.

Figure 13.12 shows the words arrow, number, and Esc changed from the original color. The cursor has been moved to the end of the last line.

Press an arrow key to move the cursor
from letter to letter.

Press a number: 1, 2, or 3 to change
the color of the character.

Press the Esc key to quit.□

Figure 13.12. Text colored by listing 13.5.

Summary

A DRAW statement contains a string of graphics commands that control the movement on-screen of an imaginary pen. The pen can draw as it moves (pen down), or it can be moved without drawing (pen raised).

The basic commands move the pen up, down, left, right (U, D, L, R), or diagonally (E, F, G, H). You can use the letters *B* (move without drawing) and *N* (move but retain the last referenced point) as a prefix to the basic commands.

You can move the pen also by using the M command. This command can move the pen to an absolute position on the screen (as in M10,10 = move to position 10,10) or to a position relative to the last referenced point (as in M-10,20 = move left 10 and down 20).

Supplementary commands include C (color), P (paint), A (draw at an angle), TA (turn a specified number of degrees), and S (scale the drawing).

You used a utility program to practice the basic drawing commands and short demonstration programs to see the effects of other commands. You used your drawing and array skills to draw arrows and GET statements to copy images into arrays.

You saw how to save arrays to disk files by using BSAVE statements with appropriate DEF SEG statements that locate the arrays in memory. In a separate program, BLOAD statements were used to load the arrays from disk into memory. Then PUT statements were used to move the images on the screen.

Another program used image arrays to create a rectangular cursor. PUT statements were used to move the cursor. You had the option of changing the color of the characters in the cursor.

Exercises

1. Draw a sketch of the figure drawn by this DRAW statement:

```
DRAW "U40 R40 NG40 D40 NL40 H40"
```

2. If the origin of the figure in exercise 1 was (160, 100), at what location did the drawing end?

3. If the last referenced point is (80, 90) and you want to move to (40, 120) with a relative M command without drawing a line, what DRAW statement do you use?

4. The equivalent move of exercise 3 can be made by moving vertically and then horizontally. What DRAW statement moves this way?

355

5. Enter the following two lines:

```
SCREEN 1: CLS
DRAW "L40 TA-120 L40 TA120 L40"
```

and execute them. Then draw a sketch of the display.

6. Use listing 13.5 to change the color of the first letter (P) of each sentence in figure 13.12.

7. Modify listing 13.3 so that the arrows are drawn horizontally, with the arrowheads pointing left and right.

8. Modify listing 13.4 so that it uses the arrows in exercise 7 to indicate where the random points are located. *Hint:* The IF statement that determines which arrow is displayed should be based on whether the column is < 160.

Chapter 14

Dynamic Debugging

So far, the programs you have used from this book have been debugged to some extent. Because these programs are for demonstration purposes only, they have not been thoroughly tested or debugged. For example, some programs do not run correctly with improper entries. Many types of errors can occur, and predetermining where and when they will occur is impossible.

No matter which computer language you use or how carefully you use it, certain programming errors are common. Some examples of these common errors are misspelled or misused variables, improper logical tests, mistakes in syntax, and failure to test for improper entry data: type, range, number, and so on.

PowerBASIC's debugging capabilities are helpful for finding and correcting program errors. To find the errors, you may need to check statements in the program, display values of variables at critical points in the program, observe the flow of the program from statement to statement, and watch the program's output as it executes. With PowerBASIC's debugging tools, you can do all these things, and more.

This chapter explains how to use debugging tools to find and fix some errors in demonstration programs. The following topics are covered in this chapter:

- Setting breakpoints to interrupt the program, and toggling off a breakpoint when you finish using it

- Tracing through parts of a program (as you did in Chapter 2, "Using PowerBASIC Lite")

- Examining variable values at points in the program where an interruption occurs. You evaluated some expressions in Chapter 4, "Statements, Expressions, Operations, and Functions."

- Adding, editing, and deleting variables that are monitored as a program is executed

- Correcting statements in which errors are found, and rerunning the revised program for additional debugging

Debugging Tools

Although PowerBASIC finds and isolates many errors while compiling or running a program, it cannot find certain kinds of errors. That is when you must find the bugs, using some clear logic, cloudy intuition, and PowerBASIC's debugging tools. One of these tools is a *breakpoint* that interrupts a program at a specific place.

Breakpoints are places you set in a program to stop execution of the program. Ordinarily, you will want to set at least one breakpoint in your program. The program executes up to (but not including) the first breakpoint it encounters. Once a breakpoint is reached, you can do the following:

- Display the value of a variable or certain expressions

- Change the value of a variable

- Clear breakpoints, set new ones, or both

- Set up a list of expressions in a window and see how the values change as the program is executed

- Single-step through the program (trace it one line at a time) from that point

- Edit the program and recompile it, or use any other menu choice

    Other debugging tools are discussed when they are used in this book.

Debugging an Errant Program

In order to set a program, you need to have a program in memory. For this demonstration, enter the program in listing 14.1, exactly as it appears here. (It contains some intentional errors that will be ferreted out by debugging tools.)

Listing 14.1. Squeeze strings and store in array.

```
REM ** Squeeze Strings and Store in Array **
' Learning BASIC, Chapter 14.  File:PBL1401.BAS

REM ** Initialize **
CLS: DEFINT A-Z

REM ** Main program **
INPUT "How many strings (1-5)"; limit
```

```
DIM Strng$(1:limit), Squeeze$(1:limit)
maxblank = limit * 20
DIM Blanks(1:limit, 1:maxblank)
FOR str = LBOUND(Squeeze$(1)) TO UBOUND(Squeeze$(1))
  LINE INPUT "String: "; Strng$
  CALL Count(Strng$)
NEXT str
PRINT "Total number of words:"; total
PRINT "Press a key to see the Squeeze array"
kbd$ = INPUT$(1): CLS
CALL PrintSqueeze(Squeeze$())
PRINT: PRINT "Press a key to see the Blanks array"
kbd$ = INPUT$(1)
CALL PrintBlanks(Blanks())
END

SUB Count(Strng$)
  STATIC words
  Squeeze$(str) = "": num = 1
  FOR number = 1 TO LEN(Strng$)
    char$ = MID$(Strng$, number, 1)
    IF char$ = " " THEN
        INCR words
        Blanks(str, num) = number
      ELSE
        Squeeze$(str) = Squeeze$(str) + Char$
    END IF
  NEXT number
  total = words + str
END SUB

SUB PrintSqueeze(Squeeze$())
FOR str = LBOUND(Squeeze$(1)) TO UBOUND(Squeeze$(1))
    PRINT Squeeze$(str)
  NEXT str
END SUB

SUB PrintBlanks(Blanks())
  FOR str = LBOUND(Blanks(1)) TO UBOUND(Blanks(1))
    FOR num = LBOUND(Blanks(2)) TO UBOUND(Blanks(1))
      IF Blanks(str, num) = 0 THEN EXIT FOR
      PRINT Blanks(str, num);
    NEXT num
    PRINT
  NEXT str
END SUB
```

This program holds a maximum of five strings. The words in each string are counted, the spaces are deleted from the strings, and each squeezed string is stored in a one-dimensional array, named `Squeeze(str)`. As the spaces are deleted, the string number and the position in the original string where the blank existed (num) are stored in a two-dimensional array named `Blanks(str, num)`.

A maximum of 20 spaces for each string is allocated when the `Blanks(str, num)` array is dimensioned.

```
INPUT "How many strings (1-5)"; limit
DIM Squeeze$(1:limit)
maxblank = limit * 20
DIM Blanks(1:limit, 1:maxblank)
```

You probably won't need 20 spaces for each string, but sometimes you may need more. You can change the number.

When the program runs, all elements of the `Blanks` array are set to zero. As each blank space is found in a string, a zero is replaced by the value of the blank's position in the original string. For example, when blanks are found in positions 5, 8, 11, and 17 in a string, the row of the `Blanks` array corresponding to that string is

```
5 8 11 17 0 0 0 0 0 0 0 0 0 0 0 0 0
```

When the `Blanks` array is printed, you do not need to print all the zeros. To avoid printing all the zeros, the `PrintBlanks` procedure tests for the first zero in the row and exits the printing loop when a zero is found, as follows:

```
FOR num = LBOUND(Blanks(2)) TO UBOUND(Blanks(1))
  IF Blanks(str, num) = 0 THEN EXIT FOR
  PRINT Blanks(str, num);
NEXT num
```

Enter and run the program. At the first prompt

```
How many strings (1-5)?
```

press **2** so that you can enter two strings to test the program. When you press Enter, a prompt for your first string appears.

```
String:
```

Type the following:

```
This is my first string.
```

When you press Enter, the `Count` procedure is called and the string you entered is passed to it, as follows:

```
CALL Count(Strng$)
```

PowerBASIC Finds an Error

When the `Count` procedure is called, PowerBASIC runs into some immediate difficulties, halts the program, and prints an error message on the status line at the top of the screen (see figure 14.1).

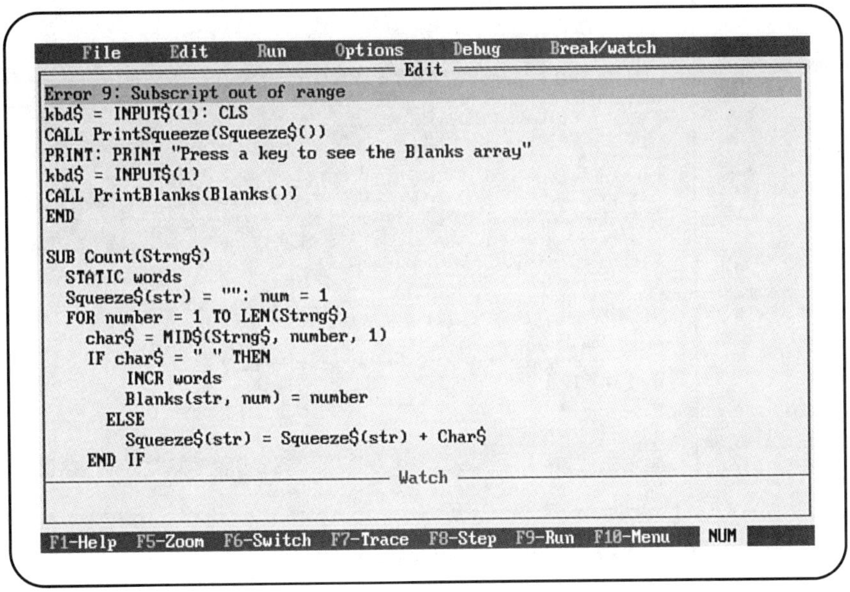

```
   File     Edit     Run     Options     Debug     Break/watch
================================== Edit ==================================
Error 9: Subscript out of range
kbd$ = INPUT$(1): CLS
CALL PrintSqueeze(Squeeze$())
PRINT: PRINT "Press a key to see the Blanks array"
kbd$ = INPUT$(1)
CALL PrintBlanks(Blanks())
END

SUB Count(Strng$)
  STATIC words
  Squeeze$(str) = "": num = 1
  FOR number = 1 TO LEN(Strng$)
    char$ = MID$(Strng$, number, 1)
    IF char$ = " " THEN
        INCR words
        Blanks(str, num) = number
    ELSE
        Squeeze$(str) = Squeeze$(str) + Char$
    END IF
=============================== Watch ===============================


 F1-Help  F5-Zoom  F6-Switch  F7-Trace  F8-Step  F9-Run  F10-Menu   NUM
```

Figure 14.1. Error message displayed on status line.

PowerBASIC recognizes an error that occurred. Errors that occur at run time are numbered below 400. Errors that occur when a program is compiled are numbered 401 and higher. Because the error code displayed in figure 14.1 indicates a runtime error (number 9), you know that the program compiled successfully and that the error occurred during the program's execution.

The cursor is at the beginning of the following line in the `Count` procedure:

```
_  Squeeze$(str) = "": num = 1
```

The cursor's position indicates that the error occurred when an attempt was made to execute this line. The error, `Subscript out of range`, occurs when you attempt to use a subscript larger than the maximum value established when the array was dimensioned. Because the only variable with a subscript on this line is `Squeeze$(str)`, this variable must be in error.

You can check the value of the subscript at the time the error occurred by accessing the Debug menu (press Alt-D). When the Debug menu is accessed, the highlight is on the Evaluate item. Press Enter to access Evaluate, type **str** in the Evaluate box, and press Enter again.

The value 1 appears in the Result box (see figure 14.2).

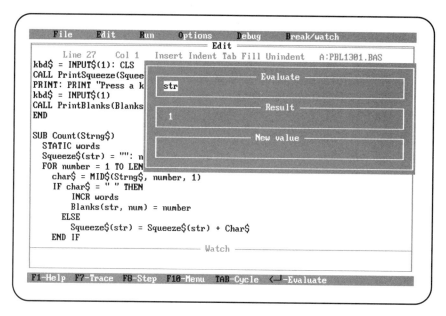

Figure 14.2. The variable, str, evaluated.

That value is correct (it equals num). The Evaluate and Return boxes have verified that the element number (str) is being evaluated correctly. Something else must be wrong with the way Squeeze$(str) is being handled. Is it dimensioned correctly?

If you check back to the beginning of the main program, you see that Squeeze$ was dimensioned for elements 1 and 2 (because limit = 2 from the INPUT statement). Remember, debugging tools are only an aid to finding bugs. They give you clues you can use; it is up to you to use the clues. The error message and cursor position provide clues in this example. They point to the line

```
Squeeze$(str) = " "; num = 1
```

The error code indicates a subscript error. Because the Evaluate box shows that str has been evaluated correctly, you must look for some other source in Squeeze$(str) for the error.

From the cursor's position, you know that the `Count` `SUB` procedure was called. Try to think of all possible requirements for using the `Squeeze$` array: dimensioning, passing to the `SUB`, and so on. The array was dimensioned before the SUB was called. Was the array passed to the SUB correctly? Aha! The program passed only the `String$` value—nothing else—to the `Count` procedure.

You can see that the `Count` procedure contains the `Squeeze$` array and another array, `Blanks`. You probably should use a SHARED option in the procedure header so that these arrays are shared. Or you can pass both arrays to the procedure. Using SHARED in the procedure header is the quickest way.

```
SUB Count(strng$) SHARED
```

However, it is better programming practice to pass the arrays. This is especially helpful when debugging.

Press Esc to remove the Evaluate box and return to the Edit window. Then change the SUB header to

```
SUB Count(Strng$, str, Squeeze$(), Blank$(), total)
```

Also, move the cursor back to the CALL statement in the main program and change it to

```
CALL Count(STrng$, str, Squeeze$(), Blank$(), total)
```

Run the program again with these changes. This time two strings are entered. They are

```
This is my first string.
```

```
This is my second string.
```

Each string is five words long, and the total is displayed correctly, as follows:

```
How many strings (1-5)? 2
String: This is my first string.
String: This is my second string.
Total number of words: 10
Press a key to see the Squeeze array
```

When you scan the strings, you see there are blanks at positions 5, 8, 11, and 17 in the first string and at positions 5, 8, 11, and 18 in the second string. These values should be stored in the two-dimensional `Blanks(str, num)` array.

When you press a key to see the squeezed strings, they are displayed. When you press a key to see the `Blanks` array, however, only one number is printed for each row of the array.

363

```
Thisismyfirststring.
Thisismysecondstring.

Press a key to see the Blanks array
  17
  18
```

Because only one number was printed for each array, either the arrays are not completely filled (5, 8, 11, 17, and 5, 8, 11, 18) or there is an error in printing the arrays. Clearly, an error exists in the Blanks array or how it is printed. Now's the time to use breakpoints so that the program runs until it reaches the section in which you think the error might be occurring.

Setting Breakpoints and Adding Watches

You can use breakpoints and variable watching to look for the missing values of the Blanks array. Two places are logical to check: the first is in the FOR/NEXT loop where the Blanks array is generated; the second, in the PrintBlanks procedure where the array is printed.

To turn on the first breakpoint, move the cursor to the FOR statement in the SUB procedure named Count.

```
_ FOR number = 1 to LEN(Strng$)
```

Access the Break/Watch menu by pressing Alt-B. (The highlight should be on Add watch.) Use the down-arrow key to move the highlight to Toggle breakpoint. Then press Enter to return to the Edit window. The line you selected is highlighted, indicating that a breakpoint has been set at this statement.

To turn on the second breakpoint, move the cursor down to the first line under the header of the PrintBlanks procedure.

```
SUB PrintBlanks(Blanks())
_ FOR str = LBOUND(Blanks(1)) TO UBOUND(Blanks(1))
```

Access the Toggle breakpoint selection from the Break/Watch menu again, and press Enter. On return to the Edit window, both selected lines are highlighted, which indicates that both breakpoints are turned on at those lines. When you run the program, it is interrupted at the first breakpoint it encounters.

When a breakpoint is encountered, you can single-step through the program to see what is happening in this section. You can watch some of the critical variables change as you single-step through the troubled area if you add some variables to the Watch window.

Variables you may want to watch are the number of the string (`str`), the number of the blank (`num`), and the number of the character in the string (`number`).

To watch a variable, access the Break/watch menu again and select `Add watch`. When you press Enter, the dialog box shown in figure 14.3 appears.

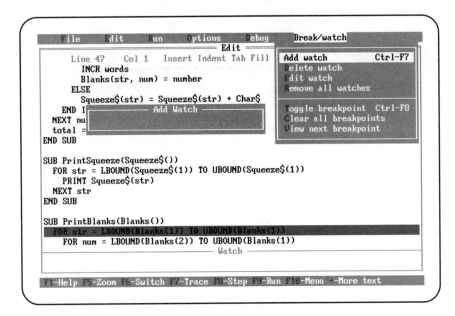

Figure 14.3. Add watch dialog box.

Type **str** and press Enter. Then access the Break/Watch menu's `Add watch` item again. Type **num** in the dialog box.

Use the same procedure to add the variable, `number`.

After you complete this step, you will notice that the Watch window (below the Edit window) has expanded and the variables you want to watch have been added. The values of the variables shown in figure 14.4 reflect the values in effect when the errant program ended. Notice that the value `num` equals 1. Only one blank was counted.

Now run the program again. At the prompts, enter the same information you entered on the first attempt, as follows:

```
How many strings (1-5)? 2
String: This is my first string.
```

When you press Enter, the `Count` procedure is called and passed the string you entered. Program execution stops at the first breakpoint.

365

```
   File      Edit      Run     Options    Debug        Break/watch
══════════════════════════════ Edit ══════════════════════════════
    Line 47    Col 1    Insert Indent Tab Fill Unindent * A:PBL1301.BAS
      ELSE
        Squeeze$(str) = Squeeze$(str) + Char$
    END IF
  NEXT number
  total = words + str
END SUB

SUB PrintSqueeze(Squeeze$())
  FOR str = LBOUND(Squeeze$(1)) TO UBOUND(Squeeze$(1))
    PRINT Squeeze$(str)
  NEXT str
END SUB

SUB PrintBlanks(Blanks())
  FOR str = LBOUND(Blanks(1)) TO UBOUND(Blanks(1))
    FOR num = LBOUND(Blanks(2)) TO UBOUND(Blanks(1))
─────────────────────────── Watch ───────────────────────────
•number:  26
 num:  1
 str:  3
──────────────────────────────────────────────────────────────
F1-Help  F5-Zoom  F6-Switch  F7-Trace  F8-Step  F9-Run  F10-Menu
```

Figure 14.4. Variables in Watch window.

The values of the variables being watched are

```
number = 0      ' position in the string
num = 1         ' blank counter
str = 1         ' string number
```

These values are correct. The FOR/NEXT loop has not entered yet.

Single Stepping

Press F7 to single step through the FOR/NEXT loop. Each time you press F7, one statement is executed and the highlight moves to the next statement. Watch the values in the Watch window as you step through the loop.

Because no blanks are encountered for the first four passes through the loop, the following sequence of statements is executed:

```
FOR number = 1 TO LEN(Strng$)
  char$ = MID$(Strng$, number, 1)
  IF char$ = " " THEN
      .
      .
      .
      Squeeze$(str) = Squeeze$(str) + Char$
      .
      .
      .
NEXT number
```

The only watched variable that changes is number, which increases, by one, each time through the sequence of statements.

On the fifth pass, the value of number changes to 5, and a blank is encountered at this string position. A new sequence of statements is executed for this pass.

```
  char$ = MID$(Strng$, number, 1)
  IF char$ = " " THEN
      INCR words
      Blanks(str, num) = number
    ELSE
      .
      .
      .
NEXT number
```

The logic of the program seems to be working. After this pass finishes, the values of the watched variables are

```
number = 6     ' incremented when NEXT number is executed
num = 1        ' blank counter unchanged
str = 1        ' still counting string 1
```

Continue single stepping through the loop until the NEXT str statement is reached. At this time, four blanks should have been counted, and the value of num should have been incremented to 5, but the final count on the first string (in the Watch window) shows

```
number = 25    ' this is correct
num = 1        ' this is not correct
str = 1        ' this is correct
```

You have learned that the number of blanks (num) is not being incremented. Look at the FOR/NEXT loop in the Count procedure. That is where the blanks should be counted, in the block IF structure.

```
char$ = MID$(Strng$, number, 1)
IF char$ = " " THEN
    INCR words
    Blanks(str, num) = number
  ELSE
```

Just before the ELSE statement, the value of num should be incremented, but it is not. Add INCR num before the ELSE statement so that this section of code is

```
char$ = MID$(Strng$, number, 1)
IF char$ = " " THEN
    INCR words
    Blanks(str, num) = number
    INCR num
  ELSE
```

To exit single-step mode, access the Run menu, move the highlight to the Program reset selection (the second item on the Run menu), and press Enter. The single-step highlight disappears from the Edit window, and you can begin the program again.

Access the Run menu, move the highlight back up to the Run item, and press Enter. Enter the number of strings and the first string.

Once again, the program stops at the first breakpoint. Use F7 to single step through the loop until the NEXT str statement is reached. This time, you see the blank counter (num) increase when a blank is found in the original string; the final count for the watched variables is

```
number = 25    ' correct
num = 5        ' correct; one more than the number of blanks
str = 1        ' correct
```

Removing a Breakpoint

Because this section of the program seems to be working correctly, you can remove the first breakpoint. To remove the first breakpoint, move the cursor to the line where the first breakpoint is highlighted. Then access the Break/Watch menu, move the highlight down to Toggle breakpoint (the fifth item on the menu), and press Enter. The highlight is removed from the line where the first breakpoint was. The breakpoint has been toggled off.

Before running the program again, access the Run menu, move the highlight to Program reset, and press Enter to leave single-step mode. Then access the Run menu, move the highlight back up to Run, and press Enter.

The program runs smoothly through the first phase. Both strings are accepted, and the words counted, as follows:

```
How many strings (1-5)? 2
String: This is my first string.
String: This is my second string.
Total number of words: 10
```

The program is interrupted by an INPUT$ statement, and the following prompt is displayed:

```
Press a key to see the Squeeze array
```

When you press a key, the squeezed strings are displayed, with another prompt, like this:

```
Thisismyfirststring.
Thisismysecondstring.
Press a key to see the Blanks array
```

When you press a key, the second breakpoint is encountered. The program stops at the following FOR statement.

```
FOR str = LBOUND(Blanks(1)) TO UBOUND(Blanks(1))
```

Press the F7 key to single step, to execute this statement and move to the next one. The values in the Watch window should be

```
number = 26    ' no longer a concern
num = 0        ' correct
str = 1        ' correct
```

Keep pressing F7 to cycle through the inner FOR/NEXT loop. The value of num increases from 1 to 2. When the first zero is found in Blanks (str, num), an exit is made from the inner loop, and the PRINT statement is highlighted. Press F7 one more time to highlight the NEXT str statement.

Before going on to the next string, press Alt-F5 to look at the output screen. As you can see from the following output, only two values are shown for the positions of blanks in the first string.

```
Thisismyfirststring.
Thisismysecondstring.

Press a key to see the Blanks array
 5  8
```

There should be four items with the values 5, 8, 11, and 17. Clearly, something is wrong in this section of the program.

You saw that four blanks were counted when you examined the Count procedure. Take a close look at the FOR statement of the inner loop in the PrintBlanks procedure.

```
FOR num = LBOUND(Blanks(2)) TO UBOUND(Blanks(1))
```

The subscripts used in the LBOUND and UBOUND functions are different. These subscripts tell which of the two dimensions is used for the function. One is 2 and the other is 1. They should be the same; the minimum and maximum value for the subscripts of the number of blanks. A look at the DIM statement for the Blanks array should tell you which is correct.

```
DIM Blanks(1:limit, 1:maxblanks)
```

The first dimension is for str; the second, for num. You should be using the lower and upper bounds of the second dimension. Change the incorrect FOR statement to

```
FOR num = LBOUND(Blanks(2)) TO UBOUND(Blanks(2))
```

Removing Watches and Breakpoints

Let's hope that is the last correction needed. Use the Run menu's Program reset item to reset the program. Then go to the Break/Watch menu, move the highlight down to Remove all watches, and press Enter. The variable names are removed from the Watch window, and the window's size is reduced.

Access the Break/Watch menu again. Move the highlight down to Clear, and press Enter. The breakpoint highlights in the Edit window should be gone.

Now run the program again to verify that it is correct. Access the Run menu, move the highlight to Run, and press Enter.

The following output shows three entries made, the words counted, and the prompt to press a key to see the squeezed array.

```
How many strings (1-5)? 3
String: This is my first string.
String: This is my second string.
String: This is the last string.
Total number of words: 15
Press a key to see the Squeeze array
```

Press a key. The squeezed array is displayed, with a message to press a key to see the Blanks array. When you press a key, the following output is displayed:

```
Thisismyfirststring.
Thisismysecondstring.
Thisisthelaststring.

Press a key to see the Blanks array
 5  8  11  17
 5  8  11  18
 5  8  12  17
```

The program now runs correctly. The corrected program is in listing 14.2.

Listing 14.2. Squeeze strings and store in array, revision 1.

```
REM ** Squeeze Strings and Store in Array Revision 1 **
' Learning BASIC, Chapter 14.  File:PBL1402.BAS

REM ** Initialize **
CLS: DEFINT A-Z

REM ** Main program **
INPUT "How many strings (1-5)"; limit
DIM Strng$(1:limit), Squeeze$(1:limit)
maxblank = limit * 20
DIM Blanks(1:limit, 1:maxblank)
FOR str = LBOUND(Squeeze$(1)) TO UBOUND(Squeeze$(1))
  LINE INPUT "String: "; Strng$
  CALL Count(Strng$, str, Squeeze$ (), Blanks(), total)
NEXT str
PRINT "Total number of words:"; total
PRINT "Press a key to see the Squeeze array"
kbd$ = INPUT$(1): CLS
CALL PrintSqueeze(Squeeze$())
PRINT: PRINT "Press a key to see the Blanks array"
kbd$ = INPUT$(1)
CALL PrintBlanks(Blanks())
END

SUB Count(Strng$, str, Squeeze$(), Blanks(), total)
  STATIC words
  Squeeze$(str) = "": num = 1
  FOR number = 1 TO LEN(Strng$)
    char$ = MID$(Strng$, number, 1)
    IF char$ = " " THEN
        INCR words
        Blanks(str, num) = number
        INCR num
```

continues

371

Listing 14.2. (continued)

```
      ELSE
         Squeeze$(str) = Squeeze$(str) + Char$
      END IF
   NEXT number
   total = words + str
END SUB

SUB PrintSqueeze(Squeeze$())
   FOR str = LBOUND(Squeeze$(1)) TO UBOUND(Squeeze$(1))
      PRINT Squeeze$(str)
   NEXT str
END SUB

SUB PrintBlanks(Blanks())
   FOR str = LBOUND(Blanks(1)) TO UBOUND(Blanks(1))
      FOR num = LBOUND(Blanks(2)) TO UBOUND(Blanks(2))
         IF Blanks(str, num) = 0 THEN EXIT FOR
         PRINT Blanks(str, num);
      NEXT num
      PRINT
   NEXT str
END SUB
```

In the next section, the program is revised to store the arrays in data files.

Revising a Debugged Program

The program in this section gives you a chance to hone your data-file tools. The arrays created in the program of listing 14.2 can be saved permanently in data files. One data file can hold the squeezed strings. Another can hold the positions of the blanks in the original string.

The task is broken into the following parts:

1. Creating arrays and storing the data in two sequential files

2. Reading and printing the data files

The first program, listing 14.3, creates the arrays and stores the data in two sequential files. Later a second program reads the data files and restores the original strings.

Listing 14.3. Create arrays and store as data files.

```
REM ** Create Arrays and Store as Data Files  **
' Learning BASIC, Chapter 14.   File:PBL1403.BAS

REM ** Initialize **
CLS: DEFINT A-Z

REM ** Main program **
CALL GetStrings
CLOSE
PRINT: PRINT "Files are closed."
END

SUB GetStrings
  INPUT "Enter drive (followed by colon)"; path$
  INPUT "Enter file name for string"; Name1$
  INPUT "Enter file name for blanks"; Name2$
  Name1$ = path$ + Name1$
  Name2$ = path$ + Name2$
  INPUT "How many strings (1-5)"; limit
  DIM Strng$(1:limit), Squeeze$(1:limit)
  maxblank = limit * 20
  DIM Blanks(1:limit, 1:maxblank)
  OPEN Name1$ FOR OUTPUT AS #1
  OPEN Name2$ FOR OUTPUT AS #2
  FOR str = LBOUND(Strng$(1)) TO UBOUND(Strng$(1))
    LINE INPUT "String: "; Sent$
    CALL WriteFiles(str, Sent$, Strng$(), Blanks(), Squeeze$())
  NEXT str
END SUB

SUB WriteFiles(str, Sent$, Strng$(), Blanks(), Squeeze$())
  Squeeze$(str) = "": num = 1
  FOR number = 1 TO LEN(Sent$)
    char$ = MID$(Sent$, number, 1)
    IF char$ = " " THEN
        Blanks(str, num) = number
        INCR num
      ELSE
        Squeeze$(str) = Squeeze$(str) + Char$
    END IF
  NEXT number
  WRITE #1, Squeeze$(str)
  num = num - 1
  WRITE #2, num
  FOR n = 1 TO num
    WRITE #2, Blanks(str, n)
  NEXT n
END SUB
```

Program 14.3 enables you to enter the names of two files and open both files at the same time, as follows:

```
SUB GetStrings
  INPUT "Enter drive (followed by colon)"; path$
  INPUT "Enter file name for string"; Name1$
  INPUT "Enter file name for blanks"; Name2$
  Name1$ = path$ + Name1$
  Name2$ = path$ + Name2$
```

Both files are opened FOR OUTPUT with different file numbers. Squeezed strings are stored in file #1, and the number of blanks and their position in file #2:

```
OPEN Name1$ FOR OUTPUT AS #1
OPEN Name2$ FOR OUTPUT AS #2
```

The strings are entered from the keyboard. When a string is entered, the WriteFiles procedure is called to write the data to the two files:

```
FOR str = LBOUND(Strng$(1)) TO UBOUND(Strng$(1))
  LINE INPUT "String: "; Sent$
  CALL WriteFiles(str, Sent$, Strng$(), Blanks(),
Squeeze$())
NEXT str
```

The WriteFiles procedure detects whether each character in the string is a blank or not. Blanks are removed, and their positions in the original string are stored in an array named Blanks(str, num). When all the blanks have been removed, the information for the string is written to the two files.

```
WRITE #1, Squeeze$(str)
num = num - 1
WRITE #2, num
FOR n = 1 to num
  WRITE #2, Blanks(str, n)
NEXT n
```

The squeezed string is written to a single record of file #1. The number of blanks (num) is written to file #2, followed by the position of each blank.

The entry of the file names and two strings looks like this:

```
Enter drive? a:
Enter file name for string? teststr.seq
Enter file name for blanks? blanks.seq
How many strings (1-5)? 2
String: This is my first string.
String: This is my second string.
```

When the second string is entered, both files are closed and a message is printed to let you know that they are closed.

The program ends with no other output. You can see what is in the two files by leaving PowerBASIC Lite and returning to DOS. Assuming that the files (still named `teststr.seq` and `blanks.seq`) were sent to drive A, you can see file #1 by typing the following at the DOS prompt:

```
TYPE A:TESTSTR.SEQ
```

The output of this DOS command is displayed and the DOS prompt returns. To see the data in file # 2, type

```
TYPE A:BLANKS.SEQ
```

The output of this DOS command is added to the screen. It now appears, as in the following output:

```
C>TYPE A:TESTSTR.SEQ
"Thisismyfirststring."
"Thisismysecondstring."

C>TYPE A:BLANKS.SEQ
4
5
8
11
17
4
5
8
11
18

C>
```

The contents of both files are displayed.

Evidently there were no errors in this program; the data files show that the files were stored as planned.

Reading the Files

Now that you know the data is stored correctly, you should write a program to read and print the data from the files. The program in listing 14.4 is a first attempt.

Listing 14.4. Read files and restore strings.

```
REM ** Read Files and Restore Strings **
' Learning BASIC, Chapter 14.  File:PBL1404.BAS

REM ** Initialize **
CLS: DEFINT A-Z
DIM Squeeze$(1:5), Blanks(1:5, 1:100), ResStrng$(1:5)

REM ** Main program **
CALL GetFile(str, Squeeze$(), Blanks(), ResStrng$())
CLOSE
PRINT: PRINT "Files are closed. Press a key to see strings."
kbd$ = INPUT$(1)
CALL PrintFile(str, ResStrng$())
END

SUB GetFile(str, Squeeze$(), Blanks(), ResStrng$())
  INPUT "Enter drive (followed by colon)"; path$
  INPUT "Enter file name for string"; Name1$
  INPUT "Enter file name for blanks"; Name2$
  Name1$ = path$ + Name1$
  Name2$ = path$ + Name2$
  OPEN Name1$ FOR INPUT AS #1
  OPEN Name2$ FOR INPUT AS #2
  str = 1
  WHILE NOT EOF(1)
    INPUT #1, Squeeze$(str)
    INPUT #2, n
    FOR num = 1 TO n
      INPUT #2, Blanks(str, num)
    NEXT num
    CALL PutBack(str, Squeeze$(), Blanks(), n, ResStrng$())
    str = str + 1
  WEND
END SUB

SUB PutBack(str, Squeeze$(), Blanks(), n, ResStrng$())
  ResStrng$(str) = "": num = 0
  FOR number = 1 TO LEN(Squeeze$(str)) + n
    IF Blanks(str, num + 1) = number THEN
        ResStrng$(str) = ResStrng$(str) + " "
        num = num + 1
      ELSE
        char$ = MID$(Squeeze$(str), number, 1)
        ResStrng$(str) = ResStrng$(str) + char$
    END IF
  NEXT number
END SUB
```

```
SUB PrintFile(str, ResStrng$())
  FOR number = 1 TO str - 1
    PRINT ResStrng$(number)
  NEXT number
END SUB
```

Both file #1 and file #2 are opened FOR INPUT so that you can read the data from the files.

```
OPEN Name1$ FOR INPUT AS #1
OPEN Name2$ FOR INPUT AS #2
```

One squeezed string is read by one INPUT # statement. The data from the Blanks file first reads how many blanks appeared in the string. Then that number is used as the upper limit of a FOR/NEXT loop to read the positions from which the blanks were removed from the original string.

```
WHILE NOT EOF(1)
  INPUT #1, Squeeze$(str)
  INPUT #2, n
  FOR num = 1 TO n
    INPUT #2, Blanks(str, num)
  NEXT num
```

The most important part of the program is the PutBack SUB procedure that places the blanks in the squeezed strings—hopefully, in positions that will restore the original strings. That is not guaranteed, however. In fact, the odds are against it happening the first time the program runs. The following output shows the results of your first attempt:

```
Enter drive? A:
Enter file name for string? TESTSTR.SEQ
Enter file name for blanks? BLANKS.SEQ

File is closed. Press a key to see strings.
This sm fi ststr ng.
This sm se ondstr ng.
```

The spaces are at the correct positions in the strings, but letters are missing, as you can see when you compare the "restored" string with the original string.

```
This sm fi ststr ng.
This is my first string.
```

377

Each time a blank is inserted, a letter seems to be dropped from the string. Time to debug again. You must find out why and where the letter is dropped and correct that part of the program.

More Debugging

The logical place to look is in the PutBack SUB procedure. Place a breakpoint at the FOR statement in the PutBack procedure, as follows:

```
FOR number = 1 TO LEN(Squeeze$(str)) + n
```

Critical variables you might watch are `Squeeze$(str)`, `ResStrng$(str)`, `number`, and `str`. Put each of these variables in the Watch window by using Add watch from the Break/Watch menu for each one.

After you add the variables to be watched, run the program again. When you do, the program is interrupted at the breakpoint. Now, use the F7 key to single step through the loop. Watch the variables as each step is made.

As you pass through the loop, you see one character added to `ResStrng$(str)` during each pass. The value of `number` is important also. Notice that on the fifth pass, the space is inserted correctly after the word *This* in `ResStrng$(str)`. On pass number 6, however, the letter *s* (the 7th letter in the original string) is appended to `ResStrng$(str)`. The letter *i* should have been appended. Continue pressing F7 until an exit is made from the loop.

Table 14.1 shows the letters that should be inserted for each pass, the letter inserted, and the difference between the letter's position now and in the original string.

Table 14.1. Analysis of Letter Positions.

Pass Number	Correct Letter	Inserted Letter	Difference Correct — Inserted	Blanks
1	T	T	0	0
2	h	h	0	0
3	i	i	0	0
4	s	s	0	0
5	blank	blank	0	1
6	i	s	6 − 7 = −1	1
7	s	m	7 − 9 = −2	1

Pass Number	Correct Letter	Inserted Letter	Difference Correct — Inserted	Blanks
8	blank	blank	0	2
9	m	f	9 – 12 = –3	2
10	y	i	10 – 13 = –3	2
11	blank	blank	0	3
12	f	s	12 – 15 = –3	3
13	i	t	13 – 16 = –3	3
14	r	s	14 – 18 = –4	3
15	s	t	15 – 19 = –4	3
16	t	r	16 – 20 = –4	3
17	blank	blank	0	4
18	s	n	18 – 22 = –4	4
19	t	g	19 – 23 = –4	4
20	r	.	20 – 24 = –4	4
21	i			
22	n			
23	g			
24	.			

An exit is made from the loop after pass number 20. By examining the Difference Correct–Inserted column of the table, you can see that the letters inserted are displaced when a blank is inserted. The error in displacement of letters accumulates as more blanks are inserted.

The value of the variable, number, is too large after a blank is inserted. This variable is used in the following statement to access the next letter to be added to the restored string:

```
char$ = MID$(Squeeze$(str), number, 1)
```

To access the correct letter, you use a value equal to number minus the number of blanks inserted. A variable containing the number of blanks (num) is available. Therefore, change the statement to

```
char$ = MID$(Squeeze$(str), number - num, 1)
```

379

After you make this change, execute the Program reset item on the Run menu. Then run the program again. When the program is interrupted by the breakpoint, single step through the loop again, using the F7 key. Watch the letters added to the restored string.

An error was encountered previously on pass number 6. Notice that the correct letter (*i*) is inserted this time. Keep pressing F7 until an exit is made from the loop. This time the logic seems to be correct. The blanks are inserted in the right places and the correct letters are appended to the restored string.

Remove the variables from the Watch window by selecting Remove all watches from the Break/watch menu. Then remove the breakpoint by selecting Clear all breakpoints from the Break/watch menu.

When the watched variables and breakpoint are removed, run the revised program. The entries and results are shown here:

```
Enter drive? A:
Enter file name for string? TESTSTR.SEQ
Enter file name for blanks? BLANKS.SEQ

File is closed. Press a key to see strings.
This is my first string.
This is my second string.
```

The results are what was expected. You should try the program with different strings from the program in listing 14.3. Enter more or fewer strings. Experiment with long strings and short strings.

If you made any typing errors in this chapter's demonstration programs, you had a few more errors to debug. Unfortunately, errors are impossible to predict. PowerBASIC Lite helps you find many errors. Appendix D lists commonly encountered error codes and their meanings.

Some computing books give you a set of program writing and debugging rules that are supposed to make errors impossible (or unlikely). This book has no such set of rules. Just remember that you can minimize and isolate errors by using functions and procedures to break the program into short logical parts. Then you can examine and debug only those parts in which you think an error has occured. Test your programs first with simple data. When the program works with simple data, try something more complex.

When you think your program is perfect, give it to a friend for testing. You have worked intensely on your project, and may assume something your friend won't. Your friend may find errors or omissions you overlooked.

Summary

Regardless of how much care you use in writing programs, programming errors are a common occurrence. PowerBASIC Lite has debugging capabilities that help you find errors. Some errors are discovered by PowerBASIC when it attempts to compile the program; others are detected when the program runs. Some runtime errors are elusive, however. In these cases, you can use PowerBASIC Lite's debugging tools.

Breakpoints are tools used to interrupt a program at strategic points. While the errant program is stopped, you can evaluate variables or expressions to see whether the variables are assigned the correct values or whether the expressions are calculating the expected values. Breakpoints can be checked from the Debug menu's Evaluate item. Breakpoints are set and cleared from the Break/watch menu.

You can step through a program, or part of a program, one statement at a time to see whether the program is being executed in logical order. Single stepping is activated by the Trace Into item from the Run menu or by pressing F7 to execute each step. To exit single-step execution mode, use the Run menu's Program reset item.

Another debugging tool is PowerBASIC's capability of watching the value of variables. Variables to be watched are entered from the Add watch item on the Break/watch menu. You can use this feature with breakpoints and single-stepping to see how variables change at critical parts of a program.

Most of this chapter focused on using the debugging tools to find and correct errors in a short program. Programs written in short, functional blocks are easier to debug than long, complex programs. After each block has been debugged, you can add code to the program and then repeat the debugging cycle for the new sections of code. You used the short program you debugged in a longer program to write strings to a disk file. Another program was created to read the stored strings from disk into memory, and then more debugging was used on this program.

Exercises

1. An array is dimensioned by the following lines:

    ```
    maxblank = limit * 10
    DIM Blanks(1:limit, 1:maxblank)
    ```

    a. How many dimensions does the Blanks array have?

    b. If limit = 5, what is the maximum subscript for the first dimension? the second dimension?

381

2. What debugging tool do you use to interrupt a program at a predetermined statement?

3. Single stepping can be activated from which menu?

4. When a program is interrupted at a breakpoint, describe what happens when you press the F7 key.

5. What debugging tools can be accessed from the Break/watch menu?

6. From the information given about the array in exercise 1,

   a. What is the value of LBOUND(Blanks(1))?

   b. What is the value of UBOUND(Blanks(2))?

   c. What is the value of UBOUND(Blanks(1))?

7. A single squeezed string has been stored in a disk file by listing 14.3. The string is

   ```
   "Puttheblanksincorrectplaces."
   ```

   What are the values placed in the Blanks array to restore the string as follows?

   ```
   "Put the blanks in correct places."
   ```

Advanced Topics

The most commonly used PowerBASIC Lite statements and functions have been explained and demonstrated in previous chapters. PowerBASIC Lite has more advanced features, as well as features that are less commonly used. These features are briefly discussed or listed in this chapter. Much of the information has been extracted from the *PowerBASIC Reference Guide* and *PowerBASIC User Manual*, which are included with the full version of PowerBASIC.

Remember, you can use the PowerBASIC Lite help system to obtain more information about any of PowerBASIC's statements and functions.

The chapter closes with a list of some of the features of the full version of PowerBASIC.

The topics discussed in this chapter are grouped into the following classifications:

- Metastatements

- General statements and functions

- The keyboard, screen, and printer statements and functions

- Numeric statements and functions

- String functions and system variable

- Graphics statements and functions

- File statements and functions

- The light pen and joystick statements and functions

- Communications and I/O statements and functions

- Error and event trapping statements and functions

- System statements and functions
- The full version of PowerBASIC

Metastatements

Metastatements are compiler directives that operate at a different level than regular language statements. They control the behavior of the compiler. All metastatements begin with a dollar sign ($). The following metastatements are available from PowerBASIC Lite:

- The $COM metastatement allocates space for the serial port receiving buffers.

```
$COM [size]
```

This metastatement sets the size of both communications buffers (COM1 and COM2). They cannot be set individually. The argument *size* is an integer constant that defines the buffer capacity in bytes (0 to 32767). *size* must be specified in increments of 16 bytes. If *size* is not specified, the buffers are allocated in increments of 256 bytes each. The $COM statement should be used only once in any program: before any executable source code.

- The $DYNAMIC metastatement declares array allocation to be dynamic by default.

```
$DYNAMIC
```

This metastatement takes no argument. It declares the default array allocation type to be dynamic. In the absence of a $DYNAMIC metastatement, the default array allocation is static. The *PowerBASIC Reference Guide* encourages you to use implied or explicit dynamic declarations in DIM statements, instead of using the $DYNAMIC metastatement. The $DYNAMIC metastatement is included in PowerBASIC for compatibility with programs written in earlier versions of BASIC.

- The $SOUND metastatement sets the capacity of the background music buffer.

```
$SOUND size
```

The argument `size` is a numeric constant that indicates the note capacity of the PLAY statement's background buffer, ranging from 1 to 4096. Increasing the capacity of the buffer to the maximum number of notes your program plays makes note-count trapping (and the attendant degradation in performance) unnecessary. Each note requires eight bytes of memory. The default capacity is 32 notes, or 256 bytes. The $SOUND metastatement should be used only once in any program before any executable source code.

- The $STACK metastatement declares the size of the runtime stack.

```
$STACK size
```

The argument `size` is a numeric constant ranging from 1536 to 32766 bytes. STACK determines how much runtime memory is devoted to the stack. The stack is used for return addresses and parameter passing. It also is used for local variables during procedure, function, and subroutine calls. Finally, it is used within structured statements such as FOR/NEXT, WHILE/WEND, and so on. The default size is 1536 bytes. This metastatement should be used only once in any program before any executable source code.

- The $STATIC metastatement declares the default array allocation to be static.

```
$STATIC
```

This metastatement takes no argument. Space for static arrays is allocated at compile time. The *PowerBASIC Reference Guide* encourages you to use implied or explicit dynamic declarations in DIM statements instead of using the $STATIC metastatement. This metastatement is included in PowerBASIC to ensure compatibility with programs written in earlier versions of BASIC.

General

The statements and functions included in this section were not discussed in earlier chapters. You may find some of them useful for special purpose programs. Some are used in advanced programming, and the actions performed by some are duplications of other statements or functions.

- The MTIMER function and statement read or reset the microtimer.

  Statement: MTIMER
  Function: y = MTIMER

MTIMER measures elapsed time, primarily for short intervals. It offers excellent resolution, because it is accurate to approximately two *microseconds* (two millionths of a second). However, the accuracy drops off sharply after approximately 54 milliseconds (which is 54 thousandths of a second).

The MTIMER statement and function must be used as a pair. You must first issue the MTIMER statement to reset the timer to 0, and then call the MTIMER function to get the result. Subsequent calls to the function return a value of zero if you haven't restarted the microtimer with another MTIMER statement. Here is how to use the pair of statements:

```
MTIMER                    ' initialize the timer
pi# = ATN(1) * 4          ' calculate the value of pi
ElapsedTime! = MTIMER     ' get the value of timer
```

- PEEK, PEEKI, PEEKL, and PEEK$ functions return the byte (PEEK), word (PEEKI), double-word (PEEKL), or sequence of bytes (PEEK$) at a specified memory address.

```
y% = PEEK(address)
y% = PEEKI(address)
y& = PEEKL(address)
y$ = PEEK$(address, count)
```

The PEEK functions and complementary POKE statements are low-level methods of accessing individual bytes in memory. The data is retrieved from memory starting at the offset *address* within the current segment.

PEEK retrieves a single byte and returns it as an integer with a value from 0 to 255.

PEEKI retrieves two consecutive bytes and returns them as a single integer:

```
(return value = second byte * 256 + first byte)
```

PEEKL retrieves four consecutive bytes and returns them as a single long integer:

```
(value = fourth byte * 2^24 + third byte * 65536 + second
byte * 256 + first byte)
```

PEEK$ retrieves *count* consecutive bytes and returns them as a string in which the ASCII code of the first character of the string is the value of the first byte retrieved, the next ASCII code is the next byte retrieved, and so on.

The argument *address* is usually a numeric expression from 0 to 65535 that indicates the offset in the current segment where the data retrieval should begin.

- The PLAY function returns the number of notes in the background music buffer.

```
y = PLAY(x)
```

The argument *x* is a dummy argument: It is functionless but necessary. PLAY returns the number of notes in the background music buffer that are waiting to be played. If music is being played in the foreground or not at all, a zero (0) is returned.

- The PLAY statement generates music.

```
PLAY string expression
```

PLAY is an interpretive mini-language that does for music what DRAW does for graphics. Use PLAY to define musical passages as sequences of characters in a *string expression* and to play them through the computer's speaker.

The *string expression* can be made up of the following commands, combined in this way:

```
note-letter [{#¦+¦-}]
```

When used in a PLAY statement, this expression plays note *note-letter*, which is a letter from A through G. Notes can be made sharp (# or +) or flat (-) by including the appropriate symbol (#, +, or -). Music definitions can be grouped into lengthy command sequences. For example:

```
PLAY "O3FGA"          '
```

387

plays notes F, G, and A in Octave 3. An octave is specified by a number following the letter O as in O3. The duration is specified by a number following the letter L as in L2 (a half note) or L4 (a quarter note).

- POKE, POKEI, POKEL, and POKE$ statements store the byte (POKE), word (POKEI), double-word (POKEL), or sequence of bytes (POKE$) at a specified memory location.

```
POKE address, byte value
POKEI address, integer value
POKEL address, long integer value
POKE$ address, string
```

POKE stores a single-byte having a *value* from 0 to 255.

POKEI stores an *integer value* in two consecutive bytes:

```
(integer value = second byte * 256 + first byte)
```

POKEL stores a *long integer value* in four consecutive bytes:

```
(long integer value = fourth byte * 2^24 + third
byte * 65536 + second byte * 256 + first byte)
```

POKE$ stores a *string* in consecutive bytes, in which the ASCII code of the first character of the string is stored in the first byte of memory, the next ASCII code is stored in the next byte of memory, and so on.

The argument *address* is normally a numeric expression from 0 to 65535 that indicates the offset in the current segment where the data storage should begin.

- The REDIM statement erases and redimensions dynamic arrays.

```
REDIM array(subscripts) [, (subarrayscripts)] ...
```

This statement for dynamic arrays is a shortcut for the two-step process ERASE arrayx(), DIM arrayx(). It has the same syntax as the DIM statement. The argument *array* is the name of the array, and the argument *subscripts* is either a group of single integers or a group of ranges, separated by commas. REDIM cannot change the number of dimensions that an array has. Only the lower and upper bounds can be redefined.

- The STOP and SYSTEM statements halt program execution.

  Either STOP or SYSTEM terminates execution of a program and returns control to PowerBASIC. Once a program is terminated by STOP or SYSTEM it cannot be continued as it can with interpreted BASIC. END, which does the same thing, is the preferred statement.

- The STR$ function returns the string representation of a number.

```
s$ = STR$(numeric expression [, digits])
```

STR$ returns the string form of a numeric variable or expression. If *numeric expression* is greater than zero, STR$ adds a leading space. For example, STR$(23) returns a three-character string. The first character is a space, whereas the second and third characters are 23. The LTRIM$ function can be used to remove the leading space. The *digits* argument permits control over the format of the result. If this option is used, the value of *numeric expression* is rounded (if necessary) to fit in *digits* places. If *numeric expression* cannot be rounded to fit, an error occurs. Allowable values for *digits* are 1 through 18. The complementary function to STR$ is VAL, which takes a string argument and returns the numeric equivalent.

- The SWAP statement exchanges the values of two variables.

```
SWAP var1, var2
```

The arguments *var1* and *var2* are two variables of the same type. If you try to swap variables of different types, compiler error 474, "Type mismatch," occurs. Swapping variables without using SWAP requires a third variable, used to temporarily hold the value of one variable while the value of the other variable is reassigned. For example, if a = 5 and b = 6, you could swap the values with these three steps:

```
temp = a
a = b
b = temp
```

Using the SWAP statement, however, reduces this to one step.

```
SWAP a, b
```

The SWAP statement is useful when you are sorting arrays.

389

- The TRON and TROFF statements turn program execution tracing on and off.

```
TRON
TROFF
```

TRON puts your program into a debugging mode that displays source code line numbers as each statement is executed. TROFF turns the debugging mode off.

You should never need to use TRON and TROFF with PowerBASIC. PowerBASIC's integrated debugger is a superior debugging tool. These statements are included for compatibility with previous versions of BASIC.

Keyboard, Screen, and Printer Statements and Functions

This section includes statements and functions that relate to the use of your keyboard, display screen, and printer. Some you will rarely use. For example, you probably rarely will use the function key line in interpretive BASIC. PowerBASIC displays active function keys on the help line of the screen.

- The CSRLIN function returns the current vertical position (row number) of the screen cursor.

```
y = CSRLIN
```

CSRLIN returns an integer between 1 and 25 that represents the current vertical position (row number) of the cursor on the display screen. Use POS to read the cursor's horizontal position (column number). Use LOCATE to move the cursor to a specified row and column.

- The INSTAT function returns the keyboard status.

```
y = INSTAT
```

INSTAT returns keyboard status information. When you press a key, INSTAT returns logical TRUE (nonzero). Otherwise, it returns logical FALSE (zero). The function doesn't remove a keystroke from the keyboard buffer, so if it ever returns TRUE, it continues to return TRUE until the keystroke is removed by INKEY$ or another keyboard-reading function. The most common use of INSTAT is in loops that suspend program execution until the user presses a key, as in the following code fragment:

```
PRINT "Press any key to continue"
WHILE NOT INSTAT: WEND
k$ = INKEY$
```

The action provided by INSTAT, the loop, and the INKEY$ function can be performed more simply with the INPUT$ function (as used throughout this book), as follows:

```
PRINT "Press any key to continue"
kbd$ = INPUT$(1)
```

- The KEY statement sets and displays function key definitions and defines key trap values.

```
KEY {ON¦OFF¦LIST}
KEY n, string expression
```

KEY ON and KEY OFF turn on and off the function key display at the bottom of the screen. The display consists of 10 key numbers, each of which is followed by the first six characters of the string, if any, that have been assigned to that key. When the function key display is on, the 25th line of the screen never scrolls.

KEY LIST displays a list of function key definitions on the screen, one per line.

KEY n, string expression assigns string expression to function key n, where string expression has a length of 15 characters or less (only the first six appear in the function key display). To disable a function key, assign it the null string.

- The LPOS function returns the number of characters on the current line in the printer buffer.

```
y = LPOS(printer)
```

The argument printer is an integer expression from 0 to 3 that selects the printer (0 or 1 = LPT1, 2 = LPT2, 3 = LPT3). LPOS reports how many characters have been sent to the printer since the last carriage-return character was output. In effect, it gives the current horizontal position of the printhead.

391

- The LPRINT and LPRINT USING statements send data to the printer.

```
LPRINT [expression list [{,¦;}]]
LPRINT USING format string; expression list [{,¦;}]
```

The argument *expression list* is a comma-, semicolon-, or space-delimited series of numeric or string expressions. The argument *format string* contains formatting information.

LPRINT and LPRINT USING statements are used identically to the PRINT and PRINT USING statements except that data is sent to the printer (LPT1) rather than to the screen. PowerBASIC inserts a carriage return/line feed (CR/LF) pair at the end of each line that it prints. The line width (the number of characters output before each CR/LF) is 80 by default, but that number can be changed by a WIDTH statement.

- The POS function returns the horizontal position (column number) of the screen cursor.

```
y = POS(x)
```

The argument *x* is a dummy argument. An argument must be used, but it has no function. The value returned by POS ranges from 1 to 80. It represents the horizontal position (column number) of the cursor on the display screen. Use CSRLIN to get the cursor's vertical position (row number). Use LOCATE to move the cursor to a specified screen position.

Numeric Statements and Functions

You have used several numeric statements and functions in earlier chapters. This section contains those that were not discussed.

- The ATN and TAN functions return the trigonometric functions arctan and tan of the specified arguments.

```
y1 = ATN(numeric expression)
y2 = TAN(numeric expression)
```

ATN returns the arctangent (inverse tangent) of the argument *numeric expression*; that is, the angle having tangent *numeric expression*. The angle is returned in extended-precision format.

TAN returns the tangent of the angle *numeric expression*. The result is returned in extended-precision format.

In both functions, *numeric expression* is expressed in radians. To convert radians to degrees, multiply by 57.2958. To convert degrees to radians, multiply by 0.017453.

- The CEIL function converts the value of a numeric variable or *expression* to an integer by returning the smallest integer greater than or equal to its argument.

```
y = CEIL(numeric expression)
```

The CEIL function rounds upward. For example, y = CEIL(1.4) places the value 2 into y.

- The CINT, CLNG, CQUD, CSNG, CDBL, CEXT, CFIX, and CBCD functions convert values to specific variable types.

```
integervar% = CINT(numeric expression)
longintvar& = CLNG(numeric expression)
quadintvar&& = CQUD(numeric expression)
singlevar! = CSNG(numeric expression)
doublevar# = CDBL(numeric expression)
extendedvar## = CEXT(numeric expression)
bcdfixedvar@ = CFIX(numeric expression)
bcdfloatvar@@ = CBCD(numeric expression)
```

Each of these functions converts *numeric expression* to a particular variable type. In each case, *numeric expression* must be within the legal range for the variable type. The argument *numeric expression* is rounded if necessary.

These conversions are rarely needed because PowerBASIC automatically performs the necessary conversion when executing an assignment statement or passing parameters. For example, the following two statements are equivalent in PowerBASIC. The value of number% is 23.

```
number% = 22.7569
number% = CINT(22.7569)
```

- The DECR statement decrements a numeric variable by a specified amount.

```
DECR variable [, size]
```

If *size* (a numeric expression) is omitted, the value of *variable* (a numeric variable) is decremented by 1. DECR is a more efficient way to subtract a value from a variable than the following statement used in other versions of BASIC.

```
variable = variable - size
```

- The EXP, EXP2, and EXP10 functions return a base number raised to a power. The base is e (2.718282...) for EXP, 2 for EXP2, and 10 for EXP10.

```
y = EXP(x)
y = EXP2(x)
y = EXP10(x)
```

EXP returns e to the *x*th power, where *x* is a numeric expression and e is the base for natural logarithms (approximately 2.718282). The following two statements produce the same value, providing the variable e has been assigned a value of 2.718282.

```
y = EXP(3)
y = e ^ 3
```

EXP2 returns 2 to the *x*th power, where *x* is a numeric variable or expression. The following two statements produce the same value

```
y = EXP2(3)
y = 2 ^ 3
```

EXP10 returns 10 to the *x*th power, where *x* is a numeric variable or expression. The following two statements produce the same value:

```
y = EXP10(3)
y = 10 ^ 3
```

- The FIX function truncates a number to an integer.

```
y = FIX(numeric expression)
```

FIX strips off the fractional part of its argument *numeric expression* and returns the integer part. Unlike CINT and INT, FIX does not perform rounding.

- The FIXDIGITS system variable controls interpretation of binary-coded decimal fixed-point numbers.

```
FIXDIGITS = numeric expression
y = FIXDIGITS
```

Use FIXDIGITS to specify how many decimal places are to be used with BCD fixed-point expressions. The default is 2. The maximum is 18.

- The LOG, LOG2, and LOG10 functions return the logarithm of their arguments.

```
y1 = LOG(numeric expression)
y2 = LOG2(numeric expression)
y3 = LOG10(numeric expression)
```

LOG returns the natural (base e) logarithm of *numeric expression*.

LOG2 returns the base 2 logarithm of *numeric expression*.

LOG10 returns the base 10 logarithm of *numeric expression*.

A logarithm of a number is the power to which the base would have to be raised to yield the number. LOG2(8) = 3, since $2 \wedge 3 = 8$

The argument *numeric expression* must be a positive value. If *numeric expression* is less than or equal to zero, runtime error 5, "Illegal Function Call," occurs. All three functions return extended-precision values.

- The MAX and MAX% functions return the argument with the largest (maximum) value.

```
y = MAX(arg1, arg2 [, argn]...)
y% = MAX%(arg1%, arg2% [, argn%]...)
```

These functions take any number of arguments and return the argument with the largest (maximum) value.

MAX handles arguments of any numeric type.

MAX% handles arguments that evaluate to integers. MAX% is more efficient than MAX. If any arguments of MAX% are outside the range of regular integers (−32768...+32767), an overflow error occurs at runtime. Any floating-point arguments of MAX% are rounded to integers before the comparison begins.

- The MIN and MIN% functions take any number of arguments and return the argument with the smallest (minimum) value.

```
y = MIN(arg1, arg2 [, argn]...)
y% = MIN%(arg1%, arg2% [, argn%]...)
```

MIN handles arguments of any numeric type.

MIN% handles arguments that evaluate to integers. MIN% is more efficient than MIN. If any arguments of MIN% are outside the range of regular integers (−32768...+32767), an overflow error occurs at runtime. Any floating-point arguments of MIN% are rounded to integers before the comparison begins.

String Functions and System Variable

The functions and one system variable discussed in this section relate to the use of strings. The system variable and several of the functions are used for advanced programming.

- The ASCII function returns the ASCII code of the first character in its argument.

```
y = ASCII(string expression)
```

ASCII returns the ASCII code (0 to 255) of the first character of the argument *string expression*. Unlike ASC, the string expression passed to ASCII can be a null string. If it is, the function returns −1.

- The BIN$, HEX$, and OCT$ functions return a string that is the binary (base 2), hexadecimal (base 16), or octal (base 8) representation of its argument.

```
b$ = BIN$(numeric expression)
h$ = HEX$(numeric expression)
o$ = OCT$(numeric expression)
```

The argument *numeric expression* must be in the range of –32768 to 65535. If it is outside this range, runtime error 6 (overflow) is generated. Any fractional part of *numeric expression* is rounded before the string is created.

BIN$ returns a string of binary digits that represent *numeric expression*. Binary is a number system that uses base 2 rather than base 10 (our decimal system). It contains only two digits, 0 and 1. One binary digit is called a *bit*. A group of eight binary digits is called a *byte*. The computer uses binary notation internally.

HEX$ returns a string that is the hexadecimal representation of *numeric expression*. Hexadecimal is a number system that uses base 16 rather than base 10. In hexadecimal, the digits 0 to 9 represent the same values as they do in decimal, whereas the letters A to F represent the decimal values 10 to 15. Hexadecimal notation is commonly used in programming because the binary bit patterns used internally by computers translate directly into hex digits. A complete byte (eight binary digits or bits) can be represented by two hex digits.

OCT$ returns a string that is the octal representation of *numeric expression*. Octal is a number system that uses base 8 with digits 0 to 7.

- The FLEXCHR$ system variable determines the character used to pad flex strings and random-access file buffers.

```
FLEXCHR$ = string expression
y$ = FLEXCHR$
```

In the first form, a single character, *string expression*, is used to fill extra space in flex strings when you are using MAP or FIELD and when you are assigning nonflex strings to random-access file buffers with LSET or RSET. The default value is a space. You also can retrieve the current value of FLEXCHR$ by assigning it to something as if it were an ordinary string variable (the second form).

- The STRPTR and STRSEG functions return the offset portion and the segment portion of a string variable.

```
x1 = STRPTR(string variable)
x2 = STRSEG(string variable)
```

The argument *string variable* is the name of a string variable (regular or flex).

STRPTR returns the offset portion of the address in memory where the string variable is stored. Such address information is sometimes called a *pointer*. For example, STRPTR(*strng$*) is said to return a pointer to *strng$*.

STRSEG returns the segment portion of the address in memory where the contents of *string variable* are stored. Note that STRSEG differs from VARSEG (and STRPTR varies from VARPTR). When used as a string variable, VARSEG returns the segment of the string's handle (a pointer to the segment of the actual data), whereas STRSEG returns the segment of the actual data.

Graphics Statements and Functions

This section discusses graphics statements and functions that were not covered in previous chapters.

- The PAINT statement (as used for tiling) fills an enclosed area with a tile pattern.

```
PAINT (x, y) [[, ][, boundary][, background]]
```

The values *x* and *y* specify the screen coordinates where tiling is to begin. For tiling, *color* is a string expression defining the tile pattern to be used. The value of *boundary* is the border color of the figure you are filling. The value of *background* is an optional string mask used when you want to repaint areas. The background mask is a tile slice to skip when checking areas that are already filled.

The pattern of each tile is defined by the byte patterns contained in *color* (from 1 to 64 bytes in length). The string expression can be formed as follows:

```
color$ = CHR$(Num1, Num2, ..., Numn)
```

where *Num* represents a hexadecimal value in the range of &H00 to &HFF. The vertical dimension of the tile depends on the number of bytes in color$. The width of a tile is either four or eight pixels, depending on the screen mode being used.

- The PALETTE and PALETTE USING statements change colors in the palette.

```
PALETTE [attribute, color]
PALETTE USING array(index)
```

To use these statements, you must have an EGA or VGA adapter and monitor.

PALETTE and PALETTE USING allow you to change colors in the current palette. The value of *attribute* represents an attribute (color number, or position) in the palette.

PALETTE lets you map color numbers greater than 15 into the palette. If no arguments are specified in PALETTE, the palette is set to the predefined default colors. The PALETTE statement allows you to change the color that is assigned to a single attribute.

PALETTE USING lets you modify all of your palette entries in a single statement. *array* is an integer array that contains the color values to be assigned to the palette. *index* specifies the element of the array to assign to attribute 0 with subsequent elements assigned to subsequent attributes. The array must be dimensioned large enough to fit all 16 palette entries after the array index.

- The PMAP function translates between physical and world screen coordinates.

```
m = PMAP(n, option)
```

In this syntax, *n* is the coordinate to be mapped and *option* is an integer expression from 0 to 3 that determines the value of the PMAP function as follows:

```
0 = map world coordinate x to physical coordinate x
1 = map world coordinate y to physical coordinate y
2 = map physical coordinate x to world coordinate x
3 = map physical coordinate y to world coordinate y
```

Physical coordinates are screen coordinates. World coordinates are the logical coordinates defined by a WINDOW statement.

399

- The SCREEN function returns the ASCII code or the attribute (color) of the character at the specified screen row and column.

```
y = SCREEN(row, column [, option])
```

The *row* and *column* arguments are integer expressions (ranging from 1 to 25 and 1 to 80, respectively) that specify the screen row and column information that is returned. For example, SCREEN (1, 1) returns the ASCII code of the character at row 1, column 1. If you set *option* to 1, SCREEN returns the attribute (color) of the character at (*row, column*) rather than the character itself. For example

```
PRINT SCREEN(10, 10)     ' prints ASCII code of character
PRINT SCREEN(10, 10, 1) ' prints attribute of character
```

SCREEN can return character information from graphics mode screens, but not attribute information.

- The VIEW statement defines the active area (viewport) of the graphics screen currently in use.

```
VIEW [[SCREEN] [(x1, y1)-(x2, y2) [, [color [, boundary]]]]]
```

Screen coordinate pairs (x1, y1) and (x2, y2) specify the upper-left and lower-right corners of the viewport being defined. The optional argument *color* fills the new viewport with this *color*. The optional argument *boundary* draws a border around the new viewport in the specified color.

VIEW defines an area on the graphics screen to which graphics output is limited. If you try to set pixels outside of the viewport, they are clipped (they will not be set). If a graphics object falls partly inside and partly outside the viewport, only the portion within the viewport shows. Text does not respect viewport boundaries. When a viewport has been defined, CLS clears only the viewport.

If the SCREEN option is omitted, future point references are taken relative to the top-left corner of the viewport rather than the top-left corner of the screen. For example

```
VIEW(20, 50)-(300, 180)
PSET(30, 60)                          ' sets pixel at (50, 110)
```

400

If you include SCREEN, you specify points in the normal way: relative to the upper-left corner of the screen. For example

```
VIEW SCREEN(20, 50)-(300, 180)
PSET(30, 60)                    ' sets pixel at (30, 60)
```

VIEW with no arguments defines the entire screen as the viewport. If you use the SCREEN statement to change screen modes, any VIEW setting is cancelled.

File Statements and Functions

This section includes a list of additional statements and functions related to files. Some are suited to more advanced programming.

- The FILEATTR function returns information about an open file.

```
y = FILEATTR(file number, {1¦2})
```

The information returned is a number (1, 2, 4, 8, 32 or a combination of these numbers).

- The FREEFILE function returns the next free PowerBASIC Lite file number.

```
x = FREEFILE
```

Using FREEFILE your program can open files and devices without keeping track of which file handles (numbers) are already in use. For example

```
x = FREEFILE
OPEN filename$ FOR OUTPUT AS x
```

x is a variable that represents the next file number, and filename$ is the name of the file that the value of *x* is assigned.

- The GET$ function reads a string from a file opened in binary mode.

```
GET$ [#] filenum, Count, string variable
```

401

filenum is the number of the file, *count* is the number of characters to be read, and *string variable* is the variable to which the string is assigned.

- The PUT$ function writes a string to a binary file.

```
PUT$[#]filenum, string expression
```

filenum is the number of the file, and *string expression* is the string written to the file.

- The RESET statement flushes all file buffers and closes all disk files and devices.

```
RESET
```

This statement performs the same function as a CLOSE statement with no arguments.

- The SEEK statement sets the file pointer position in a binary file.

```
SEEK [#] filenum, position
```

filenum is the number of the file, and *position* is the location in the file where the pointer is set.

Pen and Joystick

The statements and functions listed in this section are useful if you use a light pen or joystick.

- The PEN function reads the status of the light pen. The PEN statement controls the checking of light pen events.

Statement: PEN {ON¦OFF¦STOP}
Function: y = PEN(*option*)

Options follow:

Option	Information Returned
0	whether pen down since last check (–1 = yes, 0 = no)
1	x graphics coordinate where pen was last activated
2	y graphics coordinate where pen was last activated
3	current switch value (–1 = down, 0 = up)
4	most recent x graphics coordinate
5	most recent y graphics coordinate
6	row where pen was last activated (1-24)
7	column where pen was last activated (1-80)
8	most recent row (1-24)
9	most recent column (1-80)

- The STICK function returns joystick position information.

```
y = STICK(option)
```

Options follow:

Option	Information Returned
0	x coordinate for joystick A
1	y coordinate for joystick A
2	x coordinate for joystick B
3	y coordinate for joystick B

- The STRIG function returns the status of the joystick buttons. The STRIG and STRIG(n) statements control joystick button trapping.

```
STRIG function: y = STRIG(option)
STRIG statement: STRIG {ON|OFF}
STRIG(n) statement: STRIG(n) {ON|OFF}
```

Options follow:

Option	Information Returned
0	–1 if button 1 on joystick A has been pressed since the last STRIG(0) call; otherwise 0
1	–1 if button 1 on joystick A is currently down; 0 if not down

403

2	–1 if button 1 on joystick B has been pressed since the last STRIG(2) call; otherwise 0
3	–1 if button on joystick B is currently down; 0 if not down
4	–1 if button 2 on joystick A has been pressed since the last STRIG(4) call; otherwise 0
5	–1 if button 2 on joystick A is currently down; 0 if not down
6	–1 if button 2 on joystick B has been pressed since the last STRIG(6) call; otherwise 0
7	–1 if button 2 on joystick B is currently down; 0 if not down

Communications and I/O

Several statements and functions are related to serial port communications or other events that use input/output ports. These statements and functions are listed in this section.

- The COM(*n*) statement controls the trapping of communication (serial) port events. *n* is the number of the communications port (1 or 2).

```
COM({1¦2}) {ON¦OFF¦STOP}
```

- The INP function reads a byte from a processor I/O port. *portnumber* specifies the number of the I/O port (0 to 65535).

```
y = INP(portnumber)
```

- The IOCTL statement and IOCTL$ function communicate with a device driver. *filenum* is the file number of the device driver, and *string expression* is a string containing information sent to the device driver.

```
Statement: IOCTL [#]filenum, string expression
Function: s$ = IOCTL$([#] filenum)
```

- The OPEN COM statement opens and configures a communications (serial) port.

```
OPEN "COM{1¦2}: [baud][, parity][, data][, stop][options]"
AS [#]filenum [LEN = num]
```

- *baud* is an integer specifying the communications rate

- *parity* is a single character specifying parity status

  S (space parity)
  O (odd parity)
  M (mark parity)
  E (even parity)
  N (no parity)

- *data* is an integer (5-8) specifying the number of data bits

- *stop* is an integer (1 or 2) specifying the number of stop bits

- *options* control line handling, parity, carriage return/linefeed processing

- *filenum* specifies the communication port number

- *num* is the maximum number of bytes that can be read from or written to the port in a single operation

- The OUT statement writes a byte to a processor I/O port. *portnum* is the I/O port number (0-65535). *byte* is an integer (0-255).

```
OUT portnum, byte
```

- The WAIT statement suspends program execution until the specified hardware status condition is met. *portnum* is the I/O port number (0-65535). *n* and *m* are integers (0-255) used to control the condition to be met before continuing the program.

```
WAIT portnum, n [, m]
```

Error- and Event-Trapping Statements and Functions

The statements and functions listed in this section are related to trapping events or errors and providing information on error conditions.

- The ERADR function returns the address of the most recent error during program execution.

```
y& = ERADR
```

405

- The ERDEV and ERDEV$ functions return device driver error information. ERDEV is the error code returned by DOS. ERDEV$ contains the name of the device: 8 bytes for character devices, 2 bytes for block devices.

```
y  = ERDEV
y$ = ERDEV$
```

- The ERL and ERR functions return the program line number and error code of the most recent PowerBasic runtime error.

```
y  = ERL
y  = ERR
```

- The ERROR statement simulates the occurrence of a specific runtime error.

```
ERROR errcode
```

errcode is an integer expression (0-255). The *errcode* might be one of PowerBASIC's predefined runtime error codes or it might be a code that you define.

- The KEY statement associates a key or combination of keys with a number for key trapping.

```
KEY n, CHR$(shiftstatus, scancode)
```

The key or combination of keys are associated with a number (*n*) from 15 to 25 for key trapping with subsequent ON KEY and KEY(*n*) ON statements. *shiftstatus* is an integer expression that controls the response of the trap to the state of the Ctrl, Caps Lock, Num Lock, Alt, and both Shift keys. *scancode* is a numeric value (1-83) that defines the key to trap (see scan code table in Appendix B).

- The Key(*n*) Statement turns trapping on or off for a specific key.

```
KEY(n) {ON¦OFF¦STOP}
```

n is an integer expression (1-25, 30, or 31) that specifies the trapped key.

1-10	function keys F1 to F10
11	up arrow
12	left arrow

13	right arrow
14	down arrow
15-25	keys defined by KEY statement
30	function key F11
31	function key F12

- The ON ERROR statement specifies an error-handling routine and enables or disables error trapping.

```
ON ERROR GOTO {label¦line number}
```

Other ON... statements used with the trapping of special events follow.

```
ON COM({1¦2}) GOSUB {label¦line number)
ON KEY(n) GOSUB {label¦line number}
ON PEN GOSUB {label¦line number)
ON PLAY(NoteCount) GOSUB {label¦line number)
ON STRIG(n) GOSUB {label¦liine number}
ON TIMER(n) GOSUB {label¦line number}
```

- The RESUME statement restarts program execution after error handling with ON ERROR GOTO.

```
RESUME [{0¦NEXT¦label¦line number}]
```

System

The statements and functions listed in this section are related to computer system actions. Some of them perform the same action as DOS commands.

- The CALL INTERRUPT statement invokes a system interrupt.

```
CALL INTERRUPT n
```

- The CHDIR statement changes the current default directory.

```
CHDIR path
```

- The CHDRIVE statement changes the default disk drive.

```
CHDRIVE drive$
```

- The CLEAR statement zeros all variables and turns off event trapping.

```
CLEAR
```

- The ENDMEM function returns the address of the end of your computer's physical memory.

```
y& = ENDMEM
```

- The ENVIRON statement modifies the information in the DOS environment.

```
ENVIRON string expression
```

- The ENVIRON$ function retrieves information from the DOS environment table.

```
s$ = ENVIRON$({parameter string|n})
```

- The FILES statement displays the contents of a disk directory.

```
FILES [filespec]
```

- The KILL statement deletes a disk file.

```
KILL filespec
```

- The MEMSET statement declares the upper limit of memory that can be used by PowerBASIC.

```
MEMSET address
```

- The MKDIR statement creates a subdirectory.

```
MKDIR path
```

- The NAME statement renames a file.

```
NAME AS filespec1 AS filespec2
```

- The REG function sets a value in the register buffer. The REG statement returns a value in the register buffer.

```
Function: y = REG(register)
Statement: REG register, value
```

- The `RMDIR` statement deletes a disk directory.

```
RMDIR path
```

The Full Version of PowerBASIC

By the time you reach this point in the book, you should have had a sufficient taste of PowerBASIC Lite to decide whether you want to move on to the full version of PowerBASIC. PowerBASIC Lite is a "light" version of PowerBASIC. It is a real working system with most of the performance and functionality of the full PowerBASIC product. However, the full version has much more to offer.

By upgrading to the complete PowerBASIC V 2.1 product, you get

- The ability to create stand-alone executable (`.EXE`) files that run from DOS.

- The use of all real-mode memory for strings and arrays.

- A command-line compiler for batch-mode operation in addition to the compiler in the Integrated Development Environment.

- The ability to link `.OBJ` and PowerBASIC Unit Modules.

- The ability to `CHAIN`, `RUN`, `EXECUTE`, and `SHELL` other program segments.

- Free technical support.

- A two-volume set: The PowerBASIC Reference Guide and PowerBASIC User Manual—nearly 800 pages.

With these additional features, you can apply modular programming with separate compilation and linking of source code modules. You can link assembly code or object code from other language compilers into your programs. You can create self-contained modules (called *units*) of compiled routines, which can be used with many programs. These units make it easy to collect "libraries" of proven usable code. You can compile and run a single block of your program's code instantly to verify that it works correctly.

Additional metastatements are added to give your programs complete control over most options that appear on environment menus. Menus in the full version offer much more control over the programming environment so that you can customize the environment to fit your computer.

For just a taste, take a look at Figure 15.1, which shows the Options menu of PowerBASIC Lite.

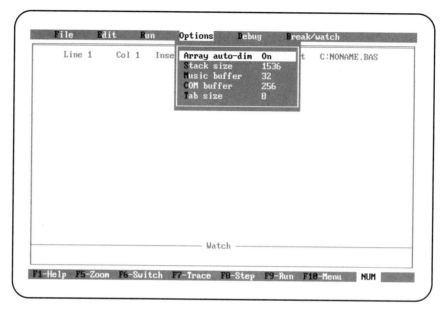

Figure 15.1. The Options menu for PowerBASIC Lite.

Notice the six items on the Main menu bar: File, Edit, Run, Options, Debug, and Break/watch. The Options menu, which contains five options, has been selected.

After you have studied Figure 15.1, look at Figure 15.2, which shows the more complete Options menu of the full version of PowerBASIC.

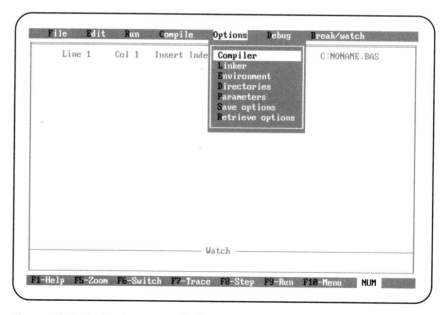

Figure 15.2. The Options menu for PowerBASIC.

A new menu item (Compile) has been added to the Main menu bar. The Options menu has been selected. The Options menu has seven items. When selected, each item on this menu displays a submenu containing other items. In addition, the Compile menu offers options for compiling the program.

In PowerBASIC Lite, your programs were automatically compiled to memory. You can use the full version of PowerBASIC to compile to memory an .EXE file, a Chain file, or a Unit file. Other menus also have additional items so that you can customize your programs and make them more efficient. If you like what you've seen in PowerBASIC Lite, you'll love the full version.

Chapter 16

PowerBASIC Lite Reference

This chapter contains the syntax for each PowerBASIC Lite statement, function, and system variable. These components are listed in alphabetical order for your convenience. Statements, functions, and system variables are the building blocks used to create programs. You can find explanations of each statement in the PowerBASIC Lite help system.

The following symbols are used to specify syntax format:

- Brackets [ ] indicate that the information they enclose is optional.

- Braces { } indicate a choice of two or more options, one of which can be used. The options are separated by vertical bars (|).

- Parentheses () indicate that the enclosed information must be supplied.

- Monospaced italic type represents placeholders for user-supplied information.

- Ellipses ... indicate that part of a command can be repeated as many times as necessary.

- Vertical ellipses

  .

  .

  .

  Three vertically spaced periods indicate the omission of one or more program lines that are not important for the example being discussed.

ABS Function

Description:

Returns the absolute value of a numeric expression. The absolute value of a
number is its magnitude, regardless of sign. In the example following the syntax,
y = ABS(–56) = 56.

Syntax:

```
y = ABS(numeric expression)
```

Example:

```
y = ABS(122-178)
```

ARRAY DELETE Statement

Description:

Deletes a single element from an array. You can specify the *index* of the element
to be deleted, how many elements to shift when deleting (*count*), and what value
to give the last element when all other elements have been shifted (*expression*).

Syntax:

```
ARRAY DELETE array([index]) [FOR count] [, expression]
```

Example:

```
ARRAY DELETE A(2) FOR 3, 17
```

ARRAY INSERT Statement

Description:

Inserts a single element into an array. You can specify the *index* at which the new
element is to be inserted, how many elements to shift to make room for the new
element (*count*), and what value to give the new element (*expression*).

414

Syntax:

```
ARRAY INSERT array([index]) [FOR count] [, expression]
```

Example:

```
ARRAY INSERT A(1) FOR 2, 23
```

ARRAY SCAN   Statement

Description:

Scans all or part of an array for the first element that satisfies an operator expression. Together, *index* and *count* specify the part of the array to be scanned. The relative *index* of the first match is stored in *ivar*, which must be an integer variable.

Syntax:

For a numeric array,

```
ARRAY SCAN array([index]) [FOR count], operator expression, TO ivar
```

Example:

```
ARRAY SCAN A&(10) FOR 20, =1, TO I%
```

For a string array,

```
ARRAY SCAN array([index]) [FOR count] [, FROM start to end]_
    [, COLLATE {UCASE¦string}], operator expression, TO ivar
```

Example:

```
ARRAY SCAN A$(), COLLATE UCASE, ="MATCH", TO I%
```

ARRAY SORT

Statement

Description:

Sorts all or part of an array in ascending or descending order. You can specify a *tag-along* array, the elements of which will be shifted along with the array being sorted.

Syntax:

For a numeric array,

```
ARRAY SORT Array1([index]) [FOR count] [, TAGARRAY Array2()]_
    [, {ASCEND¦DESCEND}]
```

Example:

```
ARRAY SORT A&() FOR 10, TAGARRAY B&(), ASCEND
```

For a string array,

```
ARRAY SORT Array1([index]) [FOR count] [, FROM start TO end]_
    [, COLLATE {UCASE¦string}] [, TAGARRAY Array2()]_
    [, ASCEND¦DESCEND]
```

Example:

```
ARRAY SORT A$(), FROM 32 TO 40, COLLATE UCASE, DESCEND
```

ASC

Function

Description:

Returns the ASCII code of the first character of the function's argument. The example assigns the ASCII code for the letter "A" to y (y = 65). The string expression cannot be a null string. Otherwise, a runtime error (5) will occur.

Syntax:

```
y = ASC(string expression)
```

Example:

```
y = ASC("Apple").
```

ASCII
Function

Description:

Returns the ASCII code of the first character of the function's argument. Unlike ASC, the string expression passed to ASCII can be a null (empty) string. If it is, the function returns –1. In the example following the syntax, the value returned to y is the ASCII code for the lowercase letter a (y = 97).

Syntax:

```
y = ASCII(string expression)
```

Example:

```
y = ASCII("apple")
```

ATN
Function

Description:

Returns the trigonometric arctangent (inverse tangent) of its argument, that is, the angle having a tangent that is *numeric expression*. The angle is returned in radians. In the example following the syntax, *angle* = .40 radians (approximately). The *numeric expression* must be expressed in radians. To convert radians to degrees, multiply by 57.29578. To convert degrees to radians, multiply by 0.0174533.

Syntax:

```
y = ATN(numeric expression)
```

Example:

```
angle = ATN(.4228)
```

417

ATTRIB

Function

Description:

Returns the DOS attribute of a file. Attribute values returned are 1 = read-only, 2 = hidden, 4 = system, 32 = archive. In the example that follows, one or a combination of the numbers 1, 2, 4, and 32 would reveal the type of the file named SOMEFILE. If zero is returned, the file is a regular file; it is neither read-only, hidden, system, or archive.

Syntax:

```
x = ATTRIB(filename$)
```

Example:

```
x = ATTRIB(A:SOMEFILE)
```

ATTRIB

Statement

Description:

Sets the DOS attribute of a file. In the example that follows, the attribute of SOMEFILE is set for a read-only. (See the attributes listed in the ATTRIB function.)

Syntax:

```
ATTRIB filename$, attribute
```

Example:

```
ATTRIB B:SOMEFILE, 1
```

BEEP

Statement

Description:

Makes the speaker sound. Plays a single quarter-second, 800-Hz tone. The optional numeric argument tells how many BEEPs. The example sounds five successive tones.

Syntax:

```
BEEP [count]
```

Example:

```
BEEP 5
```

BIN$ Function

Description:

Returns a string that is the binary (base 2) representation of its argument. The string returned in the example that follows (for the argument 12959) is 0011001010011111.

Syntax:

```
s$ = BIN$(numeric expression)
```

Example:

```
s$ = BIN$(12959)
```

BLOAD Statement

Description:

Loads into memory a file that was created with the BSAVE statement. In the example that follows, the data in the file named ARRAY.DAT is loaded into the memory assigned to the array named M%.

Syntax:

```
BLOAD filespec [, address]
```

Example:

```
BLOAD "ARRAY.DAT", VARPTR(M%(0))
```

419

BSAVE

Statement

Description:

Saves a block of memory to a disk file. In the example that follows, the block of memory beginning at the address of the array M%, which is 202 bytes long, is saved to a disk file named ARRAY.DAT.

Syntax:

```
BSAVE filespec, address, length
```

Example:

```
BSAVE "ARRAY.DAT", VARPTR(M%(0)), 202
```

CALL

Statement

Description:

Invokes a procedure. In the example that follows, the procedure named SumArray is called. An entire array named ArrayX is passed to the procedure.

Syntax:

```
CALL procname [(parameter list)]
```

Example:

```
CALL SumArray(ArrayX())
```

CALL INTERRUPT

Statement

Description:

Invokes a system interrupt (numbered 0 through 255). This is an advanced feature that should not be used unless you are familiar with the functions that are available. The IBM DOS Technical Reference Manual contains information on these functions.

Syntax:

```
CALL INTERRUPT n
```

Example:

```
CALL INTERRUPT &H21
```

CBCD

Function

Description:

Converts a numeric expression to a binary-coded decimal floating-point type. Can be used to avoid round-off errors that occur in calculations with single-, double-, and extended-precision numbers.

Syntax:

```
bcdfloatvar@@ = CBCD(numeric expression)
```

Example:

```
bcdfloatvar@@ = CBCD(a## + b##)
```

CDBL

Function

Description:

Converts a numeric expression to a double-precision, floating-point type. In the example that follows, the single-precision value of element 3 of the array named ArraySng would be converted to double-precision type, possibly for use in a double-precision calculation.

Syntax:

```
doublevar# = CDBL(numeric expression)
```

421

Example:

```
doublevar# = CDBL(ArraySng(3)!)
```

CEIL

Function

Description:

Converts a numeric variable or expression to an integer by returning the smallest integer greater than or equal to its argument. In other words, converted values are rounded up. In the following example; a! = –3.5 yields y% = –3, and a! = 3.5 yields 4.

Syntax:

```
y = CEIL(numeric expression)
```

Example:

```
y = CEIL(a!)
```

CEXT

Function

Description:

Converts a numeric expression to an extended-precision, floating-point type. In the example that follows, the single-precision value of the single-precision variable Sing! is converted to double-precision and assigned to extendedvar##.

Syntax:

```
extendedvar## = CEXT(numeric expression)
```

Example:

```
extendedvar## = CEXT(Sing!)
```

CFIX

Function

Description:

Converts a numeric expression to a binary-coded decimal fixed-point type. This data type is helpful when doing financial calculations, avoiding round-off errors resulting in calculations with single-, double-, and extended-precision numbers. In the following example, the value of the single-precision variable BigMoney! is converted to BCD fixed-point.

Syntax:

```
bcdfixedvar@ = CFIX(numeric expression)
```

Example:

```
var@ = CFIX(BigMoney!)
```

CHDIR

Statement

Description:

Changes the current default directory (similar to the DOS CHDIR command). With this statement, you can change directories from within a program. In the following example, the current default directory is changed to the DATA directory of the current default disk. CHDIR cannot be used to change the default disk drive (See CHDRIVE).

Syntax:

```
CHDIR path
```

Example:

```
CHDIR "\DATA"
```

CHDRIVE
Statement

Description:

Changes the current default drive.

Syntax:

```
CHDRIVE drive$
```

Example:

```
CHDRIVE "B"
```

CHR$
Function

Description:

Converts one or more ASCII codes into the corresponding ASCII character(s). In the syntax that follows, *int* means integer. This example assigns the string "Word" to s$.

Syntax:

```
s$ = CHR$(int expression [, int expression]...)
```

Example:

```
s$ = CHR$(87, 111, 114, 100)
```

CINT
Function

Description:

Converts a numeric expression to an integer type. In the example shown, this function converts the sum of a single-precision number and an integer to an integer result.

Syntax:

```
integervar%= CINT(numeric expression)
```

Example:

```
integ% = CINT(b! + c%)
```

CIRCLE Statement

Description:

Draws a circle or part of a circle on a graphics screen. In the example, part of a circle (an arc) is drawn with its center at (160, 100). This arc has a radius of 5 and color attribute 2. The arc begins at an angle of .2 radians and is drawn to an angle of 1.5. The aspect ratio (height to width) used is .8.

Syntax:

```
CIRCLE [STEP] (x, y), Radius [, Color [, Start, End#[, Aspect]]]
```

Example:

```
CIRCLE (160, 100), 5, 2, .2, 1.5, .8
```

CLEAR Statement

Description:

Zeros all numeric variables, sets all string variables to null, and turns off event trapping. (Also see ERASE.)

Syntax:

```
CLEAR
```

Example:

```
CLEAR
```

CLNG

Function

Description:

Converts a numeric expression to a long integer. In the example, the sum of two integers is converted to a long integer.

Syntax:

```
lngintvar& = CLNG(numeric expression)
```

Example:

```
lngintvar& = CLNG(a% * b%)
```

CLOSE

Statement

Description:

Closes an open file or device. In the example, file #1 is closed. If no file number is specified, all open files and devices are closed.

Syntax:

```
CLOSE[[#]filenum [, [#]filenum]...]
```

Example:

```
CLOSE #1
```

CLS

Statement

Description:

Clears the screen or the active viewport. When a viewport is active, CLS clears only the viewport.

Syntax:

```
CLS
```

Example:

```
CLS
```

COLOR

Statement (Graphics Mode)

Description:

Sets the colors for graphics operations. In the example for screen 1, the background color is set to 0 and the palette is set to 1. In the example for screens 7-12, the foreground color is set to 14 and the background color is set to 4.

Syntax for screen 1:

```
COLOR [Background] [, Palette]
```

Example:

```
COLOR 0, 1
```

Syntax for screens 7-12:

```
COLOR [Foreground] [, Background]
```

Example:

```
COLOR 14, 4
```

COLOR

Statement (Text Mode)

Description:

Sets the foreground, background, and border colors to be used when displaying text in SCREEN 0. In the example for screen 0, the foreground is set to color 14, the background is set to blue, and the border is set to blue.

Syntax for screen 0:

```
COLOR [Foreground] [, Background] [, Border]]
```

Example:

```
COLOR 14, 1, 1
```

COM   Statement

Description:

Controls the trapping of communications (serial) port events. In the example, communications port #1 is turned on for event trapping.

Syntax:

```
COM({1¦2}) {ON¦OFF¦STOP}
```

Example:

```
COM(1) ON
```

COS   Function

Description:

Returns the trigonometric cosine of its argument. The numeric expression is an angle specified in radians. In the example, the value returned and assigned to the variable y is approximately 0.9553.

Syntax:

```
y = COS(numeric expression)
```

Example:

```
y = COS(.30)
```

CQUD

Function

Description:

Converts a numeric expression to a quad integer. In the example, the sum of two extended-precision numbers is converted to a quad integer.

Syntax:

```
quadintvar&& = CQUD(numeric expression)
```

Example:

```
quadintvar&& = CQUD(a## + b##)
```

CSNG

Function

Description:

Converts a numeric expression to a single-precision number. In the example, the sum of a single-precision number and a double-precision number is converted to a single-precision value.

Syntax:

```
singvar! = CSNG(numeric expression)
```

Example:

```
singvar! = CSNG(a# + b!)
```

CSRLIN

Function

Description:

Returns the current vertical position (row number) of the screen's cursor. The value returned is in the range 1 to 25 for most screen modes. The maximum row is 30 in screen 11 and 12. (Also see POS.)

Syntax:

```
y = CSRLIN
```

Example:

```
y = CSRLIN
```

CURDIR$ — Function

Description:

Returns the current directory path. If *drive$* is not specified, the current drive's path is returned. From PowerBASIC Lite, the example might print C:\DOS\PBLITE.

Syntax:

```
s$ = CURDIR$ [(drive$)]
```

Example:

```
s$ = CURDIR$: PRINT s$
```

CVB — Function

Description:

Converts string data that is read from random-access files to binary-coded decimal floating-point form.

Syntax:

```
bcdflpt@@ = CVB(10-byte string)
```

Example:

```
bcdflpt@@ = CVB(bcdflpt$$)
```

CVD

Function

Description:

Converts string data that is read from random-access files to double-precision floating-point form.

Syntax:

```
doublevar# = CVD(8-byte string)
```

Example:

```
doublevar# = CVD(double$$)
```

CVE

Function

Description:

Converts string data that is read from random-access files to extended-precision floating-point form.

Syntax:

```
extendvar## = CVE(10-byte string)
```

Example:

```
extendvar## = CVE(extend$$)
```

CVF

Function

Description:

Converts string data read from random-access files to binary-coded decimal fixed-point form.

431

Syntax:

```
bcdfxpt@ = CVF(8-byte string)
```

Example:

```
bcdfxpt@ = CVF(bcdfxpt$$)
```

CVI

Function

Description:

Converts string data that is read from random-access files to integer form.

Syntax:

```
integervar% = CVI(2-byte string)
```

Example:

```
integervar% = CVI(integervar$$)
```

CVL

Function

Description:

Converts string data read from random-access files to long-integer form.

Syntax:

```
longint& = CVL(4-byte string)
```

Example:

```
longint& = CVL(longint$$)
```

CVMD
Function

Description:

Converts string variables from Microsoft-format random-access files to PowerBASIC IEEE double-precision form.

Syntax:

```
PBdouble# = CVMD(8-byte string)
```

Example:

```
PBdouble# = CVMD(MSdouble$$)
```

CVMS
Function

Description:

Converts string variables from Microsoft-format random-access files to PowerBASIC IEEE single-precision form.

Syntax:

```
PBsingle! = CVMS(4-byte string)
```

Example:

```
PBsingle!= CVMS(MSsingle$$)
```

CVQ
Function

Description:

Converts string data read from random-access files to quad integer form.

Syntax:

```
quadint&& = CVQ(8-byte string)
```

Example:

```
quadint&& = CVQ(quadint$$)
```

CVS

Function

Description:

Converts string data that is read from random-access files to single-precision floating-point form.

Syntax:

```
singvar! = CVS(4-byte string)
```

Example:

```
singvar! = CVS(singvar$$)
```

DATA

Statement

Description:

Declares constants in the source code to be read by READ statements. In the syntax form, *constant* can be a numeric constant or a string constant.

Syntax:

```
DATA constant [, constant] ...
```

Example:

```
DATA 43.3, 75.2, 93.1, 88.6
```

DATE$ System Variable

Description:

Sets or retrieves the system date. If the date is set as it is in the first example that follows, the second example would print: 02-18-1992.

Syntax:

```
set date: DATE$ = d$
```

Example:

```
DATE$ = "2-18-92"
```

Syntax to retrieve the date:

```
d$ = DATE$
```

Example:

```
d$ = DATE$: PRINT d$
```

DECLARE Statement

Description:

Explicitly declares functions and procedures. In the syntax format, *Name* is the name of the procedure or function. The *parameter list* contains the name and type of each parameter passed. The parentheses must be used, even if no parameters are passed. In the example, PrintIt is the name of the SUB procedure. NameUnit$ (a string) and NumUnit% (an integer value) are passed.

Syntax:

```
DECLARE {SUB|FUNCTION} Name([parameter list])
```

Example:

```
DECLARE SUB PrintIt(NameUnit$, NumUnit%)
```

DECR

Statement

Description:

Decrements a numeric variable by a specified amount. In the example, the value of the variable count% is decreased by 2. The default value is 1.

Syntax:

```
DECR variable [, size]
```

Example:

```
DECR count%, 2
```

DEF FN/END DEF

Statement

Description:

Defines a function. Functions can be single-line or multiline.

Syntax for a Single-Line Function:

```
DEF FNname [(argument list)] = expression
```

Example:

```
DEF FNCelToFahr! = 1.8 * Celsius! + 32
```

Syntax for a Multiline Function:

```
DEF FNname [(argument list)] [SHARED]
      [LOCAL variable list]
      [STATIC variable list]
      [SHARED variable list]

          .
          .   statements
          .

      [EXIT DEF]
          .
          .
          .
```

```
        [FNname = expression]
    END DEF
```

Example:

```
    DEF FNCount%(StringCon$)
        words = 0
FOR number = 1 TO LEN(StringCon$)
char$ = MID$(StringCon$, number, 1)
IF char$ = " " THEN INCR words
        NEXT number
        FNCount = words + 1
    END DEF
```

DEF SEG   Statement

Description:

Defines the data segment to be used by statements and functions to address memory. In the example, the defined data segment is the address of the first byte of the PointDn array. DEF SEG with no argument resets the segment value to its default segment (PowerBASIC's main data segment).

Syntax:

```
DEF SEG [= numeric expression]
```

Example:

```
DEF SEG = VARSEG(PointDn(0))
```

DEFBCD   Statement

Description:

Declares the default type for variables to be BCD floating-point. The example declares variables that begin with the letters R, S, and T to be BCD floating-point variables.

Syntax:

```
DEFBCD letter range [, letter range]...
```

Example:

```
DEFBCD R-T
```

DEFDBL   Statement

Description:

Declares the default type for variables to be double-precision floating-point. The example declares variables that begin with the letters A through C to be double-precision floating-point variables.

Syntax:

```
DEFDBL letter range [, letter range]...
```

Example:

```
DEFDBL A-C
```

DEFEXT   Statement

Description:

Declares the default type for variables to be extended-precision floating-point. The example declares variables that begin with the letters G and H to be extended-precision floating-point variables.

Syntax:

```
DEFEXT letter range [, letter range]...
```

Example:

```
DEFEXT G, H
```

DEFFIX

Description:

Declares the default type for variables to be BCD fixed-point. The example declares variables that begin with the letters P and Q to be BCD fixed-point variables.

Syntax:

```
DEFFIX letter range [, letter range]...
```

Example:

```
DEFFIX P, Q
```

DEFFLX

Description:

Declares the default type for variables to be flex string. The example declares variables that begin with the letter U to be flex string variables.

Syntax:

```
DEFFLX letter range [, letter range]...
```

Example:

```
DEFFLX U
```

DEFINT

Description:

Declares the default type for variables to be integers. The example declares variables that begin with the letters I, J, and K to be integer variables.

Syntax:

```
DEFINT letter range [, letter range]...
```

Example:

```
DEFINT I-K
```

DEFLNG

Statement

Description:

Declares the default type for variables to be long integer. The example declares variables that begin with the letters L and M to be BCD floating-point variables.

Syntax:

```
DEFLNG letter range [, letter range]...
```

Example:

```
DEFLNG L, M
```

DEFQUD

Statement

Description:

Declares the default type for variables to be quad integer. The example declares variables that begin with the letter N to be quad integer variables.

Syntax:

```
DEFQUD letter range [, letter range]...
```

Example:

```
DEFQUD N
```

DEFSNG

Description:

Declares the default type for variables to be single-precision floating-point. The example declares variables that begin with the letters D, E, and F to be single-precision floating-point variables.

Syntax:

```
DEFSNG letter range [, letter range]...
```

Example:

```
DEFSNG D-F
```

DEFSTR

Description:

Declares the default type for variables to be string. The example declares variables that begin with the letters V and W to be string variables.

Syntax:

```
DEFSTR letter range [, letter range]...
```

Example:

```
DEFSTR V, W
```

DELAY

Description:

Suspends program execution for a specified interval. Fractional values can be specified. The resolution is .054 seconds. The example suspends program execution for five seconds.

441

Syntax:

```
DELAY seconds
```

Example:

```
DELAY 5
```

DIM

Statement

Description:

Declares arrays. The example declares the MyArray% array to be an integer with a minimum subscript of 1 and a maximum subscript of 400 (400 elements).

Syntax:

```
DIM [{STATIC¦DYNAMIC}] Var(subscripts)[, Var(subscripts)]...
```

Example:

```
DIM MyArray%(1:400)
```

DIR$

Function

Description:

Returns a file name that matches the specified pattern. In the syntax format, mask$ specifies a file or path name that can include a drive name and DOS wild card characters. Subsequent calls to DIR$, with no parameters specified, return additional file name matches. In the example, matches would be found for files in the root directory of A: with the .BAS extension.

Syntax:

```
f$ = DIR$ [(mask$[, attribute])]
```

Example:

```
f$ = DIR$ (A:\*.BAS)
```

DO/LOOP

Description:

Defines a group of program statements that are executed repetitively as long as a specified condition is met. The example shows the DO WHILE...LOOP form.

Syntax:

```
DO [{WHILE¦UNTIL} expression]

        .
        . statements [EXIT LOOP]
        .

{LOOP[{WHILE¦UNTIL} expression]¦WEND}
```

Example:

```
DO WHILE count% < 10
        total% = total% + count%
        INCR count%
LOOP
```

DRAW

Description:

Draws shapes on a graphics screen. The string expression is composed of commands that control an imaginary pen. Using DRAW is analogous to drawing on a piece of paper with a colored pen. The commands control drawing, lifting or lowering the pen, and changing pen colors. In the example, a rectangle is drawn (up 10, right 40, down 10, and left 40).

Syntax:

```
DRAW string expression
```

Example:

```
DRAW "U10 R40 D10 L40"
```

END
Statement

Description:

Terminates the execution of a program (optionally returning a DOS error code) or defines the end of a structured block. If none of the options are specified, encountering an END statement closes all open files. The example shown uses the SELECT keyword to mark the end of a procedure.

Syntax:

```
END [{return expression¦DEF¦FUNCTION¦IF¦SELECT¦SUB}]
```

Example:

```
SELECT CASE
      .
      .   cases containing statements
      .
END SELECT
```

ENDMEM
Function

Description:

Returns the address of the end of your computer's physical memory. A long integer is returned. ENDMEM sees only the memory within the 640K available to DOS. It will not report on extended or expanded memory.

Syntax:

```
y& = ENDMEM
```

Example:

```
y& = ENDMEM
```

ENVIRON

Statement

Description:

Modifies the information in the DOS environment table. It is normally used in the full version of PowerBASIC to configure the environment to be passed to programs executed through the SHELL statement. The example sets the DOS *PATH* parameter to \PBLITE.

Syntax:

```
ENVIRON string expression
```

Example:

```
ENVIRON "PATH=\PBLITE"
```

ENVIRON$

Function

Description:

Retrieves information from the DOS environment table. It is used normally in the full version of PowerBASIC to configure the environment to be passed to programs executed through the SHELL statement. In the example, the second parameter from the start of the environment table would be assigned to the variable s$.

Syntax:

```
s$ = ENVIRON$({parameter string¦n})
```

Example:

```
s$ = ENVIRON$(2)
```

EOF

Function

Description:

Returns the end-of-file status of an opened file. EOF returns logical TRUE (non-zero) when the end of the specified file has been reached. Otherwise it returns logical FALSE (zero). The EOF function often is used as a condition to exit a loop, as in the example.

Syntax:

```
y = EOF(file number)
```

Example:

```
WHILE NOT EOF(1)
      LINE INPUT #1, X$
      PRINT X$
WEND
```

ERADR

Function

Description:

Returns the address of the most recent error during program execution.

Syntax:

```
y& = ERADR
```

Example:

```
PRINT "An error of type" ERR "occurred at" ERADR
```

ERASE

Statement

Description:

Deallocates dynamic arrays and resets static arrays to zero (numeric) or null (string). In the example, BigArray is the name of the array to be erased.

Syntax:

```
ERASE name [, name]...
```

Example:

```
ERASE BigArray
```

ERDEV
Function

Description:

Returns the error code from DOS. ERDEV is not the same as ERR, which returns PowerBASIC Lite's error code. See a DOS Technical Reference manual for details.

Syntax:

```
y = ERDEV
```

Example:

```
y = ERDEV
```

ERDEV$
Function

Description:

Contains the name of the device involved in the error. See a DOS Technical Reference manual for details.

Syntax:

```
y$ = ERDEV$
```

Example:

```
y$ = ERDEV$
```

ERL

Function

Description:

Returns the line number of the most recent error. When the error occurs in a statement without a line number, the number of the nearest numbered line (working backward) is returned. If there are no numbered lines, zero (0) is returned.

Syntax:

```
y = ERL
```

Example:

```
y = ERL
```

ERR

Function

Description:

Returns the error code of the most recent runtime error. This number can be tested in an error-trapping routine so that the appropriate error-handling routine can be used.

Syntax:

```
y = ERR
```

Example:

```
y = ERR
```

ERROR

Statement

Description:

Simulates the occurrence of a specific runtime error. Often used in debugging error-trapping routines to simulate an error. The value of *errcode* in the syntax format is an integer from 0 to 255.

Syntax:

```
ERROR errcode
```

Example:

```
ERROR 11
```

EXIT   Statement

Description:

Transfers program execution out of a structure. The example is used to exit from a DO/LOOP or a WHILE/WEND loop. This statement is preferred over GOTO.

Syntax:

```
EXIT {FUNCTION|SELECT|DEF|FOR|IF|LOOP|SUB}
```

Example:

```
EXIT LOOP
```

EXP   Function

Description:

Returns the value of e raised to the power of the argument. The value of e is approximately 2.718282. The value assigned to y in the example would be approximately 20.086.

Syntax:

```
y = EXP(x)
```

Example:

```
y = EXP(3)
```

EXP2

Function

Description:

Returns the value of 2 raised to the power of the argument. The value assigned to y in the example would be 8.

Syntax:

```
y = EXP2(x)
```

Example:

```
y = EXP2(3)
```

EXP10

Function

Description:

Returns the value of 10 raised to the power of the argument. The value assigned to y in the example would be 1000.

Syntax:

```
y = EXP10(x)
```

Example:

```
y = EXP10(3)
```

EXTRACT$

Function

Description:

Returns the portion of a string leading up to the first occurrence of a specified character or string. The *main string* argument is the string expression from which to extract. The search starts from the first character up to the first occurrence of *match string*. In the example, the value of x$ would be "abra" (everything up to the occurrence of "cad").

Syntax:

```
x$ = EXTRACT$(main string, [ANY] match string)
```

Example:

```
x$ = EXTRACT$("abracadabra", "cad")
```

FIELD

Statement

Description:

Defines the variables of a random-access file buffer.

Syntax 1

```
FIELD [#]filenum, width AS stringvar [, width AS stringvar]...
```

Syntax 2:

```
FIELD [#]filenum, FROM start TO stop AS stringvar
[, FROM start TO stop AS stringvar]...
```

Example:

```
FIELD #1, 2 AS IngegerVar$, 4 AS LongIntVar$,_
4 AS SingleVar$
```

FILEATTR

Function

Description:

Returns information about an open file having the specified number. The {1¦2} option returns the file's mode (1) or its DOS handle (2). File modes are combinations of 1 Input, 2 Output, 4 Random, 8 Append, and 32 Binary. The DOS handle is helpful when you are using advanced DOS-related operations.

Syntax:

```
y = FILEATTR(file number, {1¦2}
```

Example:

```
y = FILEATTR(1, 2)
```

FILES

Statement

Description:

Displays the contents of a disk directory (like the DOS DIR /W command). If the filespec parameter is omitted, all files in the current directory are displayed. In the example, all files in the current directory with the .BAS extension would be displayed.

Syntax:

```
FILES [filespec]
```

Example:

```
FILES "*.BAS"
```

FIX

Function

Description:

Truncates a number to an integer (it strips off the fractional part and does not round). The value of y in the example would be 50.

Syntax:

```
y = FIX(numeric expression)
```

Example:

```
y = FIX(50.75)
```

FIXDIGITS

System Variable

Description:

Controls the interpretation of binary-coded decimal fixed-point numbers. The default number of decimal places is 2. The second syntax format is used to retrieve the current value of FIXDIGITS.

Syntax:

```
FIXDIGITS = numeric expression
```

Example:

```
FIXDIGITS = 4
```

Syntax:

```
y = FIXDIGITS
```

Example:

```
y = FIXDIGITS: PRINT y
```

FLEXCHR$

System Variable

Description:

The FLEXCHR$ system variable determines the character used to pad flex strings and random-access file buffers. The first syntax and example set the character. The second syntax and example retrieve the current character.

Syntax:

```
FLEXCHR$ = string expression
```

Example:

```
FLEXCHR$ = "*"
```

Syntax:

```
y$ = FLEXCHR$
```

Example:

```
y$ = FLEXCHR$: PRINT y$
```

FOR/NEXT
Statement

Description:

FOR and NEXT define a loop of program statements controlled by an automatically incrementing or automatically decrementing counter.

Syntax:

```
FOR counter = start TO stop [STEP increment]
    .
    . {statements}
    .
NEXT [counter [, counter]...]
```

Example:

```
FOR num! = 1.0 TO 2.0 STEP 0.1
PRINT num!
NEXT num!
```

FRE
Function

Description:

Returns the amount of free memory that is available to your program. In the example, freemem1& would be assigned the largest continuous block of free string memory. freemem2& would return the number of bytes left for data. freemem3& would return the number of bytes left on the stack.

Syntax:

```
freememory& = FRE({string expression¦0¦-1¦-2})
```

Example:

```
freemem1& = FRE("String space")
freemem2& = FRE(-1)
freemem3& = FRE(-2)
```

FREEFILE

Function

Description:

Returns the next free PowerBASIC Lite file number. This enables you to open files and devices without keeping track of which numbers (handles) are already in use.

Syntax:

```
filenum = FREEFILE
```

Example:

```
NextFile% = FREEFILE
```

FUNCTION/END FUNCTION

Statement

Description:

Defines a function block. This statement offers more flexibility than DEF FN/END DEF.

Syntax:

```
FUNCTION name [(parameters)] [LOCAL¦SHARED¦STATIC]_
  [PUBLIC¦PRIVATE]
    [LOCAL variable list]
    [STATIC variable list]
    [SHARED variable list]
```

455

```
          .
          . {statements [EXIT FUNCTION]}
          .
END FUNCTION
```

Example:

```
FUNCTION SinOf(angle)
    PRINT angle; SIN(angle)
END FUNCTION
```

GET   Statement (Files)

Description:

Reads a record from a random-access file. The example reads the 42nd record of file number 1. If *recnum* is omitted, the next record in the sequence is read (the first record when the file has just been opened.)

Syntax:

```
GET [#]filenum [, recnum]
```

Example:

```
GET #1, 42
```

GET   Statement (Graphics)

Description:

Copies all or part of the graphics screen into an array. In the syntax format, (x1, y1) is the upper-left boundary and (x2, y2) is the lower-right boundary. The *arrayname* is the name under which the graphics information is to be stored. (See also the graphics PUT statement.)

Syntax:

```
GET (x1, y1) - (x2, y2), arrayname
```

Example:

```
GET (10, 10) - (40, 40), sprite%
```

GET$ Function

Description:

Reads a string from a file that is opened in the binary mode. `Count` is the number of characters to be retrieved from the file. This number is assigned to the specified string variable. In the example, five characters are retrieved from file #1 and are assigned to `TempString$`.

Syntax:

```
GET$ [#]filenum, Count, string variable
```

Example:

```
GET$ 1, 5, TempString$
```

GOSUB   Statement

Description:

Invokes a subroutine located at the specified label or line number. The location of the GOSUB statement is saved on the stack before the subroutine is executed so that the return location can be found. (Also see RETURN.)

Syntax:

```
GOSUB {label¦line number}
```

Example:

```
GOSUB CalcArea
```

457

Example:

```
GOSUB 110
```

GOTO
Statement

Description:

Transfers program execution to the statement identified by a label or line number.

Syntax:

```
GOTO {label¦line number}
```

Example:

```
GOTO PrintIt
```

Example:

```
GOTO 410
```

HEX$
Function

Description:

Returns a string that is the hexadecimal (base 16) representation of the argument. The string assigned to s$ in the example would be "2E" (2 * 16 + 15). (See Appendix E for hexadecimal and decimal equivalents.)

Syntax:

```
s$ = HEX$(numeric expression)
```

Example:

```
s$ = HEX$(47)
```

IF   Statement

Description:

Tests a condition and executes one or more program statements only if the condition is met.

Syntax:

```
IF integer expression[,] THEN {statements} [ELSE {statements}]
```

Example:

```
IF Income > Expense THEN PRINT "credit" ELSE PRINT "debit"
```

IF   Block Statement

Description:

Creates IF/THEN/ELSE constructs with multiple lines or conditions.

Syntax

```
IF integer expression[,] THEN
   {statements}
[ELSEIF integer expression[,] THEN
   {statements}
[ELSE
   {statements}]
END IF
```

Example:

```
IF count% < 50 THEN
  PRINT "Less than 50
ELSEIF count% < 100
  PRINT "50 through 99"
ELSE
  PRINT "Over 100"
END IF
```

INCR

Statement

Description:

Increments a variable by a specified amount. The default value is 1.

Syntax:

```
INCR variable [, size]
```

Example:

```
INCR count% 2
```

INKEY$

Function

Description:

Reads a character from the keyboard without echoing the character to the screen. It is used to capture a keypress without interrupting the program's execution.

Syntax:

```
var$ = INKEY$
```

Example:

```
DO
   kbd$ = INKEY$
   IF kbd$ <> "" THEN EXIT LOOP
LOOP
```

INP

Function

Description:

Reads a byte from a processor I/O port. It is used to read the status information of various hardware I/O ports. (See your computer's technical reference manual for port assignments.)

Syntax:

    y = INP(*portnumber*)

Example:

    StatusReg% = INP(&H61)

INPUT   Statement

Description:

Prompts the user for keyboard entry and assigns the input to one or more variables. Use LINE INPUT rather than INPUT when you need to enter string information that contains delimiters (commas or semicolons).

Syntax:

    INPUT [;] [*prompt string* {;¦,}] *variable list*

Example:

    INPUT "Enter three integers"; a%, b%, c%

INPUT #   Statement

Description:

Loads data from a sequential file into variables. The *filenum* parameter is the number assigned to the file when it is opened. *variable list* is a comma-delimited sequence of one or more string variables or numeric variables.

Syntax:

    INPUT #*filenum*, *variable list*

Example:

    INPUT #1, item$, number%

461

INPUT$
Function

Description:

Reads a specific number of characters from the keyboard or a file. The *n* parameter is the number of characters to be read, whereas *filenum* is the file to read from. When *filenum* is omitted, input from the keyboard is read. Characters read are not echoed on the screen. In the example, one character is read from the keyboard.

Syntax:

```
s$ = INPUT$(n [, [#]filenum])
```

Example:

```
kbd$ = INPUT$(1)
```

INSTAT
Function

Description:

Returns the keyboard status. If a key has been pressed, logical TRUE (nonzero) is returned. If a key has not been pressed, logical FALSE (zero) is returned.

Syntax:

```
y = INSTAT
```

Example:

```
kbd = INSTAT
```

INSTR
Function

Description:

Searches a string for the first occurrence of a specified character or string. The search begins at position *n* or (if *n* is omitted) at the beginning of the main string.

If ANY is included, *match string* specifies a list of characters to be searched for individually. The search stops at the first match found. The position of the match in the *main string* is returned. In the example, the value assigned to y would be 3, the position of "c" in the main string "abcdefg".

Syntax:

```
y = INSTR ([n,] main string, [ANY] match string)
```

Example:

```
y = INSTR("abcdefg", "c")
```

INT   Function

Description:

Converts a numeric expression to an integer. The largest integer less than or equal to the specified numeric expression is returned.

Syntax:

```
y = INT(numeric expression)
```

Example:

```
kolor = INT(freq% / 3)
```

IOCTL   Statement

Description:

Sends a control string to a device driver. The device number is *filenum* in the syntax, *string expression* contains information to be sent to the driver.

Syntax:

```
IOCTL [#] filenum, string expression
```

See the documentation for the specific driver. Also see the device driver section of a DOS technical reference manual for details.

IOCTL$ Function

Description:

Receives a data string from a device driver. The device number is *filenum* in the syntax. The format of the string information sent to or received from a device driver is a function of the driver itself.

Syntax:

```
s$ = IOCTL$([#]filenum)
```

Example:

See the documentation for the specific driver. Also see the device driver section of a DOS technical reference manual for details.

KEY Statement

Description:

Sets and displays function key definitions and defines key trap values. KEY ON and KEY OFF turn on and off the function key display at the bottom line of the screen. KEY LIST displays a list of function key definitions on the screen, one per line. The second syntax format assigns *string expression* to the function key *n*. The third syntax format associates a key or combination of keys with a number from 15 to 25 for key trapping. (See ON KEY and KEY(*n*) ON statements.) The example assigns functions to function keys 1-5. Then it turns on the function key display line, lists the functions, waits for a keypress, and turns the function key display line off.

Syntax:

```
KEY {ON¦OFF¦LIST}
KEY n, string expression
    KEY n, CHR$(shiftstatus, scancode)
```

464

Example:

```
CLS
FOR n% = 1 TO 5
    READ assign$
    KEY n%, assign$ + CHR$(13)
NEXT n%
KEY ON
KEY LIST
kbd$ = INPUT$(1)
KEY OFF
DATA Help, Return, Edit, Print, Quit
```

KEY(n)   Statement

Description:

Turns trapping on or off for a specific key. The value of *n* is 1 through 10 for function keys F1 through F10, 30 for F11, and 31 for F12. (Also see the entry for the ON KEY(*n*) statement.)

Syntax:

```
KEY(n) {ON¦OFF¦STOP}
```

Example:

```
CLS
KEY ON                          ' turn on key checking
KEY 30, CHR$(13)                ' assign carriage return to F11
ON KEY(30) GOSUB GoodBye ' set trap for F11
KEY(30) ON                      ' turn on F11 trapping
PRINT "Press F11"               ' to call subroutine trap
WHILE NOT INSTAT: WEND     ' wait for keypress
END

Goodbye:
  PRINT "Key F11 was trapped"
  KEY(30) OFF                     ' turn off trapping
  RETURN
```

KILL

Statement

Description:

Deletes a disk file. The example erases the file named SEQUENCE.DAT on drive B:.

Syntax:

```
KILL filespec
```

Example:

```
KILL "B:SEQUENCE.DAT"
```

LBOUND

Function

Description:

Returns the lower bound (smallest possible subscript) for an array's specified dimension. In the syntax format, `array` is the array's name, and `dimension` is an integer from 1 to the number of dimensions in the array. In the example, the starting value of the FOR statement is the lower bound of the second dimension of a three-dimensional array, D2Ar. (See also the entry for the UBOUND function.)

Syntax:

```
y = LBOUND(array(dimension))
```

Example:

```
FOR subsc% = LBOUND(D2Ar(2))TO UBOUND(D2Ar(2))
```

LCASE$

Function

Description:

Returns an all-lowercase version of its string argument. The example would assign the string `"quit"` to Lower$.

Syntax:

```
s$ = LCASE$(string expression)
```

Example:

```
Lower$ = LCASE$("Quit")
```

LEFT$

Function

Description:

Returns the leftmost *n* characters of a string. The example would assign "A short string" to LeftEnd$.

Syntax:

```
s$ = LEFT$(string expression, n)
```

Example:

```
LeftEnd$ = LEFT$("A short string begins long", 14)
```

LEN

Function

Description:

Returns the length of a string. The example assigns 26 to y.

Syntax:

```
y = LEN(string expression)
```

Example:

```
y = LEN("A short string begins long")
```

LET

Statement

Description:

Used to assign a value to a variable. The keyword LET is optional in assignment statements. It is included to provide compatibility with programs that were written in earlier versions of BASIC.

Syntax:

```
[LET] variable = expression
```

Example:

```
LET y = LEN("A short string")
```

LINE

Statement

Description:

Draws a straight line, a box, or a filled box on the graphics screen. The optional keyword STEP specifies coordinates that are relative rather than absolute. The example draws a filled box using color number 2.

Syntax:

```
LINE [STEP] [(x1, y1)] - [STEP](x2, y2) [, [color][, B[F]]
     [, pattern]]
```

Example:

```
LINE (10, 10)-(40, 30), 2, BF
```

LINE INPUT

Statement

Description:

Reads an entire line from the keyboard into a string variable, ignoring delimiters. You can read a maximum of 255 characters into each string variable. The entry is terminated by pressing Enter. Use LINE INPUT rather than INPUT when you need to enter string information containing delimiters, such as commas.

Syntax:

```
LINE INPUT [;][prompt string;] string variable
```

Example:

```
LINE INPUT "Enter an address"; Address$
```

LINE INPUT #   Statement

Description:

Reads a line from a sequential file into a string variable. LINE INPUT # is like LINE INPUT, except that LINE INPUT # reads data from a sequential file rather than from the keyboard.

Syntax:

```
LINE INPUT #filenum, string variable
```

Example:

```
LINE INPUT #1, Address$
```

LOC   Function

Description:

Returns the current position of a file pointer. The behavior of LOC depends on the mode in which the file was opened. For sequential files, LOC returns the number of 128-byte blocks written or read since the file was opened. For binary files, LOC returns the file pointer position. For random-access files, LOC returns the number of the last record written or read. For communications files, LOC returns the number of characters in the input buffer (which are waiting to be read).

Syntax:

```
y = LOC(filenum)
```

Example:

```
OPEN "LOC.DTA" FOR BINARY AS #1  y = LOC(1): PRINT y
```

LOCAL   Statement

Description:

Declares local variables in a procedure or function. LOCAL is legal only in function or procedure definitions. It must appear before any executable statements in the definition.

Syntax:

```
LOCAL variable list
```

Example:

```
SUB PrintIt
    LOCAL flag%, number!
    .
    .
    .
END SUB
```

LOCATE   Statement

Description:

Positions the screen cursor or defines its shape. The value for *cursor* is 0 (invisible), or 1 (visible). The values of *start* and *stop* determine the size of the cursor. The example locates the cursor at row 3, column 5, and makes the cursor invisible.

Syntax:

```
LOCATE [row][,[column][, [cursor][, start][, stop]]]
```

Example:

```
LOCATE 3, 5, 0
```

LOCK
Statement

Description:

Locks out other processes' access to part of an opened file. All locked records must be unlocked (see UNLOCK). The LOCK statement is only supported by DOS (3.0 or later) for networking. You must execute the DOS SHARE utility before attempting to use LOCK. In the example, the entire file is locked.

Syntax:

```
LOCK [#]filenum [,{record ¦ [start] TO end}]
```

Example:

```
LOCK #1
```

LOF
Function

Description:

Returns the length of a file in bytes. For communications files, LOF returns the amount of available space left in the communications buffer.

Syntax:

```
y = LOF(filenum)
```

Example:

```
NumRecords% = LOF(MyFile.DAT) / RecordLen%
```

LOG

Function

Description:

Returns the natural (base e) logarithm of its argument. A base e logarithm is the power to which e would have to be raised to yield the numeric expression.

Syntax:

```
y = LOG(numeric expression)
```

Example:

```
y = LOG(3.5)
```

LOG2

Function

Description:

Returns the base 2 logarithm of its argument. A base 2 logarithm is the power to which 2 would have to be raised to yield the numeric expression.

Syntax:

```
y = LOG2(numeric expression)
```

Example:

```
y = LOG2(3.5)
```

LOG10

Function

Description:

Returns the base 10 logarithm of its argument. A base 10 logarithm is the power to which 10 would have to be raised to yield the numeric expression.

Syntax:

```
y = LOG10(numeric expression)
```

Example:

```
y = LOG10(3.5)
```

LPOS

Function

Description:

Returns the number of characters on the current line in the printer buffer. The *printer* argument in the syntax format is an integer expression from 0 to 3 that selects the printer (0 or 1 = LPT1, 2 = LPT2, 3 = LPT3).

Syntax:

```
y = LPOS(printer)
```

Example:

```
y = LPOS(1)
```

LPRINT

Statement

Description:

Sends data to the printer. LPRINT functions identically to PRINT, except the data is sent to the printer (LPT1) rather than to the screen. The *expression list* parameter is a comma-, semicolon-, or space-delimited series of numeric or string expressions.

Syntax:

```
LPRINT [expression list [{,¦;}]]
```

Example:

```
INPUT A$
LPRINT A$
```

LPRINT USING   Statement

Description:

Sends data to the printer. LPRINT USING works identically to PRINT USING except the data is sent to the printer (LPT1) rather than to the screen. The expression list parameter is a comma-, semicolon-, or space-delimited series of numeric or string expressions. The *format string* parameter contains formatting information.

Syntax:

```
LPRINT USING format string; expression list [{,¦;}]
```

Example:

```
LPRINT USING "###.##"; Number!
```

LSET   Statement

Description:

Moves string data into a field variable that has been defined in a MAP or FIELD statement as belonging to the buffer of a random-access file. LSET left-justifies the string expression.

Syntax:

```
LSET field variable = string expression
```

Example:

```
LSET FileInt$ = MKI$(Count%)
```

LTRIM$ Function

Description:

Returns a copy of a string with the leading characters or strings removed. LTRIM$ is case-sensitive. When ANY is used, `match string` specifies a list of single characters to be searched for individually. If any of those characters are the leading character, the string is returned with that character removed. The example would trim the two leading blank spaces and the letter a from the string, leaving x$ = "bcdefg".

Syntax:

```
x$ = LTRIM$(main string [, [ANY] match string])
```

Example:

```
x$ = LTRIM$("  abcdefg", ANY " acd")
```

MAP Statement

Description:

Creates dynamic data structures and defines the variables of a random-access file buffer.

Syntax with Flex Strings:

```
MAP main$$[()] {[* length]¦[, sublength AS sub$$[()]]} [,_
   sublength AS sub$$[()]]...
```

or:

```
MAP main$$[()] {[* length]¦[, FROM substart TO subend AS_
   sub$$[()]]} [, FROM substart TO subend AS sub$$[()]]...
```

Example:

```
MAP A$$ * Length%
```

Syntax with Random-Access files:

```
MAP [#]filenum, length AS var$$ [, length AS var$$]...
```

or:

```
MAP [#]filenum, FROM start TO end AS var$$ [,_
    FROM start TO end AS var$$]...
```

Example:

```
MAP #1, 4 AS var1$$, 8 AS var2$$, 14 AS var3$$
```

MAX
Function

Description:

Takes any number of arguments and returns the argument with the largest (maximum) value. It handles arguments of any numeric type.

Syntax:

```
y = MAX(arg1, arg2, [, argn]...)
```

Example:

```
y## = MAX(1.1@, A%/B!, C#(X)^D)
```

MAX%
Function

Description:

Takes any number of arguments and returns the argument with the largest (maximum) value. Handles only arguments that evaluate to integers. Any floating-point arguments are rounded to integers before the comparison begins. MAX% is more efficient than MAX.

Syntax

```
y% = MAX%( arg1%, arg2%, [, argn%]...)
```

Example:

```
y% = MAX%(A%, B& / 4, D%(n))
```

MAX$ Function

Description:

Takes any number of arguments and returns the argument with the largest (maximum) value. The ASCII codes of the characters in a string are used to determine the value of the string. It handles string arguments, both regular and flex.

Syntax:

```
y$ = MAX$(arg1$, arg2$, [, argn$]...)
```

Example:

```
y$ = MAX$("abraca", A$, B$$)
```

MID$ Function

Description:

Returns a portion of a string. Arguments `start` and `length` are numeric variables or expressions. `start` is the position in the string expression of the first character of the string to be returned. `length` is the number of characters to be returned. If length is not included, all remaining characters of the string expression are returned. The example assigns the string "Baker" to PartString$ (start at position 6, return five characters).

Syntax:

```
s$ = MID$(string expression, start [, length])
```

Example:

```
PartString$ = ("Mary Baker-Prinz", 6, 5)
```

MID$ Statement

Description:

The MID$ statement replaces characters in a string with characters from another string. The example replaces the five leftmost zeros of TString$ with the string "Enter", giving TString$ = "Enter00000".

Syntax:

```
MID$(string variable, start [, length]) = replacement string
```

Example:

```
TString$ = "0000000000"
    MID$(TString$, 1, 5) = "Enter"
```

MIN Function

Description:

Returns the argument with the smallest (minimum) value from a list of arguments. MIN can handle any numeric argument.

Syntax:

```
y = MIN(arg1, arg2, [, argn]...)
```

Example:

```
y## = MIN(1.1@, A%/B!, C#(X)^D)
```

MIN% Function

Description:

Takes any number of arguments and returns the argument with the smallest (minimum) value. It handles only arguments that evaluate to integers. Any floating-point arguments are rounded to integers before the comparison begins. MIN% is more efficient than MIN.

Syntax:

```
y% = MIN%(arg1%, arg2%, [, argn%]...
```

Example:

```
y% = MIN%(A%, B& / 4, D%(n))
```

MIN$ Function

Description:

Takes any number of arguments and returns the argument with the smallest (minimum) value. The ASCII codes of characters in a string are used to determine the value of the string. It handles string arguments, regular strings, or flex strings.

Syntax:

```
y$ = MIN$(arg1$, arg2$, [, argn$]...)
```

Example:

```
y$ = MIN$("abraca", A$, B$$)
```

MKB$ Function

Description:

Converts BCD floating-point numbers into strings for random-access file output.

Syntax:

```
DataString$ = MKB$(BCD floating point expression)
```

Example:

```
LSET DString$ = MKB$(bcdflpt@@)
```

479

MKD$ Function

Description:

Converts double-precision floating-point numbers into strings for random-access file output.

Syntax:

```
DataString$ = MKD$(double precision floating point expression)
```

Example:

```
LSET DString$ = MKD$(dble#)
```

MKDIR Statement

Description:

Creates a subdirectory (like the DOS MKDIR command).

Syntax:

```
MKDIR path
```

Example:

```
MKDIR DirName$
```

MKE$ Function

Description:

Converts extended-precision floating-point numbers into strings for random-access file output.

Syntax:

```
DataString$ = MKE$(extended precision floating point expression)
```

Example:

```
LSET DString$ = MKE$(extend##)
```

MKF$ Function

Description:

Converts BCD fixed-point numbers into strings for random-access file output.

Syntax:

```
DataString$ = MKF$(BCD fixed point expression)
```

Example:

```
LSET DString$ = MKF$(bcdfx@)
```

MKI$ Function

Description:

Converts integer numbers into strings for random-access file output.

Syntax:

```
DataString$ = MKI$(integer expression)
```

Example:

```
LSET DString$ = MKI$(integ%)
```

MKL$ Function

Description:

Converts long-integer numbers into strings for random-access file output.

Syntax:

```
DataString$ = MKL$(long integer expression)
```

Example:

```
LSET DString$ = MKL$(longint&)
```

MKMD$ Function

Description:

Converts double-precision floating-point numbers into Microsoft-format strings for random-access file output.

Syntax:

```
DataString$ = MKMD$(double precision floating point expression)
```

Example:

```
LSET DString$ = MKMD$(dble#)
```

MKMS$ Function

Description:

Converts single-precision floating-point numbers into Microsoft-format strings for random-access file output.

Syntax:

```
DataString$ = MKMS$(single precision floating point expression)
```

Example:

```
LSET DString$ = MKMS$(sngle!)
```

MKQ$ Function

Description:

Converts quad integer numbers into strings for random-access file output.

Syntax:

```
DataString$ = MKQ$(quad integer expression)
```

Example:

```
LSET DString$ = MKQ$(quadint&&)
```

MKS$ Function

Description:

Converts single-precision floating-point numbers into strings for random-access file output.

Syntax:

```
DataString$ = MKS$(single precision floating point expression)
```

Example:

```
LSET DString$ = MKS$(sngle!)
```

MTIMER Function and Statement

Description:

Reads or resets the microtimer. The MTIMER statement and function must be used as a pair. They are used for measuring elapsed time for very short intervals.

Syntax for Function:

```
y = MTIMER
```

Syntax for Statement:

```
MTIMER
```

Example:

```
MTIMER                      ' initialize timer
pi# = ATN(1) * 4            ' calculate value of PI
ElapsedTime! = MTIMER       ' read time
PRINT ElapsedTime           ' print elapsed time
```

NAME   Statement

Description:

Renames a file (like the DOS REN command).

Syntax:

```
NAME filespec1 AS filespec2
```

Example:

```
NAME OldName$ AS NewName$
```

OCT$ Function

Description:

Returns a string that is the octal (base 8) representation of its argument. In the syntax format, *numeric expression* must be in the range –32768 to +65535. Any fractional part is rounded before the string is created.

Syntax:

```
s$ = OCT$(numeric expression)
```

Example:

```
OctString$ = OCT$(567)
```

ON COM   Statement

Description:

Declares the trap subroutine for serial port events. This function has no effect until event trapping is enabled by an appropriate COM(*n*) statement. Disable trapping by using zero (0) for *line number*.

Syntax:

```
ON COM({1¦2}) GOSUB {label¦line number}
```

Example:

```
ON COM(1) GOSUB GetComInput
```

ON ERROR   Statement

Description:

Specifies an error-handling routine and enables or disables error trapping. To disable error trapping, use zero (0) for *line number*.

Syntax:

```
ON ERROR GOTO {label¦line number}
```

Example:

```
ON ERROR GOTO Erroutine
```

ON ... GOSUB

Statement

Description:

Calls one subroutine from a list of subroutines according to the value of a numeric expression.

Syntax:

```
ON n GOSUB {label¦line number} [, {label¦line number}]...
```

Example:

```
FOR I% = 1 TO 4
        ON I% GOSUB SubOne, SubTwo, SubThree, SubFour
NEXT I%
```

ON ... GOTO

Statement

Description:

Sends program flow to one of a list of destinations based on the value of a numeric expression.

Syntax:

```
ON n GOTO {label¦line number} [, {label¦line number}]...
```

Example:

```
ON I% GOTO DecreaseIt, IncreaseIt, DoNothing
```

ON KEY

Statement

Description:

Declares the trap subroutine to get control if a specific key is pressed. The value of *n* is 1 through 10 for F1 through F10; 11 is up arrow, 12 is left arrow, 13 is right arrow, 14 is down arrow, 15 through 25 are defined by the KEY statement, 30 is F11, and 31 is F12. This statement has no effect until key trapping is enabled by a KEY(*n*) ON statement.

Syntax:

```
ON KEY(n) GOSUB {label¦line number}
```

Example:

```
ON KEY(30) GOSUB PrintIt
```

ON PEN   Statement

Description:

Declares the trap subroutine to get control when lightpen activity occurs. This statement has no effect until light-pen events are enabled by PEN ON.

Syntax:

```
ON PEN GOSUB {label¦line number}
```

Example:

```
ON PEN GOSUB PenHandler
```

ON PLAY   Statement

Description:

Declares the trap subroutine that will get control if the background music buffer note count falls below a certain number. This statement has no effect until note checking is enabled by a PLAY ON statement.

Syntax:

```
ON PLAY(NoteCount) GOSUB {label¦line number}
```

Example:

```
ON PLAY(5) GOSUB FillBuffer
```

ON STRIG   Statement

Description:

Declares the trap subroutine that will get control when a joystick button is pressed. This statement has no effect until joystick trapping is enabled by a STRIG(*n*) ON statement. Button numbers are

0 = Button 1 of Joystick A

2 = Button 1 of Joystick B

4 = Button 2 of Joystick A

6 = Button 2 of Joystick B

Syntax:

```
ON STRIG(n) GOSUB {label¦line number}
```

Example:

```
ON STRIG(2) GOSUB TriggerTwo
```

ON TIMER   Statement

Description:

Passes control to a trap subroutine every *n* seconds. This statement has no effect until time-checking is enabled by TIMER ON.

Syntax:

```
ON TIMER(n) GOSUB {label¦line number}
```

Example:

```
ON TIMER(2) GOSUB TimerSub
```

OPEN   Statement

Description:

Prepares a file or device for reading or writing.

Syntax 1:

    OPEN filespec [FOR mode] AS [#]filenum [LEN = record size]

Each mode specifies a particular kind of file (sequential, random-access, or binary) for reading, writing (or both), or appending.

Example:

    OPEN B:DataFile.DAT FOR OUTPUT AS #1 LEN = 24

Syntax 2:

    OPEN modestring, [#]filenum, filespec [, record size]

Example:

    OPEN "O", #1, B:DataFile.DAT, 24

The parameter *modestring* is a string expression with its first (and usually only) character being "O" for sequential output, "I" for sequential input, "A" for sequential append, "R" for random input/output, or "B" for binary input/output.

OPEN COM   Statement

Description:

Opens and configures a communications (serial) port. Valid *baud* rates are

75

110

150

300

600

1200

1800

2400

4800

9600

(the default is 300). The values for *parity* are

"S" = space parity,

"O" = odd parity,

"M" = mark parity,

"E" = even parity,

"N" = no parity

(the default is even parity). The number of data bits is from 5 to 8 (default is 7). The number of stop bits is 1 or 2 (the default is 1). The maximum number of bytes (*num*) that can be read from or written to the port in a single operation cannot be greater than the size of the port buffer (the default is 128).

Syntax:

```
OPEN "COM{1¦2}: [baud] [, parity] [, data] [, stop] [options]"_
    AS [#]filenum [LEN = num]
```

Example:

```
OPEN "COM1: 300, n, 8, 1, DS, RS, CS, CD" AS #1 LEN = 1
```

OPTION BASE   Statement

Description:

Sets the minimum value for array subscripts. The value of *integer expression* in the syntax format can range from 0 to 32767 (the default is 0). The OPTION BASE statement is used in conjunction with the DIM statement. In the example, the array would be dimensioned for four elements with subscripts 2, 3, 4, and 5. (See also the DIM and REDIM entries.)

Syntax:

```
OPTION BASE integer expression
```

Example:

```
OPTION BASE 2
DIM AnArray%(5)
```

OUT   Statement

Description:

Writes a byte to a processor I/O port. Because the OUT statement can write only
one byte at a time, any data stored in a two-byte integer must be sent in two parts,
as in the example.

Syntax:

```
OUT portnum, byte
```

Example:

```
OUT 12, DataByte% MOD 256
OUT 12, DataByte% \ 256
```

PAINT   Statement

Description:

Fills an enclosed area on a graphics screen with a selected color or pattern.
Painting starts at screen coordinates (*x*, *y*) in the syntax format. *color* is the
painting color, whereas *boundary* is the boundary color. An optional mask,
background, is used to skip the coloring of areas that are already filled.

Syntax:

```
PAINT (x, y) [[, color] [, boundary] [, background]]
```

Example:

```
PAINT (40, 60), 1, 3
```

PALETTE

Statement

Description:

Changes a color in the palette. It lets you map color numbers greater than 15 into the palette. To use this statement, you must have an EGA or VGA graphics adapter. The example changes color attribute 12 to color value 61.

Syntax:

```
PALETTE [attribute, color]
```

Example:

```
PALETTE 12, 61
```

PALETTE USING

Statement

Description:

Use to modify all colors in the palette. To use this statement, you must have an EGA or VGA graphics adapter. The example assigns color 5 to attribute 0, color 6 to attribute 1, and so on up to 20 for attribute 15.

Syntax:

```
PALETTE USING array(index)
```

Example:

```
DIM PalArray%(0:15)
FOR Int% = 0 TO 15
  PalArray%(Int%) = Int% + 5
NEXT Int%
PALETTE USING PalArray%(0)
```

PEEK

Description:

Returns the byte to a specified memory location. It retrieves a single byte and returns it as an integer ranging from 0 to 255.

Syntax:

```
y% = PEEK(address)
```

Example:

```
y% = PEEK(LookAddr&)
```

PEEKI

Description:

Returns the word (2 bytes equal 1 word) beginning at a specified memory location. It retrieves two consecutive bytes and returns them as a single integer (= second byte * 256 + first byte).

Syntax:

```
y% = PEEKI(address)
```

Example:

```
y% = PEEKI(PeekAddr&)
```

PEEKL

Description:

Returns the double-word (4 bytes equal a double-word) beginning at a specified memory location. It retrieves four consecutive bytes and returns them as a single long integer (= fourth byte * 2 ^ 24 + third byte * 65536 + second byte * 256 + first byte).

493

Syntax:

```
y& = PEEKL(address)
```

Example:

```
y& = PEEKL(LookAddr&)
```

PEEK$
Function

Description:

Returns a sequence of bytes at a specified memory location. It retrieves *count* consecutive bytes and returns them as a string, where the ASCII code of the first character in the string is the value of the first byte, the ASCII code of the second character in the string is the value of the second byte, and so on.

Syntax:

```
y$ = PEEK$(address, count)
```

Example:

```
y$ = PEEK$(SourceAddr&, ArrayLen%)
```

PEN
Function

Description:

Reads the status of the light pen. The *option* is a numeric option that controls the information returned. The light pen must be turned on with PEN ON before performing any PEN function requests.

Syntax:

```
y = PEN(option)
```

Example:

```
PenHandler:
    FOR Int% = 1 TO 9
        y = PEN(1): PRINT y
    NEXT Int%
    RETURN
```

PEN

Statement

Description:

Controls the checking of light pen events. The light pen must be turned on with PEN ON before performing any PEN function requests. Executing PEN ON also enables the trapping of light pen events. PEN OFF disables the PEN function and turns off pen event checking. PEN STOP turns off pen event trapping, but remembers pen events so that if PEN ON is later issued, a trap occurs immediately.

Syntax:

```
PEN {ON|OFF|STOP}
```

Example:

```
ON PEN GOSUB PenHandler
PEN ON
```

PLAY

Function

Description:

Returns the number of notes in the background music buffer. In the syntax format, *num* is a dummy argument. If music is being played in the foreground, PLAY returns 0.

Syntax:

```
y = PLAY(num)
```

Example:

```
y = PLAY(1)
IF y = 0 THEN PRINT "Music buffer is empty"
```

PLAY   Statement

Description:

Use as an interpretive mini-language to create music. With this statement, you can define musical passages as a sequence of characters in a string expression. The example plays the notes F, G, and A in Octave 3.

Syntax:

```
PLAY string expression
```

Example:

```
PLAY "O3FGA"
```

PMAP   Function

Description:

Translates between physical and world screen coordinates. Values for *option* are 0 = map world coordinate *x* to physical coordinate *x*, 1 = map world coordinate *y* to physical coordinate *y*, 2 = map physical coordinate *x* to world coordinate *x*, and 3 = map physical coordinate *y* to world coordinate *y*. PMAP has no effect if no WINDOW statement is in effect.

Syntax:

```
MapPoint = PMAP(xy, option)
```

Example:

```
MapPoint1 = PMAP(50, 2)
MapPoint2 = PMAP(100, 3)
```

POINT

Function

Description:

Returns the color of a screen pixel or information about the last point referenced (LPR). The first example returns the color attribute of the point at screen coordinates (10, 20). In the second syntax format, the *options* are: 0 returns the current physical *x* coordinate of LPR, 1 returns the current physical *y* coordinate of LPR, 2 returns the current world *x* coordinate of LPR, and 3 returns the current *y* coordinate of LPR.

Syntax 1:

```
color = POINT(x, y)
```

Example:

```
kolor = POINT(10, 20)
```

Syntax 2:

```
coord = POINT(option)
```

Example:

```
coord = POINT(3)
```

POKE

Statement

Description:

Stores a single byte (*byte value*) having a value that is 0 to 255 at a specific memory location (*address*).

Syntax:

```
POKE address, byte value
```

Example:

```
POKE DestAddr&, num%
```

497

POKEI

Statement

Description:

Stores a word (*integer value*) in two consecutive bytes (= second byte * 256 + first byte) at a specific memory location (*address*).

Syntax:

```
POKE address, integer value
```

Example:

```
POKE DestAddr&, num%
```

POKEL

Statement

Description:

Stores a double-word (*long integer value*) in two consecutive bytes (= fourth byte * 2 ^ 24 + third byte * 65536 + second byte * 256 + first byte) at a specific memory location (*address*).

Syntax:

```
POKE address, long integer value
```

Example:

```
POKE DestAddr&, num&
```

POKE$

Statement

Description:

Stores a string in consecutive bytes, where the ASCII code of the first character of the string is stored in the first byte of memory (*address*), the next ASCII code is stored in the next byte of memory (*address* + 1), and so on.

Syntax:

```
POKE address, string
```

Example:

```
POKE DestAddr&, AString$
```

POS   Function

Description:

Returns the horizontal position (column number) of the screen cursor. The value *x* in the syntax is a dummy argument.

Syntax:

```
column = POS(x)
```

Example:

```
column% = POS(1)
```

PRESET   Statement

Description:

Plots a point on the graphics screen. When no color value is specified, the background color is used (default value is 0). The optional STEP keyword specifies that the coordinates are *relative* rather than *absolute*. The example would set the pixel at (40, 50) to the background color. (Also see PSET.)

Syntax:

```
PRESET [STEP] (x, y) [, color]
```

Example:

```
PRESET (40, 50)
```

PRINT

Statement

Description:

Displays information on the screen. Expressions can be separated by commas, spaces, or semicolons.

Syntax:

```
PRINT [expression [{,| |;} [expression]]...]
```

Example:

```
A% = 1: B% = 2: C% = 3
PRINT A%, B%; C%
    Output:
1               2  3
```

PRINT USING

Statement

Description:

Sends formatted information to the screen.

Syntax:

```
PRINT USING format string; expression [{,| |;} [expression]]...
```

Example:

```
PRINT USING "###.##"; amount!
```

PRINT

Statement

Description:

Writes information to a device or a file. PRINT # sends data to a file just like PRINT sends data to the screen. The first PRINT # statement in the example puts each item in a 14-column print zone, wasting many spaces. The second PRINT # statement spaces the items close together with a leading and trailing space. The third PRINT # statement is the best way to delimit the fields because it sends the commas in quotes as delimiters.

Syntax:

```
PRINT #filenum, [expression [{,¦ ¦;} [expression]]...]
```

Example:

```
PRINT #1, 10, 20, 30
PRINT #2, 10;20;30
PRINT #3, 10 "," 20 "," 30
```

PRINT # USING   Statement

Description:

Writes formatted information to a device or a file. PRINT # USING is to PRINT # as PRINT is to PRINT USING. It sends the data in a specified format.

Syntax:

```
PRINT #filenum, [[USING format string;] expression [{,¦ ¦;}_
    [expression]]...]
```

Example:

```
PRINT #1 USING "###", 10, 20, 30
```

PSET   Statement

Description:

Plots a point on the graphics screen. If no color value is specified, the maximum color value is used. The optional STEP keyword specifies that the coordinates are *relative* rather than *absolute*. (Also see PRESET.)

Syntax:

```
PSET [STEP] (x, y) [, color]
```

Example:

```
PSET (40, 50), 8
```

PUT
Statement (Files)

Description:

Writes a record to a random-access file. The example writes record number (10) into file number 1. When *recnum* is omitted, PowerBASIC Lite uses the value in the last PUT or GET statement plus 1.

Syntax:

```
PUT [#]filenum [, recnum]
```

Example:

```
PUT #1, 10
```

PUT
Statement (Graphics)

Description:

Copies the contents of a numeric array to the graphics screen. The optional STEP keyword specifies that the coordinates are *relative* rather than *absolute*. The *option* can be one of the following:

1. PSET, which maps an exact copy of the image in the array

2. PRESET, which maps the complementary copy of the image in the array

3. XOR, which performs an XOR operation between the array image and the screen

4. OR, which performs an OR operation between the array image and the screen

5. AND, which performs an AND operation between the image and the screen

The XOR option is usually used to create animation.

Syntax:

```
PUT [STEP] (x, y), array [, option]
```

Example:

```
PUT STEP (10, 10), SpriteArray% , XOR
```

PUT$ Function

Description:

Writes a string to a binary mode file.

Syntax:

```
PUT$ [#]filenum, string expression
```

Example:

```
PUT$ #1, CHR$(Int%)
```

RANDOMIZE   Statement

Description:

Seeds the random number generator. Values returned by the random number generator (RND) depend on the initial seed value. For a given seed value, RND always returns the same sequence of values. The TIMER function is often used to provide a unique seed value.

Syntax:

```
RANDOMIZE [numeric expression]
```

Example:

```
RANDOMIZE TIMER
```

503

READ

Statement

Description:

Loads DATA statement constants into program variables. Data types in the READ statement and the DATA statement must match.

Syntax:

```
READ variable [, variable}...
```

Example:

```
READ alpha%, beta$
    DATA 23, "a string"
```

REDIM

Statement

Description:

Erases and redimensions dynamic arrays. It cannot change the number of dimensions, only the lower and upper bounds.

Syntax:

```
REDIM array(subscripts) [, array(subscripts)]...
```

Example:

```
DIM DYNAMIC MyData(40)

    .
    . {statements}
    .

REDIM MyData(5:50)
```

REG
Function

Description:

Returns a value in the register buffer. REG is usually used to pass information to and from assembly language interrupt routines and is not normally used in PowerBASIC Lite.

Syntax:

```
y = REG(register)
```

Example:

```
y = REG(1)
```

REG
Statement

Description:

Sets a register buffer to the specified value. REG is usually used to pass information to and from assembly language interrupt routines and is not usually used in PowerBASIC Lite.

Syntax:

```
REG register, value
```

Example:

```
REG 1, &H0200
```

REM
Statement

Description:

Indicates that the rest of a line in a source code file is to be interpreted as a remark or comment. It is not processed by the compiler. The apostrophe (') is an alternate form of REM.

Syntax:

```
REM comment
```

Example:

```
REM ** Main program **
```

REMOVE$
Function

Description:

Returns a copy of a string with characters or strings removed. The value assigned to Short$ in the example would be `"aceg"`.

Syntax:

```
x$ = REMOVE$(main string, [ANY] match string)
```

Example:

```
Short$ = REMOVE$("abcdefg", ANY "bdf")
```

REPEAT$
Function

Description:

Returns a string consisting of multiple copies of the specified string. The value of s$ in the example is `"HO HO HO "`.

Syntax:

```
s$ = REPEAT$(count, string expression)
```

Example:

```
s$ = REPEAT$(3, "HO ")
```

REPLACE

Description:

In a specified string, replaces all occurrences of one string with a specified string. The *main string* with replacements in the example is `"**c*efghi"`.

Syntax:

```
REPLACE [ANY] match string WITH new string IN main string
```

Example:

```
A$ = "abcdefghi"
REPLACE ANY "bad" WITH "*" IN A$
```

RESET

Description:

Flushes all file buffers and closes all disk files and devices. It performs the same function as `CLOSE` with no arguments.

Syntax:

```
RESET
```

Example:

```
RESET
```

RESTORE

Description:

Resets the READ pointer. If no label or line number are specified (as in the example), RESTORE places the READ pointer at the first item in the first DATA statement.

Syntax:

```
RESTORE [{label¦line number}]
```

Example:

```
RESTORE
```

RESUME
Statement

Description:

Restarts program execution after error handling with ON ERROR GOTO. The optional parameters are

0 = Resume at statement that caused the error.

NEXT = Resume at statement following the one that caused the error.

label = Resume at statement identified by the label.

line number = Resume at statement identified by the line number.

Syntax:

```
RESUME [{0¦NEXT¦label¦line number}]
```

Example:

```
RESUME  NEXT
```

RETURN
Statement

Description:

Returns from a subroutine to the place that called the subroutine. If no label or line number is specified, the return is made to the statement directly following the calling GOSUB statement. With one of the options, the return is to the specified label or line number.

Syntax:

```
RETURN [{label¦line number}]
```

Example:

```
RETURN
```

RIGHT$ Function

Description:

Returns the rightmost *num* characters of a string. In the example, s$ = "ghi".

Syntax:

```
s$ = RIGHT$(string expression, num)
```

Example:

```
s$ = RIGHT$("abcdefghi", 3
```

RMDIR Statement

Description:

Deletes a disk directory (like the DOS RMDIR command).

Syntax:

```
RMDIR path
```

Example:

```
INPUT "Enter name of directory to be removed"; Dr$
RMDIR Dr$
```

RND

Function

Description:

Returns a random number. Given the same seed, the RND algorithm always produces the same chain of "random" numbers. The performance of RND depends on the optional numeric value you supply as an argument. With no argument (or with a positive argument), RND generates the next number in sequence based on its initial seed value. With 0 as the argument, RND repeats the last number generated. With a negative argument, the random number generator is reseeded (See also RANDOMIZE). The example produces a random integer from 1 through 5.

Syntax:

```
y = RND[(numeric expression)]
```

Example:

```
num% = INT(RND * 5) + 1
```

ROUND

Function

Description:

Rounds a numeric value to a specified number of decimal places. The value of x in the example is .667.

Syntax:

```
x = ROUND(numeric expression, num)
```

Example:

```
Extpre## = 2 / 3
x = ROUND(Extpre##, 3)
```

RSET
Statement

Description:

Moves string data into a random-access file buffer, right-justifying *string expression*. The string data is moved into *field variable*, which has been defined in a previous FIELD or MAP statement.

Syntax:

```
RSET field variable = string expression
```

Example:

```
RSET FileInt$ = MKI$(Count%)
```

RTRIM$
Function

Description:

Returns a copy of a string with the trailing characters or strings removed. When no *match string* is specified, all trailing spaces of the main string are removed. If *match string* is included without ANY, the characters of *match string* are removed from the main string if they match the trailing characters of the main string. If ANY is included, *match string* is a list of single characters to be searched for individually. A match for any one of the characters as a trailing character causes its removal. In the example, the space at the end of the string "1234 " is removed. Thus, x$ = "1234".

Syntax:

```
x$ = RTRIM$(main string [, [ANY] match string])
```

Example:

```
x$ = RTRIM$("1234 ")
```

511

SCREEN

Function

Description:

Returns the ASCII code or the attribute of the character at the specified screen row and column. If an *option* of 1 is used, the attribute of the character is returned. In the example, 65 (the ASCII code for A) is printed in the first print field, and 7 is printed in the second print field (white type on a black background is attribute 7).

Syntax:

```
y = SCREEN(row, column [, option])
```

Example:

```
LOCATE 2, 15: PRINT "A"
PRINT SCREEN(2, 15), SCREEN(2, 15, 1)
```

SCREEN

Statement

Description:

Sets the screen display mode. Legal values for *mode* are: 0, 1, 2, 3, 7, 8, 9, 10, 11, and 12. The *colorflag* parameter controls whether color information will be passed to the composite monitors that are connected to the composite video port of CGA. The *apage* parameter (0 to 7) controls which text page is being written to when PRINT and other output commands are given. The *vpage* argument selects which of the possible screens (0 to 7) is actually displayed. The *apage* and *vpage* parameters are only valid with CGA, EGA, and VGA in screen modes 0, 7, 8, 9, and 10. Normal use specifies the mode only as in the example.

Syntax:

```
SCREEN [mode] [,[colorflag]] [,[apage]] [,[vpage]]
```

Example:

```
SCREEN 2
```

512

SEEK   Statement

Description:

Sets the file pointer position in a binary file. This means that the next GET$ or PUT$ performed on the file will occur *position* bytes deep into the file.

Syntax:

```
SEEK [#]filenum, position
```

Example:

```
SEEK #1, Start%
```

SELECT   Statement

Description:

Controls program flow based on the value of an expression.

Syntax:

```
SELECT CASE expression
  CASE test list
    (statements)
  CASE test list
    (statements)

    .
    .
    .

  CASE ELSE
    (statements)
END SELECT
```

Example:

```
INPUT "Enter an integer less than 100"; Int%
SELECT CASE Int%
  CASE < 33
```

513

```
      PRINT "Lower 1/3"
   CASE 33 TO 66
      PRINT "Middle 1/3"
   CASE ELSE
      PRINT "Upper 1/3"
END SELECT
```

SGN

Function

Description:

Returns the sign of a numeric expression. When *numeric expression* is positive, SGN returns +1; when it is negative, SGN returns –1. When numeric expression is zero, SGN returns 0.

Syntax:

```
y = SGN(numeric expression)
```

Example:

```
ON SGN(balance!) + 2 GOSUB InRed, EvenUp, InBlack
```

SHARED

Statement

Description:

Declares shared (global) variables within a main program and between procedures and functions in a program.

Syntax:

```
SHARED variable list
```

Example:

```
SHARED Mynum!, Yournum%
```

SIN

Description:

Returns the trigonometric sine of its argument. `numeric expression` is an angle in radians.

Syntax:

```
y = SIN(numeric expression)
```

Example:

```
FOR x! = -6.28 TO 6.28 STEP .1
    PSET (x!, SIN(x!))
NEXT x!
```

SOUND

Description:

Generates a tone of specified frequency and duration.

Syntax:

```
SOUND frequency, duration
```

Example:

```
FOR freq% = 150 TO 175
    SOUND freq%, 2
NEXT freq%
```

SPACE$

Description:

Returns a string of a specified number of spaces. It is useful in formatting output for the screen or printer. In the example, five spaces would be printed between *xx* and *yy*.

515

Syntax:

```
s$ = SPACE$(Count%)
```

Example:

```
s$ = "XX" + SPACE$(5) + "YY"
PRINT s$
```

SPC

Function

Description:

Prints a specified number of spaces. SPC can be used only in an expression list of a PRINT #, PRINT, or LPRINT statement.

Syntax:

```
SPC(num%)
```

Example:

```
PRINT NumItems%; SPC(5); Cost!
```

SQR

Function

Description:

Returns the square root of its argument.

Syntax:

```
y = SQR(numeric expression)
```

Example:

```
PRINT var!; SPC(5); SQR(var!)
```

STATIC

Description:

Declares static variables in a procedure or function. This statement is only legal within a procedure or function. Static variables have a fixed address in memory. The value of the variable (Int%) in the example is known only within the procedure. Another variable of the same name could be used outside the procedure and would not be affected by the value inside the procedure. Static variables retain their value between calls to the procedure or function.

Syntax:

STATIC *variable list*

Example:

```
SUB CountUp
    STATIC Int%
    FOR Int% = 1 to 3
        PRINT Int%
    NEXT Int%
END SUB
```

STICK

Description:

Returns joystick position information. Values for *option* in the syntax format are

0 returns the x-coordinate of joystick A

1 returns the y-coordinate of joystick A

2 returns the x-coordinate of joystick B

3 returns the y-coordinate of joystick B.

Syntax:

y = STICK(*option*)

Example:

```
LOCATE 3, 15
PRINT STICK(0), STICK(1), STICK(2), STICK(3)
```

STOP
Statement

Description:

Halts program execution and returns control to PowerBASIC Lite. END does the same thing and is preferred.

Syntax:

```
STOP
```

Example:

```
STOP
```

STR$
Function

Description:

Returns the string representation of a number. The string is comprised of ASCII characters with a leading space for positive values. LTRIM$ can be used to remove the leading space. The optional *digits* argument specifies the number of digits to appear in the result. The example prints .66666666666666667.

Syntax:

```
s$ = STR$(numeric expression [, digits]
```

Example:

```
a## = 2.0 / 3.0
PRINT STR$(a##, 18)
```

STRIG

Function

Description:

Returns the status of the joystick buttons. Before making any STRIG function calls, you must enable joystick button checking with the STRIG statement. Use STICK to read the position of the joystick. The values of the *option* argument are 0 through 7 which return the status of joystick buttons. The example returns –1 if button 2 on joystick A is currently down. Otherwise it returns 0.

Syntax:

```
y = STRIG(option)
```

Example:

```
y = STRIG(5)
```

STRIG

Statement

Description:

Controls joystick button trapping. In the first syntax format, STRIG ON turns on trigger-event trapping so that the STRIG function requests can be made. Trapping is performed by the routine specified in an ON STRIG statement. STRIG OFF turns off trigger-event checking. In the second format, *n* is the value of the button to trap. Once STRIG(*n*) ON has been executed, a check is made before the execution of every subsequent statement to see whether the specified button has been pressed. If so, control passes to the statement that was specified in an ON STRIG statement. With STRIG(*n*) OFF, joystick trapping is turned off.

Syntax:

```
STRIG {ON¦OFF}
```

Example:

```
STRIG ON
```

519

Syntax:

```
STRIG(n) {ON¦OFF}
```

Example:

```
STRIG(1) ON

    .
    . {statements}
    .

STRIG(1) OFF
```

STRING$ Function

Description:

Returns a string consisting of multiple copies of the specified character. `Count` and `code` are integer expressions. STRING$ with a numeric argument returns a string of `Count` copies of the character with ASCII code `code`. STRING$ with a string argument returns a string of `Count` copies of `string expression`'s first character.

Syntax:

```
s$ = STRING$(Count, {code¦string expression})
```

Examples:

```
s$ = STRING$(8, 32)    ' eight spaces
s$ = STRING$(8, "*")   ' eight asterisks
```

STRPTR   Function

Description:

Returns the offset portion of the address of a string variable. (Also see STRSEG.)

Syntax:

```
x = STRPTR(string variable)
```

Example:

```
x = STRPTR(Alpha$)
```

STRSEG
Function

Description:

Returns the segment portion of the address of a string variable.

Syntax:

```
y = STRSEG(string variable)
```

Example:

```
Alpha$ = "PBLite"
DEF SEG = STRSEG(Alpha$)
offset& = STRPTR(Alpha$)
PRINT PEEK$(offset&, LEN(Alpha$))
DEF SEG
```

SUB/END SUB
Statements

Description:

Defines a PowerBASIC Lite procedure.

Syntax:

```
SUB procname [(parameter list)] [{STATIC¦SHARED¦LOCAL}] [{PRIVATE¦PUBLIC}]
    [LOCAL variable list]
    [STATIC variable list]
    [SHARED variable list]
    {statements}
    [EXIT SUB}
    {statements}
END SUB
```

Example:

```
SUB PrintIt (Int%, Long&, Single!) PRINT Int%, Long&, Single!
                    END SUB
```

SWAP   Statement

Description:

Exchanges the values of two variables of the same type. The example would print the smaller of two variable values first, then the larger.

Syntax:

```
SWAP var1, var2
```

Example:

```
IF Able(1) > Able(2) THEN
    SWAP Able(1), Able(2)
END IF
PRINT Able(1), Able(2)
```

SYSTEM   Statement

Description:

Terminates a program in the same manner as STOP or END. END is preferred.

Syntax:

```
SYSTEM
```

Example:

```
SYSTEM
```

TAB   Function

Description:

Moves the printing position to the specified column (*num*). Can be used only in PRINT, PRINT #, or LPRINT statements.

Syntax:

TAB(*num*)

Example:

PRINT Friend$ TAB(25) Phone$

TALLY   Function

Description:

Counts the number of occurrences of specified characters or strings within a string. If ANY is not included, TALLY counts all occurrences of *match string* in *main string*. If ANY is included, *match string* specifies a list of characters to be searched for individually. The value of x is increased by one for each occurrence of each character. The example finds 2 characters (one "a" and one "e").

Syntax:

x = TALLY(*main string*, [ANY] *match string*)

Example:

PRINT TALLY("abcdefgh", ANY "ae")

TAN   Function

Description:

Returns the trigonometric tangent of its argument. The argument *numeric expression* is an angle specified in radians.

523

Syntax:

```
y = TAN(numeric expression)
```

Example:

```
y = TAN(2.5)
```

TIME$ System Variable

Description:

Used to read or set the system time. TIME$ contains an eight-character string in the form "*hh*:*mm*:*ss*", where *hh* is hours (based on a 24-hour clock), *mm* is minutes, and *ss* is seconds.

Syntax:

to set time:

```
TIME$ = string expression
```

to read time:

```
s$ = TIME$
```

Example:

```
TIME$ = "13:01"
t$ = TIME$
```

TIMER   Function

Description:

Returns the number of seconds since midnight.

Syntax:

```
y = TIMER
```

Example:

```
start! = TIMER
WHILE TIMER < start! + 1.5
     SOUND 500, .1
WEND
```

TIMER   Statement

Description:

Controls the trapping of timer events.

Syntax:

```
TIMER {ON|OFF|STOP}
```

Example:

```
TIMER ON
.
. {statements}
.
TIMER OFF
```

TROFF   Statement

Description:

Turns off the display of line numbers as the program is executed. It is included for compatibility with earlier BASIC versions. You should use PowerBASIC Lite's debugging tools if possible.

Syntax:

```
TROFF
```

Example:

```
TROFF
```

TRON

Statement

Description:

Turns on the display of line numbers as a program is executed. It is included for compatibility with earlier BASIC versions. You should use PowerBASIC Lite's debugging tools if possible.

Syntax:

```
TRON
```

Example:

```
TRON
```

UBOUND

Function

Description:

Returns the largest possible subscript for an array's specified dimension. The example would print "The array's first dimension is from 1900 to 1990".

Syntax:

```
UBOUND (array(dimension))
```

Example:

```
DIM MyArray(1900:1990, 1:500)
PRINT "The array's first dimension is from";_
    LBOUND(Myarray(1)); "to "; UBOUND(Myarray(1)
```

UCASE$ Function

Description:

Returns an all-uppercase version of its string argument. The example would print `"MAKE ALL LETTERS CAPS."`.

Syntax:

```
s$ = UCASE$(string expression)
```

Example:

```
PRINT UCASE$("Make all letters caps.")
```

UNLOCK Statement

Description:

Restores other processes' access to an opened file that was previously locked with a LOCK statement. This statement is only supported by DOS (3.0 or later) for networking.

Syntax:

```
UNLOCK [#]filenum [, {record¦[start] TO end}]
```

Example:

```
UNLOCK #1
```

USING$ Function

Description:

Formats numeric or string data like `PRINT USING`. Use `USING$` when you want to format data but don't want to print it immediately. (See `PRINT USING`.)

Syntax:

```
x$ = USING$(format string, expression)
```

Example:

```
x$ = USING$("##.###", alpha#)
.
. {statements}
.
PRINT x$
```

VAL

Function

Description:

Returns the numeric equivalent of a string. The example would print the value of *price$* with the dollar sign ($), commas, and spaces removed from the entry. For example, the entry $ 13,214.45 would be printed as 13214.45.

Syntax:

```
y = VAL(string expression)
```

Example:

```
LINE INPUT "Enter price"; price$
Cost! = VAL(REMOVE$(price$, ANY "$, "))
PRINT Cost!
```

VARPTR

Function

Description:

Returns the offset portion of the address of a variable. A segment value also must be specified.

Syntax:

```
y = VARPTR(variable)
```

Example:

```
DEF SEG = VARSEG(Int%)
address& = VARPTR(Int%)
```

VARPTR$ Function

Description:

Returns a pointer to a variable in string form. The function is used primarily with DRAW and PLAY statements to include numeric variables within command strings.

Syntax:

```
s$ = VARPTR$(variable)
```

Example:

```
DRAW "M= " + VARPTR$(Int%) + ", 40"
```

VARSEG Function

Description:

Returns the segment portion of the address of a variable. VARPTR returns the offset portion of the address.

Syntax:

```
y = VARSEG(variable)
```

Example:

```
DEF SEG = VARSEG(Int%)
address& = VARPTR(Int%)
```

VERIFY

Function

Description:

Determines whether each character of a string is present in another string. It returns the position of the first non-matching character in *main string*. VERIFY is case-sensitive. The example would return 4, because the decimal point (the fourth character in *main string*) is not in *match string*.

Syntax:

```
x = VERIFY([start,] main string, match string)
```

Example:

```
Alpha$ = "123.625"
PRINT VERIFY(Alpha$, "0123456789")
```

VIEW

Statement

Description:

Defines the active area (viewport) of the graphics screen. The optional *color* parameter fills the viewport with the specified *color* attribute. The optional *boundary* parameter draws a border around the viewport in the specified *color* attribute.

Syntax:

```
VIEW [[SCREEN] [(x1, y1)-(x2, y2) [, [color [, boundary]]]]]
```

Example:

```
VIEW (100, 50)-(300, 180)
```

530

WAIT
Statement

Description:

Suspends program execution until the specified hardware status condition is met. The byte read from the port is exclusively ORed with *m* and ANDed with *n*. If the resulting value is FALSE (zero), the process repeats. If the resulting value is TRUE (nonzero), PowerBASIC Lite proceeds with the next statement. WAIT has no time limit. It can be used to poll an input port until a set of conditions is met. The example polls port 11 until the resulting value is TRUE.

Syntax:

```
WAIT port, n [, m]
```

Example:

```
WAIT 11, 1, 1
```

WHILE/WEND
Statements

Description:

Define a loop of program statements that is executed repeatedly as long as a certain condition is met.

Syntax:

```
WHILE integer expression
    .
    . {statements}
    .
WEND
```

Example:

```
WHILE NOT EOF(1)
   INPUT #1, data$
   PRINT data$
WEND
```

531

WIDTH

Statement

Description:

Sets the logical line size on your printer, screen, or communications port.

Syntax:

```
WIDTH [{device name¦#filenum},] size
```

Example:

```
SCREEN 0
WIDTH 40
PRINT "Wide letters, 40 per line"
WIDTH 80
"Normal letters for SCREEN 0, 80 per line"
```

WINDOW

Statement

Description:

Redefines the graphics coordinate system. If the optional parameter SCREEN is used, the coordinates used are "screen" coordinates. Otherwise "world" coordinates are used. The coordinate pairs (*x1*, *y1*) and (*x2*, *y2*) define opposite corners of the display screen.

Syntax:

```
WINDOW [[SCREEN] (x1, y1)-(x2, y2)]
```

Example:

```
WINDOW (-6.28, -2)-(6.28, 2)
```

WRITE   Statement

Description:

Sends data in delimited format to the screen. WRITE is like PRINT; however, WRITE inserts commas between each expression, puts string data in double quotations, and doesn't output a space before positive numbers.

Syntax:

```
WRITE [expression [{,¦;} expression]...]
```

Example:

```
WRITE number%, word$
```

WRITE #   Statement

Description:

Outputs data in delimited format to a sequential file. It is similar to PRINT #; however, WRITE # inserts commas between each expression, puts string data in double quotations, and doesn't output a space before positive numbers. WRITE # with a file number and comma, but with no expressions, outputs a carriage return to the file.

Syntax:

```
WRITE #filenum, [expression [{,¦;} expression]...]
```

Example:

```
WRITE #1, person$, address$, phone$
```

533

Answers to Chapter Exercises

Chapter 1 Answers

1. Compiling, like PowerBASIC Lite, and interpreting.

2. PowerBASIC Lite programs are compiled to machine language before they are run.

3. The first, or top, line in the Edit window.

4. The F10 key is used from the Edit window to activate the Main menu. The cursor moves from the Edit window and one of the Main menu items is highlighted.

5. The Write To command should be used when a file has no name.

6. The maximum number of displayed characters on one line is 77.

7. The Ctrl-Q Y key combination erases the line from the cursor position to the end of the line.

8. The New command is located on the File menu.

9. Alt-F5 is used to move from the User screen window to the Edit window.

10. Exit from PowerBASIC to DOS with the Quit command of the File menu.

Chapter 2 Answers

1. The F7 key is used to step through a program.

2. a. right-arrow key

   b. left-arrow key

   c. down-arrow key

   d. up-arrow key

3. Ctrl-F moves the cursor one word to the right, so the cursor would move to the S of the word, Sum.

4. This statement will vary for different users.

5. There are many ways to delete a line. You must first move the cursor to the line to be deleted. The quickest way to delete the line would be to use Ctrl-Y, which deletes the entire line on which the cursor lies. The slowest way would be to use the Del or Backspace key to delete each character.

6. The apostrophe (') is the alternate for REM.

7. CLS should be used to remove any data left on the User output screen from a previous output.

8. The exclamation point (!) declares a variable or a numeric value to be single-precision.

9. DEFINT A-Z declares all variables beginning with a letter in the range of A through Z to be an integer. You can override DEFINT by appending a different type declaration character to a variable.

Chapter 3 Answers

1. Write, test, and debug.

2. The error number and name are displayed on the status line in the Edit window. The cursor is placed at the beginning of the line where the error exists.

3. ? _ (Question mark, space, and cursor)

4. `Enter your name? _` (Prompt, question mark, blank, and cursor)

5. `1   4   7   10   13`

6. `1`

   `2`

   `3`

   `4`

   `5`

7. Programs vary. Run your program to see whether it works.

8. Programs vary. Run your program to see whether it works.

Chapter 4 Answers

1. Yes

2. Yes, but a maximum of 77 characters are displayed on one line of the screen at a time.

3. The plus sign (+) is an operator (arithmetic).

4. $3 * 6 - 12 / 2 \char`\^ 2 = 3 * 6 - 12 / 4 = 18 - 3 = 15$

5. TRUE

6. TRUE

7. TRUE because 5 < 6 is TRUE.

8. `INT(RND * 20)` returns integers 0-19, inclusive.

9. TRUE, since 93 > 80 and 30 < 40.

10. -1 for TRUE and 0 for FALSE.

11. The underscore character is used to break a long program line into two or more parts.

Chapter 5 Answers

1. Integer number types are fastest.

2. a. long integer (greater than 32,767)

   b. integer

   c. long integer (greater than 32,767 but less than 2,147,483,647)

   d. quad integer (greater than 2,147,483,647)

3. 32,158,269

4. 1.3143215E+07 or 1.3143215E+7

5. The underscore character (_)

6. Answers will vary. %STOP = 25 should replace the previous %STOP value. More data is needed. More than one DATA statement can be used, as

   ```
   DATA 95, 80, 75, 85, 80, 70, 90, 85, 80, 85
   DATA 75, 80, 95, 80, 85, 85, 100, 75, 80, 85
   DATA 60, 75, 80, 85, 75
   ```

7. ```
   DEFINT A-K

   DEFLNG L-P

   DEFSNG Q-W

   DEFDBL X-Z
   ```

8. Add the single-precision specifier to the variable name Money!

Chapter 6 Answers

1. A label is used to mark a specific location within a program. The normal flow of sequential statement operation can be changed by a jump (such as GOTO) to the label.

2. INPUT$(1) interrupts the computer to wait for one keypress. INPUT$(2) interrupts the computer to wait for two keypresses.

3. a. The control of the program is passed to the label (LoopHere:).

   b. The sequential execution of statements continues to the line following the IF statement.
   ```

4. INPUT "Enter an integer (1-10)"; number%

5. LOCATE 5, 3   ' row first, then column

6. LTRIM$ removes the leading blanks, or characters, from a string. RTRIM$ removes the trailing blanks or characters from a string.

7. The value is rounded to three decimal places and printed as 23.264.

8. The format$ and PRINT USING statements cause the value to be printed as $123.78.

9. The value is "rig" because MID$ returns 3 characters starting at position two in the string.

10. The resulting string is "Some dogs are small".

Chapter 7 Answers

1. The value of number% is 11. The value of number% is increased by one each time a loop is completed. At the end of the tenth pass, number% is increased by 1, to 11. This causes the exit from the loop.

2. The numbers printed are

1	1
1	2
2	1
2	2
3	1
3	2

3. Insert an IF statement containing EXIT LOOP between the calculation of SquareValue% and the PRINT statement.

   ```
   SquareValue% = number% ^ 2
   IF SquareValue% > 5000 THEN EXIT LOOP
   PRINT number%, SquareValue%
   ```

4. Examples

   a.

   ```
   CLS: amount! = 0.1
   DO UNTIL amount! = 0
     INPUT "amount"; amount!
     Total! = Total! + amount!
   LOOP
   PRINT Total!
   ```

539

b.

```
CLS
DO
   INPUT "amount"; amount!
   Total! = Total! + amount!
LOOP UNTIL amount! = 0 PRINT Total!
```

c.

```
CLS
DO
   INPUT "amount"; amount!
   Total! = Total! + amount!
LOOP WHILE <> 0
PRINT Total!
```

5. Programs will vary.

6. Programs will vary.

Chapter 8 Answers

1. There is no END statement. The date and time will be printed, the numbers 1 through 7 will be printed, then the program will run into the subroutine, print the date and time again, and a "RETURN without GOSUB" error message will result.

2. GOSUB statement including a label or line number to specify the location of the beginning of the subroutine.

3. The value returned will be –2. (–8 + 16 +20 –30)

4. LEN prints the length of the specified string, which is 8 in this example (the space is counted).

5. First line: DEF FNHeatOff(Temp!)

   Last line: END DEF

6. Answers will vary. Try your program to see if it works.

7. Answers will vary. Try your program to see if it works.

Chapter 9 Answers

1. a. 0, 1, 2, and 3
   b. 3, 4, 5, and 6

2. Change DIM to `DIM day!(1:31)`

   Add more data

   Change FOR to `FOR number = 1 TO 31`

   Change Average! to `Average! = Sum! / 31`

3. Answers may vary. Here is one way:
   ```
   PRINT "Day"; SPC(5); "Temperature"
   FOR number = 1 TO 7
     READ day!(number)
     PRINT number; SPC(7); day!(number)
   'etc.
   ```

4. a. When `INPUT` is used, no commas may be used within the entry. A comma is interpreted as a data separator (delimiter).

   b. When `LINE INPUT` is used, commas may be used in the entry. The entire string, including the commas, is input.

5. Eight

6. Three

7. Product(1) = 45
   Product(2) = 35
   Product(3) = 98

   The value previously in Product(3) is lost.

8. Sales(1) = 35
   Sales(2) = 98
   Sales(3) = 123

Chapter 10 Answers

1. FOR OUTPUT in all cases or FOR APPEND if there is no other file with the specified name.

2. Press Enter.

3. LINE INPUT will accept commas, spaces, and other punctuation without considering these characters as field separators.

4. INPUT # should be used to read records from a file when WRITE # has been used to write the records to the file.

5. FOR APPEND

6. To determine if and when the end of a file has been reached when reading its data.

7. Programs will vary.

Chapter 11 Answers

1. String data is stored as ASCII text, numeric data is stored in strings in IEEE format.

2. Sequential files (all ASCII text) are the most portable.

3. It is not necessary because the default value of 128 bytes will be used. However, this may waste much space. It is better to use only the number of bytes that fit your longest record.

4. 640 bytes; 5 records * 128 bytes/record

5. GET #1, 4

   PRINT FName$, CVI(FPhone$)

6. Methods will vary. The numbers of each record should be input and the GET statements should reflect the variable names used to get the input.

7. Methods will vary. One way is to use

```
FOR RecNum = 1 TO 4
```

In addition the GET and PUT variables that were RecNum −1 should be changed to RecNum +1.

Chapter 12 Answers

1. Zero for column, and zero for row (0, 0)

2. Black background (color 0), palette 1 (cyan, magenta, white)

3. a. LOCATE specifies row first, then column—row 12, column 5

   b. PSEAT specifies column first, then row—column 14, row 30

4. a. (0, 0) is the lower-left corner, (100, 10) is the upper-right corner

   b. (0, 0) is the upper-left corner, (100, 10) is the lower-right corner

5. a. Draws a single line from (10, 10) to (100, 40)

   b. Draws a rectangle with (10, 10) as one corner and (100, 40) as the opposite corner

   c. Draws the same rectangle as part b, but fills the rectangle with the same color as the boundary

6. a. The rectangle is filled with the same color as the boundary; therefore appears as a solid block

   b. The rectangle is drawn with one color, and the interior painted with another

7. $4 + 9 * INT((49 * 2 + 7) / 8)$
   $= 4 + 9 * INT(105 / 8)$
   $= 4 + 9 * 13 = 121$ bytes
   $121 / 2 = 61$ elements (rounded up)
   62 elements for safety

8. Programs will vary.

Chapter 13 Answers

1. Your sketch should look something like figure A.1.

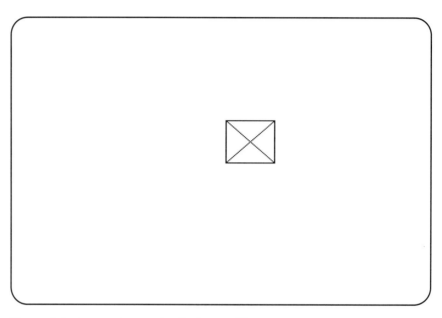

Figure A.1. Answer to question 1, chapter 13.

2. Drawing ends at (160, 60), 40 pixels up from start.

3. DRAW "BM-40,30"

4. DRAW "BL40 BD30"

5. Your sketch should look something like this.

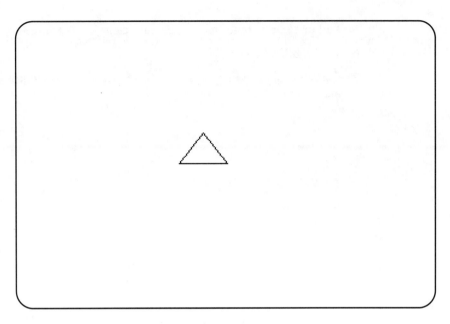

Figure A.2. Answer to question 5, chapter 13.

6. Your display shows the result.

7. Statements will vary. Run your statements to see if they work.

8. Programs will vary.

Chapter 14 Answers

1. a. Two dimensions: (1:limit, 1:maxblank).

   b. 5 for first dimension, 50 for second dimension.

2. A breakpoint interrupts a program at a predetermined statement.

3. The Run menu (Trace into item) provides single stepping.

4. The statement at the breakpoint is executed, and the highlight moves to the next statement. The F7 key produces a single-step in the program.

5. Add or clear watches and toggle and clear breakpoints.

6. a. 1   b. 50   c. 5

7. 5 (the number of blanks) and 4, 8, 15, 18, and 26 (the positions of the blanks in the original string).

ASCII, Extended Key, and Scan Codes

ASCII Codes

The American Standard Code for Information Interchange (ASCII) translates alphabetic and numeric characters, symbols, and control instructions into the codes shown in table B.1.

Table B.1. ASCII table.

ASCII Value		ASCII Character	ASCII Value		ASCII Character
Dec	Hex		Dec	Hex	
000	00	null	016	10	►
001	01	☺	017	11	◄
002	02	☻	018	12	↕
003	03	♥	019	13	‼
004	04	♦	020	14	¶
005	05	♣	021	15	§
006	06	♠	022	16	▬
007	07	●	023	17	↨
008	08	■	024	18	↑
009	09	○	025	19	↓
010	0A	■	026	1A	→
011	0B	♂	027	1B	←
012	0C	♀	028	1C	FS
013	0D	♪	029	1D	GS
014	0E	♪♪	030	1E	RS
015	0F	☼	031	1F	US

continues

Table B.1. (continued)

| ASCII Value | | | ASCII Value | | |
Dec	Hex	ASCII Character	Dec	Hex	ASCII Character
032	20	SP	072	48	H
033	21	!	073	49	I
034	22	"	074	4A	J
035	23	#	075	4B	K
036	24	$	076	4C	L
037	25	%	077	4D	M
038	26	&	078	4E	N
039	27	'	079	4F	O
040	28	(	080	50	P
041	29	)	081	51	Q
042	2A	*	082	52	R
043	2B	+	083	53	S
044	2C	,	084	54	T
045	2D	-	085	55	U
046	2E	.	086	56	V
047	2F	/	087	57	W
048	30	0	088	58	X
049	31	1	089	59	Y
050	32	2	090	5A	Z
051	33	3	091	5B	[
052	34	4	092	5C	\
053	35	5	093	5D	]
054	36	6	094	5E	^
055	37	7	095	5F	–
056	38	8	096	60	`
057	39	9	097	61	a
058	3A	:	098	62	b
059	3B	;	099	63	c
060	3C	<	100	64	d
061	3D	=	101	65	e
062	3E	>	102	66	f
063	3F	?	103	67	g
064	40	@	104	68	h
065	41	A	105	69	i
066	42	B	106	6A	j
067	43	C	107	6B	k
068	44	D	108	6C	l
069	45	E	109	6D	m
070	46	F	110	6E	n
071	47	G			

| ASCII Value | | ASCII Character | ASCII Value | | ASCII Character |
Dec	Hex		Dec	Hex	
111	6F	o	146	92	Æ
112	70	p	147	93	ô
113	71	q	148	94	ö
114	72	r	149	95	ò
115	73	s	150	96	û
116	74	t	151	97	ù
117	75	u	152	98	ÿ
118	76	v	153	99	Ö
119	77	w	154	9A	Ü
120	78	x	155	9B	¢
121	79	y	156	9C	£
122	7A	z	157	9D	¥
123	7B	{	158	9E	P_t
124	7C	¦	159	9F	ƒ
125	7D	}	160	A0	á
126	7E	~	161	A1	í
127	7F	DEL	162	A2	ó
128	80	Ç	163	A3	ú
129	81	ü	164	A4	ñ
130	82	é	165	A5	Ñ
131	83	â	166	A6	ª
132	84	ä	167	A7	º
133	85	à	168	A8	¿
134	86	å	169	A9	⌐
135	87	ç	170	AA	¬
136	88	ê	171	AB	½
137	89	ë	172	AC	¼
138	8A	è	173	AD	¡
139	8B	ï	174	AE	«
140	8C	î	175	AF	»
141	8D	ì	176	B0	▒
142	8E	Ä	177	B1	▓
143	8F	Å	178	B2	█
144	90	É	179	B3	│
145	91	æ	180	B4	┤

continues

Table B.1. (continued)

ASCII Value Dec	Hex	ASCII Character	ASCII Value Dec	Hex	ASCII Character
181	B5	╡	216	D8	╪
182	B6	╢	217	D9	┘
183	B7	╖	218	DA	┌
184	B8	╕	219	DB	█
185	B9	╣	220	DC	▄
186	BA	║	221	DD	▌
187	BB	╗	222	DE	▐
188	BC	╝	223	DF	▀
189	BD	╜	224	E0	α
190	BE	╛	225	E1	β
191	BF	┐	226	E2	Γ
192	C0	└	227	E3	π
193	C1	┴	228	E4	Σ
194	C2	┬	229	E5	σ
195	C3	├	230	E6	μ
196	C4	─	231	E7	τ
197	C5	┼	232	E8	Φ
198	C6	╞	233	E9	θ
199	C7	╟	234	EA	Ω
200	C8	╚	235	EB	δ
201	C9	╔	236	EC	∞
202	CA	╩	237	ED	ø
203	CB	╦	238	EE	∈
204	CC	╠	239	EF	∩
205	CD	═	240	F0	≡
206	CE	╬	241	F1	±
207	CF	╧	242	F2	≥
208	D0	╨	243	F3	≤
209	D1	╤	244	F4	⌠
210	D2	╥	245	F5	⌡
211	D3	╙	246	F6	÷
212	D4	╘	247	F7	≈
213	D5	╒	248	F8	°
214	D6	╓	249	F9	•
215	D7	╫	250	FA	·

| ASCII Value | | | ASCII Value | | |
Dec	Hex	ASCII Character	Dec	Hex	ASCII Character
251	FB	√	254	FE	∎
252	FC	η	255	FF	
253	FD	2			

Extended Key Codes

Extended key codes are returned by those keys or key combinations that cannot be represented by the standard ASCII codes listed in table B.1. The extended codes are returned by the system variable INKEY$ in a two-character string where a null character is the first character. Table B.2 shows the second code and what it means.

Table B.2. Extended key codes.

Second Code	Meaning
3	NUL (null character)
15	Shift Tab
16-25	Alt-Q/W/E/R/T/Y/U/I/O/P
30-38	Alt-A/S/D/F/G/H/J/K/L
44-50	Alt-Z/X/C/V/B/N/M
59-68	F1-F10
71	Home
72	Cursor up
73	PgUp
75	Cursor left
77	Cursor right
79	End
80	Cursor down
81	PgDn
82	Ins
83	Del
84-93	Shift-F1 to Shift-F10

continues

	Second Code	Meaning
	94-103	Ctrl-F1 to Ctrl-F10
	104-113	Alt-F1 to Alt-F10
	114	Ctrl-PrtSc
	115	Ctrl-Cursor left
	116	Ctrl-Cursor right
	117	Ctrl-End
	118	Ctrl-PgDn
	119	Ctrl-Home
	120-131	Alt-1/2/3/4/5/6/7/8/9/-/=
	132	Ctrl-PgUp
	133	F11
	134	F12
	135	Shift-F11
	136	Shift-F12
	137	Ctrl-F11
	138	Ctrl-F12
	139	Alt-F11
	140	Alt-F12

Table B.2. (continued)

Keyboard Scan Codes

Keyboard scan codes are the codes returned from the keys on a PC keyboard as they are seen by PowerBASIC. The scan codes are shown in table B.3.

Table B.3. Keyboard scan codes.

Key	Scan Code	Key	Scan Code
Esc	01		15
! 1	02	Q	16
@ 2	03	W	17
# 3	04	E	18

Key	Scan Code	Key	Scan Code
$ 4	05	R	19
% 5	06	T	20
^ 6	07	Y	21
& 7	08	U	22
* 8	09	I	23
(9	10	O	24
) 0	11	P	25
_ -	12	{ [	26
+ =	13	}]	27
Backspace	14	Enter	28
Ctrl	29	| \	43
A	30	Z	44
S	31	X	45
D	32	C	46
F	33	V	47
G	34	B	48
H	35	N	49
J	36	M	50
K	37	< ,	51
L	38	>	52
: ;	39	? /	53
" '	40	Rgt Shift	54
~ '	41	PrtScr	55
Lft Shift	42	Alt	56
Spacebar	57	7 Home	71
Caps Lock	58	8 CursorUp	72
F1	59	9 PgUp	73
F2	60	-	74
F3	61	4 CursorLft	75
F4	62	5	76
F5	63	6 CursorRgt	77
F6	64	+	78
F7	65	1 End	79

continues

553

Table B.3. (continued)

Key	Scan Code	Key	Scan Code
F8	66	2 CursorDn	80
F9	67	3 PgDn	81
F10	68	0 Ins	82
F11	217	. Del	83
F12	218	Num Lock	69
		Scroll Lock	70

PowerBASIC Lite Components

This appendix contains lists of the components that are used in creating PowerBASIC Lite programs. The components are divided into four major categories: Operators, Statements, Functions, and System Variables.

Operators

PowerBASIC Lite's operators are classified into three major groups: arithmetic, relational, and logical.

Arithmetic Operators

Arithmetic operators perform the normal mathematical operations shown in table C.1.

Table C.1. Arithmetic operators.

Operator	Action	Example	Procedure
^	Exponentiation	12 ^ 3	1
–	Negation	–32	2
*	Multiplication	45.2 * 9.7	3
/	Division	22.8 / 13.4	3

continues

Table C.1. (continued)			
Operator	**Action**	**Example**	**Procedure**
\	Integer division	23.1 \ 7.2	4
MOD	Modulo	23.1 MOD 7.2	5
+	Addition	75 + 18	6
–	Subtraction	65 – 62	6

The following applies to the two operations in table C.1 that are uncommon in elementary school arithmetic.

The backslash (\), the integer division operator, returns a truncated quotient of two operands. For the example in the table, 23.1 and 7.2 are first rounded to integers (23 and 7). The truncated quotient (23 \ 7) evaluates to 3. This is the same quotient produced by the paper and pencil division of elementary school. The integer division operator ignores any remainder.

The remainder of an integer division can be determined by using the MOD operator. It operates in a manner similar to integer division, but returns the remainder. Thus the example in the table would return a value of 2 (23 MOD 7 = 2).

If either operand of an integer division or MOD operation is outside the range of a quad integer ($-2\wedge63$ to $2\wedge63-1$), an overflow occurs.

Relational Operators

Relational operators enable you to compare the values of two strings or two numbers (but not one of each) to obtain a Boolean result of TRUE or FALSE. The result of a comparison is assigned an integer value of –1 when the relation is TRUE and 0 when the relation is FALSE. Table C.2 lists the relational operators.

Table C.2. Relational operators.		
Operator	**Relation**	**Example**
=	Equality	5 = 5
<>	Inequality	6 <> 5
<	Less than	5 < 6
>	Greater than	6 > 5
<= or =<	Less than or equal to	5 <= 5 and 5 <= 6
>= or =>	Greater than or equal to	5 >= 5 and 6 >= 5

When arithmetic and relational operators are combined in an expression, arithmetic operations are always evaluated first.

Logical Operators

Logical operators perform logical (Boolean) operations on numbers of any type. Before a Boolean operation takes place, PowerBASIC Lite automatically converts floating point numbers to integers. Table C.3 lists the logical operators.

Table C.3. Logical operators.

Operator	Logic	Example
AND	TRUE if both operands are TRUE; otherwise FALSE.	TRUE AND TRUE = TRUE TRUE AND FALSE = FALSE FALSE AND TRUE = FALSE FALSE AND FALSE = FALSE
OR	FALSE if both operands are FALSE; otherwise TRUE	TRUE AND TRUE = TRUE TRUE AND FALSE = TRUE FALSE AND TRUE = TRUE FALSE AND FALSE = FALSE
XOR	FALSE if both operands are the same; otherwise TRUE	TRUE XOR TRUE = FALSE TRUE XOR FALSE = TRUE FALSE XOR TRUE = TRUE FALSE XOR FALSE = FALSE
EQV	TRUE if both operands are the same; otherwise FALSE	TRUE EQV TRUE = TRUE TRUE EQV FALSE = FALSE FALSE EQV TRUE = FALSE FALSE EQV FALSE = TRUE
IMP	FALSE only if the first operand is TRUE and the second is FALSE	TRUE IMP TRUE = TRUE TRUE IMP FALSE = FALSE FALSE IMP TRUE = TRUE FALSE IMP FALSE = TRUE

Note that all logical operators operate on all types of integers, but not on floating point values. If the operands of a logical expression are outside the range of a quad integer (-2^{63} to $2^{63}-1$), an overflow occurs.

In addition to performing complex tests, logical operators permit control over the bit patterns of their integer operands. For example, to clear the extreme left 2 bits of an integer value, use AND with a *mask* of &H3FFF; that is, an operand that is all

1s except for the positions you wish to force to zero. Each bit in the mask is ANDed with the corresponding bit of the operand whose extreme left 2 bits are to be cleared, as follows:

```
    1101 0111 0100 0001          (first operand)
AND 0011 1111 1111 1111          (mask)
    ───────────────────
    0001 0111 0100 0001          (result = first operand
                                  with extreme left 2 bits
                                  cleared)
```

Statements

Statements are the building blocks used to create programs. PowerBASIC Lite has over 130 statements. You can find explanations of each statement in the PowerBASIC Lite help system. Here is a list of PowerBASIC Lite statements in alphabetical order.

PowerBASIC Lite statements

ARRAY	ATTRIB	BEEP	BLOAD
BSAVE	CALL	CALL INTERRUPT	CHDIR
CHDRIVE	CIRCLE	CLEAR	CLOSE
CLS	COLOR	COM	DATA
DECR	DEF FN	DEF SEG	DEFBCD
DEFDBL	DEFEXT	DEFFIX	DEFFLX
DEFINT	DEFLNG	DEFQUD	DEFSNG
DEFSTR	DELAY	DIM	DO/LOOP
DRAW	END	ENVIRON	ERASE
ERROR	EXIT	FIELD	FILES
FOR/NEXT	FUNCTION	GET	GOSUB
GOTO	IF	INCR	INPUT
INPUT #	IOCTL	KEY	KILL
LET	LINE	LINE INPUT	LINE INPUT #
LOCAL	LOCATE	LOCK	LPRINT
LPRINT USING	LSET	MAP	MID$
MKDIR	MTIMER	NAME	ON COM
ON ERROR	ON GOSUB	ON GOTO	ON KEY
ON PEN	ON PLAY	ON STRIG	ON TIMER
OPEN	OPEN COM	OPTION BASE	OUT
PAINT	PALETTE	PALETTE USING	PEN
PLAY	POKE	POKEI	POKEL
POKE$	PRESET	PRINT	PRINT USING
PRINT #	PRINT # USING	PSET	PUT

RANDOMIZE	READ	REDIM	REG
REM	REPLACE	RESET	RESTORE
RESUME	RETURN	RMDIR	RSET
RUN	SCREEN	SEEK	SELECT
SHARED	SOUND	STATIC	STOP
STRIG	SUB	SWAP	SYSTEM
TIMER	TROFF	TRON	UNLOCK
VIEW	WAIT	WHILE/WEND	WIDTH
WINDOW	WRITE	WRITE #	

Functions

PowerBASIC Lite offers three kinds of functions: predefined functions (more than 125 functions defined by the language), and two kinds of user-defined functions. Here is an alphabetical list of the predefined functions.

PowerBASIC Lite predefined functions

ABS	ASC	ASCII	ATN
ATTRIB	BIN$	CBCD	CDBL
CEIL	CEXT	CFIX	CHR$
CINT	CLNG	COS	CQUD
CSNG	CSRLIN	CURDIR$	CVB
CVD	CVE	CVF	CVI
CVL	CVMD	CVMS	CVQ
CVS	DIR$	ENDMEM	ENVIRON$
EOF	ERADR	ERDEV	ERDEV$
ERL	ERR	EXP	EXP2
EXP10	EXTRACT$	FILEATTR	FIX
FRE	FREEFILE	GET$	HEX$
INKEY$	INP	INPUT$	INSTAT
INSTR	INT	IOCTL$	LBOUND
LCASE$	LEFT$	LEN	LOC
LOF	LOG	LOG2	LOG10
LPOS	LTRIM$	MAX	MAX%
MAX$	MID$	MIN	MIN%
MIN$	MKB$	MKD$	MKE$
MKF$	MKI$	MKL$	MKMD$
MKMS$	MKQ$	MKS$	MTIMER
OCT$	PEEK	PEEKI	PEEKL
PEEK$	PEN	PLAY	PMAP
POINT	POS	PUT$	REG
REMOVE$	REPEAT$	RIGHT$	RND
ROUND	RTRIM$	SCREEN	SEEK
SGN	SIN	SPACE$	SPC

SQR	STICK	STR$	STRIG
STRING$	STRPTR	STRSEG	TAB
TALLY	TAN	TIMER	UBOUND
UCASE$	USING$	VAL	VARPTR
VARPTR$	VARSEG	VERIFY	

System Variables

System variables are variables that relate to the interior computer system. You can set or read system variables within legal parameters. Four system variables are available from PowerBASIC Lite. They are:

- DATE$ is used to set and retrieve the system date. Note: DATE$ cannot be used to read or set the battery operated clock/calendar found on many PC expansion cards.

```
DATE$ = d$   '(sets system date according to d$)
```

To set the date, your date string (d$) must be formatted in one of the following ways:

```
"mm-dd-yy"
"mm/dd/yy"
"mm-dd-yyyy"
"mm/dd/yyyy"
d$ = DATE$   '(d$ retrieves the system date)
```

The date is returned in the following format:

```
mm-dd-yyyy
```

- FIXDIGITS is used to set the number of "fixed" decimal places for a BCD fixed-point number. The default value is 2 but can be increased to a maximum of 18.

- FLEXCHR$ determines which character is used to pad extra spaces in a flex string. The default character is a single space.

- TIME$ is used to read or set the system time. Note: TIME$ cannot be used to read or set the battery operated clocks found on many PC expansion cards.

```
t$ = TIME$   '(reads the time)
```

The time is returned in the following 24-hour military form:

```
hh:mm:ss  '(where hh is hours, mm is minutes, and ss is
seconds)
```

TIME$ will not be accurate unless the DOS clock was set correctly when the computer was last booted up.

```
TIME$ = string expression
```

This statement sets the time. The *string expression* must be in 24-hour format; minute and second information may be omitted.

PowerBASIC Lite Selected Error Codes

Two types of errors can occur in PowerBASIC Lite programs: compile-time and run-time. Compile-time errors are errors in syntax discovered by the compiler before the program is run. Run-time errors are caught at run-time by error-detection mechanisms that the compiler places in your object programs.

Common Run-Time Errors

You can write error-handling routines into your programs to take care of many run-time errors. If run-time errors are not explicitly trapped by your code, your program will abort upon encountering an error condition. An error number and brief message describing the condition is displayed. The cursor in the Edit window will be positioned at the statement that caused the error. Run-time errors have numbers less than 400.

Table D.1 contains a list of common run-time errors, their error numbers, and an explanation of the condition causing the error.

Table D.1. Common run-time errors.

Error and Message	Meaning
2 Syntax error	A run-time syntax error has been created by a READ statement trying to load string data into a numeric variable.
3 RETURN without GOSUB	A RETURN was encountered without a matching GOSUB.
4 Out of data	A READ statement ran out of DATA statement values.
5 Illegal function call	A catch-all error related to passing an inappropriate argument to some statement or function.
6 Overflow	A value resulted that is too large to be represented by the indicated number type.
7 Out of memory	Many different situations cause this message, including dimensioning too large an array or using up all string space.
9 Subscript out of range	An attempt was made to use a subscript larger than the maximum value established when the array was dimensioned.
10 Duplicate dimension	You attempted to dynamically dimension an array for the second time, without first erasing it.
11 Division by zero	You attempted to divide by zero or to raise zero to a negative power.
12 Type mismatch	You used a string value where a numeric variable was expected, or vice versa.
50 Field overflow	Given the file's record length, you attempted to define too long a set of field variables in a FIELD statement.
52 Bad file number	The file number given doesn't match one given in an OPEN statement, or the number may be out of the valid range.
53 File not found	The file name specified cannot be found on the indicated disk drive.
54 Bad file mode	You attempted a PUT or a GET on a sequential file.

Error and Message	Meaning
55 File already open	An attempt was made to open a file that was already open, or you tried to delete an open file.
58 File already exists	The new name argument specified in a NAME statement already exists.
61 Disk full	Not enough free space on the disk to carry out a file operation.
64 Bad file name	The file name specified in a FILES, KILL, or NAME statement contains invalid characters.
70 Permission denied	You attempted to write to a write-protected disk.
71 Disk not ready	The door of a floppy disk drive is open, or there is no disk in the indicated drive.

Common Compile-Time Errors

Most compile-time errors are errors of syntax, caused by missing symbols, misspelled commands, unbalanced parentheses, and so on. When the compiler finds something in a source program that it cannot understand or permit, you are automatically placed in the editor, with the cursor positioned at the point of the error. At the top of the screen, PowerBASIC Lite lists the error number and a brief description of the error. Compiler errors have error codes of 401 and above. Table D.2 contains a list of common compiletime errors, their error numbers, and an explanation of the condition causing the error.

Table D.2. Common compile-time errors.

Number and Message	Meaning
411 "," expected	Statement syntax requires a comma.
412 ";" expected	Statement syntax requires a semicolon.
413 "(" expected	Statement syntax requires a left parenthesis.
414 ")" expected	Statement syntax requires a right parenthesis.
415 "=" expected	Statement syntax requires an equal sign.

continues

565

Table D.2. (continued)

Number and Message	Meaning
416 "-" expected	Statement syntax requires a hyphen.
417 "*" expected	Statement syntax requires an asterisk.
418 Statement expected	A PowerBASIC Lite statement was expected. Some character could not be identified as a statement, metastatement, or variable.
419 Label/line number expected	A valid label or line number reference was expected in an IF, GOTO, GOSUB, or ON statement.
420 Relational operator expected	The compiler has found a string operator in a position where a numeric operand should be.
423 Array variable expected	An array variable was expected in a DIM statement or in the GET or PUT graphics statements.
424 Numeric variable expected	A numeric variable was expected in an INCR, DECR, or CALL ABSOLUTE statement.
425 String variable expected	A string variable was expected in a FIELD, GET$, PUT$, or LINE INPUT statement.
426 Variable expected	A variable was expected in a statement such as VARPTR, VARSEG, and so on.
427 Integer constant expected	An integer constant was expected in a named constant assignment.
430 Integer variable expected	An integer variable was expected as a parameter in a statement such as ARRAY SCAN.
434 End of line expected	No characters are allowed on a line (except for a comment) following a metastatement, END SUB, or a statement label.
437 AS expected	The AS reserved word is missing in either a FIELD, MAP, or OPEN statement.
438 FROM expected	The FROM reserved word is missing in either a FIELD or MAP statement.
439 GOSUB expected	An ON statement is missing its accompanying GOSUB part.
440 GOTO expected	An ON statement is missing its accompanying GOTO part.

Number and Message	Meaning
441 IN expected	The IN reserved word is missing in a REPLACE statement.
442 THEN expected	An IF statement is missing its accompanying THEN part.
443 TO expected	A FIELD, FOR, or MAP statement is missing its accompanying TO part.
444 WITH expected	The WITH reserved word is missing in a REPLACE statement.
447 IF expected	The compiler found an END IF or EXIT IF statement without a beginning IF statement.
448 DO LOOP expected	The compiler found a LOOP or EXIT LOOP statement without a beginning DO statement.
449 SELECT	The reserved word SELECT is expected missing or the compiler ran into an END SELECT or EXIT SELECT without a beginning SELECT CASE statement; or you tried to use the reserved word CASE as a variable name in your program.
450 CASE expected	When a SELECT CASE statement was defined, the reserved word CASE was not included; or you tried to use the reserved word SELECT as a variable.
451 FOR loop expected	The compiler found an EXIT FOR statement without a beginning FOR statement.
452 SUB expected	The compiler found an END SUB statement without a procedure SUB statement.
453 END DEF expected	A DEF FN function wasn't terminated with an END DEF statement.
454 END FUNCTION expected	A FUNCTION definition wasn't terminated with an END FUNCTION statement.
455 END IF expected	An IF block wasn't terminated with an END IF statement.
456 LOOP/WEND expected	A DO or WHILE loop was not terminated with a LOOP or WEND statement.
457 END SELECT expected	A SELECT CASE statement was not terminated with an END SELECT statement.
458 END SUB expected	A procedure was not terminated with an END SUB statement.

continues

567

Table D.2. (continued)

Number and Message	Meaning
459 NEXT expected	A FOR loop was not terminated with a NEXT statement.
460 Undefined name constant	A named constant was used without defining it.
461 Undefined FN function reference	An FN function name was used in an expression without defining the DEF FN function.
462 Undefined SUB procedure reference	CALL was used to call a procedure that was not defined.
463 Undefined label/line reference	A line number or label was used in an IF, GOTO, GOSUB, or ON statement that was not defined.
464 Undefined array reference	An array was referenced but never defined in a DIM statement.
465 Duplicate definition	A program element that should appear only once was duplicated.
466 Duplicate name	A SUB, FUNCTION, DEF FN, label, or variable name was defined more than once.
468 Duplicate named constant	Two named constants were defined with the same name.
470 Duplicate variable	Two variables with the same name declaration have been declared with a LOCAL, STATIC, or SHARED statement.
472 Invalid label	Label contains invalid characters.
473 Invalid numeric format	A number was declared with more than 18 digits, or a floating point number was declared with an E component with no exponent value.
474 Invalid name	A function, procedure, or label has an invalid name.
475 Metastatements not allowed here	Metastatements must be the first statement on a line.
476 Block/Scanned statements not allowed here	Block statements (like WHILE/WEND, SELECT CASE, and so on) are not allowed in single line IF statements; you cannot have a procedure or function definition nested within the body of another definition.

Number and Message	Meaning
477 Syntax error	Something is incorrect on this line—the compiler could not determine a proper error message.
478 Array subscript error	An array was dimensioned with a number of subscripts and used with another set of subscripts.
479 Array bounds error	For a static dimensioned array, the program referenced the array with a literal value out of range.
480 Type mismatch	The parameters passed to a procedure or function are not of the same type that was defined in the definition or DECLARE statement.
481 Parameter mismatch	The type or number of parameters does not correspond with the declaration of the function or procedure.
482 CLEAR parameters not allowed	The additional parameters available in interpretive BASIC are not available in PowerBASIC.
483 CLEAR not allowed here	CLEAR is illegal within a procedure or function.
484 LOCAL requires DEF FN/FUNCTION/SUB	You can only declare LOCAL variables in a function or procedure.
485 STATIC requires DEF FN/FUNCTION/SUB	You can only declare STATIC variables in a function or procedure.
487 LOCAL arrays must be dynamic	Arrays defined as LOCAL cannot be defined as STATIC.
488 Array is dynamic	If you have two DIM statements in a program for the same array, or if you dimensioned an array using variables as indices, the array is automatically declared to be DYNAMIC.
489 Array is static	You issued a DIM STATIC statement to dimension a static array, then later attempted to dimension that array again. Static arrays may be dimensioned only once in a program.
504 Flex variable expected	A flex string variable was expected in a FIELD or MAP statement.

continues

569

Table D.2. (continued)

Number and Message	Meaning
505 Flex array expected	A flex string array variable was expected in a MAP statement.
506 Declaration must precede statements	A metastatement was preceded by some executable code.
601-606 Internal error	If this error occurs, report it immediately to Spectra Publishing's Technical Support group.

Editing Aids

PowerBASIC Lite has many aids to assist you in editing your programs. Because the editor is an integral part of the integrated development environment, you don't need to use the menu bar to use more than 50 editing commands. Instead you use keys or combinations of keys to move within your file, insert, copy, and delete text, and search and replace text. The commands are grouped into four main categories:

- Cursor movement
- Insert and delete operations
- Block operations
- Miscellaneous editing operations

Cursor Movement

Movement of the cursor in your file can be accomplished in short, intermediate, or long steps. The keystrokes used for moving the cursor are listed in Table E.1.

Table E.1. Cursor movement commands.

Command	Movement
Ctrl-S or Left arrow	Left; character
Ctrl-D or Right arrow	Right; character
Ctrl-A	Left; word
Ctrl-F	Right; word
Ctrl-E or Up arrow	Up; line
Ctrl-X or Down arrow	Down; line
Ctrl-W	Scroll up; line
Ctrl-Z	Scroll down; line
Ctrl-R or PgUp	Up; page
Ctrl-C or PgDn	Down; page
Ctrl-Q S or Home	Beginning of line
Ctrl-Q D or End	End of line
Ctrl-Q E	Top of window
Ctrl-Q X	Bottom of window
Ctrl-Q R	Top of file
Ctrl-Q C	End of file
Ctrl-Q B	Beginning of block
Ctrl-Q K	End of block
Ctrl-Q P	Last cursor position

Note: A word is defined as a sequence of characters separated by one of the following characters: space < > , ; . ( ) [ ] ^ ' * + [neg]/ $

Insert and Delete Commands

The commands in Table E.2 are used to insert or delete text.

Table E.2. Insert and delete commands.

Command	Action
Ctrl-V or Ins	Insert mode on/off
Ctrl-H or Backspace	Delete character left of cursor
Ctrl-G or Del	Delete character under cursor
Ctrl-T	Delete word right
Ctrl-N	Insert line
Ctrl-Y	Delete line
Ctrl-Q Y	Delete to end of line

Block Commands

A block of text is any amount of text, from a single character to hundreds of lines, that has been surrounded with special block-marker characters. There can only be one block in a document at a time. Once marked, the block may be copied, moved, deleted, printed, or written to a file. Blocks that have been marked are highlighted.

The commands listed in Table E.3 are used to perform actions on blocks of text.

Table E.3. Block commands.

Command	Action
Ctrl-K B	Mark block begin
Ctrl-K K	Mark block end
Ctrl-K T	Mark single word
Ctrl-K C	Copy block
Ctrl-K V	Move block
Ctrl-K Y	Delete block
Ctrl-K R	Read block from disk
Ctrl-K W	Write block to disk
Ctrl-K H	Hide/display block
Ctrl-K P	Print block

Miscellaneous Editing Commands

The commands in Table E.4 cover editing commands that do not fit into the previous categories.

Command	Action
Table E.4. Miscellaneous editing commands.	
Command	**Action**
Ctrl-U	Abort operation
Ctrl-O I	Autoindent on/off
Ctrl-P	Control character prefix (see note 1)
Ctrl-Q *n* (see note 2)	Find place marker
F3	New file
Ctrl-K P	Print file
Ctrl-K D, Ctrl-K Q,	Quit edit, no save or F10
Ctrl-L	Repeat last search
Ctrl-Q W	Restore error message
Ctrl-Q L	Restore line
Esc	Return to Main menu bar
Ctrl-K S or F2	Save and continue edit
Ctrl-Q F	Search
Ctrl-Q A	Search and replace
Ctrl-K N	Set place marker
Ctrl-I or Tab	Tab
Ctrl-O T	Tab mode
F10	Toggle editor/menu bar
Ctrl-O U	Unindent mode

Note 1: Enter control character by first pressing Ctrl-P, then press the desired control character. Control characters appear as low-intensity capital letter on-screen (or inverse, depending on your screen setup).

Note 2: Where *n* represents a number from 0 to 3.

Number System Equivalents

The information in table F.1 shows the equivalent values of binary, octal, decimal, and hexadecimal number systems.

Table F.1. Number system equivalents.

Binary		Octal	Decimal	Hexadecimal
0000	0000	0	0	0
	0001	1	1	1
	0010	2	2	2
	0011	3	3	3
	0100	4	4	4
	0101	5	5	5
	0110	6	6	6
	0111	7	7	7
	1000	10	8	8
	1001	11	9	9
	1010	12	10	A
	1011	13	11	B
	1100	14	12	C
	1101	15	13	D
	1110	16	14	E
	1111	17	15	F

continues

Table F.1. (continued)

Binary		Octal	Decimal	Hexadecimal
0001	0000	20	16	10
.		.	.	.
.		.	.	.
.		.	.	.
0010	0000	40	32	20
.		.	.	.
.		.	.	.
.		.	.	.
0100	0000	100	64	40
.		.	.	.
.		.	.	.
.		.	.	.
1000	0000	200	128	80
.		.	.	.
.		.	.	.
.		.	.	.
1111	1110	376	254	FE
1111	1111	377	255	FF

Index

C

E

F

G

H

types, 140
values
  assigning, 77
  modifying, 78
watching, 364-368
zeroing all, 408
VARPTR function, 344-345, 528
VARPTR$ function, 529
VARSEG function, 344, 529
VERIFY function, 166, 530
Video Graphics Array Adapter (VGA), 177, 296-297
VIEW statement, 400-401, 530

W

WAIT statement, 405, 531
Watch window, 5, 12
watches, variable
  removing, 370-372
  setting, 364-368
WEND statement, 86, 181
WHILE
  keyword, 98
  statement, 86, 181-184
WHILE/WEND
  loop, 85-88, 181-182
  statement, 531
WIDTH statement, 297, 532
wild cards, 38
WINDOW statement, 303-304, 532
windows
  Change Dir help, 30-31
  Directory help, 30

drawing on screen, 175
Edit, 5-11, 105, 202
Get Info help, 30-32
Load help, 28-29
menu, 321-323
Run help, 32-33
scrolling, 55
Trace into help, 34
User screen, 19
User Screen help, 34-35
Watch, 5, 12
words
  inserting/deleting shortcuts, 50-52
world screen coordinates, 399
WRITE # statement, 249, 533
WRITE statement, 533
Write to... command, 29
WriteFiles procedure, 374
writing
  bytes to I/O ports, 405
  information to files, 249
  programs, 94-95
  strings to binary files, 402

X-Z

XOR operations, 112

zeroing all variables, 408

601

Sams Guarantees Your Success In 10 Minutes!

The *10 Minute Guides* provide a new approach to learning computer programs. Each book teaches you the most often used features of a particular program in 15 to 20 short lessons—all of which can be completed in 10 minutes or less. What's more, the *10 Minute Guides* are simple to use. You won't find any "computer-ese" or technical jargon— just plain English explanations. With straightforward instructions, easy-to-follow steps, and special margin icons to call attention to important tips and definitions, the *10 Minute Guides* make learning a new software program easy and fun!

10 Minute Guide to WordPerfect 5.1
Katherine Murray & Doug Sabotin
160 pages, 51/2 x 81/2, $9.95 USA
0-672-22808-4

10 Minute Guide to MS-DOS 5
Jack Nimersheim
160 pages, 5 1/2 x 81/2, $9.95 USA
0-672-22807-6

10 Minute Guide to Windows 3
Katherine Murray & Doug Sabotin
160 pages, 5 1/2 x 8 1/2, $9.95 USA
0-672-22812-2

10 Minute Guide to PC Tools 7
Joe Kraynak
160 pages, 5 1/2 x 8 1/2, $9.95 USA
0-672-30021-4

10 Minute Guide to Lotus 1-2-3
Katherine Murray & Doug Sabotin
160 pages, 51/2 x 8 1/2, $9.95 USA
0-672-22809-2

**10 Minute Guide to Q&A 4,
Revised Edition**
Arlene Azzarello
160 pages, 51/2 x 81/2, $9.95 USA
0-672-30035-4

**10 Minute Guide
to Harvard Graphics 2.3**
Lisa Bucki
160 pages, 51/2 x 81/2, $9.95 USA
0-672-22837-8

SAMS

See your local retailer or call 1-800-428-5331.

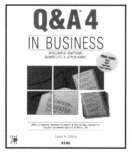

Installation Summary

Before trying to use PowerBASIC Lite, first make a backup copy of the PowerBASIC Lite disk. Once you have successfully copied the disk, store the original disks in a safe place. When you run PowerBASIC Lite on a floppy disk system, use the backup disk.

To use PowerBASIC Lite on a hard disk system, make a new subdirectory on your hard disk. Use the DOS Make Directory command and type the name of the subdirectory (PBLITE in this example), as follows:

```
C:>MD \PBLITE
```

Next, copy the files from the backup disk to the PBLITE subdirectory.

```
C:>CD PBLITE
C:\PBLITE>COPY A:*.* C:\PBLITE
```

Two of these files are used to create programs and provide explanatory material:

- PBLITE.EXE—contains all that is necessary to write, run, and modify your PowerBASIC Lite programs.

- PBLHELP.PBH—contains help material to assist you with writing or modifying programs.

The example programs in the book are also included on the disk. These files are compressed and combined into one file: BAS.COM. When BAS.COM is uncompressed, many files with the .BAS extension will appear in your PBLITE directory. These files are the correct PBLITE programs found in the listings throughout the book. Therefore, you should place the .BAS files in the subdirectory, \PBLITE\ANSWERS. While you are in your \PBLITE directory, type the following:

```
C:\PBLITE>MD ANSWERS
```

Now change to this subdirectory and copy the file BAS.COM into it by typing

```
C:\PBLITE>CD ANSWERS
C:\PBLITE\ANSWERS>COPY A:BAS.COM C:\PBLITE\ANSWERS
```

Finally, to uncompress the file, type

```
C:\PBLITE\ANSWERS>BAS
```

If your computer uses 3 1/2-inch disks . . .

Although many personal computers use 5 1/4-inch disks to store information, some newer computers are switching to 3 1/2-inch disks for information storage. If your computer uses 3 1/2-inch disks, you can return this form to SAMS to obtain a 3 1/2-inch disk to use with this book. Complete the remainder of this form and mail to:

Learning BASIC
Disk Exchange
SAMS
11711 N. College Ave.
Suite 140
Carmel, IN 46032

We will send you, free of charge, the 3 1/2-inch version of the book software.

Book Title _____

Name _____ Phone _____

Company _____ Title _____

Address _____

City _____ St _____ ZIP _____

> "It's a killer product. Faster than the Quick Basic native-code compiler, blessed with some incredible array-handling features and unheard of accuracy ..."
>
> *Tom Campbell - Compute Magazine - 1991*

New! PowerBASIC 3.0

Speed, Power. Flexibility.

Programmers asked for bit operations, mouse support, integrated debugging of BASIC, and Assembler code. We've listened and responded with PowerBASIC 3.0.

Firsts for BASIC

PowerBASIC 3.0 is the first to offer both User-Defined TYPES and UNIONS! The first with Unlimited Strings! The first and only BASIC to offer a true handle-based string memory manager. With PowerBASIC 3.0, there are no artificial limits. Use all real mode memory for any and all dynamic strings.

Integrated Environment

Use true compiled code to develop and debug - the same code as your .EXE file. Plus, you'll never need to deal with a slow, threaded p-code interpreter. That means faster development, and the elimination of subtle differences between interpreted and compiled results.

New Bit Operations!

PowerBASIC 3.0 offers a full complement of bit operations including; SHIFT, ROTATE, TEST, SET, RESET, and TOGGLE.

Easy TSRs

Forget the magic wand, you won't need it to make POP-UP programs. Creating TSRs has never been easier; everything you need is built-in. Your TSR can POP-UP from any stimulus you choose: keystrokes, timers, non-activity, even a call from the foreground program! Any size program can be a TSR. PowerBASIC keeps a few k of your TSR resident, just enough to initiate the rest of the TSR when you call it. At last, a TSR generator that won't make you jump through hoops.

New Data Types

Unsigned byte, word, and double word variables. Integers of 16, 32, and even 64 bits! Single, double, and extended floats. Fixed and Floating-point BCD. Fixed and dynamic strings. You can even MAP Flex strings into dynamic structures; they're defined, created, and sized at the time of program execution.

Array Manipulation

Built-in Array, Sort, Scan, Insert, Delete, and Fill, with optional collate sequencing for foreign or special character sets.

BCD Variables

Eliminate round-off errors, even those problems associated with CURRENCY variables! Choose floating-point BCD or fixed-point with user definable precision from zero to 18 digits. Automatic rounding to the precise level YOU need, not an arbitrary 4 digits as found in other compilers.

BCD variables, as always, are implemented as scaled integers for FAST calculation.

Structure

Create BASIC programs with any level of structure desired. Free form or absolute, the choice is yours. If desired, you can even require variable declaration before use! Another first in popular BASICs!

Built-In Assembler

Need assembler routines for blazing speed? PowerBASIC 3.0 won't slow you down. Just include assembler code in your BASIC program. The built-in assembler handles all the messy details.

Fast Math!

An optional procedural float package offers startling speed. Without an '87 chip, it's 40% to 500% faster than emulation! Yet it still uses the '87 when available. It's IEEE-compatible, so procedural, emulated, or '87 specific code can be intermixed as needed.

PowerBASIC 3.0 - It's Not Your basic BASIC

To ask about special pricing for Learning BASIC readers, call (800) 245-6717 and ask for Operator M.

☐ Yes, Please send me information on PowerBASIC 3.0.

Name:_____

Address:_____

_____

City, state, Zip, _____

Fold Here

From:

_____

_____

_____

SPECTRA Publishing
1030D East Duane Avenue
Sunnyvale, CA 94086

Staple or tape here